ADVANCE PRAISE

"Witty, wise, helpful, and humane, this clear and engaging book is most timely. *Coming Out Atheist* is a great resource for the many Americans out there who have rejected religious faith and are moving towards embracing, acknowledging, and proclaiming their atheism."

—Phil Zuckerman, Ph.D., author of *Faith No More: Why People Reject Religion* and *Society without God: What the Least Religious Nations Can Tell Us About Contentment*

"There's no doubt that it's hard to be an atheist in America, but Greta Christina's message will make you rethink keeping your beliefs to yourself. There's an optimistic truth that ties her book together: By coming out publicly as non-religious, we are doing something courageous, powerful, and important. Given the choice between simply handing someone a copy of *The God Delusion* and telling that person you don't believe in God, Greta reminds us that the personal message may be the most powerful weapon in the atheist arsenal."

—Hemant Mehta, blogger at FriendlyAtheist.com and author of *The Young Atheist's Survival Guide*

"What an accomplishment! In *Coming Out Atheist*, Greta Christina has pulled together a great resource for emerging atheists. She very thoroughly captures the reality that atheists are people too, including non-believing clergy."

—Catherine Dunphy, Acting Executive Director, The Clergy Project

"Millions of Americans are discovering that life without religion and superstition can be rewarding, fulfilling, and joyful. Greta Christina has done that growing demographic a great service, with this thoughtful and entertaining book that will inform and inspire those who embrace personal secularity."

—David Niose, author of *Nonbeliever Nation: The Rise of Secular Americans*

"Greta Christina is unmatched in passion and clarity of thought. Her writing manages to be both friendly and confrontational. *Why Are You Atheists So Angry?* quickly became the #1 book that I recommend to atheists and curious believers alike, and I can't imagine a better or more complete guide to telling someone that you don't believe than *Coming Out Atheist.*

—Gem Newman, Life, the Universe & Everything Else Podcast

"Greta Christina knows that the philosophy of atheism is incomplete without practical and sensible advice about how to live in a world full of believers. Her fascinating life experience and astute observations of atheists, in or out of the closet, offers readers some of the most potent testimony for why coming out as an atheist will make a godless life better."

—Hector Avalos, professor of Religious Studies at Iowa State University, author of *The End of Biblical Studies* and *Slavery, Abolitionism, and the Ethics of Biblical Scholarship*

"Make the world a better place. Start living your life. Greta Christina shows you why and how (and how not) to escape the atheist closet. A must read for every new atheist and anyone who is considering becoming one."

—David Fitzgerald, author of *Nailed: Ten Christian Myths That Show Jesus Never Existed At All* and *The Complete Heretic's Guide to Western Religion Book One: The Mormons*

"Coming out is one of the most important decisions a person can make. Greta walks readers through that decision in a straightforward step by step process: if, when, how, to whom, and—perhaps most importantly—why. A guide for atheists and allies alike."

—Lyz Liddell, Director of Campus Organizing, Secular Student Alliance

"Greta's new book gives advice on how to come out atheist to pretty much everyone you know—and even to those you don't. Greta's take-away message from reading and hearing thousands of coming out-atheist stories? Most of the time, despite the initial awkwardness or fear, it turns out all right. This is a great how-to-guide for cautious nonbelievers who may fear the consequences of coming out godless."

—Annie Sapucaia, New Books in Secularism podcast

"Not only is *Coming Out Atheist* a valuable compendium of information on the how and why of coming out, it is also a unique book on the importance of living an authentic life. Beautifully woven within its pages is a priceless collection of deeply touching coming out stories. It's one of those rare books that is both an essential resource and a fantastic read. I highly recommend it."

—Bill Lehto, editor of *Atheist Voices of Minnesota*

COMING OUT ATHEIST

COMING OUT ATHEIST

How to Do It, How to Help Each Other, and Why

GRETA CHRISTINA

PITCHSTONE PUBLISHING
Durham, North Carolina

Pitchstone Publishing
Durham, North Carolina 27705
www.pitchstonepublishing.com

Portions of this book were originally published in Greta Christina's Blog, *Alternet*, and *Free Inquiry*.

To contact the publisher, please e-mail info@pitchstonepublishing.com
To contact the author, please e-mail gretachristina@gmail.com

Printed in the United States of America

21 20 19 18 17 16 15 14   1 2 3 4 5

Library of Congress Cataloging-in-Publication Data

Christina, Greta.
  Coming out atheist : how to do it, how to help each other, and why / Greta Christina.
    pages cm
  ISBN 978-1-939578-19-8 (pbk. : alk. paper)
  1. Atheism. I. Title.
  BL2747.3.C473 2014
  211'.8—dc23
                        2013045158

Cover design by Casimir Fornalski, casimirfornalski.com

For Ingrid.

TABLE OF CONTENTS

PART ONE: WHY COME OUT AS AN ATHEIST?

— ✷ —

"Atheists have to come out! Coming out is the most powerful political action we can take! It's how we change people's perceptions of us! It's how we counter the myths and bigotry against us! It's how we find each other! It's how we create communities and give each other a safe place to land! It's how we're forging ourselves into a political force to be reckoned with!"

People in the atheist movement have been saying all of this for as long as I've been an atheist. Probably for longer. And there's a reason: It's all true.

But when atheists talk about coming out, a surprisingly common reaction is, "Why is this so important? Why does the whole world need to know about people who don't believe in God?" This reaction doesn't just come from religious believers, either. It sometimes comes from atheists. Many people see their atheism as private, none of anybody's business. Some atheists even compare coming out to evangelizing. "I'm sick of all those Christians shoving their Christianity in my face. Why should I shove my atheism in theirs?"

If you're thinking that, I'd like to change your mind.

When I started collecting "coming out atheist" stories for this book, a remarkable pattern emerged that I noticed right away. I based this book on over four hundred "coming out atheist" stories. I posted an invitation on my blog,[1] asking people to tell me how they'd come out: who they told, how that went, what happened right away, what happened weeks or months or years later, what they would do differently if they could do it over again, what they think they did right and would do exactly the same. I got colleagues and friends to spread the word about the project, so I wouldn't just be gathering data from people who read my blog. (Quotes in this book come from those stories, unless otherwise noted.) I also collected stories from the websites of the Coming Out Godless Project,[2] the Clergy Project,[3] the Military Association of Atheists & Freethinkers,[4] and Reddit,[5] as well as several books about atheism. And for years, I've been listening to "coming out" stories: at conferences, at talks, in pubs after conferences and talks, at parties, in deep conversations with friends, on my blog, on other people's blogs, on Facebook, in online forums, in one-on-one heart-to-hearts everywhere.

And in all these stories, a single pattern appears again and again, with a consistency that surprised even me: When atheists come out of the closet, they're almost always glad that they did.

For most of this book—Parts Two and Three—I'm assuming that readers already want to come out, and just want ideas and encouragement on doing it (and on helping each other do it). But if you're not there—if you're not convinced that you want to come out, and you're looking for reasons to do it—that's what this first section is about. If you want the "25 words or less" version:

Coming out atheist can make your life better.

Coming out helps other atheists.

Coming out cultivates other atheists.

And coming out creates a better world.

Let's talk about how.

CHAPTER ONE

— ✺ —

Making Your Own Life Better

This is the crux of it:

Coming out atheist will very likely make your life better.

This, by far, is the most important reason to come out. There's no point in coming out solely as a noble sacrifice. It's great to want to be a role model for other atheists—but you're going to be a lousy role model if being out makes you miserable. You have to do this for you. You have to do your own cost/benefit analysis, and weigh the plusses and minuses yourself.

Fortunately, there are lots of plusses.

For most atheists, coming out improved their lives—*even if they alienated friends and family in doing so*. In all the coming-out stories that I've read and heard, this is the consistent pattern, the conclusion the stories overwhelmingly point to. And this conclusion is backed up by good sociological research (although this research is somewhat limited in scope, and more needs to be done).[1] There's often an initial period of trauma, just as there often is when people become atheists in the first place. But once that's passed, most atheists are happier after they've come out. Even if their worst fears are realized—even if they do lose people they love, even if they are alienated from their community and have to find a new one—for the most part, they're still happier. I've read and heard literally hundreds of "coming out atheist" stories—and almost none of them ended with, "This was a bad idea, and I wish I hadn't done it." Some people regret the particular way that they came out, and if they had it to do over again they might do it differently—but almost nobody says they wouldn't do it at all. In fact, in all the coming out stories I read for this book, only one person said they regretted it. (That was Snowball, by the way—you can read her story in the chapter on coming out to family.)

Why would this be?

Given the discrimination and bigotry many atheists face, given the myths and misinformation and flat-out lies that get spread about us, given how divisive religious differences often are—why would this be?

For starters, living in the closet can be really hard. Having to keep silent about something that's important to you? Worrying about what could happen if people found out? Keeping track of who knows what about you, and worrying about how people might hurt you if they decided to tell? Covering your tracks when you go on the Internet, and worrying what might happen if you slip up? Constantly measuring your words, even in atheist spaces, to make sure nobody could trace your words back to you? Feeling like you're being dishonest with the people you care about most? That's a hard way to live.

Being out of the closet, on the other hand... well, I'm not going to say that it's easy. Very little in life is easy. But when you're out of the closet, you can relax. You can be more open. You can be less afraid, even unafraid. You can connect with people more deeply. You can find friends, partners, communities, who share your values and your world-view, and who not only accept you but appreciate you as you are. The people who love you will really love *you*—not some other person walking around with your face and your name, pretending to be you. You can feel more honest. You can feel more like yourself.

There are happy stories about coming out atheist, and about being an out atheist, in almost every chapter of this book. There are extra heaps of them in the "Coming Out Is Fun" chapter. But if you're still in doubt, ask your LGBT friends (or yourself, if you're an openly LGBT person): Was life easier and better while they were still closeted, or after they came out? Do they regret coming out? Even if it caused a family fight, even in a homophobic society that treats them as second-class, are they happier now that they're out of the closet?

There are lots of other reasons to come out: noble reasons, moral reasons, political reasons. But ultimately, you need to do this for yourself.

CHAPTER TWO

Helping Other Atheists

But what if you want a little more inspiration?

Let's say you're one of those hyper-compassionate do-gooders who always feels a little selfish when you do something just for yourself. (Yeah, I wouldn't know anything about that...) Let's say you've done the cost/benefit analysis, and you've looked at the research showing that coming out makes most atheists happier, and you've read the happy stories, and you've decided that you want to come out—but you need a little push to just do it already. Here's a good one:

Coming out helps other atheists.

For starters, and for enders, and for many places in between: Coming out makes it easier for other atheists to come out. As you read this book, you'll see these stories again and again. So many atheists say they were emboldened to come out simply by seeing other open atheists: family members, friends, co-workers, people on online forums, even atheist writers or public figures they've never met. And again and again, atheists tell the flip side of this story. They tell friends or colleagues or family members that they're an atheist—and the reaction is, "Me too!" The reaction is ecstatic relief, because the person they told doesn't believe in God either, and *they've* been in the closet, and *they've* been scared to tell *us*.

It's easier to come out when you know you're not the only one. It's easier when you see other atheists leading happy, meaningful lives. It's easier when you know that you'll have other people to talk with about your atheism, and can get advice and support from them. It's easier when you know that you'll have a supportive community that can give you some or all of what you got from religion.

You'll see a lot of these stories in this book. I'll especially be talking about it in the chapter on visibility and role models. But I'll give you a little taste now.

Lexie, a university student from a religious community in Australia, says of coming out to her parents, "It did help that my brother had also come out as atheist... so I had someone to chat to about it. Initially we both went and hid in a bedroom to chat about religion and atheism but we started actually chatting in the living room and stopped being so secretive. We've finally got to the point where mum at least accepts what we are even if she doesn't understand it."

Daff came out to her family when she told them she was going to an atheist convention. "Dad has since admitted," she says, "when pressed by Mum and sister, that he doesn't believe in God. He's never said anything like that previously."

In her interview for *The Ebony Exodus Project: Why Some Black Women Are Walking Out on Religion—and Others Should Too* by Candace R. M. Gorham, Mandisa says that seeing other out black atheists made it easier for her to come out more, to the point where she's now a serious activist in the atheist movement. "If you would've told me a year ago," she says, "or a month ago, that this would be the direction that I'm in now, where I would be interviewed as someone who, I guess, is viewed as key to this movement, I would've said you were lying. After doing some research, I see that there are other black atheists who have been out longer and have been more vocal about it than I have. So, you couldn't have told me that I would be someone who is looked at as an inspiration in this thing... So, we're trying to let people know that we are here and there are other black atheists, other humanists. And there are more people coming out; so, you are not alone in your thought process. There are others who struggle with the same things."[1]

Lisa, whose family lives in upstate New York, came out to her mother when her mom initiated the conversation—about how *she* was an atheist. "Emboldened by this," she says, "I initiated a conversation with my dad. He believes St. Patrick and Jesus were sorcerers and wants to follow in their footprints, but respects my atheism." She also says that when she was in the military, the presence of an openly atheist non-commissioned officer gave her the courage to come out to everyone. "I guess the big lesson in my stories," she says, "is other atheists coming out helped me come out repeatedly."

In *The Young Atheist's Survival Guide: Helping Secular Students Thrive*, Hemant Mehta tells the story of Daniel, a high school atheist at Wekiva High School in Florida, who was emboldened by the presence of an openly atheist teacher, not only to come out, but to start an atheist student group. "When I visited my Psychology teacher-to-be during orientation," Daniel says, "I noticed the wonderful *The God Delusion* on his 'List of Books that Influenced My Life'... In addition to his atheism, I later found him to have a sort of activist demeanor about him and [he] eagerly accepted my request [to become the group sponsor]."[2]

And WilloNyx, who's a teacher, an out atheist, and a parent in a small town in Tennessee, says, "Often when I come out I am met with the 'I thought I was the only one in this town' theme. Actually there are probably about 30 atheists I have personally met here. We are not alone but being out is the only way to know that."

Coming out has a snowball effect. Each person who comes out makes it easier for the next person... and they make it easier for the next person, and so on, and so on... until eventually, atheism will become entirely uncontroversial, and every atheist who wants to be out can do it without fear.

How else does coming out help other atheists? Well, coming out changes people's minds about us. You're probably familiar with the misinformation and bigotry about atheists: that we have no morality, that we have no meaning or joy in our lives, etc. The single best way to counter these myths is simply to come out: to be living, breathing counter-examples proving that the myths are just flatly wrong. We can make arguments showing that the myths are irrational; we can show research showing that they're unsubstantiated; and all of that is useful. But ultimately, what changes people's minds about atheists is simply coming into contact with us: seeing that someone they know, someone they love or respect or just think is a basically decent person, is an atheist.

This has repeatedly been shown to be true for every other marginalized demographic (Google "contact hypothesis" to see what I mean[3]), and it's true for us. In fact, in the United States, public opinion of atheists is already going up. It's still way lower than it should be, but it's risen noticeably in just the last few years.[4] I don't think it's a coincidence that those same years have also seen a huge rise in atheist visibility, and in atheists coming out.

As former Southern Baptist Rocky Oliver says on the Coming Out Godless Project website, "One of my closest friends that I hang with locally is a devout Christian who listens only to Christian radio, is very involved in his church, and who really does live his faith. We have great discussions, and we have learned a lot from each other—and I believe he has a newfound respect for me as an atheist because I have shown him that you can be a 'good,' 'just,' and 'moral' person without having a belief in a deity." And in *The Young Atheist's Survival Guide*, author Hemant Mehta says, "If young atheists can make themselves known to their classmates, there's a good chance atheism will become more acceptable—and significantly less demonized—as they all grow older."[5]

And in fact, for atheists specifically, there's research supporting the conclusion that anti-atheist prejudice is reduced in places where atheists are more common—or where we're perceived to be more common.[6] As the number of atheists—and perceived atheists—goes up, prejudice against us goes down. For atheists, overcoming bigotry isn't just about people getting to know us. At least part of it is simply about people seeing how many of us there are.

So when you come out as an atheist, you're putting a little dent in anti-atheist bigotry. And that makes life easier for other atheists. The atheists who feel that they can't come out now, because they might lose their job or their home or custody of their kids... well, they'll be less likely to lose their job or their home or custody of their kids. They'll be less likely to have an anti-atheist boss, or landlord, or custody judge. And even if they do have an anti-atheist boss or landlord or judge, and they really can't come out, they'll be less likely to have anti-atheist co-workers, teachers, school administrators, county clerks, store clerks, car mechanics, neighbors, friends, family members, all grinding them down and forcing them to bite their tongue and adding to the stress of being a closeted atheist. Every piece of anti-atheist bigotry that you chip away at by coming out is a piece of bigotry that some other atheist doesn't have to deal with.

Being an out atheist also means you can do work that other atheists aren't able to do—again, atheists who really can't come out. Every time you're at a party or an online forum and say, "Hey, I'm an atheist, and the things you're saying about atheists just aren't true"; every time you go to a community meeting and say, "Can we please have an atheist on the interfaith panel?" or, "Can we please not open our meetings with a prayer?"; every time you write to an elected official or go to a school board meeting and say, "I'm an atheist, and I don't want religion taught to my kids in the public school"—you're speaking for other atheists who feel the same way you do, but can't say so.

In *The Young Atheist's Survival Guide*, Hemant Mehta tells the story of high school atheist Matthew LaClair, who fought back against illegal religious proselytizing from a teacher in his public high school—and who took the shrewd step of making audio recordings, not only of the proselytizing, but of the subsequent meeting he had with this teacher and the school principal. "In Matthew LaClair's situation," Mehta writes, "a teacher had been making religious and political comments in the classroom for *over a decade*, but no one ever did anything about it. We don't know why they all kept silent, but it's very likely that some of those students sat uncomfortably in class, *knowing* their teacher's actions were wrong. Maybe they considered telling an adult, but they thought their word would never be believed." LaClair's willingness to be an out atheist made it possible for him to fight this fight.[7]

As you speak out more, and change more people's minds about us, you'll be making the world better for these other atheists. You'll be making it easier for them to eventually come out if they want to. And even if they never come out, you'll still be making their lives better, a little less full of bigotry.

And, of course, being an out atheist makes it easier for you to participate in atheist communities if you're so inclined—and community building is one of the most powerful things we can do to help other atheists. (I'll talk more about that in the chapter on building community.)

Don't come out to be a martyr. That's one of the best things about atheism—we don't need martyrs, and we don't want them. But if you need a nudge of encouragement, and if knowing that you're helping others will help you take that step, keep this in mind. Think about all the atheists who came out before you, and who made it easier for you to even contemplate coming out. Think about the fact that you're reading this book—a book you might not have even heard about if it hadn't been for a visible, vocal atheist community talking about it. And think about how good it feels to pay it forward.

Quick tangent: Since I've now started quoting people, I'm going to take a moment to explain how I'm doing it. When I quote people in this book,

I'm respecting people's wishes about how they want to be attributed. Some people who told me their stories didn't want their names used—for them, I used a made-up name. Some wanted to be quoted by first name only. Some wanted their full names used. And some wanted to be attributed by their online handles. In all cases, I'm respecting their wishes. (If they didn't specify, I'm erring on the side of caution.)

I'm quoting people's comments exactly as they wrote them, except for very small changes for clarity (shifts in punctuation, correcting some spelling errors, etc). This means I'm respecting people's preferences about capitalizing religious words. Many atheists have strong feelings about whether words like "God," "Christianity," or "Muslim" should be capitalized. Some think this gives religion respect it doesn't deserve; others prefer to go along with the linguistic convention. Some capitalize these words, but also capitalize "Atheism." I want atheists to speak in their own voices here—so I'm quoting them however they wrote.

And when I quote someone, and I don't know their gender, I use the singular "they." Deal with it.

Okay. Back to why coming out is awesome.

CHAPTER THREE

— ✦ —

Cultivating Other Atheists

Coming out atheist is not evangelizing. I'm going to say that right off the bat. If it is, than it's evangelizing to simply say, "I'm a Christian," or "I'm a Hindu." If it is, then it's evangelizing to say anything at all about what we think about the world, ever. And I don't think that's a particularly useful definition of the word. Simply disclosing that you're an atheist doesn't make you an irritating proselytizer knocking on people's doors asking if they've heard the good news about Charles Darwin.

But it is true that coming out doesn't just make you happier, and it doesn't just make other atheists happier. Coming out *actually helps create other atheists.* Even if you never argue with anyone about their religion, even if you never once try to persuade anyone that their religious beliefs are mistaken, the simple act of telling people "I'm an atheist" puts cracks in people's faith, or widens cracks that are already there. If you ask atheists what made them become an atheist, many will tell you that simply seeing other atheists, or hearing about them, is part of what made them question their beliefs.

You may not care whether there are more atheists in the world. And that's fine. If you're unconcerned about other people's beliefs, if you'd be totally okay with religion if it weren't for faith healing and homophobia and stoning adulterers and so on—that's fine. You can skip this chapter.

But if you think religion is a harmful idea, or simply an incorrect one, and you'd like to see fewer people think it (as you would with any other harmful and/or false idea), then coming out is a powerful way to help make that happen. Maybe even *the* most powerful way.

Here's why.

Religion relies on social consent to perpetuate itself. And coming out atheist denies it that consent.

Religion—the hypothesis that the world is the way it is because of supernatural beings or forces acting on the natural world—is a bad idea. At best, it's almost certainly wrong; at worst, it's incoherent. Religious beliefs are either unfalsifiable—in which case we should reject them on that basis alone—or they've been falsified. It has never turned out to be the right answer to anything. It may have made sense thousands of years ago, when we didn't understand the world as well as we do today, but it makes no sense now. Of course we don't know everything there is to know about the universe—but given the fact that natural explanations of phenomena have replaced supernatural ones thousands upon thousands of times, and supernatural explanations have replaced natural ones exactly never, assuming that one particular supernatural explanation will turn out to be right is clearly a sucker's bet.

Religion is a bad idea. It can't stand up on its own. But it can—and does—perpetuate itself through social consent. It perpetuates itself through people not asking hard questions, or indeed any. It perpetuates itself through dogma saying that asking questions about religion is sinful and will result in punishment, and that trusting religion without evidence is virtuous. It perpetuates itself through dogma saying that joy and meaning and morality can only be found in religion, and that leaving religion will automatically result in a desperate, amoral, pointless life. It perpetuates itself through parents and other authority figures teaching it to children, whose brains are extra-prone to believing whatever they're taught. It perpetuates itself through social conventions and even legal protections that keep religious leaders and organizations from suffering consequences when they behave despicably. It perpetuates itself through religious communities and support systems that make believing in religion—or pretending to believe in religion—a necessity to function and indeed survive. Etc. Etc. Etc.

Religion perpetuates itself through social consent.

And coming out atheist denies it that consent.

This, in my opinion, is one of the best reasons for atheists to come out. You don't have to argue with people about their beliefs. If all you do is tell people "I'm an atheist," you're denying religion your social consent.

And as the years and decades roll on, this will have a snowball effect. The more of us there are who deny consent to religion, the harder it'll be to ignore difficult questions about it, or to ignore the option of atheism. And as it gets harder to ignore difficult questions about religion, more people will become atheists... and as more people become atheists and come out about it... oh, you get the picture.

You'll see a lot of stories like this in this book. It isn't the primary focus—the focus of this book is on telling people you're an atheist, not on becoming one in the first place. But for lots of atheists, the process of accepting atheism is interwoven with the process of telling people about it. And for lots of atheists, a big part of accepting atheism is simply seeing other atheists, and realizing that it's an option.

You'll see a lot of these stories in this book. Here are a couple to whet your appetite.

Rosie, who was raised Catholic in a small town in southwestern Minnesota, became an atheist as a sophomore in high school after she started dating her boyfriend. "His older brother was an atheist," she says, "which influenced my boyfriend. He and I talked about it, and it was a revelation to me (forgive the pun). It had never occurred to me before that a person could not believe."

Wayne Schroeder, whose family were all very devout Christians (his father was a church minister and later a chaplain), says that simply knowing other atheists existed made a big difference in his acceptance of atheism. "I had actually had struggled with God beliefs some time," he says, "and over those years I had come to realize that there were fewer and fewer reasons to believe in God; that the simpler explanation is a universe without it. But I clung to the belief for some time. Everyone in my world believed, it appeared, so it seemed like it had to be true. It was only when I discovered that there are Atheists in the world, that I realized that that one *could* believe in a universe without a supernatural, and then I realized that that was what I believed too. It just fell together so nicely."

In the book *Mom, Dad, I'm an Atheist: The Guide to Coming Out as a Non-believer* by David G. McAfee, Julia Sciple from Kingwood, Texas says that when she realized she was an atheist, telling her husband wasn't easy. "Most Christians believe that when two people marry they become one," she says, "and I feared that this could possibly tear us apart." But after she came out to him, she says, "my husband started to research how the Bible was formed, and along the way, discovered that he may have questions after all. After much study, we finally came to the realization that it wasn't crazy of us to question things... I'm happy to say that my husband and I now live godless lives and enjoy what each day has to bring."[1]

For Angela Rey, part of her process of re-thinking her fundamentalist Christianity was simply meeting atheists. On the Coming Out Godless Project website, she says that she enrolled in a Judaic Studies program, with the intention of better understanding Jewish people so she could convert them. "Instead of finding a community of people lost and empty in their own self-deceit," she says, "everyone seemed totally normal. What's more, a lot of them were atheists, and no one seemed to have a problem with that." And she adds that an important part of her deconversion was "my cosmically important friendship with a reformed jew turned atheist."

And on the Coming Out Godless Project website, Mia tells her story of a lonely and difficult Catholic upbringing, in which convoluted religious teachings were closely intertwined with her depression and doubts about her self-worth. "In college," she says, "I met an atheist who asked me why I believed in God. My answer was that people had told me all my life that there is a God, so I just took it as fact. I have always been open-minded and accepting of others and their beliefs. Despite constant rejection from my family, I was able to grow into a person completely open and accepting, respectful and aware of other people's beliefs and opinions. I was nice to everyone—too nice, people have often said. But I was deeply sad and I didn't know why.

"I treated people well but why did I always feel worthless? Why did I always feel like dying? Why did God make me feel these things?

"In my darkest moments I would call out to God and ask him to help me feel better, make me happy because I never was. I would cry and wish to die and wonder why I felt so terrible for no reason at all. I prayed to God for an answer, for respite, but neither came. I remembered my atheist friend who believed there was no God.

"And atheism came upon me as an epiphany. It felt like a gigantic weight had been lifted off me.

"There is no god.

"That is why everything is the way it is. That is why nothing happens no matter how hard I pray: there is no recipient. I feel terrible because the people around me treat me terribly, not because God thinks I deserve to feel bad all the time. And with this realization came pure bliss. I came to realize that I was in control of my actions, that there was no one manipulating me, that I was 100% responsible for what happened to me. It was exhilarating. Millions of possibilities came before me, and it was up to me to decide where my life went. I would decide how I felt, how I acted and thought.

"Feelings of total wrongness and self-hatred transformed into feelings of assurance and confidence in myself and my capabilities. My apostasy took mere seconds, and they were the most revitalizing seconds of my life."

"I remembered my atheist friend who believed there was no God. And atheism came upon me as an epiphany."

This. Remember this. Even if you don't argue with your friend, even if all you do is ask your friend why they believe in God—heck, even if all you do is be open about your atheism so your friend knows it's an option—you might be part of them leaving their religion.

Coming out atheist almost certainly won't, by itself, get someone to reject their religion. But it can plant the seeds of doubt. It can start people asking questions. And it can get people who are already on the fence to move along in their process, and take that final leap out of faith.

Ultimately, people need to accept atheism on their own, for their own reasons. But other people can help. And the most important help you can give may simply be to come out.

CHAPTER FOUR

— ✹ —

Creating a Better World

So yes. Coming out makes your life better. Coming out makes life better for other atheists. Coming out makes more people question, and eventually abandon, the mistaken idea of religion. If these were the only ways that coming out atheist made the world better, it would be enough.

But these aren't the only ways.

Coming out atheist is what changes believers' minds about atheists. It's what makes people realize they've been fed lies about us, and that we're not who they've been told we are by their pastor or their parents or the media. It's what shakes loose people's bigotry against us. And a less bigoted world is a better world.

Jason, from Tampa, Florida, came out at work when some of his colleagues began promoting a Bible study course endorsing Christian nationalism and wildly inaccurate science. He attended the course—and during the "questions and comments" section, he said to the group, "'My twin brother and I were raised in a secular household by a single mother. Her number one priority was working hard and effectively managing her time and money to make sure that we were taken care of. Through her guidance and example, we learned the importance of integrity, honesty, work ethic, compassion, friendship, and responsibility.

We learned these important virtues without religion. I am an atheist and my brother identifies as non-religious, and we both grew up to be good citizens; my brother is a phenomenal father; we both treat people with respect and kindness; and we live fulfilling lives. I reject the idea that without faith in a god, we would not have these attributes or that anyone here would be incapable of leading the lives that you do if your life was without god or religion.'"

Afterwards, he says, "the facilitator and a few other attendees were eager to hear what I, the only atheist in the group, had to say. It seemed that they were being exposed to an entirely new line of thought... I'm not saying that they accepted everything I said or information I presented or that I changed their minds. What I did show them is that an atheist can be confrontational yet professional, witty, patient, intriguing, challenging, informative, diligent, good-natured—really not that different from what they consider a good person." What's more, he says, "One woman who had attended the Bible study group for years later told me that she was glad that I shared my thoughts about being raised in a secular home and being influenced by the morality of a hard-working single parent. To this woman, I was a real-world example of an atheist who is just as kind, pleasant, caring, hard-working, and thoughtful as her religious friends, family, and co-workers. The next time she confronts the stereotype of the immoral atheist, I trust that she will not remain silent. This is one way that we can slowly erode the stigma of atheism."

So coming out atheist is a big part of what makes people less bigoted against us. And that doesn't just make the world better for atheists. It makes the world better for everyone.

Being bigoted makes you treat people badly. Being bigoted adds to the hatred in the world. And being bigoted screws up your own life. It closes you off to people and possibilities. It closes you off to ideas. It makes you sour and nasty, small-minded and unpleasant.

Less bigotry against gay people is good; less bigotry against African Americans is good; less bigotry against people of Middle Eastern descent is good; less bigotry against women is good. Repeat, for other bigotries. And less bigotry against atheists is good.

As it happens, I think there are other ways that coming out makes the world better. I do think religion is both a mistaken idea and a harmful one; I think the world will be better as fewer people believe in religion; and I think coming out about our atheism is an important part of making that happen. But even if you don't agree with me about religion being harmful, I hope you'll agree that coming out changes people's minds about atheists—and that's a constructive act. That makes a better world.

CHAPTER FIVE

— ✺ —

Should You Even Come Out at All?

There are good reasons to come out as an atheist.
There are also good reasons not to.

I do a lot of cheerleading in this book. Much of the book is centered on practical information and specific tips about coming out as an atheist. But a fair amount of it consists of encouragement, reassurance, and "Rah! Rah!" exhortations to come out, come out, wherever you are, if you can, as much as you can.

There's a reason for that. I'm assuming that if you're reading this book, you've already decided that you want to come out. I'm assuming that you're reading this book to get information and ideas on how to come out—and to get a gentle nudge of encouragement to just do it already. So for the most part, I'm comfortable skewing my advice in that direction.

But I also have some biases. The information I'm basing my advice on has some biases. These biases are skewing me in the direction of encouraging atheists to come out, and emphasizing the benefits of doing it. Before I move ahead with the cheerleading, I need to acknowledge these biases, and spell them out.

I'm basing this book on hundreds of stories that I've read and heard about atheists' experiences with coming out. And in reading the stories that I've gathered, I've been startled by how overwhelmingly positive most of them have ultimately been. Some people have expressed regrets about how exactly they came out, or when, or where, or in what tone of voice. But of the hundreds of coming out stories that I've read and heard, literally one person said that they regretted having done it. Virtually everyone said they're glad they came out. Even if the experience was traumatic, even if they lost communities or alienated family and friends, they still think it was the right decision. And this isn't just anecdotal evidence from the atheists I happen to have run across—there's research backing up this conclusion as well.[1]

But in the interest of full disclosure, I should make it clear: These stories were not—repeat, *not*—collected with any sort of statistically representative sampling method. I did work hard to cast as wide a net as I could. When I posted the solicitations on my blog for coming out stories, I did everything I could to spread the word as far as possible. I also made it clear that I wasn't just looking for a certain kind of story: I wanted to hear any coming out stories that any atheist wanted to tell—sad or happy, dramatic or dull, from every demographic I could find. And I didn't just use stories that I got through my blog: I gathered plenty of coming out stories from books and other websites. But the stories here are not a statistically accurate representation of "coming out atheist" experiences. Or, if they are, it's only because I got really, really lucky.

"People who read Greta Christina's Blog" are over-represented here. "People who read atheist blogs and forums that publicized my call for stories" are over-represented. "People with Internet access" are, obviously, very much over-represented. "People who speak English" are over-represented, as are people from the United States. I've collected stories from around the world, and have done my best to make my advice relevant to as many atheists as possible—including atheists from different nationalities. But most of my own experience has been in the United States, and most (although by no means all) of the atheists I know and work with are from the U.S. or Canada. That's the experience I'm most familiar with, and I'm sure it's coloring my ideas.

And very importantly, these stories are coming from people who are connected in some way, even if it's just a small way, with the atheist community and the atheist movement. They're coming from people who attend atheist talks or conferences or other events, who participate in online atheist forums, who follow other atheists on Facebook or Twitter, who at the very least read atheist blogs once in a while.

All of this creates a significant selection bias. I have no idea what coming out atheist is like for people who aren't connected in any way with organized atheism. It may well be that there are atheists whose lives have been destroyed by coming out, who are now jobless or homeless or bankrupt, who have been abandoned by friends and family and are emotionally shattered by the experience, who think coming out was the worst decision they ever made—and who I haven't heard from and am never going to hear from. If those people exist, they aren't likely to attend atheist events, read atheist blogs, or do any of the things that would get me listening to their stories.

There's another important bias that's almost certainly at work here: the bias of rationalization. Human beings are wired to start rationalizing our decisions the second we make them. No matter what action we take, our brains immediately rush in to explain why it was obviously the right thing to do. And the larger the impact is of that decision, the more stubbornly we rationalize it. It's the psychology behind hazing—when you go through a horrible experience in order to join a group, it makes you feel more invested in that group, and more committed to it. And it's the psychology behind doomsday cults actually getting stronger when their end-of-the-world predictions don't come true. If you thought the end of the world was nigh, and you prepared by taking a couple of days off work, you might be willing to admit that you were a fool. But if you thought the end of the world was nigh, and you prepared by quitting your job and selling your house and taking your kids out of school, your brain is going to have a hard time letting you accept that this was a bonehead move. (To find out more about why our brains do this and how, read the excellent book *Mistakes Were Made (But Not by Me): Why We Justify Foolish Beliefs, Bad Decisions, and Hurtful Acts*, by Carol Tavris and Elliot Aronson).[2]

So when I hear all these hundreds of atheists say how happy they are that they came out, I have to remember: Of course they'd say that. It's the decision they already made—of course they're going to think it was the right one. And when I hear atheists say that they're happy they came out, even though the experience was traumatic and caused great loss in their life, I have to remember: Those are the people who *really* would say that. They gave up a lot for their decision. It's going to be hard for them to think it was a mistake. (This rationalization bias is less prevalent in the research done on this topic—the study relies on measurements of general distress, as well as self-reporting on specific distress caused by living as an atheist—but again, this research is somewhat limited in scope, and more needs to be done.)[3]

And I have one more bias, a more personal one, that I should acknowledge here as well: I'm a movement atheist. I care about the atheist community and the atheist movement, and I want them to flourish. And I know that things will be better for the atheist community and movement if more atheists come out. I know that things will improve, both for organized atheism and for most individual atheists, if more atheists come out to more people. So I have a vested interest in encouraging atheists to come out.

But that doesn't mean *you* should come out.

Yes, there are good reasons to come out. There are also good reasons not to. Some of those:

You think it would seriously endanger your safety, or the safety of the people in your life: if, for instance, you're living in a theocracy, where coming out as an atheist could get you or your family imprisoned, beaten, or killed.

You think it would seriously endanger your livelihood or your home: if, for instance, you're living in a very religiously conservative region, where religion is deeply woven into the social and economic and political structure, and coming out atheist could mean losing your job or your home.

You or your family are financially dependent on intensely religious relatives, who might cut off support if they discover your atheism.

You're emotionally dependent on intensely religious family or friends or community, who might cut off contact if they discover your atheism.

You think coming out as an atheist could cut you off from family members who aren't necessarily the religious ones: if your atheism could create problems in custody battles, for instance, or if your religious children might not let you see your grandchildren.

You're already in one or more other marginalized groups, and you don't need another stigma piled onto the ones you already have.

You're already in one or more other marginalized groups, and you think coming out would disconnect you from the social, emotional, and practical support that religion provides in your community.

Your life in general is very stressful, and you don't need the extra stress of coming out.

You're dealing with an unusual amount of stress right now, and you don't need the extra stress of coming out.

You have work that you care about, and coming out atheist would create a distraction or otherwise make your work more difficult.

You just don't want to.

These are all good reasons not to come out. They're good reasons not to come out to a particular person, or to anyone at all; they're good reasons not to come out right away, or not to come out ever.

Later on in this book, I have a chapter on how to encourage each other to come out without pressuring or guilt-tripping. I want to make sure that I'm not pressuring you myself. So I'm spelling this out as clearly as I can, before I say a word about how to come out: I am not—repeat, NOT—writing this book to talk you into coming out if you seriously think it would be a bad idea.

Now, if you've decided not to come out, I do think it's worth looking carefully at that choice. Even with all these biases factored in, I still think that coming out is generally a good decision. The overwhelmingly positive experiences that most atheists report about it are... well, pretty overwhelming. I'd add to that the experiences of LGBT people and the LGBT movement. Most openly LGBT people are glad they've come out, and coming out is a big part of how LGBT people have gained so much in acceptance and rights, and how we've made coming out easier. And there are risks of staying in the atheist closet—and benefits of coming out of it—which you might not have considered. I talk about some of these throughout the book. (If nothing else, staying in the closet creates a risk of being outed—and being outed against your will is almost always a crappy experience.)

But once you've weighed those risks and benefits, you'll need to decide for yourself if this is something you want to do—and if so, how much you want to do it. If you've decided against it—for the time being, or indefinitely—that is entirely your business and none of my own, and I support you in that choice.

If you do want to do it, though...

PART TWO: COMING OUT

— ✹ —

Okay," you say. "I get it. I'm on board. Coming out atheist is good. It'll probably make my life better, it'll make things better for other atheists, it'll fill the world with puppies and sunshine. So how do I do it? How do I tell my Baptist parents, my New Age boss, my Muslim sister, my Hindu best friend, the other students at my Catholic school, that I'm an atheist?"

This is it. This is the nuts and bolts, the part of the book I'm guessing 80% of you flipped to first.

I'll be talking here about a lot of specific situations: coming out to your family, your spouse or partner, your friends, your colleagues, strangers on the street. I'll be talking about coming out in conservative communities, progressive communities, theocracies, the U.S. military, the Internet. I'll be talking about coming out for parents, students, and people who are already marginalized, such as women, people of color, and LGBT people.

I encourage everyone to read all these chapters. Not all these categories are clear-cut. There are stories in the Friends chapter that shed light on coming out at school; stories in the Internet chapter with ideas about coming out at work. And even if a chapter doesn't apply to you directly, it'll almost certainly have ideas you can use to help other atheists, or simply be more empathetic with them.

I'll also talk here about some general philosophies of coming out, as well as some controversies: what language to use, whether to argue about religion and when, the difference between coming out versus simply being out. And I'll be telling my own "coming out atheist" story—it wouldn't be much of a coming out book without that!

But first, let's touch on some basics.

CHAPTER SIX

The Basics

So now that you've bought this book on how to come out as an atheist, and you've invested a certain amount of time and money in it, I have a confession to make:

I can't really tell you how to come out as an atheist.

I can't tell you how to come out as atheist in a way that will make it happen perfectly, for every atheist, every time. No matter what I tell you, you could still have bad conversations, angry and hurt family members, hostile communities, lost jobs, and more. Coming out atheist can be hard—it isn't always, but it can be—and there's nothing I can say that's going to change that. Sorry.

And coming out atheist is different for everyone. What's worked for me may not work for you; what failed for me might turn out great for you. That's one of the reasons this book is structured the way it is: with chapters for parents and for students, for people in conservative and progressive communities, etc. And even though the collective wisdom of hundreds of atheists is gathered here, it isn't going to speak to every aspect of your experience.

So I'm just about never going to tell you, "Here is the right way to come out." There is no right way to come out. Instead, I'll be saying, "Here are some right ways to come out. Here are some situations that could arise, some questions you might not have thought about. Here are some mistakes other people made. Here are some things other people think they did right." Throughout this book, I'll be saying things like, "You could do X—or you could do Y. Decide that for yourself, based on your personality and your situation." That's very deliberate. I'm not trying to give you specific directions. I'm trying to give you a map of the territory—so you can have some preparation and information that'll help you decide how to proceed.

But there are a few guidelines that seem to apply to most people who are coming out as godless. I can't guarantee that they'll make your coming out go perfectly, with no hitches or hurt feelings. But following these guidelines will probably help the process go smoother, with better relationships and a better life in the long run.

Let's talk about those first. Here are eighteen basic principles for coming out as an atheist.

1. Coming out atheist is different for everyone.

I said that already, didn't I?

Well, it's true, and it's important. So I'm going to repeat it. And it's important for a couple of reasons.

For one thing: If your friend is telling you their coming out story and talking about what worked for them, and your instincts are telling you, "Okay, but my situation is totally different, there's no way that would work for me"? *Listen to those instincts*. And yes, that applies to this book. If you're reading a piece of advice here and are thinking, "That wouldn't be right for me at all"—you know yourself and your circumstances better than I do. Take what you need, and leave the rest.

The reverse is every bit as true. What works for you may not work for other people. So when you're giving advice and encouragement to other atheists on coming out, bear that in mind.

What's more, different ways of coming out don't just have personal impacts in people's lives. They have political implications as well. And those will vary from person to person. Some people want their coming out to make a gentler, blending-in, "we're just like everyone else" statement. Others want their coming out to be more radical, more confrontational, less about merging with the status quo and more about challenging it. As Alex Gabriel of the Godlessness in Theory blog said to me, "Less obvious ways to come out, including as an atheist, are worth considering. How we choose to express our non-belief affects how public life imagines us. Soap operas and primetime dramas show LGBT comings-out predominantly as tearful, fragile confessions. Many queer people's experience is different; likewise there are many ways to be an atheist, and equally many ways to say you are."

Bottom line: There isn't one magical coming out formula that's right for everyone. So while it's great to encourage each other to come out, we all need to do it on our own timetable, and in our own way. And we need to support each other in that.

2. Coming out is a spectrum, and a process.

Coming out isn't a single step we take once and are done with. It's an ongoing process, a series of decisions we make every day. Each time you come out to a different person, it's a different "coming out" moment. Plus, with some people, you may have to come out more than once—if they don't believe you the first time, or don't accept it.

And even after you've come out to all the central people in your life, coming out is still an ongoing series of choices you make every day. Do you chat about your atheism at the basketball game? Do you wear an atheist T-shirt to the airport? Do you cross "In God We Trust" off your money—and do you do it right in front of the store clerk, or wait until you get home? When someone asks you, "What church do you belong to," do you say something vague like, "I haven't decided"; or do you say something more specific like, "I'm not really religious"; or do you flatly say, "I don't go to church, I'm an atheist"?

Kate, who grew up in a fairly extreme Christian background, says that since coming out to her immediate family, "I have 'come out' to lots and lots of other people. Every so often I still have to do it, because a family friend or distant relative has not heard the news, or because I'm in a situation where faith may be assumed, such as at a baptism." And Paul, who grew up in the relatively non-religious United Kingdom and moved to the more religious United States, puts this idea really well. "For me," he says, "it has not been a single event. Every new job, new address, new acquaintance, etc. has been somewhat of an event."

So being an out atheist isn't an either/or thing. It's a continuum. And we all get to make our own choices about where to be on that continuum. I, for instance, am about as out an atheist as you can be—but I don't always tell strangers in the airport that I'm an atheist. I don't necessarily want to have that conversation for five hours on the plane. And I'm not going to beat myself up over that.

A useful way to look at this is the difference between secrecy and privacy. We don't consider it bad to have things in our lives that are private: things we don't share with everyone, or indeed with anyone. It doesn't mean we're hiding or faking. It means we have a private life. But if we're keeping secrets—especially big secrets about important parts of our identity—that can be a serious emotional burden. Especially if it involves deception: taking active steps to conceal something, or even outright lying.

There's a useful analogy here with coming out queer. As an out bisexual, I don't share the details of my sex life with my family. That's private. But it was important to tell my family that I'm bisexual—because not telling them was keeping a secret, hiding an important part of myself. And when it comes to atheism, each of us has to decide where the line is between secrecy and privacy, and whether the burden of secrecy outweighs the risks of coming out.

3. Give the people you're coming out to some credit.

When I first started researching this book, I'd expected to read story after story of shattered families, ruptured marriages, broken friendships, ruined careers. And I did read those stories. Too many of them. Anti-atheist bigotry is a real thing, and it can seriously screw up lives.

But those stories were the exception—not the rule. Most "coming out atheist" stories that I've read and heard have turned out okay. The atheists who have come out are mostly on good terms with their families. They mostly get along with their co-workers. They've mostly kept most of their friends. It often took time, they sometimes went through fights and tears and long conversations—but as a rule, it eventually worked out okay. Sometimes it's worked out great, and they're closer to the people they came out to than ever; sometimes it's worked out less great, and it's kind of awkward, with subjects they stay away from. But even intensely religious people, or people in very conservative religions, have generally wound up being okay with it. And a lot of the time, the process didn't involve any fights or tears, and didn't take that much time.

When Eric Paulsen came out to his parents at age ten, he says, "We had a very long talk, something like an hour or two, where they asked me all manner of questions trying to understand how I had come to my conclusions and if there was not some more childish reason I didn't want to attend church (like I would rather watch TV)." Once they realized that his atheism was serious, they not only accepted it, but agreed that he wouldn't have to go to church. "I am still astounded how reasonable my parents were," he now says.

So give the people who care about you some credit. Don't assume that their religion will trump their relationship with you. Sometimes it will, and you should be prepared for that. But most of the time, it won't.

4. In general, sooner is better.

If it's at all possible, it's generally better to come out sooner rather than later. The sooner you come out, the more likely it is that you'll be able to pick the time and place. The sooner you come out, the less likely it is that someone else will out you (accidentally or intentionally); that someone in your life will force the issue (pressing the question and not accepting a vague answer—it happens more than you might think); or that a crisis will make it necessary for you to come out right away, even though the timing is lousy (such as a health crisis or a death in the family, where religious beliefs and the lack thereof suddenly become very relevant). And if you come out sooner, the people in your life will have more time to get comfortable with the idea—and you'll have more time with them to have an honest, open, "not keeping your atheism a secret" relationship.

Chris Hallquist, of the Uncredible Hallq blog, kept his atheism a secret for years so he could finish becoming an Eagle Scout. He now says, "Now having made Eagle rank affects my life for nada, beyond being able to tell this story. I regret even caring about it when I was in high school. I regret not coming out to everyone earlier."[1] And Alan, who was raised in a Jewish household in Minneapolis, echoes this sentiment. He came out to his parents somewhat by accident, when he was at college; he'd let go of his religious practice, so he didn't notice when it was Yom Kippur, one of the holiest days in the Jewish calendar. His advice now: "Come out as early as you are comfortable with, so you can control the circumstances and minimize the risk of being outed by accident."

There are obvious exceptions, of course. If you're in a situation where coming out atheist would seriously screw up your life—like if you're a college student whose parents might cut off your tuition—then yeah, hold off for now. (See #14 below: "Have your practical and financial ducks in a row—within reason.") And if you're pursuing a plan of softening the ground before you come out, or if you're being strategic about who to come out to first, then obviously, waiting is going to be part of that plan. (See #11 and #15 below.)

But in general, sooner is better. Sooner gives you more control—and sooner gives you more time.

5. Have patience.

Coming out is a process. And it's not just a process for you. It's often a process for the people you come out to. It can take time for them to get used to it. One of the most important lessons about coming out—another lesson we can learn from LGBT experiences—is patience.

As atheist activists, and in our public life, I think it's fine to demand justice and acceptance right now. In fact, I think it's more than fine. I think it's essential. If we wait until people accept us before we speak up and fight for our rights, we're going to wait forever. Speaking up and fighting for our rights is exactly how we get people to accept us. If we don't start demanding justice and acceptance now, we're never going to get it.

But in your personal life, with people you care about and are in it with for the long haul, you probably want to... well, plan to be in it for the long haul. You don't have to be a doormat—more on that in a moment—but you need to understand that this process often takes time.

William, who was raised as a non-denominational Christian in a small town in the Midwest, says that when he first came out to his parents, there were some hard conversations, with tears and recriminations and even threats. "I think hearing that their child was an atheist was such a shock at first," he says, "because they had never known any atheists before and thought we were immoral, unhappy people. They became much more accepting once some time had passed and they saw I was the exact same person I had always been. Changing negative perceptions like those of my parents is why coming out and being visible as an atheist is so incredibly important. It makes it easier for everyone after us to come out and just be themselves without fear."

There's a coming out story that I think is very instructive here. It's a story about coming out as gay, but it connects strongly with coming out atheist. When the sex advice writer Dan Savage first came out to his mother as gay, her reaction was not good, and one of the things she said was that she never wanted him to bring his boyfriends home, and she never wanted to meet them.[2] I know. Harsh. But years later, when Dan had been with his partner Terry for some time, his mom was the one noodging them to get married. They were the ones who were dithering, and she was the one being a typical mom, saying "Come on, guys, give me a wedding already."[3]

She totally came around. It just took time.

So be willing to give it time.

If you're feeling doubtful or despairing about whether your relationships will improve with time, I encourage you to read the many stories throughout this book where atheists were just as doubtful and despairing as you are—and they found that time healed, often faster and more deeply than they'd expected. It doesn't always get better—but it often does.

Related to this: Know when to stop the conversation. If things are going south, you may need to drop it and come back to it later. Again: This process may take time, for the people you're coming out to as well as for yourself, and you may not get closure in one conversation. (There is a potential danger, though, in cutting off a conversation. If one of you pulls the plug because things were getting upsetting, it may be hard to bring it up again, and the topic can start to feel taboo or like it's off the table permanently. So if you decide to shut down the discussion for now, make sure you keep the door open for the future.)

6. Be the bigger person.

Being patient means giving the process time. But sometimes, it also means that you have to be the bigger person.

When you come out as an atheist, people will sometimes be—how shall I put this?—total assholes. They may be bigoted, manipulative, guilt-tripping, cruel. If you want relationships with these people, you need to be willing to be the bigger person.

Lexie, who comes from a religious community in Australia that she would rate as "on the conservative side," has this to say from her experience: "Don't expect religious family or friends to accept or even be nice when you first come out. If they get angry or upset, you have to rise above it and not retaliate in kind because this spirals out of control. Stay calm and answer questions, explain that you do understand that this is hard for them (this really helps) and if it's all going pear shaped walk out of the room (just say, 'I don't think this is constructive, let's talk about it later')."

The people you come out to may be jerks about it. It won't help if you're a jerk back. Being a jerk tends to escalate things, and it can push people out onto a limb that they have a hard time walking back from. And besides, being a jerk makes you... well, a jerk. If people are being horrible to you when you come out, presumably you don't want to take them as your role model. So if they're getting overwrought, try to stay calm. If they're being manipulative, try to be straightforward. If they're being cruel, try to maintain your empathy. You don't need to be a doormat; you don't have to put up with abuse, and you should ultimately expect fairness in your relationships with believers. But two wrongs don't make a right, and mistreating people who are mistreating you does not equal justice. So keep your eye on the bigger picture—the fact that you care about these people, and want to maintain a relationship with them.

On the other hand, it's also a good idea to:

7. Decide how much crap you're willing to take.

The reality is that you're probably going to deal with at least some anti-atheist hostility and bigotry. This sucks, but it's true—whether you come out or not. The only way to avoid it is to never have anything to do with anyone who isn't an atheist. You can try that if you like. If atheist separatism isn't up your alley, though, then some anti-atheist crap is almost certainly in your future.

But you get to decide how to respond to it. You get to decide where to draw the line—and how.

When you run into anti-atheist bigotry, you get to decide when to let it slide, and when to gently say, "Hey, I'm an atheist, and that's not true or fair," and when to say, "Screw you, I'm an atheist, and that is some totally bigoted bullshit." And you get to decide who you're willing to be patient with and who you're not; who you're willing to hang in there with over months or years, and who you're willing to write off after their second chance (or indeed their first). You might, for instance, decide to put up with more crap from your mom than you do from the friend of a friend you meet at a party.

It's important to remember that there's a difference between being patient and being a doormat. You may have to be patient with ignorance; you may have to be patient as people change their minds about atheists and atheism, and as they learn more about us. But you don't have to let people walk on you. You don't have to put up with insults or hatred, bigotry or abuse. Again, you probably want to be the bigger person; stay calm, be straightforward, maintain empathy. But you can do all that while still drawing clear boundaries about what you're willing to deal with. And again—you get to decide where that line is.

When Terri Garrett came out to her fundamentalist family, some family members handled it better than others. "I have had to have several talks with one sibling in particular," she says. "After more than twenty years of this, and dealing with a several-hours long, emotionally draining conversation the day after my mom died, I finally told her. 'Two decades of having the same conversation with you needs to end. You and I can talk about anything but religion from now on.'"

Where and when you draw that line may change over time. As your life changes, you may find your patience with anti-atheist hostility increasing. Or you may find it decreasing. As you get more accustomed to being an out atheist and more familiar with anti-atheist bigotry, you may find that it irritates you less, and that you're more willing to engage with it patiently or even shrug it off. Or the reverse may be true. As you get more support from an atheist community, you may feel less need for religious friends, and thus be more willing to confront them on their bigotry.

That's up to you. But don't let people tone-troll you. If they're treating you badly, you have a right to be angry, and it's their bigotry that's the problem—not your anger about it.

8. Don't apologize.

There is not a damn thing wrong with you being an atheist. So don't apologize for it.

When people you care about act as if you've wounded them by not believing in God and by telling them about it, it can be painful to deal with. After all, when people tell us that we've hurt them—especially people we care about—our instinct is often to feel guilty, and to apologize. That instinct is understandable, and as a general rule, it's even admirable.

But you haven't done anything wrong by being an atheist. And you aren't doing anything wrong by being honest about it.

Marnie, who was raised in a generically Christian household, says, "I try to never give the impression that I am defensive or uncomfortable with my views. I come by them honestly and I feel that I should be able to defend what I believe on its own grounds."

If people get upset when you tell them you're an atheist, you can express compassion for their upset, without accepting responsibility for it. You can say, "I feel bad that you're so upset about this," without saying, "I'm sorry that I did this to you." But if they're upset because they have bigoted ideas about atheism—that's their fault, not yours. If you apologize for your atheism, or for your honesty about it, that feeds the idea that there really *is* something wrong with it. And ultimately, that's going to make it harder for people to accept it.

9. Expect fairness.

Religion is very privileged in much of the world, and that sense of privilege is often internalized—even by atheists. So in relationships between believers and atheists, it's easy to fall into a pattern where you're making all the concessions to their religion, and they're not making any concessions to your atheism.

Don't let this happen. If you're going to keep attending religious services or rituals with people in your life, expect them to attend some atheist events with you. If they want you to lay off criticizing religion, expect them to lay off criticizing atheism. If they want to debate your atheism and try to persuade you out of it, you should be able to do the same with their religion. If they want to tell you about their religious activities, you shouldn't have to stay quiet about your atheist ones. Etc.

On the Coming Out Godless Project website, Emmanuel Donate tells of coming out to his family, a Latino family that took their Catholicism seriously—even more seriously when their teenage son turned out to be an atheist, to the point where they forced him to go to church with them. "After mass every Sunday," he says, "I would get the ladder from the toolshed and climb up to the roof for exactly one hour. I thought that if I was going to be forced into an hour of mass that I deserved to take an hour away from my family.

"After a few weeks my family eventually found my hour away strange. My father was the first to approach me and one Sunday he asked if he could come up to the roof with me. I wanted to say no, but I knew I did not have a choice. I said yes and up he came. The conversation was long but the general idea was him asking for an explanation. Again forced into honesty, I told him why I took an hour for myself every Sunday. I explained that being persecuted for having different beliefs was precisely what happened to Christ and that I thought forcing me to go to church was ironically reminiscent. Luckily my father is a reasonable man and after that he decided against forcing me to go to church."

Concessions and compromises are important in any relationship. But it's important that they not all go in one direction.

10. Give them space to have a reaction.

When you're coming out to the people you're closest to—family, close friends—it's usually a good idea to be thoughtful about the time and place. Choose a place where they can have their feelings with some privacy, and a time when you'll have some time to hash things out if you need to. As tempting as it might be to have the conversation in a restaurant where they can't throw a fit, that's not really fair.

Midori, who has come out as queer and trans as well as atheist, has this advice: "If there may be consequences to coming out or being outed, take a little time to think ahead about how you could handle this. Pick a time to come out when there is relatively little else going on, so there won't be any unusual distractions or stressors to complicate things. If you or the person you are coming out to is upset, it's not a good time, especially if it's you that's upset—the other person might think that being an atheist is upsetting to you, which is probably not the sort of impression you want to make. Make sure you will have some time available afterwards to answer questions or explain things, if needed."

Now, this doesn't necessarily apply to more casual acquaintances, or to people you work with. If you don't care about processing someone's innermost feelings about your atheism, and you just want them to have the information, it can make more sense to come out more matter-of-factly, and more publicly—so people are more likely to treat it as ordinary, or at least are less likely to pitch a fit. (See Chapter 7: The "No Big Deal" Method.) And if you're coming out at the workplace, there are practical reasons to come out with more than one person around. If you get hostile or bigoted reactions, and they don't go away over time, having witnesses may be useful.

But with the people you deeply care about, let them have their fit if they're going to have one. It may not be a fun conversation, but if you want a real relationship with these people, it may be necessary.

11. Consider softening the ground first—but be prepared for it to collapse.

If the people you're coming out to are intensely religious, and you think they're going to be upset about your atheism, you might try softening the ground first. You can start saying things like, "I'm having some questions about religion," "I haven't really been going to church," "My ideas about religion are changing." That way, when you do end up telling them flatly, "I'm an atheist," or, "I don't believe in God," it won't come as such a shock.

Lexie, a university student in Australia, knew that her parents would have a hard time with her atheism. She came out about it in stages: first saying that she had doubts, then saying she didn't want to go to church, and later saying she was an atheist. Her family had huge problems with these initial "doubting" stages, with "lots of yelling and screaming." But by the time she finally told them she was an atheist, she says, "they were a bit upset, but the previous 'I doubt the church,' and the things I did to slip in the hint before this chat, made it so much easier, they were almost expecting it when it happened rather than it being out of the blue... We've finally got to the point where mum at least accepts what we are even if she doesn't understand it, she even uses the word atheist now and will now tell other people."

But if you do decide to soften the ground, be prepared for direct questions. If you say things like, "I'm having doubts about religion," the people you're coming out to might evade the topic, or go into denial about it, or file it away to process later. But they might also start asking immediate, direct questions, like, "What do you mean? Don't you believe any more? Are you an atheist?"

Beth Presswood, of the Godless Bitches podcast and the Atheist Community of Austin, told me a fascinating and deeply sad story that dramatically underscores this point. When she moved away from her family, her father didn't just ask her, "Which church are you going to in your new town?" He grilled her on the topic of the sermon that Sunday. *Every* Sunday. Beth actually had to research the church she'd lied to her father about going to, and find out what the preacher had been preaching about. She'd wanted to simply keep her atheism private, at least for a while—but her father wouldn't let her. He forced her into a position where privacy wasn't an option. She had to either actively keep her atheism a secret, to the point where she was lying and going out of her way to deceive—or come out. (Or else wind up with someone else outing her—which is, in fact, what happened.)

You need to be prepared for these questions. And I strongly urge you not to lie. The whole point of this exercise is that you don't want to lie anymore. So don't go the "softening the ground" route unless you're prepared to go the whole way.

12. Do your homework.

When you come out as an atheist, you'll probably be in for a round of Atheism 101—Myths and Facts. Maybe more than one round. Even the most supportive believers often have misunderstandings about us. And the more people you come out to, the more mythbusting you'll have ahead of you.

So do some homework first. Get familiar with the common myths about atheists—that we don't have any morality, that we left religion because we're angry at God, that there are no atheists in foxholes, etc. And be prepared to counter them. (Several atheists have written pieces debunking the myths about us: Amanda Marcotte,[4] Sam Harris,[5] and Austin Cline[6] have particularly good ones, and I'm fond of my own[7] as well.)

David Viviano, who grew up non-religious in a liberal area of New York but later moved to the Bible Belt, shares his advice on coming out, based both on what he thinks he did right and what he did wrong. "Allow yourself time to think, research, question and think some more," he says, "until you are comfortable with it yourself and confident." And he adds, "If you know/feel like the other party will become angry, prepare for it well beforehand. The more informed and calm you are the easier it MAY be. Prepare what you will say; also prep for what you think they may say back. If you prepare for the worst you will be ready for anything."

But when you're countering anti-atheist misinformation, remember: Coming out isn't about proving to some jerk that they're wrong. It's about reassuring the people who care about you that you're okay. Stand up for yourself—but stay calm. Try to see things from their perspective. And remember that you do actually care about these people, and that they care about you. Don't treat them as adversaries.

Which brings me to:

13. Don't get sucked into fights about whether God exists.

It may surprise some people to hear me say that. I'm normally a big advocate of arguing with people about whether God exists. I think these arguments are awesome, and I think they can be very effective. But the "coming out" conversation is not the time for them.

When you come out to the people you care about, it's not just about them accepting you. They need to know that you're going to accept them. And for a lot of believers, their religion isn't just an idea. It's an identity. Many people associate it with culture, family, historical tradition, racial or ethnic identity, even national pride. So when you tell them you're an atheist, it can seem like you're rejecting that identity.

Sebastian, who had been a Christian at an evangelical church in London, says that one of his regrets about coming out is that he tried to drag his religious friends into atheism with him. "I was visiting my Christian friend Will," he says, "after a prolonged period of reading Dawkins, Dennett, etc.; and had decided to myself that I was actually an atheist. We got—as you do—into a philosophical discussion about the Bible and God; and we both got damn angry when I demanded proof of the various tenets of Christianity. Long story short: Will and I have a rather icy acquaintancy these days and I no longer attend my erstwhile church, as he, through general chit-chat (though I doubt maliciously) informed the rest of the church that I was atheist. An involuntary coming-out I suppose... I think I could have 'come out' more smoothly rather than belligerently insisting on proof to poor Will."

I talk a lot in this book about parallels between coming out atheist and coming out LGBT. There's a reason for that; the LGBT community has decades of experience in coming out, we've come up with a battalion of strategies and support systems for it, and atheists can learn a lot from that. But there are real differences as well. And one of the most important differences is this: When you come out as queer, you're not telling straight people they're wrong to be straight. But there is no way to say, "I don't believe in God," without implying, "If you do believe in God, you're wrong." And even if we see this as a simple disagreement about an idea, many believers will experience it as a personal rejection. From your perspective, you're telling them, "I don't believe in God"—but what they may hear is, "I don't love you the way you are."

I don't think there's any way around that. But you don't have to exacerbate it by trying to argue them out of their religion. Instead, focus on any misconceptions they might have about atheism, and on any fears they might have for you. After they've gotten used to your atheism—then, if you want to, you can have the arguments about whether God exists. (Do note, however, that there's a somewhat blurry line between explaining your atheism and arguing about religion. For more on that, see the chapter specifically devoted to arguing about religion.)

14. Have your practical and financial ducks in a row—within reason.

As positive as coming out generally is, the reality is that it can create serious practical problems. It doesn't always—but it can. Creating friction with people you care about is hard enough. It's harder still when your livelihood is jeopardized.

So have your practical and financial ducks in a row first, as much as you can. If you're coming out atheist at work, and it might endanger your job—make sure you could cope with that financially. If you're in a conservative religious community, and coming out might isolate you—find an atheist community, and put down roots there first. If you're a college student and your parents are supporting you—you might wait to come out until you're out of college.

Corey A. Henderson knew that coming out would mean being completely cut off from his community and his livelihood. He had been a Jehovah's Witness, a sect that preaches the complete shunning of anyone who leaves the faith. So he prepared a space to go to, as best he could. "I worked in Toronto at the time," he says, "and I had secretly rented an apartment there in the days leading up to when I left… I planned it out, and did it at a time of my choosing when I had a place to live, and enough money hidden to live on for a short time."

Now, there are some obvious limits to this advice. Coming out means accepting some risk. There's really no way around that. If you wait to come out until everything is perfectly safe, you're going to wait a long time.

But it's important to remember that staying in the closet has risks as well.

For one thing: The longer you wait to come out, the greater your chance is of being outed by someone else—accidentally or intentionally. And it's much, *much* better to come out voluntarily than to be outed against your will. When you come out voluntarily, you can have the conversation when you want, where you want, with whom you want. You can do it when you're calm, when you're prepared. You can do it when you're not in the middle of finals or right after your mother has died. You can do it when you've found a supportive community and have gotten your ducks in a row. When you're outed by someone else, you don't get to control any of that. And even if all the circumstances are reasonably okay, being outed can still be traumatic. It takes your coming out away from you. It can feel like a violation.

What's more, staying in the closet doesn't just involve the risk of being outed. It involves the risk and stress of living a lie. And that can do real damage.[8]

So when you're doing your cost/benefit analysis about coming out versus staying in, remember: Neither choice is risk-free.

15. Be strategic about who you come out to first.

You don't have to make one big announcement to everyone all at once. If you think your dad will handle your atheism better than your mom—tell him first. If you think your mom will cope better, tell her first. (Again, there's a lesson we can learn from the LGBT community; gays and lesbians have a long history of coming out to Mom before Dad.) If you think your siblings will handle it better than your parents, or that your roommate will handle it better than your best friend—tell them first.

This accomplishes a couple of things. It gets you allies you can get support from if you run into a harder time with other people. And it gets you practice in coming out, and makes you more comfortable and familiar with doing it.

On the Coming Out Godless Project website, Michael Brownstein has a very instructive "what not to do" story about who to come out to first, and in what order. He initially came out to friends at college, which worked out fine. But then, he says, "I drunk dialed my super religious cousin on Purim [an important Jewish religious holiday], which was soon after my coming out to my roommate. I ended up coming out as an atheist to him. He called me back the next day, and confronted me on it. This, I realized, was a bad idea. Firstly, he was considered somewhat of a hero in the Jewish Community because he had moved to Israel at one point. I realized that he also had a big mouth, and I perceived that my secret was now out in the Jewish Community." Michael's big-mouthed cousin forced him to come out to the rest of his family, more hastily than he'd planned. "A few were supportive," he says—including his parents, who were fairly good about it. "Others I have not talked to since."

This principle is especially true in the workplace. I'll go into more detail about that in the chapter on coming out at work. But I'll touch on the basic principles here: Identify someone at work who has some kind of authority and is likely to be supportive. Come out to them first. Get them used to the idea. Get them on your side. And *then* start coming out to the rest of the folks.

But when you're doing your strategic planning about who to come out to first, bear this in mind as well:

16. Be prepared for the dam to burst.

It's smart to be strategic about who you come out to first. But you can't always predict how people are going to react. And they might react by outing you—either unintentionally, because they made a stupid computer mistake or didn't know who knew and who didn't, or intentionally, out of malice or misguided concern.

Daniel Fincke, of the Camels With Hammers blog, says, "With my college friends, I came out in person usually through one on one conversations. Quickly word spread through the grapevine so I did not need to tell everyone directly myself... I have since always voluntarily outed myself." And Alice tells a heartbreaking story of coming out to her best friend/former boyfriend, who saw her atheism as a betrayal— and took revenge by outing her to her family, who reacted terribly. "If there's one thing I can prescribe to those who aren't out yet," she says, "it would be to tell no one until you're ready to tell everyone."

So once you start coming out, be prepared—emotionally and practically—for word to get out.

17. If you can, find an atheist community—first.

This can be hugely helpful in coming out. It's especially important if you live in a very religious region, where religion is tightly interconnected with social life, and leaving it means leaving that support. But even if you don't live in a super-religious community, coming out can be stressful and alienating—sometimes surprisingly so. People can be jerks who you might not expect to. Having support from other atheists can make it much easier.

When Corey A. Henderson came out as an atheist, he became totally isolated from his family and community; he had been in the Jehovah's Witnesses, a sect that requires its members to shun anyone who leaves the church. He now wishes he'd known that atheist communities existed when he was deciding to leave. "I had no support network of any kind," he says. "If I had known atheist communities even existed 20 years ago in Canada I would've tried to reach out to them after I made my break."

Online atheist communities can be a wonderful place to start—and to continue. They're easy to find. They're plentiful. They're varied, with focuses and vibes and conversational styles to suit many personalities. You can participate in them at your leisure and on your timetable. You can stay connected with them if you move, giving you stability and continuity. If you're careful about clearing your browser history, they're as private as you want them to be. (Usually. More on that in the chapter on the Internet.) And online atheist communities are making it impossible to keep atheism a secret. If you have an Internet connection, you can't grow up not knowing that atheists exist, and you'll be able to connect with as many as you want. These communities are hugely important. As Poodles says on the Coming Out Godless Project website, "The internet is a great tool for people looking for like minds and helpful information; I wish it had been around when I was reverting back to my birth state of atheism."

But as awesome as they are, online communities aren't the same as in-the-flesh ones. They're better in some ways, worse in others, but they're not the same. A virtual hug isn't the same as a physical one. An online discussion isn't the same as a group picnic or a drink with friends in a bar. And people who live in your area are... well, they're familiar with your area, and with the particular culture you live in. They

can give you specific, fine-tuned guidance on living as an atheist: who in the Chamber of Commerce is sensitive to bigotry issues, who on the school board is going to pitch a fit if you bring up evolution, who in the church choir is secretly an atheist. A local community can help you in ways that nobody else can even begin to.

Marshall Davis was born into a Southern Baptist family. On the Coming Out Godless Project website, he explains that when he began questioning Christianity, he explored the possibilities of Wicca and Buddhism. "Then," he says, "I found the Jacksonville Atheist Meetup and went and found I was an atheist and among friends." And former Baptist Terry Cupp, also on the Coming Out Godless Project website, says, "I have found a wonderful group of Atheist friends in Las Vegas and now know I do not need a church or belief in a God for comfort."

If you're not into groups? That's fine. Not everyone is. But it's a good idea to make contact with an atheist community anyway, or at least to make yourself aware of what options you have. A lot of people thought they didn't need community until it started to disappear from under their feet. You don't want to be scrambling to find contacts and connection right when you're at your most vulnerable.

If you're thinking, "There's no atheist community where I live"? Don't assume that. I travel a lot around the United States, and I've found that almost every major city in the country has some sort of atheist/humanist/godless community. Many smaller cities have them as well. In conservative regions like the Bible Belt, they're actually more prevalent than they are in progressive areas, and typically stronger as well. And more are popping up all the time: not just in the United States, but around the world. Check out the resource guide at the end of this book—in particular, check out the organizations that sponsor local communities, and ask for information about how to find a group. Or just go to Meetup.com, and search for "atheists" + your area. Lots of local atheist groups aren't affiliated with any national organization.

And if you really don't find any atheist groups where you live? Consider starting one.

About 5[9]–15%[10] of all Americans are atheists or other nonbelievers. Those numbers are even higher in many other parts of the world; in some countries, it's as high as 65%, and possibly even 85%.[11] That's according to fairly conservative estimates, and it doesn't take into consideration the stigma against atheism, and the fact that many nonbelievers are uncomfortable saying so—even to themselves. And those numbers are on the rise.[12] So the chances that you're the only atheist in your neck of the woods are pretty darned small. The chances are excellent that other folks are out there, not far from you, wondering the same things you're wondering, and feeling just as alone as you are.

So check out the organizations in the resource guide that sponsor local communities, and ask for information about how to *start* an atheist group. Or heck—just go to Meetup.com, and hit "Start group."

There's a whole chapter in this book about building atheist communities. There are lots of people who can give you lots of information about it. But the first step is to just do it.

"Start group." It's not as hard as you think.

18. Remember that it's not always that big a deal.

So far, I've mostly been focusing on the difficulties. That's often what atheists talk about when we talk about coming out. And that makes sense. If I'm writing a guide on how to come out, of course I'm going to focus on overcoming the obstacles. If we're working on ways to make coming out easier, of course we're going to pay attention to all the ways that it's hard.

But there's a flip side that's really important to remember: Sometimes, coming out isn't as traumatic as we fear.

I can't tell you how many atheists I've talked to who have told me their coming out stories, and ended them with, "It really wasn't that bad." And often the reaction is in the middle: "No, they didn't love it, but they got over it sooner than I thought, and now it's pretty much fine."

bubba707, who lives in a pretty conservative, mostly Catholic small town in Wisconsin, says, "It's just not a real subject of conversation. The closest to it was a while after my Dad's funeral an Aunt asked if I was religious at all and I told her no, not at all. Nothing more was said and we still get along fine."

Thais Camargo, who lives in Rio de Janeiro, Brazil, says, "Since high school, people have mostly reacted in a very positive way (except for one person who said 'Oh no!,' I can't think of a single bad comment)."

Chris Hallquist, who was raised liberal Protestant in Oshkosh, Wisconsin and now writes the Uncredible Hallq blog, says, "I had some legitimate excuse for not going to church that day, but then my mom asked, 'But you still want to go to church, right?' and I said, 'No, because I don't believe in God anymore.' My parents weren't necessarily happy with it, but didn't make a fuss."[13]

Coolred38, who was raised in the Middle East, says, "After being muslim for 20 years, I eventually 'converted' to atheism several years ago. The first person I told was my girlfriend, who is still muslim. She has encouraged me every step of the way and supported me against others who just want to condemn me. I have not directly told my children (who are still muslim, mostly... all nearly grown) that I am an atheist but they understand from my new direction in life, my online comments etc. It actually went smoother than I thought though there have been haters."

And finally, Kristin: "My brother died some years ago, in his mid twenties. And his death was a very hard blow for our family. One of the difficulties concerning his funeral was that we simply didn't know what he would have wanted.

"So it was a few weeks after the funeral, I was driving with my mother, and as we passed the cemetery I told her I would prefer a humanist funeral and cremation in case I died.

"She shrugged and said, 'ok.'

"It was all very dramatic..."

There's one more story I want to tell that illustrates this point beautifully. It's a story about coming out gay that someone wrote in to the sex advice columnist Dan Savage. It was from a teenage boy who finally got up the courage to tell his parents he was gay, something he was really scared to do. When he finally did, his father started crying—and when he stopped crying and was able to talk, he explained that he wasn't crying because his son was gay. He was crying because he didn't know what he had done wrong to make his son think this would be a problem, or to make him think that he wouldn't love him and support him no matter what.

Obviously, that doesn't happen to everyone who comes out—as gay, or as atheist. But it happens more than you might think. If you're scared to come out, maybe you should give the people you love the benefit of the doubt, and not leap to the conclusion that they're going to freak out about it.

And sometimes when atheists come out, the reaction is, "Me too!" I have heard this story from so many atheists, I can't even tell you. They tell their friends or colleagues or family members that they're an atheist—and the response is ecstatic relief. *They* don't believe in God either, and *they've* been in the closet, and *they've* been scared to tell *us*.

Wendy Hughes was raised in a Reform Jewish congregation, but left religion in college (although her Jewish cultural identity is still important to her). On the Coming Out Godless Project website, she tells this story: "One day, my dear ex mother-in-law and I were getting ready to take a swim. I had been married to my ex-husband for only six years, but I'd remained friends with his mother, a very nice Jewish lady, for over 30 years after we were divorced. We used to go to get Jewish deli together, and she made the best chopped liver I ever ate. One day I decided to tell her how I feel. I said, 'You know, I don't believe in God.' She looked over her shoulder, and all around... we were alone in her apartment, but she whispered, '... neither do I.' And it started an important dialog. I think there are a lot of Jewmanists."

So don't go into the conversation with a giant black cloud over your head, assuming that it's going to be dire, with tears and recriminations and years of tension between you. It may play out that way—but it may not. And going into the conversation with dire expectations may make things worse. It can set a grim tone that might not have to be there.

You know the people you're coming out to better than I do. You know better than I whether they're likely to be angry, insulted, relaxed, worried, relieved, hurt, delighted, unsurprised. You know better than I whether the conversation will take five minutes or five hours or five months or five years; whether you'll need to be ready to get out of the house and check into a motel, or will be happily hanging around that night talking about the ball game.

I'm just saying: Give the people who care about you some credit. They may react better than you think. They may not react badly at all. Or they may react badly at first, and then get over it quicker than you think.

Which leads me to the next chapter.

CHAPTER SEVEN

— ✸ —

The "No Big Deal" Method

So far, the "coming out" basics I've been talking about have mostly assumed that you're going to sit down with the people you know and have a Serious Talk about your atheism. But there's an entirely different approach that many people take, and it's worth discussing before we get much further:

Instead of coming out, you can just *be* out.

Instead of sitting people down and having the Serious Talk About Atheism, you can just mention it when it seems appropriate. If someone asks you, "What did you do this weekend?," you can tell them, "I went to this great atheist conference in Missouri—the car broke down on the drive back, but otherwise it was awesome," or, "I stayed home and read *Why Are You Atheists So Angry?*—interesting book, have you read it?" If someone asks how your dating life is going, you can say, "It's been going well—I thought being an atheist on OKCupid was going to limit my options, but I think it's actually turning out to be an advantage." If someone says they'll pray for you, you can tell them, "Actually, I'm an atheist—but I appreciate the thought." (Oklahoma tornado survivor Rebecca Vitsmun became a national atheist hero when CNN's Wolf Blitzer asked if she was thanking the Lord for her family surviving the tornado, and she replied, "I'm actually an atheist.")[1]

The "no big deal" method has some real advantages. One of the biggest is that it normalizes atheism—not just yours, but everybody's. Instead of making atheism seem like something weird and scary, it presents it as an entirely ordinary way to be and to think. Which it is.

I like what 1000 Needles says about this method. "Believe it or not, I can't remember my coming out! Neither as an agnostic (I was still a teenager) nor as an atheist (22 or 23). Of course I can remember discussing the subject, but the point is this. Being not religious always has been normal for me and for the people around me, even if they disagreed. The few dorks who reacted in an intolerant way always have been the exception."

In fact, the "no big deal" method doesn't just "normalize" atheism. It calls into question the very idea that being religious should be considered the norm. Here's what Sally M, an atheist for almost her entire life (ever since she was a kid), has to say about this: "Ever since I realized being an atheist wasn't the default state (something I still wrongly assume about people I meet), I've always just been upfront about it, with friends, family, co-workers, everyone. If religion comes up in conversation, I just say 'well… I'm an atheist,' with a hint of 'I'm sorry, I don't understand why you asked me such an obvious question?' I've found that if I say it as though it's the normal, proper, obvious thing, most people become a little bit embarrassed and start trying to downplay their own religious beliefs. I'm the normal one, they're the weird one who has to explain themselves."

And I love this take on it from John Horstman, who was raised non-religious in mostly non-religious circles and who still has a mostly atheist social set. "Since my default assumption," he says, "is that a given person I don't know doesn't believe in any given god(s), when I'm NOT interacting with other atheists, the coming out happens on the part of the religious, and MY coming out occurs as a response to that (along the lines of: ME "Wait, Jesus? Seriously?"; ZE "Yeah, wait, you DON'T believe in God?"; ME "No, of course not."; ZE "Oh…"

(subject change to something unrelated to religion))." *(Note: "Ze" is a gender-neutral personal pronoun, parallel to "he" or "she.")*

LGBT people have been doing this for years. We may have sat down with our parents and had a heart-to-heart about our sexual orientation or gender identity. But for many of us, in our everyday lives with friends and acquaintances and colleagues, we're just... out. We talk about our girlfriends or boyfriends, our wives or husbands, the time we worked for the trans rights organization or our weekend rehearsing with the gay chorus. We don't sit down with everyone we meet, look them in the eye, and say, "I have something important to tell you." And it works. In much of the world, anyway. In much of the world, it really isn't that big a deal. And treating it as no big deal is part of how we've made it less of a big deal to other people.

The downside of this method is that if people do react badly, you may not be in a good place for it. If you've casually mentioned your atheism on your way to class, and your friend bursts into tears or starts telling you that you're going to burn in Hell—do you have time and energy to deal with that before you get to class? And if there are people in your life for whom religion is deeply important, they may see your casual dropping of the A-bomb as disrespectful—not just to their religion, but to their deep feelings about it. And that may exacerbate the other bad feelings they were probably already going to have.

What's more, LGBT people have a big advantage in this area that atheists don't. The LGBT community has been highly visible and vocal for many decades now, and we've had decades to work on changing society's attitudes about us. So if you're a gay person who's doing a "no big deal" coming out, chances are excellent that the people you're coming out to are already pretty familiar with gay people. They've already met lots of other gay people. They've seen lots of gay people in movies and on TV. So when you tell them you're gay, they're not as likely to react with horror or shock, or to pepper you with ignorant and insulting questions, the way people routinely did fifty years ago, or thirty, or even ten.

That's a lot less true for atheists. Especially in the United States, or other countries that are very religious and where atheism isn't that common or visible. (Yet.)

You know your colleagues and friends and family better than I do. You have a better sense than I do of how they're going to react to your atheism. So use your own judgment about this. And you don't have to use the same method with everyone. You might, for instance, sit down with your intensely Catholic parents to have the Serious Talk About Atheism, but be more casual and "no big deal" with your friends and acquaintances.

There are also atheists who settle on a somewhat different version of "no big deal." They don't try to keep their atheism a secret, they come out as atheist if it comes up in conversation, but they don't go out of their way to bring it up. Some people are more comfortable with this method, as they find it less confrontational. Others like it because it limits the number of people who'll find out and be upset, but it still doesn't make them feel like they're keeping a Big Secret. Kimberly, a 19-year-old business major in the northeastern United States, says, "I generally don't hide my atheism from people but I also don't mention it, mainly because as a business major I feel that it would be best for my future career to appear non-controversial. You never know who will be looking over your application and what might offend them, and I need every chance I can get to get a good job." And Taran Meyer, who grew up in a liberal and secular community in urban Western Canada, says, "I've always been matter-of-fact about my atheism when it does come up (which isn't often). Some of my friends find it puzzling, but we don't really get into it—either it's not important, or it's upsetting to discuss, so we don't."

This "mention it if it comes up, don't bring it up if it doesn't" method doesn't have the same political punch as the "just being out to everyone" method. If for no other reason, you simply won't be out to as many people. But you get to decide if that matters to you—and if so, how much.

If you do use the "no big deal" method, I still suggest being prepared. Be emotionally prepared for scenes and storms. Be practically prepared for rifts and alienation. Be financially prepared for loss of jobs or parental support. The "no big deal" method isn't a replacement for all the rest of the advice in this book—it's a supplement to it. But it's a useful tool in your coming out toolkit. Don't forget about it.

CHAPTER EIGHT

— ❋ —

A Few Words About Language

"Atheist." "Agnostic." "Humanist." "Skeptic." "Freethinker." "Naturalist." "Materialist." "Nonbeliever." "Godless."

There are at least a dozen different words that roughly mean, "Person who doesn't believe in any gods." And atheists/agnostics/humanists/skeptics/freethinkers/naturalists/materialists/nonbelievers/godless people often love to squabble about which word is best, and which one we should all be rallying behind, and what exactly they even mean.

I don't want to get into that squabble here. Or anywhere, really. I usually use the word "atheist" for myself—I think it's strong and clear, and pretty much everyone knows what it means. (More or less. I'll get to that in a sec.) And it is the word I'm mostly using in this book. But if you identify as an agnostic, a humanist, a freethinker, a naturalist, a nonbeliever, or some other term meaning "person who doesn't believe in any gods or in the supernatural"—this book is still for you. When I say "atheist," please feel free to do a mental search-and-replace, and replace it in your mind with whatever term you prefer to use for yourself. I titled this book "Coming Out Atheist" rather than "Coming Out Atheist/Agnostic/Humanist/Skeptic/Freethinker/Naturalist/ Materialist/ Nonbeliever/Godless/Other," not for ideological reasons, but for aesthetic ones. The thought of giving my beloved book a twelve-word title made me nauseous. But I don't really care what word other godless people use to describe their godlessness. When you're talking with other heathens, use whichever one you like. I do, however, have strong thoughts about which kind of language to use when we're coming out.

I'm not going to argue in favor of any one word. What I am going to argue in favor of is clarity.

If you tell your fundamentalist aunt that you're a freethinker or a bright, she may literally have no idea what you're talking about. What's more, if the language you use is vague or open to misinterpretation in any way, do not underestimate the power of people to misinterpret things they don't want to hear. And if the people you're coming out to have no idea what you're talking about, or if they completely misinterpret and misunderstand it, that's missing the whole point of coming out in the first place.

So when you're coming out, use words that the people you're coming out to will understand. You don't want your coming out conversation to degenerate into a muddle-fest about what exactly you're trying to tell them. And you don't want a situation where you think you've told people about your nonbelief—and weeks or months or years later, it turns out that they didn't get it.

Flora, whose family are all very conservative Christians living in East Texas, tells a story that illustrates this point beautifully. "I brought the topic up with my mom," she says, "but to her I said only that 'I don't believe anymore.' She was concerned, but wanted to assure me that she still loved me. I was so relieved, wow. All of this worrying was for nothing. So several months later when I was discussing the plans for my upcoming wedding and I casually dropped into the conversation that it was going to be an atheist wedding, I was somewhat surprised by the heavy silence from my mom.

"'What do you mean?' she finally asked.

"'Well, there won't be any prayers, any mention of God, any pastor or priest,' I said, maybe a little flippantly.

"'But, does that mean YOU are an atheist?' she asked.

"'Yeah, remember, I told you all about it several months ago.'

"'Well, yes, I know you didn't believe anymore. But I had no idea you were an atheist. That's just gross.'"

After a couple of weeks, though, Flora and her mom were back to normal. And now, when asked if there were anything she'd do differently about coming out, she says, "If I could change it, I wouldn't have been so afraid of 'the A word.' Claiming it is the only way to overcome the negative stigma associated with it. It's not any more 'gross' than any other philosophical position."

Now, it's certainly true that some words are more likely to push buttons than others. The word "atheist," especially, often shocks and upsets people—probably because it *is* so blunt—in a way that other words don't. And the word "atheist" often comes with baggage. There's stigma associated with it, myths and misinformation about who atheists are and what we think and do. Yes, the word "atheist" is clear, in the sense that pretty much everyone understands that it means, "I don't believe in any gods, seriously, no fooling." But people will sometimes interpret it to mean things that you didn't intend at all. And I'm not just talking about the whole "if you acknowledge even the tiniest sliver of hypothetical possibility that some god might exist, you're not really an atheist" thing. I'm not even talking about the assorted debates within the atheist community about the precise definition of the word. I mean that many people hear the word, and use it, with a whole set of nasty associations tacked on. People will interpret "I am an atheist" to mean things like, "I have no morality." "I hate Christmas." "I worship Satan." In her extraordinary one-woman performance piece, *Letting Go of God*, Julia Sweeney has a wonderful line about her parents' reaction: "I think my parents had been mildly disappointed when I'd said I didn't believe in God anymore—but being an atheist was another thing altogether."[1]

But again, this stigma and baggage are probably there precisely because the word *is* so clear, and so descriptive. Some of the stigma is attached to the word "atheist"—but most of it is attached to the very idea of atheism. The word has baggage because the idea has baggage. Whatever word we commonly use to describe ourselves is going to pick up stigma. (Look at how the word "gay" has become an insult.) And honestly? Chances are that when you come out as a nonbeliever, you're going to be dealing with stigma and misinformation no matter what language you use.

And using the word more is a big part of what's going to de-stigmatize it. Marnie, who grew up in southern New Hampshire in a generically Christian family, says, "I try to avoid hedging and avoiding the topic, when it's brought up. I feel strongly that when ostensibly 'normal' people say they are atheists without immediately ripping the head off a nearby child, or invoking a dark lord, I think it subtly changes the way people view atheists. I don't think atheists need to be perfect or exceptional in any way, I think the most powerful thing they can be is relatable."

Being vague or imprecise about your language can also make things difficult if you decide later on that you want to be more open. Stephanie, who grew up and lives in the fairly non-religious country of France, says, "These days, if beliefs come up in conversation I am comfortable prefacing my opinion with 'I am an atheist,' whereas in the past I would have said 'I have many doubts,' 'I have serious issues with organised religion but I'm not sure about divinity/spirituality,' or 'I am an agnostic'... My close friends, my sister (a practising Christian but not a devout or bigoted one) and my aunt (who believes lots of new-age-y nonsense), when I said this to them for the first time, responded by dismissing it. 'You? No, you're not really an atheist.' Several people had that reaction. This is presumably based on previous conversations we had had. I let it go, but it annoyed me."

Now, I will say here that some people prefer gentler words like "humanist," in part, for the very reason that it *isn't* smack-you-in-the-face clear. They say that the word "humanist" opens doors, while the word "atheist" closes them. They say that if they tell people, "I'm an atheist," people think they know what an atheist is, and they think it's scary and bad, and the conversation shuts down before it starts. If, on the other hand, they tell people, "I'm a humanist," people will often respond with, "What does that mean?"—and it can start a conversation. The very fact that the word isn't universally understood, they say, is exactly what opens the door.

And some atheists will try to avoid the whole "Coming out as atheist means telling them they're wrong" thing by saying more non-committal things, like, "Religion isn't for me." That can be okay if you're talking with people you don't have ongoing relationships with, in casual situations where you don't feel like getting into a big thing about your atheism and it doesn't matter that much anyway. And it can also work as a soft opening, to gradually get people used to the idea. But the problem with this language comes from the exact reason that it's less button-pushing—it frames religion and atheism as subjective opinions. Saying, "Religion isn't for me," is like saying, "Opera isn't for me," or, "Broccoli isn't for me." And that's not how it is. Atheism and religion are conclusions about the real, non-subjective world. We *do* think believers are mistaken. We may or may not care very much about that mistake, but we still think they're mistaken. If you don't accept that, if you don't eventually come out and clearly say who you are and what you think, it can create real confusion and problems. (Look at Flora and Stephanie's stories again if you don't agree.)

You need to make your own decision about that balance between button-pushing and clarity. You might even decide to use different words in different situations, depending on who you're talking with and whether you're in the mood for a fifteen-minute conversation about what humanism is. And of course, if you do primarily identify as a humanist—or as a skeptic, or an agnostic, or a materialist, or whatever—rather than an atheist, then that's the word you should use. Just remember: The people you're coming out to may not know what you're talking about. You may have to do some explaining, and some spelling out of what it is you actually do and don't believe, if you don't want your coming out conversation to muddy the waters even further.

But if you're in doubt—don't lie. Use whatever language is most honest, and most clear, and expresses who you are most accurately. "Atheist" means subtly different things to different people—but for most people who call themselves atheists, it means some version of "person who doesn't believe in any gods." If you feel like that's the best word for you, if that's the word that most correctly describes who you are and what you think—use it. And don't evade direct questions. If you're using gentler language to soften the conversation, and the people you're talking with ask you directly, "Are you an atheist?"—and the answer is "Yes"—say, "Yes."

The whole point of coming out is to be true to yourself. Being evasive is missing the point.

CHAPTER NINE

Family

This is, by far, the longest chapter in the book. And there's a reason for that. When I was collecting "coming out atheist" stories for this book, I got more "coming out to family" stories than any other kind—by a significant margin. I got more "coming out to family" stories than all the other stories put together. Given a chance to tell stories about coming out as atheist to friends, to co-workers, to teachers, to fellow students, to little old ladies on the street, people overwhelmingly wanted to talk about their families.

And that makes sense. If your friends flip out when you come out as an atheist, you can ultimately decide to get new friends. If your boss or your colleagues flip out, you can ultimately look for a new job.

If your mom flips out? You only get one mom. Okay, some of us get more than one. But we usually don't have more than two or three. And however many you have, moms are entirely unique. It's an irreplaceable relationship.

Coming out atheist to family is different from just about any other coming out experience you're going to have. Assuming that you do actually care about your family and have a halfway decent relationship with them (which I realize isn't universally true—I'll get to that in a bit), these are irreplaceable relationships. They're relationships you're pretty much stuck with. They're relationships you're going to have for a good long while. And they're probably relationships that matter to you a great deal.

So with family members, I'm inclined to counsel more preparation, more caution with timing, more patience, working harder to be the bigger person, being willing to put up with somewhat more crap for longer. You're hopefully going to have these people in your life for a long time. That's probably worth putting more work into, and it's probably worth putting up with a little more crap.

At the same time, though, when it comes to families, I'm also more inclined to counsel honesty. I'm more inclined to counsel coming out eventually, and as soon as you reasonably can. And the reason is exactly the same. You're hopefully going to have these people in your life for a long time. It's not like workmates or classmates, who you might never see again after a couple/few years. So the elephant in the room isn't going anywhere. It can't be avoided by postponing it. You either have to come out to them eventually, or live with the secret. Forever.

And because families are (usually) fairly dedicated to loving each other, thinking well of each other, and getting along reasonably well, the chances are good that both your honesty and your patience will pay off. Remember in the chapter on the basics, how Basic #3 was, "Give the people you're coming out to some credit"? That applies even more strongly to families. I have heard and read hundreds of "coming out atheist to my family" stories, and the overwhelming majority have ended with some version of, "Things are basically fine now." "They love me and accept me." "It's sometimes awkward and contentious, but most of the time we get along great." Some of these stories started with tears or fights or even threats—but most of them have wound up in a pretty good place.

Will, who started coming out as a nonbeliever at age five in Bozeman, Montana, says, "My uncle and I are now in the small minority of confessed atheists/agnostics in the larger family of my mother's siblings. But fortunately our family is as warm and accepting as they are intelligent, even despite their varying degrees of indulgence in such antiquated superstitions. So it has never been a divisive issue among us."

Coolred38, who became an atheist after being Muslim for twenty years, has had a similar experience. "My kids," he says, "the ones I most cherish how they think of me, have handled it well. My sons are the more devoted muslims but after the initial awkwardness they have accepted it more or less. I'm assuming their love for me allows them to push aside the beliefs Islam has instilled in them about apostates... but who knows."

And Jessica, who was raised in a fairly liberal Christian family in Australia, tells this story of coming out to her mother: "The conversation went something like this:

"Scene: Mum and I.

"Me: 'Mum, I need to talk to you. I won't be coming to church with you at Christmas. I'm... not a Christian anymore.'

"...

"'Sorry?'

"Mum: 'That's OK.' (slight puzzled face)

"(silence)"

Here's what Dale McGowan, editor of *Parenting Beyond Belief: On Raising Ethical, Caring Kids Without Religion* and co-author of *Raising Freethinkers: A Practical Guide for Parenting Beyond Belief,* said to me about this: "In my experience, and in the experience of most people I've talked to, coming out goes much better than you think it will. There are important exceptions, but we too often assume the worst and miss the opportunity to normalize disbelief and to live honestly. Parents in particular should think about the importance of modeling that kind of honest courage for their kids."

One of the most common fears about coming out atheist to families is the fear of total alienation: the fear that once your religious family knows you're an atheist, they'll never see you or even speak to you again. But based on the coming out stories I've seen, this extreme response seems to be very rare. It does happen, and if your family is intensely religious (or if they belong to a sect where total ostracism of apostates is required, such as Jehovah's Witnesses), you should be prepared for that possibility. But most of the time, even intensely religious people don't stop loving their godless relatives, and don't cut them out of their lives. You may have shouty arguments or painful conversations; you may have ongoing disputes or awkward silences or topics you just don't talk about; your family may totally ignore your atheism or even deny it. But you'll probably still have a family.

So. All that being said. What are some good ways to come out to your family? What are some of the reactions you're likely to get? And what are some good ways to deal with those reactions—or head them off at the pass?

Tradition, or, That's Just What We Do In This Family

You'd think that for most religious families, any strife or upset they had over atheism would be about... you know, religion. But in many families, when atheists come out, the problems that arise have less to do with religion, and more to do with... well, with family. For many families, being religious is less about spiritual beliefs, and more about family identity. More than anything else, going to religious services is a family togetherness activity, or even a family duty. And many people have absorbed the idea that being religious is what makes you a good person—so making sure the whole family stays religious gets treated as a moral obligation. Like making sure the whole family brushes their teeth and says "thank you" for presents.

For these families, conflicts over coming out atheist aren't about your eternal soul burning in Hell. They're much more about family cohesion and responsibility. Sally M, who was brought up Catholic but has been an atheist since childhood, says, "The whole family has always treated church like a chore, so they probably assumed I was claiming atheism to get out of wasting my Sunday. If my mother had to drag herself and the rest of my siblings out of bed, there was no way I was getting out of it. It honestly didn't ever occur to me that being an atheist would work to get me out of church until I moved out, and it didn't occur to them either. They wanted to stay home as much as I did. It wasn't about believing or not. It was about my father's enormous Catholic guilt complex."

Kimberly, who was raised by a Catholic mother and an atheist father, has a similar story. "My mom was actually OK with me being an atheist," she says, "but she was really, really upset when I told her I would not go to church anymore. She wouldn't talk to me. She got over it though," she adds, "and our relationship was not damaged." And in her performance piece *Letting Go of God*, Julia Sweeney says this was one of the hardest things about coming out as a nonbeliever to her parents. "My mom said, 'This doesn't mean that you've stopped going to church, does it?' I suddenly felt so guilty about this religion: my parent's religion, the religion that they had given to us kids, and that I was now handing back to them."[1]

Religion can also have a connection to place, to social class, to an ethnic identity—all of which can get tied up with family as well. In *Letting Go of God*, Sweeney talks about a newspaper that reported on her appearance at an atheist conference—the newspaper in her parents' town, the town where she grew up. "Spokane," she says, "where I had recently hosted the Catholic Charities luncheon, where I had spoken repeatedly at my Catholic high school, where my parents took such pride in their Catholicism and their children and, who I believe now in retrospect, felt that my Catholicism was what connected me to my hometown, to my social class, and to them in spite of having moved away." Sweeney's father even spelled this out in words: "My dad called and said, 'You have betrayed your family, your school, your city.' It was like I'd sold secrets to the Russians."[2]

To some extent, this hurt may be unavoidable. If religion is central to your family's identity, then it's central to your family's identity, and there's not much you can do about that. And there is, in fact, no way to say, "I don't believe in God," without implying, "If you do believe in God, I think you're wrong." You have the right to reject that identity, of course, just like you'd have the right to not stay in the family business—but it's not surprising that they'd be hurt about it.

But you can mitigate this hurt. When you come out as atheist, you may be very focused on your own fears that your family will abandon you—and that's reasonable. But they may be having their own fears that your atheism might make you abandon them. So make it clear that you love your family, and respect them, and have no intention of deserting them. Follow through on that; continue to call, write, email, visit, whatever it is you do to stay connected—just as often as you did before you came out. Focus on other things your family has in common: family stories, activities, recipes, values, traditions, non-religious rituals, the secular aspects of religious rituals (like Christmas trees or latkes). And make it clear that these are things you value and treasure.

In these situations, some atheists are okay with going to religious services and participating in religious events—as long as the family knows that they're atheist, and knows that they're doing it for the family and not for any gods. When Liz H., who grew up in suburban Massachusetts, came out as atheist to her parents, they didn't have much problem with it (although they did pull Pascal's Wager on her). But, she says, "I do remember them telling me to go along with church services when we visited conservative relatives. Their logic was as follows: We see them very rarely, let's not turn this 'once every few years' visit into a big argument. I understood the notion that in the interest of my parents' peace with their siblings, I did them this favor." She goes on to say, "Once I moved out it became a non-issue. I spend the big holidays with them, including Christmas and Easter, and I've made it clear that I like the tradition and sense of family and the food, and the holiday is an excuse. And in return they come over to my place sometimes for 'because I felt like making a multi-course meal' feasts that are just as fun and important." (That last bit points to another important principle, one we talked about in the chapter on the basics—fairness. If you're going to compromise and keep participating in your family's religious rituals, don't let it be a one-way street. Get them to compromise as well, and to participate with you in secular rituals of your own.)

Other atheists feel that going to religious services or participating in religious ceremonies would be dishonest, like they're giving public support to an idea they don't agree with and even passionately oppose. Or else they just find religious services unpleasant, even offensive. If that's true for you, and you're not willing to go to services with your family—that is totally reasonable. Just make it clear that your rejection of religion isn't a rejection of the family. And again, suggest other activities you could do together—ones that actually reflect your shared interests and values.

And you get to decide where to draw that line: which religious rituals you're willing to participate in, and which ones you're not. When LD's father was alive, she'd had some painful disputes with him about her atheism. When he was dying, she says, "I stood around his bed with my mother and the priest and said the 'Our Father' with him (which now sounded utterly ridiculous to me) so as not to upset anyone. At his funeral the same priest requested we all do readings and I was open to it, if I could read something poetic from Psalms, maybe.

"Instead," she says, "I was handed John 3:16. ['For God so loved the world that he gave his one and only Son, that whoever believes in him shall not perish but have eternal life.'] Family and friends knew about my apostasy and I didn't care if they thought me hypocritical or not, but then all those memories of my dad calling me an asshole in front of these same people were now being dredged up. I declined, angered a few relatives, and was angry myself that now because of the interfering priest, the bad memories of my father were at the top of my mind."

This story brings up another point: You may run into problems or communication breakdowns with your family over rites of passage, like weddings or funerals. There's a common cultural assumption that these rituals will be religious, or at least held in religious institutions and presided over by clergy. Even families who aren't very religious will often make that assumption. It's like a family version of ceremonial deism. So if that's not your plan, you should probably spell it out—clearly, and early. And again, even if nobody cares that much about the God part of these rituals, there may be an element of family tradition or history that feels like it's being broken. If your parents and aunts and uncles and sisters and brothers all got married in the church or the synagogue, they may feel hurt if you decide not to. Again, emphasizing other family traditions can be a good way to mitigate this.

Rejection, or, You Don't Love God—Do You Still Love Me?

So some families may see atheism as a rejection of the family. And reactions to that can play out in a variety of ways, from hurt feelings to guilt-tripping to an invasive violation of your own values. But in addition to that, you might have family members who'll see your atheism, not just as a wholesale rejection of the family, but as an individual rejection of them.

Some of this is because, for many people, their religion is an important part of their personal identity—so saying you think their religion is wrong feels like you're saying part of them is wrong. But some of it may happen if religion was a personal bond between you. If you and your dad had a tradition of getting ice cream after church, or if your mom has a fond memory of reading you religious stories when you were a child, rejecting their religion can feel like you're dissing those memories and those bonds. Jessica, who was brought up in Australia in a fairly liberal Christian tradition, says that her mom was entirely okay with her atheism, and her coming out was undramatic, even anti-climactic. But, she says, while she has no regrets about the fact that she came out, "I regret that, before I moved out of home, I returned to her her confirmation necklace, which she had given to me. I felt at the time that I didn't deserve to carry it, and she should keep it and give it to some other, unspecified descendant. I didn't tell her that was what I thought, though, I just said 'I can't keep this anymore.' I think that really hurt her, but we haven't spoken about it. Since then she seems to assume I'm on an Angry Atheist Quest against religion, which I'm not."

These hurt feelings may be unavoidable. Again: When you say, "I don't believe in God," you are in fact implying, "If you do believe in God, I think you're wrong." And that can be true for progressive believers as well as conservative ones. gbjames, who was born into a relatively liberal and educated family in Wisconsin, talks about simply wearing a red "A" pin from the Out Campaign. "What I came to realize," he says, "was that my wearing an 'A' is seen by others (my brother, my mother, and probably many neighbors who know what it means) as a critique of them. They take it as an insult of sorts. It has contributed to a rift between me and my surviving sibling: my brother who holds some sort of fuzzy notion of religion, the point of which mainly seems to be that atheism is dogmatic and Richard Dawkins is scary."

But it's also important to remember: Yes, telling them you're an atheist implies that they're wrong to believe. But the reverse is also true. When they tell you about their religion, *they're* implying that *you're* wrong to be an atheist. And neither position is inherently more insulting than the other.

So when you tell your family that you're an atheist, be as clear as possible that you're not rejecting them or trying to insult them. (Assuming that's true, of course!) Remind them that your atheism isn't about them, any more than their religion is about you. It may help to make it clear that your atheism isn't a whim: that it's something you've thought about carefully, and that you do understand the religion you're rejecting. When Michael came out to his mother, a convert to Catholicism, he says that "at first she dismissed my atheism as me being a rebellious teenager. We had several discussions along the lines of 'it's just a phase you're going through, you'll soon return to Holy Mother Church.' After she realized that I had given the matter a great deal of thought and my atheism wasn't just an excuse to sleep in on Sundays, we had a series of discussions about specific Catholic dogma. When I told her about how the idea of the Assumption of Mary came about she accepted that I was knowledgeable about Catholicism."

And explain why it's important for you to be out: that your intention isn't to criticize or ridicule them, but to be honest with them and the rest of the world. gbjames again: "My 'outness' provoked, perhaps a year or two ago, a conversation with my mother during which, in response to her complaint that my 'A' was ridiculing her beliefs, I pointed out that she had never actually asked me why I wore that red letter. Since that time she seems to be a bit less disturbed by it."

This also worked for Kimberly, who lives in Tulsa, Oklahoma and whose mother and sister are both devout Protestants. She came out in an email to them, suggesting that they watch a news show about Julia Sweeney's one-woman show, *Letting Go of God*. In that email, she said (among other things), "I hope that you both know me well enough to understand that my intent in mentioning this piece is not to insult or belittle anybody's religious beliefs. You've both always been very open and honest with me about your beliefs, and I think I owe you the courtesy of being open and honest with you about my lack thereof." She says, "My mom responded by email promptly and lovingly. She'd read the transcript of the 'Sunday Morning' segment, and like Julia Sweeney's mother, said she and I could 'agree to disagree.' She said she respected my views and appreciated that I treat her beliefs with respect.

(I don't mind that she misinterprets my respectful treatment of her as 'respect for her beliefs.') The line that I like best from her email message is, 'I'm especially grateful that our differences don't keep us apart!'" In fact, Kimberly's mother trusts her so much, she's named her as her legal advocate if she's unable to express her wishes about her health care. (Her sister was chilly for a while, but warmed up later on.)

This story brings up another possible coming out strategy: If someone else has explained their atheism in a way that resonates with you and comes close to expressing your views—and you think that their book, movie, podcast, blog post, juggling act, etc. is more articulate or calm than you think you can be—you might ask your family to read/watch/listen to it, and then have a conversation about it. That probably should be the start of the conversation rather than the end of it—after all, your family needs to know about *your* atheism, not Julia Sweeney's or Richard Dawkins' or mine—but it can be a good starting place.

Failure, or, Where Did We Go Wrong?

For many deeply religious parents, the hardest part about their children coming out as atheist is their sense of failure. In most religions, one of the most important parental duties is raising the children to keep the faith. (This is actually one of the cleverest and most powerful ways that religion perpetuates itself.) So when your parents find out that you've left the faith, they may not just have anxiety over your immortal soul—they may have guilt over having failed as parents. Depending on their religion, they might think that it was their job to get you into Heaven, and that their failure will condemn you to Hell. And if they have fears that your atheism will lead you into misery and debauchery and no-goodnik-ism, chances are they'll have guilt on that front as well. This can be very painful for them—and it can be painful for you as well. If you've been a good person and a good daughter or son, it can be hard to have your parents treat you as a failure simply because you no longer believe in their invisible friend.

William, who grew up in the Midwest in a non-denominational Christian family, came out to his mother as a teenager, after she confronted him about his staying away from church. "She cried," he says, "and tried to talk me into going to church again, to give it another shot. I vividly recall her saying 'Where did we go wrong?' at one point. As the golden child who excelled in school and never got in trouble, it was pretty upsetting to know that my parents were so disappointed in me."

If this happens, do your best to reassure them: not just that you'll be okay, but that they didn't fail. Point out other ways that they brought you up right; if you're kind, smart, hard-working, well-mannered, funny, a good cook, good with animals, passionate about doing the right thing—and if that came from your parents—tell them. Emphasize that they brought you up to be honest and to care about the truth (assuming that's true, of course)—and that your honesty about your atheism proves that they did a good job. If it won't make you feel dishonest or like you're caving in to the idea that religious wisdom matters, you might even give them examples from their religion—texts, words from leaders, examples from their friends and community—backing up the idea that their god cares more about people being good than he does about being worshipped.

Alan was raised in Minneapolis, in a family that took religious observance and their Jewish identity seriously. When he first came out as atheist to his parents, he says, they were "surprised and disappointed." But, he says, "months later, my dad came to grips with this. We discussed things like where I get my sense of morality from, and he accepted that I was atheist and became totally cool with it. He's a scientist, and my phrasing it as 'you raised a good scientist, and I went where the evidence led me' helped, I think." (This particular story has an even happier ending: "Years later, he even admitted to me that he is atheist, too, but still goes to synagogue and celebrates holidays and stuff in order to feel closer to his ancestry.")

Time can do wonders for this particular wound. Once your parents have a chance to see that you're still the same good and happy person you always were, it'll go a long way towards alleviating their guilt over their supposed failure.

Andrew, who grew up in a very conservative Pentecostal family in Ontario, used a "spoonful of sugar helps the medicine go down" method to good effect: giving good news he knew would make his mother happy at the same time he told her about his atheism, which he knew would upset her. He says that when he and his wife were both leaving religion, and were expecting their first child, "I thought it was time my mother knew where I was at. I live in Toronto, she lives in Sarnia, about three hours away. We met halfway at a restaurant and I told her that I no longer believed in God, Jesus, or Christianity. She immediately went on to urge me to consider the awful repercussions of such a decision, clearly saddened that I would be going to hell, and trying to convince me based on the 'what if you're wrong?' argument.

"I didn't dwell on that though, and immediately told her the wonderful news that she would be a grandmother. We all decided to focus on that, and it went very well, turning a time of potential conflict and sadness into a time to share joyful news. My mother is still a hard-line Christian, but we have learned to accept our differences, and no significant negative situations have arisen."

Timing, or, Who Knows What and When Do They Know It?

In the chapter on the basics, on of my pieces of advice is to be strategic about who you come out to first. Think about who will probably deal with your atheism better, and start by telling them. Get a little softball practice in before you start playing hardball—and find allies who'll support you if you run into a harder time with other people.

This can be especially powerful with families. If you can get some family members to accept your atheism, it can help smooth things over with the rest of the family. Flora, who comes from a conservative Christian family in East Texas, says, "I started by talking to my sisters, who are a lot more liberal-minded than my parents. I told them how much I hated the hypocrisy of religion, how the hatred of people who were different was just more than I could take. And on certain points they even agreed with me: they both have gay friends, they've dated guys from different races. Anyway, I finally just said 'I'm an atheist' to them, and they accepted it. It was no big deal. I was floored. With their help I brought the topic up with my mom." Her mom had a harder time than her sisters—she was concerned, and was more upset with the word "atheist" than she'd been with "I don't believe anymore"—but she mostly wanted to assure Flora that she still loved her. And even after the scary "A"-word, they were back to normal after a couple of weeks.

It's also worth thinking about the timing of your conversation. Are you coming out at a time and place when your family will feel comfortable talking? If it turns into a long conversation, will you have time for that? If things get upsetting or heavy, will you have the emotional energy for it? Are you coming out at a time that's going to be unusually difficult?

Kate was brought up in what she describes as the fairly extreme evangelical/fundamentalist wing of the Church of England; her father was (and still is) a vicar, as is her brother. "I was torn," she says, "between going through Christmas on false pretenses, and having to tell my family something which would devastate them. As it happened, we had a really nice and positive family dinner together on the 23rd of December, and I ended up derailing it by telling them then about my loss of faith. Which of course ruined the mood! We had a quite stressful and emotional discussion at the time (the thought that a family member is destined for hell must of course be upsetting)." Things are better now, though. "All of us still respect each other," she says. In fact, she adds, "My Dad took me aside and apologised to me because he had already written his Christmas sermon which was somewhat critical of atheists, and he didn't have time to rewrite it but didn't want me to feel hurt by it."

Many atheists decide to come out to their families gradually: talking first about doubts and questions about faith, pointing out problems with organized religion, even using language like, "I'm not religious." The idea is that if they soften the ground first, and gradually get their families used to the idea, it won't be so upsetting when they finally use the "A" word. Wayne Schroeder was brought up by very devout Methodist parents—his father was a church minister, and later a chaplain. Wayne chose to come out gradually, by softening the ground. "In some of my pre-high school years," he says, "I began to have different views and I would express those views during discussion periods in Sunday school classes, which sometimes would have Dad as the teacher. These were heated discussions at times, but not shouting arguments. Dad and I would also sometimes discuss, debate or argue at home." And so, he says, "When I finally told my parents that I really didn't believe in God, they knew I had been moving in that direction. I had decided that it was more important for me to be open and honest with them (and myself), than to spare their feelings and possible disownment or other recrimination. And I'm glad I did... They didn't like my non-belief, but they accepted it, and continued to love me.

"Over time, we didn't discuss it much, but our relationships were and are fine. My father passed away quite a few years ago now, but I have a good relationship with my mother and sisters even though they and their families are quite religious. So I'm happy with my decision about coming out and I think it was done in a good way, at least for my family."

Denial, or, I Can't Hear You, I Can't Hear You, La La La La La

This "softening the ground" technique can be very effective. But if you go that route, you're eventually going to have to be explicit, even blunt, about your nonbelief. It's not uncommon for family members to deny your atheism—no matter how clearly you tell them about it. Comments like "you're just searching," "you're going through a phase," and other flat-out denials of reality are fairly common. Much of the time, this is just an initial reaction, and families eventually accept that you're an atheist, even if they don't like it. But sometimes, this denial can last indefinitely. Christopher Stephens started seriously doubting Christianity when he was eleven years old. "To this day," he says, "my parents still answer their fellow church-goers' questions of what their son believes with 'he's searching.'" And when Brennan told his moderately religious and very liberal father about his nonbelief, he says, "he gave a slight, condescending chuckle and said that he was 'ok with the fact that you're Agnostic, as long as you still believe in god.' After that I just dropped the issue because I knew he was not going to be able to engage me in a worthwhile conversation on the issue."

This denial can be intense. It can go on for a long time. It can make family members put you in difficult or embarrassing positions, because you thought they understood about your atheism and they understood nothing of the kind. If this happens, you may have to come out more than once—and you may have to come out more bluntly, even harshly, than you'd intended. Alexandria Farris, a 23-year-old Hispanic woman born and raised in Los Angeles, was brought up Catholic for eleven years; her father then became a born-again Christian, and persuaded her mother to convert as well. "Early in 2011," she says, "I had come out to my mother as an eclectic after she placed a rosary on the rear-view mirror of my car, and I had taken it off. She seemed to accept my beliefs, and afterward didn't give me too much trouble. It was during December of 2011 that I had come out as a Naturalistic Pantheist (to avoid using the dreaded 'A' word)." Then, when Alexandria was preparing to go away to college in Texas, her parents and their pastor arranged what she thought was going to be a simple church service to pray for her success at college.

"Keep in mind this was in front of all the church people," she says. "The pastor asked me if I believed in god. I turned to my mom, wondering why I'm being questioned like this. She just nodded, as if telling me to say yes when she knew very well the answer was no. The pastor asked me if I would be more comfortable if he spoke to me in English (everything that was said previously was in Spanish). I said yes and then he asked me again, in English, if I believed in god, and again I turn to look at my mom, expecting her to jump in and stop this because I had only come out for a prayer. Again she nodded yes. I turn to look at my dad who was still teary-eyed. I told him I'm a Naturalistic Pantheist. He told me it doesn't matter. I thought he meant that it was ok. I didn't know that what he really meant was that it was ok, I can still be saved. So I turn to the pastor and tell him that my view of god is way different from what his is. He said that it was fine, and that I didn't have to repeat the prayer he said; I just had to close my eyes. So I did, thinking that all was going to be well, and that everyone had accepted my non-belief in their deity. But that wasn't the case.

"The pastor prayed to god, asking him to make me see the error of my ways, to make me see the truth, make me believe in him, make me confess that I was in the wrong and that I needed him in my life to guide me. During this prayer the other people were saying things like 'amen' and 'praise be to the lord' and other such things Christians say while a person is praying or preaching. I had opened my eyes after the prayer had started, feeling my face getting warm with silent fury. The prayer then focused on my trip to Texas, and how it was god's plan to send me there to serve him, and that I will find god in this new chapter of my life... I had come out to my religious family and they just thought I was misinformed and that god hadn't called me to serve him yet."

Alexandria's mother did have a talk with the pastor about her beliefs. But the denial continued. When her boyfriend proposed to her, she says, "I had called my parents to tell them the wonderful news. During the FaceTime call, my dad asked me if I wanted his pastor to marry me and my fiancé. I had no words. I thought, 'why would he suggest that after I had come out as not being a Christian?'... In a more recent phone call my dad asked the same question. Again, I didn't know how to respond. My mom told me that I needed to have a Christian wedding because I was part of the church. I told her I wasn't part of the church and she looked stunned. Had my parents forgotten about the whole coming out thing or did they think that after the praying I would become a Christian?"

So she's decided that she has to be more blunt. "Now," she says, "I've decided that if my previous coming out wasn't enough, I would have another coming out, and this time it would be to more people and family and I won't care if they disown me. I'll be starting my own family soon... a freethinking family. This next time I come out, I'll make sure everyone knows damn well that I have no intention of becoming a Christian, and that I am happier and my life is much more fulfilled being an Atheist. And yes, this time I will most definitely be using the 'A' word."

It's important to remember, though: You can be super-clear about your atheism, and some families still won't get it. You can hold up a sign that says "I AM AN ATHEIST" in six-inch red letters, and some families will still ignore it or misunderstand it or conveniently not remember it. Some families need to hear it multiple times, in six-inch red letters, and several more times accompanied by marching bands and fireworks, before they get the message. When rodriguez came out to their mother, a fully committed Catholic with no liberal or even moderate leanings, "she didn't believe it. She said I would surely change my mind as I got older... Later I realized that she probably forced herself to forget it. I came out to my uncle, her brother, in her presence. Her face told me that she was surprised all over again." If that happens, it's not your fault. Do what you can to be as clear as you can—but if they persist in their denial, don't blame yourself.

Denial doesn't just take the form of denying your atheism. It can even involve religious believers denying the realities of their own religion. "I remember a particularly vivid conversation with my mom," says Christopher Stephens, "when I had just read 1 Samuel 18 (this is verse 27): 'Wherefore David arose and went, he and his men, and slew of the Philistines two hundred men; and David brought their foreskins, and they gave them in full tale to the king, that he might be the king's son in law. And Saul gave him Michal his daughter to wife.' I was just curious what a foreskin was! The Bible actually has kind of a weird fixation on foreskins, eh? So in all innocence, I asked my mom. Without any context for my question, she answered primly that it's a part of a boy's private parts, and we don't really talk about it in public. Of course, I'm completely horrified. I think I was around fifteen years old at the time, give or take a year or two.

"The disturbing part is that I tried to explain to my mom why I was so disgusted, and she literally refused to believe that the Bible contained such a horrible story. She said that I was 'smart enough to talk about the Bible intelligently, without resorting to making up nasty stories.' I argued, and pretty soon I just went and got the Bible that I had been reading, and she wouldn't look at it. She had caught on that I wasn't just making up horrible stories, and sent me to my room instead of admitting that she was wrong about the Bible."

This flat-out denial of reality can be very frustrating, and even hurtful. It can make people feel invisible, like their own families don't see who they are even when they're jumping up and down and waving signs. But there's another form of denial that can be frustrating as well.

Some families are masters at ignoring, or simply not talking about, the things they don't want to think about. The degree to which people will ignore the elephant in the room can be remarkable.

Keith Hughes, who had been an atheist for years after being rather religious through high school, was nervous about telling his evangelical parents, but finally decided he had to be honest with them. "The Reason Rally and the Lobby Day before the Reason Rally," he says, "gave me what I felt was an excellent opportunity because I could talk about being in DC and slip in why I was there without a glaring 'Hey Mom and Dad, I am an Atheist, God doesn't exist, So whatdyathink.' I wrote them an email describing the weekend and how much fun my wife and I had, mentioning the Lobby Day, briefly saying what it was, how interesting I had found the entire process meeting Congress folks, and how I felt being on the Mall for the Reason Rally and what it was, all very low key. I nervously hit the Send button and waited.

"Email to my parents is never answered quickly, so I waited nervously for a few days, wondering if I had been excommunicated from the family. Finally, one day I see a response from my Mom in my Inbox and I nervously clicked on it.

"'Did you see the cherry blossoms?'

"That was it.

"My mother has always been very big on ignoring chunks of my emails, so I wasn't sure whether telling her was a non-event, something she'd always known, or was a case of 'I can't hear you... nah, nah, nah.' So, after a birthday greeting from her a week or so later I wrote another letter thanking her for continuing to include me in her life as I had heard about many people telling their family that they didn't believe in God and found themselves booted from the family.

"Nothing was ever acknowledged. I went to visit her for Mother's Day since I was on the West Coast. Nothing came up. I rode with my Dad to the restaurant. Nothing. So, all in all, a non-event."

While this can be frustrating for people who value honesty and being understood, it can contribute to family peace. And it does let your family process your atheism on their own timetable. So if your family is in denial about your atheism—whether they're openly denying reality, or simply ignoring it—you'll need to decide whether you want to press the issue or drop it. You'll have to make that decision based on your own values, and what matters to you more in your relationships with your family: whether you place higher value on honesty and understanding, or on peace and getting along. You'll have to make it based on practical matters, too; will religion be an issue when it comes to things like weddings, child-rearing, health care decisions? When these issues come up, will it screw things up if your family doesn't clearly understand your atheism and the values and preferences that go along with it? And you'll have to make the decision based on your own assessment of reality: whether your family is likely to keep their fingers in their ears indefinitely, or whether they'll eventually get the memo.

Forcing the Issue, or, Tell Me What I Don't Want to Hear—Now!

But some families will go in the other direction. Rather than ignoring or denying the reality they're not happy with, some families will actually force the issue. They'll pressure their family members to confirm their religiosity—often because they already suspect that it's weakening or gone. In doing so, they force the nonbelievers to either lie—or tell them a truth they don't want to hear.

This is one of many good arguments for coming out sooner rather than later. The problem with your family forcing the issue is that you don't get to come out on your own timetable. All those wonderful ideas about picking your time carefully, doing it when emotions aren't running high, deciding who to tell first, etc.—it all goes out the window. So you either have to lie, and tell the truth later—which means you'll get to pick a better time, but you'll have the burden and complication of having lied. Or you have to be honest, even though the timing is lousy. (You can try to be vague or dodge the question—but families who are forcing the issue can be very persistent.)

When her mother forced the issue, Amy took the "being honest when asked" route. She was raised in a conservative southern state, in a multigenerational household; her mother is from the Philippines and grew up Catholic, and Amy describes her own upbringing as "sheltered and warmly Christian." She became an atheist in college, but didn't come out to her family—until she started planning her secular wedding. "I had barely said hello," she says, "before my mother began to aggressively question the wedding plans, especially the fact that we were not planning to marry in a church. I mentioned that we had considered a church—UU [Unitarian Universalist] of course—but that it was out of our price range. She would not hear of any excuses about money or availability in Manhattan. She even suggested a temple or a mosque. Any house of worship would be better in her eyes than none. She continued to harp and demand to know why we weren't having the wedding in a church.

"And here is where things got dicey. After several minutes of this interrogation and lack of response to my rational rebuttals, I felt pushed to my limits and responded emotionally, 'Because I'm not a Christian.' At first there was silence. And then the recriminations started. I don't remember much of the resulting conversation besides the fact that I cried and that my father had to eventually take the phone away from my mother, but it was unpleasant and my mother was incredulous and we were both audibly upset."

The rest of Amy's family were reasonable, and even supportive. But the argument put a strain on her relationship with her mother. "I can say for certain," she says, "that just blurting it out during an emotional conversation was not the best way to come out to my mother. I felt attacked and responded defensively. Maybe I should have ended the conversation when it seemed like she wasn't paying attention to my valid rational reasons. Maybe I should have calmed down and later told her of my non-belief while feeling calm and in control. As it was, all that outpouring of negative emotion took its toll on our relationship. It took weeks for us to even consent to talk to each other on the phone again, and that particular conversation was strained and ultimately unproductive." (They've now gotten over it, though. "These days," she says, "years after my coming out, my mother and I have basically the same relationship we had when I was in college. I talk to her on the phone less often, but we can talk pleasantly about nothing and religion never enters into the conversation.")

Terri Garrett, who at one time had been the most devout of a fundamentalist family, took the other route. She tells this story of an incident that took place during a terrible family crisis. "My mom had always been a very emotional person," she says, "and this was absolutely carrying her away. She grabbed hold of me, her face just a few inches from mine and pleaded. 'Pray for me. Pray for Gramma.'

"One thing about me. I never lie. Not ever. And mom knows this. She also knows... right now, she's got me. What could I say to this?

"I said, 'I love you mom. So much. Please be careful.'

"She repeated, 'Will you pray for me?'

"I tried to dodge again. 'I want to come with you. Are you SURE I can't come and help you drive?'

"She grabbed my face with both her hands. 'I know you and I believe differently. But you do believe in GOD, don't you?' She's shouting at me at this point. Her face is wet with tears and her eyes look almost feral.

"And what could I do, standing there, looking in her eyes on the worst night ever? I lied. 'I believe in god, mom.'

"And THAT was what she needed.

"But it bothered me. Though the situation was extreme, I'd been manipulated into lying to my mom. Lying about a fundamental part of who I was in front of my kids. Denying my beliefs as though they were something to be ashamed of.

"The next summer when they came to visit, I was ready. I got them alone and had a separate talk with both mom and dad. I talked about why I lied, and why it bothered me that I lied.

"I was very, very prepared. I had done the talk in my head so many times, even written it out, so I was over-ready when it happened. I told them that I loved them, a lot. I also addressed 'the elephant in the room.' I told my father (who was being treated for prostate cancer at the time), 'I know that the most important legacy you would leave for me is your faith, and I've rejected that. I know it causes you great pain. But you should know dad, it causes me pain too. I love you.' I reminded him that his legacy, his life lessons, will continue in my life and in the lives of my children. That I'm the same daughter with the same morality. I just have one key difference.

"I reminded them that they already have close friends who have very different religious beliefs than their own. I assured them that they were loving and accepting of differences and told them that they'd taught me about accepting others and I knew they could accept me as well. (OK, I was idealizing it, but sometimes a little optimism goes a long way.)

"My parents grew more accepting as time went on. My siblings have generally mellowed as well. This process took a few years and I feel was primarily influenced because some of their own children have also embraced atheism."

When Miguel's mother forced the issue, he took a middle road. He didn't give her an answer the moment she demanded one—but he gave her one soon after, when he'd had time to collect his thoughts, and was able to choose a time and place. A 23-year-old lawyer from Recife, Brazil, he still lives with his mother, who is a devout Christian. "She started noticing I was kind of leaving the faith," he says, "so she just came up to me and asked whether or not I believed in God. I hesitated at first, because I didn't want to bum her out or anything, so I just clammed up. I actually had no idea what to answer, because I wasn't ready for that kind of approach. Obviously, she knew it, but she didn't hear it from my lips.

"The next day, though, I thought it would be better if I just got it out of my system, so I went for it. I waited until she went to bed, I shut the door, sat her down and said I wanted to talk. I calmly explained to her I didn't believe in God anymore, that I couldn't accept the Bible as the word of god and I thought the whole thing was just bullshit. I tried my best not to offend her, because I know just saying the word 'atheist' would be a disaster. Strangely, I wasn't as nervous as I thought I'd be."

She didn't react well. She "went nuts," Miguel says, and "she just kept on saying how that was the worst thing that could have happened to her." And after that conversation, he says, "it was just her trying to change my mind." She's tried to restrict his access to atheist books and videos, and even told him that "she would rather have a not-so-smart and not-so-good son than an atheist son."

And yet, even with all that, Miguel says that becoming an atheist and coming out about it "was the best thing that could've happened to me. It was awful at first, when I realized I had built my life around a lie, but it's fulfilling to know that I dragged my way out of this delusion all by myself... Now I feel free to really enjoy life."

In a Crisis, or, The House Is On Fire—Oh, and God Doesn't Exist

Having the issue forced on you is a hard way to come out about your atheism. But it's not always something that your family does on purpose. Sometimes a family crisis or trauma—such as job loss, illness, or death in the family—can force the issue for all of you. (Again, this is one of many good arguments for coming out sooner rather than later if you can. When a crisis arises, it's better if the "I'm an atheist" conversation is already behind you.)

Coming out during a family crisis isn't the best timing in the world. Emotions are high, tempers are short, patience is thin. And yet, family crises are often when the topic of religion comes up. People often rely on religion to help them through difficult times—so families who don't ordinarily discuss religion will often do so in a crisis. Illness or death in a family can spark conversations about God or the afterlife—even among people who don't usually talk about it. And illness or death is often when families discuss their wishes for things like funerals, medical emergencies, end-of-life care—topics that often involve religion.

So even if you don't want to bring up your atheism while your uncle is in surgery or you're sitting shiva for your grandmother, your family may force the topic on you—or the situation itself will force it on you. And you'll have to decide whether to lie outright, dodge the question, or tell the truth. Kimberly from Tulsa, Oklahoma says, "Shortly before my uncle's death from cancer in 2006, my mom, my sister and I had been discussing his refusal of any kind of spiritual counseling and his request that there be no funeral for him. (I suspect he was an atheist but unfortunately I never got to talk to him about his beliefs.) My mom and sister are both devout Protestants, and my uncle's antipathy toward religion clearly distressed them. While not referring to myself as an atheist at that time, I voiced my sympathy for my uncle's position."

Robert, a never-very-religious atheist in a family that's mostly not very interested in religion, tells of a conflict he had with his niece—a convert to the Jehovah's Witnesses—when his uncle died. "He was, so far as I know, the only gay member of the family," he says. "His will specified that his funeral was to be conducted by the [LGBT-oriented] Metropolitan Community Church. She wanted me to help her set aside that stipulation of the will and have a Jehovah's Witness funeral. Of course I refused and there were problems. We became estranged and I haven't seen her in about 17 years. Yes, my views contributed to the estrangement but I don't feel any responsibility for it nor do I feel any real loss. She just wasn't my kind of person. The 'closeness' of genetic connection isn't enough to overcome the total lack of mutual interests."

Immediate crises aren't the only issue. Past crises and traumas can also make coming out atheist difficult—especially if your family has been using religion to cope. Kelly, who was raised in a conservative evangelical Protestant home by very devout parents, finally came out to her parents at age 24. "I was terrified to tell my parents," she says, "particularly my mother, due to both a fear of rejection and our unusual family history. When I was 16, my younger brother Matthew died suddenly in a freak accident. Though my family had always been religious, Matthew's death made them more vocal and enthusiastic about it. My parents have made it clear that the only thing that allowed them to recover from my brother's death was the belief that my family would be re-united in Heaven. I knew that by coming out as an atheist I was taking that hope away from my parents—and that terrified me. I didn't want to see them fall back into the deep grief and pain we all felt immediately after his death. I was particularly concerned about my mother who has a history of depression and tends to take the 'failings' of her children as a personal affront to her abilities as a mother. It seemed almost selfish to tell them the truth. However, the pressure of lying and hiding myself was making me miserable and eventually became unbearable."

In Kelly's situation, coming out atheist didn't just mean implying, "You're wrong to believe in God." It meant implying, "You're wrong to believe that you'll be reunited with your dead child." That's a hard thing to say. She scoured the Internet looking for advice on how to have this conversation, but didn't find anything she could use. So she asked her former therapist. "She suggested I write a letter," she says, "explaining that I loved them but I just do not share their religious beliefs. She also told me to explain specifically what they were doing that hurt me, why it hurt me, and what behaviors they would need to change to feel comfortable going home again.

"I took my therapist's advice and it worked better than I ever could have hoped. I am glad I chose to write a letter (instead of calling or talking in person) so that I didn't have to see their initial looks of hurt or outrage. It also gave my parents time to digest the information before having to discuss or act on it. My mother did call me about a week after receiving the letter expressing that she was glad I told her but was confused as to how this had happened. She was clearly hurt but she didn't want me to disappear from her life either. My father has never directly discussed my coming out as an atheist with me. Now, I am able to go home without the horrible, distancing awkwardness. There are obviously still a lot of tense and hurtful moments. They beg me to read books by Christian apologists, express concerns about the state of my soul, disapprove of my having a sex life, and pray for me—but at least I am not hiding anymore. I am very happy I came out."

I wish I had some great advice on how to manage coming out as an atheist in the middle of a family crisis. I don't. All I can suggest is to take the rest of the ideas in this book, and dial them up to eleven. Be clear, and don't use language that can easily be misinterpreted. Keep the conversation focused, as much as possible, on how much you love your family, and why, in this crisis, it was important to you to be honest. Reinforce other forms of tradition and continuity—family crises can make these feel extra-fragile. Reassure them that they're not failures. Be calm but firm about your boundaries. Don't get sucked into debates about religion; if you think they're important, save them for later. And above all, remember that they love you too, and want to maintain their relationship with you.

In situations like these, some atheists will be selective about who they come out to and who they don't. Lisa has come out to her father, her mother, her siblings, her friends, and her co-workers in the military. However, she says, "I did not come out to my step-mom, because she is pretty insistent that God planned that her son had to die so others could be saved, which she claims helps her cope. She turned her tragedy into an organization devoted to saving people (with no religious requirements). The fact that her god doesn't make her act helpless or discriminatory makes it hard for me to even come up with an argument that her god is hurting her."

Arguments, or, If This Is Your First Night at Fight Club…

So what about arguments over religion? When you come out as an atheist, chances are excellent that somebody's going to try to talk you out of it. Should you get into those debates? If so, how? If not, how do you avoid them? Should you try to do some persuading yourself, and try to argue your family into atheism?

I actually have an entire chapter on arguing about religion. That's mostly where I'll be talking about theological debates, and how they do or don't fit into coming out as atheist. But family arguments about religion can be… let's say, unique. So I want to take a moment here to talk about them.

It is true, unfortunately, that arguments about religion can be very divisive in families, even creating permanent or long-term rifts. This is something Daniel Dennett talks about in his book, *Breaking the Spell: Religion as a Natural Phenomenon*. He points out that the less evidence people have for a belief, the more fiercely they'll cling to it[3]—since you don't have to fiercely defend an idea that's obviously true. This makes disagreements over religion more heated than other kinds of arguments—ironically, for the very reason that religion is groundless, and believers can't give any good evidence to back up their side. So you can't assume that because your family has a fine tradition of lively debate, therefore your reasonable dismantling of their faith is going to go over without a hitch.

You may want to do it anyway. And I'm not going to try to talk you out of that. You have to decide for yourself whether "agreeing to disagree" feels sensible or dishonest; whether pressing the debate feels honest or obnoxious. Yes, family relationships are unique, and irreplaceable. But you get to decide whether that means, "This relationship is too important, I don't want to start a fight that might turn ugly and cause a permanent rift"—or whether it means, "This relationship is too important, I don't want to have to bite my tongue about things that really matter to me."

What's more, for some atheists, holding back on arguments about religion won't just seem dishonest—it'll seem unfair. Especially with parents. If they spent years forcing you to listen to their views, it may feel unacceptably unfair that they can now turn the conversation off. As Alex Gabriel of the Godlessness in Theory blog said to me, "No one should be interrogated against their will, of course, but when was I allowed to opt out? Before I could speak, my mother enlisted me as part of her church (a membership which, on the books, I can't undo). Before I could tie my shoelaces, she told me Satan had possessed me; that unbelieving relatives of hers were now in Hell; that I, having sworn before God something she thought was a lie, would burn there too. When, as she poured her dogma down my unresisting throat, was *I* allowed to abstain from discussion—to change the subject, leave the room or fall conspicuously silent, as she now does when God comes under fire?

"I know it would be equally unfair to force the issue," Alex continues, "thrusting a conversation on her which she doesn't wish to have. I know it causes her distress, and I'm not entitled to discussions she's unwilling to pursue. But I do *feel* entitled—cheated, at least. I resent her expectation that I honour, as a matter of détente, her deafness to rebuttals of her faith, while she expected me for years to listen as she preached; I resent that she was all too keen to play chess on the side of Christendom when I had no voice of my own, knew nothing of the facts and took her word as gospel, but deigns not to sit down at the board now I've a chance of winning. I resent the notion *I* am the aggressor, bullying her for a faith grown meek since she lost the power to force it on me. Most of all, I resent that I won't force my complaints on her—that I, subjected to preachments unethical in the extreme, with no ethical way to air my grief today, am punished emotionally for being kinder."

You have to make that decision for yourself. If you do want to pursue these debates, though, I would advise you to hold off until after you've come out. Like I said in the chapter on the basics: A lot of believers associate their religion with familial, racial, cultural, or historical identity. Telling them you're an atheist can seem like you're rejecting that identity. I don't think there's any way around that—but you don't have to compound it by trying to persuade them that their faith is ridiculous. Hold off until you've been out for a bit, until you've had some time to show each other that you're not rejecting each other and that the love and respect are still there. Then, if you want to, you can try to persuade them that their faith is ridiculous.

So when you come out to your family (or to anyone, really), you may decide to avoid arguments about religion—either initially, or indefinitely. You may decide to keep your coming out conversations focused on explaining your atheism, countering myths about it, letting them know your limits about things like proselytizing or participating in religious events, and reassuring them that you're okay and still want a relationship with them,

That's a totally reasonable decision. But if you do that, remember that it's very easy for those "coming out" conversations to drift into debates about whether God exists. After all, it's hard to explain why you became an atheist without getting into an explanation of... well, why you became an atheist: the lack of evidence for religion, the logical flaws in religious arguments, and so on. And even the most touchy-feely, "atheism doesn't make me a bad person" conversation can turn into a theological debate if your family's religion holds that... well, that atheism by definition makes you a bad person. It's a fuzzy line between explaining your atheism and arguing for it, and I can't tell you how or where to draw it. (Although I do explore the conundrum in more detail in the chapter on arguing about religion.) I'll just suggest that you be aware of that line, and keep an eye on it. If the conversation is drifting away from who you are and how you feel about your family, and is turning into a back-and-forth about Pascal's Wager and biblical inconsistencies and "I feel it in my heart"—and if you don't want to go there—you're going to have to re-direct. You may even have to say so, in words: "I really don't want to get into a debate about God—we can have that argument later if you want. Right now, can we just talk about the wedding?"

And don't assume that because your family's religion isn't conservative or strict, therefore debates about it won't be divisive. Karla grew up in Marin County in the late '60s and early '70s, with a blend of New Age religion and Unitarianism. But as her sister was getting deeper into her New Age belief, Karla's atheism was developing. She says of their conversations, "I talked with her a lot and asked her all kinds of questions, wanting her to explain what she believed and why she believed it. I have to admit I was a hell of a pest—didn't help that I worshipped her and her knowledge—and she got annoyed with me as time went on. And the reason she got annoyed with me is that you don't ASK questions like that of believers—they don't have a clue why they believe, they just do, and she told me so—'In order to understand, you have to believe first, and then you can understand,' she told me one time. Which wasn't much help to me at all—I wanted a REASON to believe in the first place! And so I pressed her, and the more I pressed, the more she withdrew, and the more she withdrew, the more I pressed.

"And my sister was getting more and more frustrated with me, especially since I was getting more and more enthusiastic about science, which kept giving me more and more genuine understanding of the world around me the harder I looked at it. I started sending her books and articles, trying to show her the neat stuff I was finding out about the world. Finally, the last straw was *Consciousness Explained* by Daniel Dennett, which I sent to her the year it came out, in 1991. She was furious with me, furious just about the title, which she interpreted as a personal attack against her and her beliefs. (I can't imagine she ever actually read the book!) At that point she cut off all contact with me, and literally hasn't spoken to me since."

Because of this potential for divisiveness, because it can be such a contentious subject, many families with differences about religion simply don't discuss it. But some families do get into arguments about religion—and are totally fine with that. When Josh came out to his devoutly Catholic family in Australia, his father initially tried to insist that he go to church, and even threatened to make him change schools. But now, he says, "My parents are fine with my atheism. We've even had discussions during which I've criticised religion, and especially the Catholic church, quite strongly."

I can't predict whether your family will be okay with you trying to argue them out of their religion. What I can say is this: If you do want to get into one of these arguments, pay attention to how it's going—not to how it's proceeding logically (or not only to that), but to how it's going emotionally. Tune in to people's emotions. If they're treating the argument as a simple debate about differing ideas, then go for it. If they're getting upset and treating the argument as a personal attack, you might want to dial it back. And if they start in one emotional place and shift to another—if they start out saying, "Sure, let's debate, I want an honest interchange of ideas, my faith can withstand scrutiny," but then start getting upset during the course of the conversation—pay attention to that as well.

And pay attention to your own feelings, too. Are you getting disproportionately invested in this argument? Are you starting to get less cerebral and more heated? How important is this argument to you, anyway? I'm seriously asking. Not everyone wants a relationship with their family if it means some topics always have to be kept off the table—especially if it means that believers can talk about religion, but atheists can never talk about atheism. Karla again: "So, of course, the question of 'would I have done it differently' comes up... But I wouldn't KNOW how to do it differently—if what I have learned really is true, there is no other way to say it, no other way to put it, no other way to tell someone what's going on, other than to be direct and truthful about it. If they believe that two and two are five, and you can demonstrate that no, two and two make four, and they get huffy and upset, what can you do?

"I'm really sad in some ways," she says, "in how it all turned out. It's lonely. It's a hard decision, a hard choice, between your family members and your own honest, genuine understanding of how the world really is. But believing in something doesn't make it true, no matter how hard you—or they—might wish it to be so."

But depending on who you are—and who your family is—you don't have to come to an agreement about religion to have a good, close, loving relationship. Person after person has told me about their families who continued to believe in religion—and continued to love them, support them, and accept them. Sometimes these families talk about religion or even debate it; sometimes they set it aside and just don't discuss it. Some atheists' families keep trying to persuade them to return to religion; some completely accept their heathens' heathenocity, and are even proud of it. And some manage to do both.

Jesse Daw is a 33-year-old gay man living in Fort Worth, Texas, whose mother is very spiritual and whose father is the minister in a conservative Church of Christ congregation. Here's what he says about their relationship: "Despite being raised with some classic fundamentalist Christian ideas, like creationism, heaven, and hell, I was always taught to think for myself and that integrity was the highest virtue I could have... I don't think there was ever a specific 'I'm an atheist' conversation, except one where I told my dad that I didn't think an all-wise being who fine-tuned the universe would hold up faith without evidence as the pinnacle of virtue. He told me I was relying on human ideas about god and that the comparison was flawed. My mom still puts books like 'The Shack' in my stocking, hoping that I'll eventually find my way back. My parents are very loving people though, and I rarely regret honesty with them for long."

And sometimes, when people come out atheist, the family's response can be complete and utter lack of surprise—because they've already figured it out. Icaarus was raised largely secular by a liberal Christian father and a reform Jewish mother, but he nevertheless came out to his parents with trepidation and a long explanation of why exactly he didn't believe. "They thought on this for a few moments," he says, "and then the conversation moved on. Nothing further was said that night, at all.

"So there I was," he says, "feeling a huge weight lifted off my shoulders, thinking that it would be a big deal, and the whole thing came off as meh. The next morning my mother asked me a little more, then said something that really surprised me. To this day I don't know how or why she came to this conclusion but she said 'due to your education and knowledge I'd have been really surprised if you believed in a god.' It still sticks to me."

And Michael, who grew up Catholic in Oshkosh, Wisconsin and went to Catholic school for twelve years, had a very similar experience. "I first came out to my father," he says. "His response was quite literally, 'I was wondering how long it would take for you to tell me about your atheism.'"

Trauma, or, Making the Best of a Bad, Bad Situation

Positive experiences aren't universal, though, and I'm not going to pretend that they are. For some people, telling their family "I'm an atheist" has meant coldness, guilt-tripping, ongoing fights, manipulation, proselytizing, disrespect, ignoring limits and boundaries, using children or other family members as weapons, and in some cases permanent rifts.

And while most atheists think coming out was a good idea even if it caused rifts or fights or bad feelings, not all of them do.

Snowball says, "Yeah, I regret telling my parents... When I came out as atheist to my parents, I was a first-year university student. It was actually an extended coming-out following an equally drawn-out realization of my loss of faith, which I tried to soften (unsuccessfully) by hinting that I had doubts some time before the actual announcement and indulging my parents by approaching church leaders and reading works of apologetics. My memory of that night is a little fuzzy, because I've tried hard to forget it, but basically I said I didn't believe, and got into a long argument about *why*. I do recall I repeatedly emphasized I still respected my parents' faith and had no wish to damage it, I only wanted my own (lack of) belief to be respected in turn—though eventually I got so pissed off I did pull out the stops and pour on the criticism that Mom and Dad basically went 'lalala' and 'why don't you want to be in Heaven with your loved ones?!' too.

"It's been two years since then and we don't really talk about it. I still go to church and attend weekly youth group meetings, and basically pretend my confession never happened. My mother alludes to it now and then, ascribing all the unfortunate events in my life to my being 'against God' and constantly pushing me to serve in church. (I'm gonna start on the PA crew this week. Cheers.) No one else in church knows. And it sucks, because sometimes I want to tell somebody... and I'm scared that history will repeat itself."

It's worth noting here, however, that in the hundreds of "coming out atheist" stories I've read for this book, Snowball is literally the only person to say they regret doing it. It's common for people to regret how they came out, or when, or where—but as difficult as it often is, very few people regret doing it at all.

It can definitely be difficult, though. It can be painful, upsetting, even traumatic. So what do you when coming out sucks?

In the chapter on the basics, one of the things I counseled was patience. I said it sometimes takes time for people to get used to our atheism, to learn about it, to get over their fears and prejudices about it, to accept it. And at the beginning of this chapter on family, I counseled having even more patience with family than we might with other people in our lives—since family relationships are probably special and important, and we're likely to have them for a long time.

But I want to emphasize something crucial here: Being patient and loving doesn't mean being a doormat. It's completely fine for you to expect fairness: to expect that concessions and compromises you make about religion or atheism be met with concessions and compromises they make for you. And it's fine for you to set limits—such as no yelling, no proselytizing, no anti-atheist bigotry—and to calmly but firmly enforce them. In fact, it's more than fine. It's desirable, and it's necessary. Terri Garrett had some terribly upsetting conversations when she came out to her fundamentalist family about her atheism, and she had to set clear, firm limits in order to have a relationship with them at all. "The final, most important rule," she says, "was to insist upon a calm and fair discussion place. This means that I refused to allow tempers in the conversation. The instant that siblings would start to flip their shit, I'd say 'I love you too much to have this conversation in anger' and I would physically leave the room, effectively enforcing my 'no yelling' rule.

"I also learned," she says, "after being far too patient with siblings, to stop allowing it to be a one-way conversation. If they insist I read a certain book or watch a DVD, I would only agree if they would be willing to watch one of mine. If they pushed me to answer a series of questions, I'd be fine with that, as long as I was free to ask them questions in return. THIS little aspect I should have instituted from the start. It would have saved me rereading a lot of circular crap by C.S. Lewis."

And in her interview for *The Ebony Exodus Project* by Candace R. M. Gorham, Raina makes a similar point about setting limits. When her uncle chose to proselytize to her in a birthday e-card, she wrote back to him saying, "'Okay, so now you choose to be self-righteous on my birthday about me. It's the one day that's about me and you decided to make it about you. I feel offended. Please don't do that again.'"[4]

Plus there's an important point to remember about ugly family fights—which is that, as no-fun as they are, it can actually be better to have them openly than to imagine and internalize them. As Alex Gabriel of the Godlessness in Theory blog said to me, "The vitriolic drama of a fighting family can be easier to cope with, actually, than the inner drama of the closet. Coming out is a declaration of independence, liberating and empowering; a refusal to internalise the views of others; a statement that we needn't measure up to their ideals and won't try. Families fight at times when the person coming out hands back their loved ones' enmity. 'Your antipathy to how I live,' we say, 'is your cross to bear, not mine. You have to live with it; I don't.'"

When it comes to fairness, though, there's an unfortunate reality we do have to face. Sometimes, with some people, we have to choose between fairness and having a relationship. Some relationships are going to be unfair: either because the other person doesn't get it about us and is never going to get it, or because the bad stuff that happened in the past is large enough that justice would be impossible (or reprehensible). It's in the nature of forgiveness that it's unfair. And it's in the nature of being the more ethical person that you're sometimes going to get shafted. Of course being ethical has its own rewards, in many ways it *is* its own reward—but in the moment when you're being hard done by, that can be difficult to remember.

I don't have a miraculous way to fix this. All I can say is that the way we get our power back is to recognize that we have the choice between expecting fairness or forgiving and moving forward with a relationship. We get to decide when to forgive and when to draw the line, and with whom.

It is true that most families do come around, and do become accepting—or accepting enough, anyway, and definitely more accepting than they originally were. But some families don't ever change their attitudes about atheism. You have to be prepared for that possibility. Markus Ismael, who was brought up in a strict Protestant family in Indonesia (a predominantly Muslim country), says, "In the end, my parents gave us their blessings, and they came to attend our wedding, but their attitude and stance toward our lack of faith never changed. Every time we spoke on the phone since then was an opportunity for my mom to reiterate how much she would like to be able to see me and my wife in heaven after we've all died, which of course, was only possible if I regained my faith in Christ. Her tenacity only grew after our kids were born; then it became an excuse to tell me how much they'd like to be able to see their grandchildren in heaven someday. Even mere moments after my dad died, while we were at his bedside, the first thing my mom told me was how my dad's last wish was for me to 'come back to the Lord.' My mom was relentless all the way to her death. I suppose she probably brought her disappointment in me to her grave."

Sometimes, coming out atheist can make family members even more aggressive about their religion. IasasaI tells of trying to quietly reject a gift of a rosary from their intensely religious Catholic grandparents—a rejection that wasn't accepted and that turned into a confrontation. "The main result of all this," IasasaI says, "is that my grandparents then expended a LOT more effort on making religious commentary towards me, mainly in the form of cards in the mail, birthday cards and holiday cards. For the next couple years I attended the family functions, but as it got increasingly annoying dealing with the jesus talk, I just stopped going and have seen them only a dozen or so times since."

Religious differences in families can also have serious practical consequences, and these can include medical decisions or legal ones. rwahrens has three daughters, one of whom he says is intensely Catholic, almost fundamentalist. "The biggest worry for the future," he says, "is the issue of if/when my wife or I get sick, and the kids have to get involved—my middle daughter will, of course, take the Catholic line of 'pro-life,' while I and my wife have explicitly, both verbally and in writing (living wills) noted our desires to not have extraordinary methods used to keep us alive should the worst happen. We just don't trust her any more to follow our wishes. Since she is the only one of the three to live here, that could turn into an issue someday."

Daniel Schealler, who grew up in Australia and currently lives in New Zealand, is mostly out as an atheist to everyone in his life, including his family. He's generally come out casually, when it happens to be relevant to the discussion, and it's mostly been no big deal. But he says that the "only really big exception is with my fiancée's family. We go out of our way to hide both my atheism and also the fact that my fiancée is basically a weak pantheist and cultural Muslim from her parents. Pressure here is worse than usual because my partner has lupus, which is an incurable autoimmune disease. Every now and again my fiancée needs looking after. If I get hit by a bus tomorrow, her support network is gone. For health reasons she cannot afford to risk being disowned by her parents."

As enthusiastic as I generally am about coming out atheist, I'm not going to tell you to do it if it'll screw up your sick fiancée's relationship with her religious family. The whole point of coming out is that it makes life better for you and the people around you. There's no point doing it if it's going to muck things up.

What I will say is this: Bear in mind that there's a difference between holding off temporarily on coming out until your practical ducks are in a row, and holding off indefinitely. It's one thing to wait to come out until you graduate, or get a new job with a more accepting work environment. It's another thing to wait until your fundamentalist parents die, or stop being fundamentalists. Remember that the longer you wait to come out, the more likely it is that someone will force the issue on you, that someone else will out you, or that a crisis will force you to come out right away. And *not* being out about your atheism can have practical consequences as well. Yes, it would completely suck if you got hit by a bus tomorrow, and your family wasn't there to help because they'd cut the infidels out of their life. It would also suck if you got hit by a bus tomorrow, and your family didn't respect your health care or end-of-life decisions, because they didn't know about your atheism and you'd never told them about your values and wishes.

I wish I had a magic formula for making that choice. I wish I had a magic formula for making those choices unnecessary. But I don't. We're atheists—we know that magic isn't real. It's your life, and you have to do that cost/benefit analysis for yourself.

All of this assumes, by the way, that you actually do care about your family, and have a tolerable relationship with them, and want them in your life. But I'm aware that this isn't true for everyone. Some people have abusive families, hateful families, seriously dysfunctional families. And religion will often play a role in that abuse or dysfunction. Religion, unfortunately, can be a uniquely powerful tool to control people or even terrorize them.

Safron, who was raised Mormon in the Midwest, makes this point all too clearly. "My dad was emotionally abusive to my mother," she says. "My parents were both very religious. I would classify my dad as a fanatic. I pretended to be religious as a child/teen because life would have been even more unpleasant if I had not. While I didn't go around proclaiming beliefs I didn't have, I did what was expected of me: I went to church every week, attended Seminary in the mornings, etc. Then, even though I knew that I was an atheist, I attended BYU (a religious college) for two years. I was manipulated by my dad and too young or naive to realize I had other options."

But even in that situation, Safron found ways to push back. At Brigham Young University, she says, "I practiced a kind of passive resistance. Starting out as a Mormon and becoming atheist could have gotten me kicked out of school, so I was not open with my beliefs unless I completely trusted the person. I went to church with my assigned church group as infrequently as I thought I could get away with it, and broke church rules with only a small group of trusted friends." And she eventually transferred to another school, where, she says, "it was very liberating for me to not have to confront religion and religious culture every day."

Some atheists have had families restrict access to other family members, or even cut it off altogether. Their religious parents won't let them see their siblings; their religious siblings won't let them see their nieces and nephews; their religious children won't let them see their grandchildren. Or else families will enforce a less extreme version of this isolation: allowing access to other family members, but putting tight restrictions on it. rwahrens again: "My middle daughter married a Catholic, and they have been getting more and more fundamentalist until they are now pretty similar to the Quiverfull group (there is a Catholic equivalent). (They have six kids now.) My wife and I are forbidden to visit and see the grandkids unless both parents are there to 'supervise' to be sure we don't say anything inappropriate. My wife has since refused to visit at all (she is German Lutheran, but estranged from the organization) and is very insulted. I am sad about it, but do go over occasionally just to keep in touch. Visits are often awkward."

On the Coming Out Godless Project website, Scarlett Letter tells this heartbreaking story about adopting a baby and coming into contact with the birth family. "We found out after the fact," she says, "that there was a large, intact, really nice extended family who was open to having a relationship with their Grandson/Nephew/Cousin. We got together last Christmas, grandma visited several times, we had a few playdates with small cousins. Then we became Facebook friends (i.e., they found out I was an Atheist liberal.) They have stopped communicating with me in any way. I feel bad for my son, who is only three, that he will not have a relationship with his birth family because I am an Atheist."

In some families, coming out atheist really can mean being completely shunned, even disowned. Michael, who was raised in a Catholic family in Oshkosh, Wisconsin, says, "My twin brother is estranged from me because I fail to give the Catholic Church the respect he feels it warrants." It can get even worse than that. In *The Young Atheist's Survival Guide*, Hemant Mehta tells the story of Chelsea, a high school atheist who refused to stand during the Pledge of Allegiance and forced her school to accept her legal right to do this. But while Chelsea is basically glad that she took this stand, she also says, "The worst part of this entire thing is that I was kicked out of my house the day I graduated. My father's girlfriend refused to have an atheist living with her. She thought God would set the place on fire I guess."[5]

And Damon Fowler—and his family's reaction to his atheism—made national news when he complained to his public high school administration about the school-sponsored prayer being planned for his upcoming graduation. His complaint was publicly leaked, including the part about his atheism—and his parents disowned him, kicked him out of the house, and dumped his belongings in the front yard.[6]

If your family really does shun you when you come out, there is no way that's not going to suck. One of the hardest things about writing this book has been accepting that sometimes, coming out atheist is going to have crummy consequences—and there's nothing I can do to make that not be true. All I can do is repeat the point I keep making: Most atheists who have come out say it was the right decision, and they're happy they did it—even if it did alienate their families and the other people in their lives. rwahrens is obviously sad about his limited relationship with his grandchildren. But when he talks about coming out atheist, he also says, "Over all, I've been happy with this change in my life." This is a pattern we see again and again throughout this book; you'll see a lot of it in the "Coming Out Is Fun" chapter, and it's a pattern that's backed up by research. Even when the worst happens, even when coming out atheist does estrange people from their families, most of the time they're still happier.

And frankly—it may not be your family who cuts you off. You may decide that *you* have to cut *them* off.

If family members react to your atheism with intractable hostility, disrespect, manipulation, evangelizing, or otherwise unacceptable behavior, you may have to draw a line. Being patient does not mean being a doormat. Unless you're willing to put up with an infinite amount of crap forever, you may have to draw boundaries, and calmly but firmly enforce them. And if a family member keeps crossing that line, or won't even recognize it, you may decide to shut them out.

Aaron Wiebusch was raised in a religious home. "Church on Sundays," he says, "bible study at other church members' houses on Wednesday and Friday, and over the Labor Day weekend our church would host a 'Bible Retreat' every year." When he finally came out to his parents, he says, "about three months went by, during which I received dozens of emails, phone calls, and letters, with most of them containing lengthy bible verses, numerous requests to go back to church, and mom saying she was constantly praying for me, and that she couldn't figure out where she and dad went wrong. She also said she was very upset that I was so angry at god and Christianity and said that it was obvious to her that I just didn't understand what Christianity was. She said that I was being misled by satan, and that all I needed to do was to talk to Jesus, and he'd show me the way.

"After three months of this, I decided enough was enough. I won't include my reply to her, but it was very much like the video 'Nothing more to talk about' by The Thinking Atheist.[7] That was nearly four years ago, and I haven't spoken to her since. Me and my dad talk, mostly about how my college classes are going (I'm studying Biology, with the intent to become a science teacher) but every time I call, mom leaves the room."

The decision was hard, he says—but he thinks it was the right one. "I suppose that a part of me is sad that my mom and I haven't spoken in so long over something as trivial as whether or not I believe in god, but religion does things like that. I'm happy that my parents know the truth, even if their reaction to hearing it wasn't favorable. Overall, I do not regret my decision to tell my parents I'm an atheist, and if I had it to do again, I'd probably do it the same way."

An open rift with your family can be painful. Obviously. That's an understatement. But for most atheists, being honest about their atheism has been a relief—even if it did mean alienating their family. For them, the burden of secrecy was too much. H. Beaton is a former Jehovah's Witness—a sect that forbids its members to have contact with apostates, even if they're close family. When he began dropping hints about his atheism to his parents, they pressured him into moving in with his brother, in an attempt to keep him connected with the religion. But when he told his ex-girlfriend about his atheism, and when she told his parents, "they moved my brother out, and I was finally free.

"The feeling I got when I first came home to that empty apartment was almost indescribable," he says. "For the first time in my life, I felt like a normal person. I didn't have to hide who I was anymore. I felt like I could finally start moving on with my life."

Happy Endings, or, The Best of All Possible Worlds

Coming out atheist can be hard. Even if it's the right decision—and for most atheists, it seems to be—it can be a painful decision. So now that I've thoroughly bummed you out, let's wind up this chapter on a happier note. Let's bring back the flowers and rainbows and happy dancing unicorns. And let's talk about some of the happiest surprises that atheists get from their families when they come out.

One of the biggest benefits of coming out atheist is that it helps atheists in families find each other. I have heard this story more times than I can recount. It happens with atheist friends and colleagues, class-mates and acquaintances, as well as family members. Coming out em-boldens other atheist family members to come out—and it gets family members who have been discreet about their atheism to finally talk to each other. And that makes things better, for both them and you.

"I don't remember specifically coming out to my dad," says otrame. "At the time he was away on TDY (temporary duty—he was in the Air Force) quite a bit. I don't think I knew at the time that he had been an atheist since he was a young kid, but I did know that he did not attend church and rarely said anything at all about religion. Today all of my family are either atheists or very progressive Christians, with the excep-tion of two nephews and their wives."

In her interview for *The Ebony Exodus Project* by Candace R. M. Gorham, Crystal says, "I actually told my dad the first time last sum-mer. We were at a restaurant and the strangest thing happened. We prayed for our meal and then I thought, *This is my dad and we're very close so let me just tell him.* And the shocking thing was he told me, 'Well actually, Chris, I no longer believe either. The reason I asked you if you wanted to pray is because I thought you believed.' I said, 'Actually I don't. I was praying just because of you.'"[8]

And Speedwell has a funny (in a gallows-humor way), unusual sto-ry about how this can work. Her mother was the first devout Christian in a Jewish family, and when she was dying, she had persuaded her own mother to accept Jesus—or so she thought. But after the funeral, Speedwell told her grandmother that she wasn't religious. "My grand-mother said brightly, 'Oh, yeah, honey, neither am I.' After picking my jaw up out of my lap, I asked her, 'Um... Mom said you prayed with her and accepted Jesus, did you really do that?' And she responded, 'Yeah, I did that. It didn't mean anything to me; it just made your mother feel better and that's all I really cared about.' I absolutely couldn't laugh, though I really wanted to.

"However, when we got back into Grandma's apartment where everyone was gathering, Grandma told everyone in the family I was an atheist. It was rather like being the ugly duckling finding the swan family. My uncle told me everyone in the family was basically an atheist (not even Jewish, except culturally), and they had all been holding their tongues about it for more than thirty years out of respect for my parents. It was the first time I really felt close to my mother's family and I've been glad ever since that they embraced me like that. I'd been scared of what they thought but at the time it was more important to tell the truth, and now they have a lot more respect for me because of it."

Coming out atheist can also embolden family members who aren't necessarily atheist per se, but who aren't crazy about the family religion. Liz H.'s family varies in their religious affiliation, from liberal Christian to fundamentalist. She says, "Once word trickled around the extended family that I'm an atheist (it's useful having a mother who's a gossip sometimes, I didn't have to break it to grandma that I wasn't going to do the high school religious affirmation whatever) I had other relatives come up to me and basically tell me they didn't agree with the fundamentalist members of the family either. Once again the eldest breaks the ground, and everyone else plants seeds."

Amanda Knief, managing director at American Atheists, had a very similar experience. "Telling my family was one of the best things I have ever done," she says. "It was while I was home for Christmas one year after college and we were discussing our holiday plans. The family was talking about going to church for the Christmas Eve service. I said I wouldn't be going. My dad, who was and is the most overtly religious person in the family, was aghast and insisted that I would be going. I said, no—I didn't believe in god and any of that stuff so I didn't see any reason for going. The rest of the family was quiet. A few hours later, bundled against the cold, they all left for church. I stayed home and read a book with the family dog cuddled beside me. The next year at Christmas, everyone stayed home from church except my dad. Coming out as I did was freeing." And, she adds, "I just officiated my younger sister's wedding as a humanist celebrant—because, as she put it, her and her new husband's ideas and beliefs 'are closer to yours than to any church's.'"

And coming out atheist doesn't just make your already-atheist family members feel safer coming out. It can actually help turn the believers in your family into atheists. Seeing the existence of other atheists is often a big part of what makes people change their minds about religion.

Kat Car says that when she started coming out as an atheist, "As it turned out, my sister was beginning to lean that way, so I lent her *The God Delusion* and she agreed."

Eric Paulsen says that in his mother's family, "it would have been unheard of to turn your back on religion—hell, both sides of my family are lousy with ministers, reverends, pastors, and the fanatically devout." And yet, he says that after he came out to his parents, "The only thing that has changed over time is that I now see my mother is a skeptic as well."

And here's otrame again: "The first person I came out to was my mom (who was a non-specific Christian). I was sixteen. I said, 'It just doesn't make sense.' She shrugged and said, 'You'll figure it out.'

"Actually, she figured it out. She is an atheist today."

CHAPTER TEN

Spouses and Partners

Like coming out atheist to family, coming out atheist to spouses or partners is a unique experience. For many people, their romantic relationships are even more important than their relationships with family—especially if the relationship is a serious, committed one of long standing. Even people who are very close to their families commonly feel even closer to their partners. Relatives are the people we got stuck with loving. Partners and spouses are the people we chose to love. (To the degree that we choose to love anyone, of course.)

So just like I did with family members, I'm counseling more preparation, more caution with timing, more patience, working harder to be the bigger person, being willing to put up with somewhat more crap for longer, when you come out as an atheist to your partner. (Or, as may be if you're polyamorous, your partners.)

And just like I did with family members, I'm also counseling more honesty. In fact, I'm going to go even stronger here. With spouses and partners, I'm definitely advising you to come out about your atheism if you possibly can—and I'm advising you to do it as soon as possible. It's pretty standard for family members to keep a lot of things private from each other. But partners typically expect a greater degree of honesty.

The longer you keep your atheism secret from them, the more likely it is that they'll feel deceived or betrayed—and the stronger those feelings are likely to be.

Here's what zero6ix says about this: "Coming out was terrifying. Especially with my fiancée (now wife). She is 'catholic,' but only in the sense that she claims the label. We had been dating for six years. Six years of warmth and life and happiness. I had never really been subtle about myself and my stances in life, yet this one term, 'ATHEIST,' always stuck in my throat. I made comments here and there, but never came out in unambiguous terms. Really, it had all come down to an episode of Family Guy. The specifics are unimportant. At one point, Richard Dawkins' *The God Delusion* had been shown, sans author's name. By correctly recalling his name, I had planted a red light right on top of myself. The wife looked at me sideways, and asked bluntly; 'Since when are you an atheist?'

"To which I replied; 'Since before the day you met me.'

"This was a shock to her. I was confused, of course. Hadn't I left all the clues? I never spoke highly of religion, never bowed my head at family prayers, and anytime I found myself in a church, I did nothing more than what was asked. I never sang or took communion, just stood when told, and sat when told. In my mind, this was enough evidence to show what I did, or rather didn't, believe. But it wasn't enough. She heard this, me claiming my godless nature, and reacted. She questioned if we should get married.

"I reacted in turn. But I reacted poorly.

"'So, in all the years you've known me, just now, I am filth. I am the same person that I was yesterday, and yet, now that a label has been attached to me, everything before means nothing. Nothing. All the happiness I have given, all the secrets I have shared, all of ME, now gets rejected because a word gets associated with me. Fine then. Turn your back on me. Make your decisions. Choose if you want to throw this all away because I refuse to believe in myths.'

"Our hearts shattered then. I had lashed out because I felt attacked. She shrunk back, having actually been attacked. And in that moment, I would have taken it back. Not my shiny new label, just my piss poor reaction. I apologized, saying that nothing changed. I was still the same, and that is all I wanted to let her know. A word that was stuck to me didn't matter, didn't change me, especially after all those years of just not saying. That new openness brought us back together, after my bad mood washed away. The only concern she really had was our potential children and what we would teach them.

"'We teach them to be good people. No more, no less. Stories are stories, but decency is decent.'

"We married two months later."

This story points to an important principle of coming out atheist: to anyone, really, but especially to spouses or partners. That principle: Be clear. Don't drop hints or leave a trail of clues. If you think it'll go over better, you can soften the ground first—but eventually, you'll need to spell it out. Even if you think your hints are pretty obvious, people's ability to ignore what they don't want to see is pretty close to infinite. And even if you think your hints are obvious, partners will still often feel betrayed or lied to, if the way you communicate about your atheism is to scatter puzzle pieces and hope they put it together. So be clear. Use the most accurate, explicit, impossible-to-ignore language you can.

Chad in Wichita Falls, a somewhat conservative Christian community in North Texas, has a story that shows how important it is to be clear from the get-go. "My wife's cousin was over visiting," he says, "and we were all talking in the living room. The cousin had been to church with my wife, I had stopped attending, and [she] was commenting about how devout the service had seemed to her. She asked me if I was that way, and without thinking I replied, 'Me? No, I'm an atheist.'

"My wife's initial response was, 'no you aren't, you're just searching.'

"I assured her later that I was in fact an atheist. For a month or so there was a tension in the house, but that was the extent of it. In retrospect, I think I may have been more tense than her because in a way, I felt as though I had let her down. I in no way regret telling her how I did. I was up front and I didn't have to deal with her feeling as though I didn't trust her enough to tell her. I had learned in my first marriage that it is better to be oneself and deal with others than to hide and be miserable. This one principle more than anything guided me. I had found it to be true in other areas of my life, and it just naturally carried over to atheism."

Honesty about your atheism—and sooner rather than later—is almost always the best policy with marriages or other long-term committed relationships. The only reasons I can think of for waiting are if there's some practical consideration—like if you think your spouse might use your atheism against you in a custody battle—or if it's in the middle of a crisis. (Even I wouldn't counsel telling your religious spouse that you're an atheist the day after their mom died.)

And honesty, as early as you can, is definitely the best policy if you're in the earlier stages of a relationship, or are just starting to date. If the person or people you're involved with are going to be upset about your atheism, you want to know—before you get deeply invested. You want to know, sooner rather than later, how important your differences over religion are: not just to them, but to you as well. You might not even realize until you start discussing it how important your atheism is to you; differences over religion might be a deal-breaker for you. For that matter, you might not realize how unimportant it is; you might be dating a religious person, and realize that their religion is just not that big a deal to you. And if the person/people you're seeing are going to be upset by your atheism, you don't want to compound that by keeping it a secret and making them feel like you've betrayed and deceived them.

So again—be clear. It's not fair, or useful, to just leave a trail of hints and hope they figure it out. Again, people have a remarkable ability to not pick up clues, even obvious ones, when they don't want to see where those clues lead. And for some reason, the word "atheist" often upsets people—even when they basically understand that you're not religious. If the "A" word applies to you, if it's the most honest description of your position on religion—use it, and soon.

So how do you use that word? If you're an atheist who's involved with a religious believer or believers, how do you bring it up?

For this question, I was lucky enough to consult with an expert. Dale McGowan (editor of *Parenting Beyond Belief: On Raising Ethical, Caring Kids Without Religion*, and co-author of *Raising Freethinkers: A Practical Guide for Parenting Beyond Belief*) has an upcoming book specifically on relationships and marriages between believers and nonbelievers: *In Faith and In Doubt: How Religious Believers and Nonbelievers Can Create Strong Marriages and Loving Families*. (As of this writing, it's scheduled for publication in August 2014.) To write this book, he surveyed 994 people currently or formerly in secular-religious mixed marriages and romantic relationships.

Dale told me that a number of different variables—variables that you don't have much control over—can affect how much conflict or tension couples experience over religious differences in secular-religious mixed relationships. The specific religion of your partner makes a difference; if they're in a more conservative denomination, there'll probably be more problems, especially if both of you were in a conservative denomination when you got together. Your own past experience with religion can affect how much conflict there is over your religious differences. And how intense your worldviews are—both the intensity of your partner's religiosity, and the intensity of your own atheism—can have a very big effect. As Dale put it, "Two partners with low to moderate intensity of worldview identification usually experience relatively low tension around these issues. When one partner is intensely engaged, tension varies considerably based on other things. When both are intensely engaged, tension is usually through the roof." All of which is stuff you can't do much about.

But that being said, Dale does have useful information on how to communicate about your atheism with your religious partner or partners. "The most important elements of the actual conversation," he says, "are these:

"1. There's often a fear that everything has changed. Reassuring one's partner that this isn't the case is important—that most of your values and priorities are exactly the same as they were.

"2. Also important for the changing partner is to let the other partner know that his/her own religious choices will still be respected. Continuing to attend religious services together or similar concessions can help bridge the transition.

"3. If there are children, it's crucial to come to an agreement about how to proceed. Will they continue to go to religious services, pray, identify with a religious identity? Will they ultimately have the right to choose their own religious identity? It's ideal if both parents are permitted to be entirely open with the kids about their beliefs, while always pointing them to the other partner for another opinion on religious questions."

And some patterns he observed reinforce the importance of coming out early. "All of those variables," he says, "spike *much* further if the change happened after marriage. There's a commonly expressed feeling of a broken covenant—that the understanding they had on their wedding day had been violated by the change. It's also common for the partner who changed to express feelings of profound guilt about that."

Now, obviously, if you were religious when you started your relationship and became an atheist later on, that's not something you can control. But if you know you're an atheist going in, it's important to say so, and soon.

But what about this business of continuing to attend church or other religious services together?

In the chapter on coming out to family, I pointed out that for many believers, the "family togetherness" aspect of religion is as important as the belief in the supernatural. For many people, it's actually more important. That's often true of marriages and relationships as well. And like I said in the chapter on family: You get to decide what you're okay with. You get to decide if attending religious services with your partner, or participating in religious rituals with them, would feel dishonest or unpleasant or offensive—or whether it would feel like a loving compromise in your relationship, and a reassurance of your commitment to them.

I'll say all that again now. I will also say this:

Concessions and compromises are important in any relationship. But it's important that they not all go in one direction. The privilege that religion enjoys in much of the world is often internalized—even by atheists. So it's easy to fall into a pattern where you're making all the concessions to your partner's religion, and they're not making any concessions to your atheism. And I assume you don't want that. When you come out as an atheist, you don't want to start right off with a dynamic where atheism is reflexively, even unconsciously, treated as second class.

So if you're going to keep going to religious services with your partner, suggest that they attend some atheist events with you. If you have kids, and your partner wants them to attend religious services or get religious training, suggest that they also go to events for kids of secular families, like Camp Quest. And if you decide against attending religious services, suggest other activities you could do together: ones that give you both a sense of continuity and commitment, involving interests that both of you share. (Or that all of you share, if you're poly. And if you're poly, make sure that tensions over religion and atheism don't result in some partners getting prioritized and others shut out.)

CD from TX, a former passionate Christian and worship leader who lives "smack in the middle of the Bible Belt," says that his devoutly Christian wife noticed when he started reading atheist books, but wasn't really interested in discussing them. The conflict started when he decided to stop going to church. "When the day came that I decided I wasn't going back to church," he says, "I sat my wife down to talk about it. The conversation went something like this:

"Me: 'I've decided that I'm not going to church any more.'

"Her: 'I know you haven't been happy with our church—what other church would you like to visit?'

"Me: 'You don't understand, I'm not going to church any more. Not any church.'

"Her: 'Oh.'

"She was shocked, to say the least. She had been confident that all of my reading and searching would lead me back to God. We had a few more conversations about my reasons why, but I couldn't get too far into it without her collapsing into tears. Over the next few months we did consider divorce, but eventually decided that we could make it work. She still goes to church every week, I stay home on Sunday mornings, and for the most part we just don't discuss it. It's been hard, and it will get harder as the kids get older and start to ask questions.

"Regardless," he says, "I'm glad that I did it—continuing to go to church would have been dishonest of me and disrespectful."

Of course, if you have religious differences with your partner or spouse—including the difference that they're religious and you're not—and if you have kids or plan to, one of the biggest points of contention can be over how to raise your kids. That's a very large topic, and addressing it thoroughly is outside the scope of this book. Fortunately, there are good resources available. Again, read Dale McGowan's books on parenting, as well as his new book on mixed secular-religious relationships.

And there are lots of communities of atheist parents, both online and in the flesh, that can help you.

But if I had to boil this issue down to a few words, here's what I'd say: Work out compromises that suit both of you. Work out compromises that respect both worldviews equally. Work out compromises that make everyone in the relationship—including your kids—feel loved and treasured. And work out compromises that don't make your kids feel like they're in the middle of a battlefield.

Rosie, a former Catholic in the Midwest, talks about issues she's had with her husband, who "believes in god but is not religious. I made sure he was aware of my stance when we first started dating. When our first child was baptized, I felt suckered into participating. I told him I would never do that again. For our second child, he is having him baptized (mostly for my mother-in-law's sake). I don't care, as long as I don't have to stand up in front of people and agree to it. I don't care if my children attend church with their grandma occasionally, but I will not have them indoctrinated at Sunday school. I intend to raise my children to have open minds, think rationally, use reason, and become educated about as many religions as they can."

Often, even if your partner or spouse is totally fine with your atheism—or indeed is an atheist themselves—in-laws can still present a problem. This can be especially difficult when one partner comes from a family that doesn't believe or is more relaxed about religion, and the other partner comes from a stricter religious background. Seh, a 14-year-old who lives in a small town in northern Wisconsin, has a family that's fairly relaxed when it comes to religion, and they're all pretty accepting of his atheism—or else they're nonbelievers themselves. However, he says, "I've struggled with my girlfriend's parents heavily. At first they liked me, seeing me as a respectable person for their daughter to be with, but when they saw my awkwardness at their prayer before a meal one time at their house, things changed. After I left for my house that day, they asked my girlfriend about it." When she told them that Seh was an atheist, he says, "I was forbidden to see her for quite a while, and now it's calming to the point where we're allowed to 'be friends.' Not trying to get too personal with this section of it, but of course my girlfriend and I have secretly been together throughout this. It just pains me that all this conflict is caused simply because I do not share beliefs with the parents of my girlfriend."

If your partner's family is deeply religious, these problems can be exacerbated, to the point where they might actually withdraw love and support from your partner if they learn about your atheism. In the chapter on family, I quoted the story of Daniel Schealler, who is out as an atheist to almost everyone in his life—but who's chosen to keep his atheism private from his fiancée's Muslim family, because she has a chronic illness, and he doesn't want to risk her being disowned for marrying an atheist. "Which means," he says, "that I will have to go through with a Muslim 'conversion' for a smaller wedding-before-the-actual-wedding to maintain the illusion with her parents. I am less than thrilled about this." (The things we do for love...)

Of course, not all relationships with religious in-laws are fraught. Often they work out fine, even if they're somewhat contentious. On the Coming Out Godless Project website, Larro tells this story: "My father-in-law is over and we are partaking of some beers (I rather enjoy having a few beers with him and discussing politics and current events). Most of what I remember is just flat out telling him 'I'm an atheist. I don't believe...' after getting into some debate about a secular issue. His answer was 'I feel sorry for you.' My retort: 'I feel sorry for *you*.' And I honestly do." But Larro goes on to say that he and his father-in-law "are still on speaking terms and we still love to engage in political discussions. He's pretty open-minded about that. Though he'll never change his stance as a true-blue Blue Dog Democrat."

Issues with in-laws are, of course, common in lots of relationships and marriages—not just ones between atheists and believers. And writing an entire manual on blending your families is definitely outside the scope of this book. (Again—look at Dale McGowan's book, *In Faith and In Doubt*. He can tell you a lot more about this than I can.) What I mostly want to say, once again, is this:

When it comes to in-laws, you and your partner or partners get to make whatever decisions work for you. Just make sure you're on an equal footing. Make sure your compromises work for both of you, and respect both of your worldviews equally. It's all too easy to let "they'll be upset by your atheism" be the trump card, the be-all and end-all of the discussion. Don't let it be. It might help to make "if the shoe were on the other foot" analogies; would your partner be okay keeping their religion a secret if you had an atheist family who'd be upset by it? What compromises would they be willing to make to get along with your godless clan? Of course it's fine to make compromises in relationships—it's essential—and you don't even need to have a strict "tit for tat" about it. If your in-laws have a problem with your atheism or are likely to, and you think the right thing to do is compromise to show your love and devotion, I'm the last person to talk you out of it. Just make sure you're not doing all the giving, and your partner's not doing all the taking. And make sure your compromises aren't being made with a reflexive respect for religion that atheism isn't getting.

Of course, depending on the intensity of your partner's faith—or the specifics of their religion—coming out about your atheism might actually mean the end of the relationship. This can happen with people who have been dating a few weeks or months—and it can happen with people who have been married, or otherwise seriously committed, for years.

When Dale McGowan surveyed 994 mixed secular-religious relationships, he came to the conclusion that for these relationships to work, atheists need to reassure their partners that they haven't radically changed, and that most of their values and priorities are the same. They need to reassure their partners that they still respect their right to make their own religious choices. And if they have kids, there needs to be agreement about how to raise them. But what if none of that is true? What if becoming an atheist *has* changed your values and priorities? What if you *don't* have respect for your partner's religion—even if you respect their right to make their own choices about it? What if you *do* radically disagree with the religious upbringing your partner wants to give your kids? Becoming atheist sometimes takes people very far from who they were when they believed—especially if their religion was conservative, dogmatic, or simply very intense. And it can take people very far from the religious people in their lives—especially if *their* religion is conservative, dogmatic, or simply very intense.

When coming out atheist means trouble for a relationship, it may be because of anti-atheist bigotry from the believer. But it can also be because of genuinely differing values. Many religious believers—not all, but many—place a high value on faith, respect for religious authority, and clan loyalty. Many atheists—not all, but many—place a high value on evidence and reason, independent thinking, and accepting reality even when it means changing your mind. And shared values is one of the foundations of a relationship. When you realize that your values have changed, and you and your partner don't share the same values anymore—or you realize that you always had different values, and you didn't notice it until your values led you to atheism—it can create a genuine rift.

And that can happen from either side. It can be either you or your partner who decides that you just don't have enough in common anymore to make your relationship work. And I'm going to go out on a limb here, and say that that's okay. I know this isn't a popular opinion in advice to couples, but some relationships can't be saved. Some relationships shouldn't be saved. If you do still have enough values and priorities and plans and memories and interests in common to make things work—that's great. And if your relationship is of long standing, or if you have kids together, then you'll probably want to put a lot of effort into making it work. But if your atheism and the values that led you to it are important enough to you that you can't share a life with someone who doesn't share them—it's sad, but it's your right. And if your partner's religion and the values connected to it are important enough to *them* that they can't share a life with someone who doesn't share them—it's sad, but it's their right, too. Breaking up is hard to do, but sometimes it's the right thing to do. For some couples (or triads, or other poly relationships), there may be no way for the people to be authentically themselves, and still be together.

William Brinkman, an atheist since college, has mostly had good experiences coming out atheist. But there was one time when it led to a breakup. "I leaped into a relationship," he says, "with a woman who believed in the Catholic faith. After I moved to Chicago to be closer to her and get into a better job market, I came out as an atheist to her. It was quite a shock to her. She asked me why I couldn't believe, and said it was OK. However, she didn't think we'd be together in Heaven. So we broke up. Sure I could have lied or pretended to believe, but I wouldn't have been true to myself. You should be able to show your true self to your partner. So while it hurt, I think the breakup made me a better person."

Corey A. Henderson had an even more intense and traumatic experience. He had been in a rural congregation of Jehovah's Witnesses—who demand that its members completely cut off any contact with anyone who has left the faith. For Corey, this meant that "I 'came out' by leaving that faith at the same time I left my wife and children... Leaving the Witnesses immediately made my marriage impossible.

"I told my wife that I was leaving her because I had to leave the Witness faith. There was no way for me to do one or the other and not both. I was sick of living a lie, going to meetings at the Kingdom Hall when I no longer believed, and hiding my 'worldly' lifestyle from everyone." The shunning required by Jehovah's Witnesses was nearly complete. After Corey came out, he says, "I lost contact with my four younger siblings, my parents, and my large extended family. Most of the friends I grew up with have never spoken to me again. It's been 20 years. I had to start my life completely over from nothing." This experience was so traumatic that at one point, he even attempted suicide.

And unfortunately, spouses or partners will sometimes use religious differences as a weapon in custody battles or other disputes. Corey again: "After about a month [after coming out] I contacted my estranged wife to pay support, start a divorce and get access to my children. That led to several years of court fights over trying to have regular access to my children, while my family and my ex-wife's family were systematically trying to keep me from 'polluting' them by interfering with my access." Although he did eventually re-connect with his children, it took years. "I lost contact with my children and everyone else for over ten years. My son (now 20 years old) finally searched for me online (where I had left a way for him to reach me) and we have reconciled. We are now close friends. In my absence he discovered he was also an atheist and I was surprised to find that he and my daughter are not active in the Jehovah's Witness faith anymore."

And yet, even after such a prolonged traumatic experience, he still says that coming out was the right decision. "I would not have survived," he says, "if I had tried to stay in the Witness faith for the past two decades... I had lived a 'double life' for about two years before I decided I could not hold on until my children were teenagers. It was killing me."

Breakups are hard. Breakups over religion are hard in special ways. But it's not always how things work out. It's not even usually how things work out. Even if there's an initial period of trauma and upset, coming out to religious partners often turns out okay. So give the people you love some credit.

Secular Skeptic comes from a family of seventh-generation Mormons, and married his wife in a special secret ceremony, making a covenant with God as well as each other to stay faithful on pain of hellfire. But even then, he was having doubts. On the Coming Out Godless Project website, he says that when he finally acknowledged his lack of belief and told his wife about it, the news initially "went over in my household like a lead balloon." But he says that since then, "she's been a real trooper about it. She has always been fairly liberal, unlike the majority of Mormons, and has been able to accept my transition with open arms. She even reads all of the content of this space [his Secular Skeptic blog], which has served as good discussion fodder."

Ex-Muslim Omaar Khayaam says, "My wife was slightly aware of my struggle. I told her one night just before we slept. I simply said that I didn't believe in God anymore. She thought I was going through a phase and said that surely I'll snap out of it. This was her initial reaction. She did in time come to accept that this was the conclusion of a long struggle."

Nicole Kippel was raised in a conservative evangelical charismatic home. On the Coming Out Godless Website, she says that when she came out as atheist, "I felt nothing but liberation and knew then that I could face any reaction. Luckily, I've got nothing but support... I am lucky my husband is a very liberal non-literal Christian who is 100% supportive of my path."

In the book *Mom, Dad, I'm an Atheist* by David G. McAfee, Nickolas Johnson of O'Fallon, Missouri says, "My wife and I have been married for nearly five years now and I think religion plays a bigger role in my life than it does in hers... Sometimes my opinions of her religion may seem reflective of her but I'm not brash because of some sort of disdain for that part of her personality; more so I have an open, honest relationship with her and nothing is too taboo to talk about... When it all boils down to it, if you share the same core values and put importance in the same values it really isn't that hard to be with someone that disagrees with you on other things."[1]

And Jamie G. was raised in a religious home, and belonged to various Christian churches for many years—including an Assembly of God church that practiced speaking in tongues. On the Coming Out Godless Project website, he says that while the change to atheism was difficult at first, he feels better having let go of religion—and his wife is happy about the change as well. "My wife," he says, "though no longer a Christian, takes an agnostic theist position... for now. She has told me that she thinks that I am so much a better husband now. That makes me glad."

When you come out as atheist to a religious partner or partners, they may feel an initial sense of betrayal. But the same commitment that might at first make them feel upset or betrayed is likely, in the long run, to inspire them to stick with it and make it work. For better and for worse.

CHAPTER ELEVEN

Friends

I said it about family, I said it about spouses and partners, and I'll say it again about friends: Coming out atheist usually turns out fine. It usually ends up better than we expect. It doesn't always—coming out atheist can injure friendships with believers, or even end them—but most of the time, that doesn't happen. And even when it does, most atheists still think it was the right decision.

Sometimes, coming out atheist to your friends is not a problem in the slightest. Daniel Schealler says, "They all know. But it's not an issue, except inasmuch as they know it winds me up to repeat bad creationist arguments while pretending to be serious. My friends are assholes."

Sometimes coming out atheist will lead to unpleasant fights or put some strain on a friendship—but without ending the friendship, or even putting a serious dent in it. Erasmus, who first came out as a child in Catholic school when he refused to be blessed, says, "At University I had to break it to a friend that not only was I atheist but almost everyone else he knew was too. He tried to convert me then, which is the only time he and I ever had a vitriolic argument: as he ended up in tears over the offensive shit in his holy book, we agreed not to discuss it again. His father is a bishop: he went on to lead the CU at our uni and does Christian outreach. I happily turn up to some of his programs to tell people what he is peddling is crap. We've been friends a decade."

And in some cases, coming out atheist can even strengthen friendships. It's hard to be really close with someone when you're keeping secrets from them, especially secrets about things that are important to you. And taking a risk to share something can, in itself, build a bond of trust.

Malani, who lives in Mexico in a society where Catholicism is the dominant religion, tells the story of coming out to one of her oldest friends. At first, she says, when she started explaining her atheism and pointing out the questions about religion that led her to it, her friend "was petrified. I started pouring questions and she tried to answer them all but she couldn't respond to most of them, at the end she said 'that's what happens when you let yourself think and question stuff'... That left ME petrified." But Malani goes on to say, "She remained being my friend and I actually feel we are much closer now... I am really glad I was able to come out to her, that gave me peace of mind and allowed me to come out to my sister later on."

Sarah, a former Catholic, tells a similar story. "Three or four friends and I were talking at a party," she says, "and the conversation turned to religious beliefs. One of my friends said something about being okay with whatever people want to believe, even if they don't believe in anything. She said, 'I don't know anyone who's an atheist, but that would be okay.' I debated for a split second but then thought, Oh what the hell, put my hand up and said 'I am.' My friend exclaimed, 'Oh my God!' and hugged me! She said, 'Wow, I didn't know you were an atheist.' And I think I said something like 'Yeah, it's good to know I can talk to you guys about it.' I wasn't expecting this kind of reaction. I live in Arkansas, the middle of Bible Belt country, and I knew this friend of mine was a pretty devout Christian (goes to church almost every week and thanks/praises God in every other Facebook status update). The others in the group reacted the way I expected, with silence or conversation topic changes.

"None of us were very close to start with," she says, "but since my coming-out, I think a couple of those others avoided me for a while. But the friend who hugged me and I became much closer after that conversation."

And, of course, just as with family members and partners or spouses, telling your friends that you're an atheist will bring other atheists out of the woodwork. If you're not out to your friends, you probably have no idea how many of them are atheists themselves. When you come out, it'll embolden them to come out, too. In *The Young Atheist's Survival Guide*, Hemant Mehta tells of the time high school atheist Allison came out to a friend at a homeschooling event. "The friend responded back, 'Hey, that's really cool! I am, too!'"[1] And Sam, a pilot, says, "Friends at the airport, fellow pilots, event volunteers who are also friends on Facebook have seen my posts about atheism. Three have come up to me on the side and said that they don't believe either."

You can't always predict, though, which friends will be accepting and supportive, and which ones will turn away. Omaar Khayaam, an ex-Muslim living in northern England in a city with a large Pakistani Muslim minority, says that even friends who knew he was having doubts were shocked and upset to discover he was an atheist—to the point where it ended the friendships. "This turned out pretty sour and bitter," he says. "Two of my best friends expressed huge concern and in the end it led to the breakdown of our friendship. I am aware that their concern was sincere and genuine. The irony was the sheer surprise that they showed considering the fact that they were privy to my doubts. We had discussions every time we got together. They had spoken to the clerics and were advised to break contact with me and not keep my company." He accepted the rift, even though he was saddened by it. "In the end," he says, "it was their choice. If they wanted to sacrifice our friendship then fair enough." But it's made him cautious about coming out to other friends—since their reactions are so unpredictable. "It's like playing Russian Roulette. I have to be careful who I tell and who I don't. Especially when over ninety percent of my friends are Muslims."

And yet, even with these sour experiences, he still thinks coming out was the right choice. "On the whole," he says, "I am happy and glad that I came out. I no longer try to square the circle anymore... The only regret I have is that I should have come out much earlier. Preferably before my marriage."

When you're coming out to friends—just as when you're coming out to most people—it's often a good idea to think about who you'd like to tell first. For one thing, coming out to friends can be a good way to get in a few practice rounds before coming out to your family—especially if you think your friends are likely to have an easier time with it. That's often the case; we don't choose our families, but we do choose our friends, and we typically choose people whose worldview is pretty similar to our own. If you tell your friends first, you'll get some practice, and coming out will get easier and more comfortable. Plus you'll have people to support you if things with your family go south.

And for the same reasons, it's worth thinking about *which* of your friends you want to tell first. Coming out to supportive friends can help you come out to other people more confidently, and more publicly, even more defiantly if that's your style. Ralph Serrano, who lives in Quezon City in the Philippines, says that when he came out to his friends in culinary school, some of them invited him to Bible study and asked him to turn to God. But on the whole, they've been accepting. "Because of my very accepting friends and family," he says, "I've become more confrontational and more geared towards debating theists. I've become more open and not afraid of the backlash now thanks to my friends."

But when you do start telling some of your friends that you're an atheist, be prepared for the dam to burst. Friends can gossip, often even more than family. And friends may assume that if you're out to them, you're out to everyone. If that's not true—be sure they know that. Let them know that you'd rather keep it private for now, and that you'd rather do your own coming out. That's especially true if you're worried about serious consequences if word gets out, and you're keeping your atheism private with all but a few people.

And then be prepared for the news to get out anyway. If they tell just one friend and swear them to secrecy, and that person tells just one friend and swears *them* to secrecy, and so on and so on... your secret may not be secret for very long. This is especially true if you're communicating via email, Facebook, or anywhere on the Internet. (I talk more about this in the chapter on the Internet.)

One of the biggest questions you'll likely be facing is whether to get into arguments about religion. Many people are more prone to debate with friends than they are with their family, or even with their spouses and partners. For a lot of people, that's one of the things they value about their friendships; they like the back-and-forth, the exchange of differing ideas, the opening and expanding of minds, that can come from debating smart people they disagree with. With family, or with spouses and partners, many people feel a greater need to focus on common ground—but with friends, the differences are a big part of what they value. And they like the sense of acceptance and continuity they get from being able to disagree with someone and still stay friends.

But unfortunately, debates about religion can be very different from debates about politics or art or Star Trek vs. Star Wars. The point Daniel Dennett made in *Breaking the Spell* is worth noting again: The less evidence people have for a belief, the more fiercely they'll defend it—since you don't have to fiercely defend an idea that's obviously true.[2] I know, I know. It's totally unfair. The very thing that should make these arguments easy for you to win—the unbelievable weakness of the case for religion—is the exact thing that's likely to make these arguments upsetting for the people you're arguing with. And that's extra-true if it's a belief that deeply matters to people: when it's central to their philosophy of life, their cultural and family identity, how they cope with death, and so on.

So just like with your family, you can't assume that because you and your friends have a good history of friendly disagreement, therefore your debates about religion won't be a problem. You'll have to decide what your priorities are: whether you're okay biting your tongue around your friends, or whether speaking your mind is worth it even if it disrupts or ends the friendship. That's going to differ depending on you and your personality. It may also differ depending on your friend, and their personality. And it may differ depending on what kind of friendship you have, and how close you are, and what both of you value in your friendship. Just like with family, you get to decide whether valuing your friendship means, "This relationship is too important, I don't want to start a fight that might turn ugly"—or whether it means, "This relationship is too important, I don't want to have to shut up about the things that matter to me." (I cover this in more detail in the chapter on arguing about religion.)

In her interview for *The Ebony Exodus Project* by Candace R. M. Gorham, Heather says that arguing with her religious friends was often very frustrating. When she started discussing her atheism on Facebook, she says, "I still had friends from my hometown and friends from church. So, when I started putting these questions up and I started saying, 'Hey! What about this? What about that?' everybody was like, 'Girl, you going off the deep end. There's no contradiction in the Bible.' But I said, 'Yes there is! I'm trying to show you right here! There is a contradiction!' And they said things like, 'Well, I don't know where you getting your information from.' It was like I was talking to a brick wall."[3]

Sometimes, though, arguments with friends about religion can be difficult and upsetting, and yet still be productive and eventually turn out well. Patrick Walsh was raised Catholic, but later became Presbyterian; he describes himself as having been "really into Christianity," and went to a religious youth group with many of his friends. He told a select group of his friends about his atheism when they went on a cabin trip to the mountains—close friends who knew him from their Christian activities, who were intensely Christian and assumed that he still was, too. He decided ahead of time to come out on this trip—and looked for an opening to bring it up.

"So a couple nights into the trip," he says, "we set up an awesome fire outdoors, and we were all sitting around it talking about whatever. The topic of Ouija boards came up, and I saw it as my opportunity to somewhat get into the topic. I very forwardly stated that I did not believe Ouija boards actually worked and asked others what they thought. Stephen said there was no way he would ever touch one, just in case. Then we got deeper into talking about ghosts and such and I again openly stated that I didn't believe in ghosts or spirits. Then Stephen asked, 'Do you believe in God?' And he didn't ask it as an actual question, but instead with kind of a laughing tone, knowing 100% that I've always been big into believing in God, and that obviously I would say yes, and he would be able to use that to prove that spirits exist. This was the moment. Although I had hoped this would happen and had looked forward to it, I was extremely nervous. But I knew that this was my chance, and I had to take it. I responded, 'No.' Instant, awkward silenced ensued. At that moment, the way these people had always viewed me, this image they'd created of me, was completely shattered. I don't remember what was actually said directly following this, or by whom, because I was so in the moment of what I had just done. But eventually, we all started talking again. Instead of being bombarded by questions (I think most of them were still shocked), I instead did a lot of the questioning. I questioned why they believed in God, and talked about all of the inconsistencies in the Bible that I had recently discovered, etc.

"At one point in the conversation, Kyle started getting defensive, and as a result of him not being able to answer some questions, he got up and went into the cabin. I felt bad, but I didn't feel that I had done anything wrong. I was simply expressing my opinions and questioning his. Stephen stayed though, and a couple of us stayed out by that fire late into the night. Stephen was pretty cool about it, asking me many questions about Atheism, rather than getting defensive. The couple of us that stayed up late all went to bed with smiles on our faces, still as good as friends as before. For the rest of the trip, the topic didn't really come up again, and I wondered how Kyle now thought of me.

"Fast forward to this summer [2013], after I have come home from college. Kyle and I have now had many talks about religion and Christianity, and I think now he is starting to think for himself about it, rather than just accepting what he had always been taught."

So it often turns out fine, even when it starts out being difficult. But sometimes it's fine without ever being difficult. Lisa says that coming out to her friends in her Illinois college town was "pretty easy. Oh so easy. This is one of the few situations in which I was confident bringing the subject up. I had conversations with christians asking, 'Exactly what do you believe anyways? You aren't mean enough to my queer self to believe in the literal truth of the bible, so is it just the version the preachers filter to you? How do you even decide which preachers are the good prophets and which will selectively choose quotes to control you?' and not ruining friendships with such prodding."

Also—remember that your friends are grownups, and can decide for themselves which arguments they're willing to get into and which ones they're not. Lauren, who came out at age 12 when preparing for her confirmation in the Lutheran church, now says, "It usually doesn't come up until a friendship is well established. My devout friends learn quickly not to proselytize too much, because they will be asked uncomfortable questions they can't answer. Mostly they just pray for me—that's a handy escape hatch for believers who want to remain friends with a godless heathen."

It is true that coming out atheist may mean the end of some friendships. If you have friends from conservative religions, religions that require the shunning of apostates (such as Jehovah's Witnesses), or simply friends who are passionate about their faith, the reality is that those friendships may end when you tell them you're an atheist.

That might be because of anti-atheist bigotry. And if it is, it might not be your friend who ends the friendship. You might decide that you can't be friends with someone who thinks you're amoral, miserable, or doomed to be tortured in fire. If so—that is totally fine. It might be sad, but it's completely reasonable. If you wouldn't expect gay people to stay friends with homophobes, or black people to stay friends with racists, don't pressure yourself to stay friends with anti-atheist bigots. If you want to stick with them and try to persuade them out of their bigotry, that is awesome. It might even work—it has before. But you're not morally obligated to do it. And you get to decide what your limits are, and how much crap you're willing to put up with in the name of Atheism 101 education.

And while coming out atheist does sometimes mean the end of friendships, many atheists feel that those friendships weren't worth preserving. If their friends didn't want to stay friends with an atheist, they say, they weren't true friends in the first place. CD from TX, a former passionate Christian and worship leader who lives "smack in the middle of the Bible Belt," says that when he stopped going to church, "I've definitely found out which of those church people were really friends and which were just church friends. To be frank most of those people I wouldn't really want to hang out with anyway—most of them think Barack Obama is a socialist Muslim from Kenya and all of the other tripe that goes along with far-right-wing politics."

Kat Car agrees. Most of her friends don't particularly care about religion—but, she says, "I do have one friend that is an ardent Christian. She keeps posting pictures of pregnant women and stomping over her own rights and those of others, or claiming Einstein to be a Christian. If it were not for her, my atheism would have been one post. And yes, it has wrecked our friendship, and no, I don't regret it. It has shown me her true colours. Prevent rape victims getting abortions? Sneer at those who don't believe in your one true god? Not a person with whom I want to be friends."

But when coming out atheist means the end of a friendship, it might not be because of anti-atheist bigotry. It might be because of genuinely differing values. I said this about marriages and romantic relationships, and it's true of friendships as well. Even if your religious friend isn't bigoted against atheists—even if they don't think you're amoral or miserable or doomed to be tortured in fire—believers and atheists often have very different values. And shared values are one of the foundations of friendships. When becoming an atheist means you don't share the same values anymore—or it makes you realize that you never shared the same values—it can put strain on a friendship.

Jason Sciple lives in the Bible Belt, and he feared that when he came out as an atheist, it would create problems and even rifts with his family and friends. In David G. McAfee's book *Mom, Dad, I'm an Atheist*, he says, "Regarding my friendships, I was mostly right. Since many of our [his and his wife's] relationships were with friends we met through churches, we lost what we had in common. There were very few instances where people just quit talking to us strictly because they couldn't stand to be friends with atheists, but rather we weren't the people they knew before. We had changed."[4]

That can happen from either side, theirs or yours. And while it might be sad, it's completely reasonable. You get to decide which of your values are... you know, most valuable to you. If you and your friend have other priorities and interests that you share, and those are enough to make the friendship worthwhile—that's great. It'll certainly make the world a better place if there are friendships between atheists and believers. But if that's not going to work for you, if your atheism and the values that led you to it are important enough that you can't be close to someone who doesn't share them, don't beat yourself up. (And by the same token, if your friend's religious values make it impossible to keep their friendship with you, they have that right as well. Even if they're basing that decision on messed-up ideas, they still have the right to make it. Don't beat them up for exercising it.)

Also, depending on who you are, it might be important to you not only to be open about your atheism, but to speak out against religion. And that's likely to put a damper on your friendships with believers. If you're not a "live and let live" atheist—if you're passionately opposed to religion, to the harm done in the name of religion, to the very idea of religious faith—that's going to be hard on your religious friends. I can't blame them. If I had a friend who was posting on Facebook every day about why my most cherished beliefs were toxic bullshit, I'd probably get sick of it, too. But I won't blame you, either. You have the right to speak out against ideas you find repugnant. If you're a Democrat, you have the right to speak out against Republicanism—even if you have Republican friends. If you're an environmentalist, you have the right to speak out about global climate change—even if you have friends who are climate change denialists. And if you're an atheist, you have the right to speak out against religion—even if you have religious friends. I hardly have any religious friends anymore. I don't really blame them. But I don't blame myself, either.

Again, though—this isn't what usually happens. Usually when people tell their friends that they're atheists, it turns out fine. It can turn out in all different degrees of fine: tense but okay, no big deal, stronger than ever, "it turns out that she was an atheist too," "now he's become an atheist himself." But it usually turns out fine. Presumably, you're friends because you like each other, and respect each other, and enjoy each other's company. So give your friends some credit. Have some faith—small-f faith—that they like you and want to keep being your friends. And give them the respect of assuming that they can cope.

CHAPTER TWELVE

Work

Coming out atheist at work has a whole special set of challenges—and risks.

When you come out as atheist at work, you probably won't be worrying so much about questions like, "Will they still love me? Is this going to make them feel rejected? Will we be able to have an honest and authentic relationship?" You'll probably be worrying more about questions like, "Is the fundie in the next cubicle going to make my life miserable? Will this create tension when we work on projects together? Will this keep me from getting promoted? Will this get me fired?"

So coming out atheist at work will probably not be so much about warm fuzzies and intense philosophical conversations. Some people do develop close bonds and personal friendships with the people they work with, of course; if that's true for you, read the chapter on friends as well as this one, and consider whatever mix you usually apply to managing personal differences with your work friends. But for many people, maybe even most people, coming out at work will probably be about practical considerations more than personal ones. It'll probably be more about fairness, equality, getting along—and possibly the law.

But coming out at work also has a whole special set of rewards. The workplace can be an amazing place to come out into. In many workplaces, people are thrown together who would never have any connection otherwise. It's not like family, where you share a common history; or friendships, where you seek out people who already share your values. There's a good chance that your workplace will have people with very different backgrounds from you, and very different outlooks on life. So at work, you have a great chance to do Atheist Visibility 101 with people who might not otherwise be exposed to it. You have a great chance to be the great atheist counter-example to all the myths people have about us. And that has huge potential to ripple out into the rest of the world.

Sam first came out atheist at his job in the late '90s, in response to an engineering co-worker who joked about what atheists say when people sneeze. "I have one Catholic co-worker," he says, "who will question and joke with me about it which shocks others sometimes, especially since I hold my own and joke back at her. But then I've had one come to me on the side and agree with some of my replies, Facebook rants or a comment from the news, especially when it concerns the Pope... My morals are probably what has surprised them the most. Why am I so nice? Why don't I just want to rape and murder? What keeps me from trying that? Seeing the charity things I do used to just baffle them. I had to explain how altruism benefits a population and that it is natural for me to be good."

Even if you don't want to be the great atheist educator, though, it's often worth coming out at work—simply because, for lots of people, that's where they spend most of their waking life. If you want the benefits of being an out atheist anywhere—being more relaxed, more un-afraid, not constantly measuring your words and biting your tongue, not stressing about what might happen if people discover your secret, etc.—having these benefits at the place where you spend eight hours a day can be especially beneficial. And if you don't want to be the great atheist educator, work can be a great place to be an out, visible athe-ist—and still have a built-in escape valve if things start to get hairy. At most workplaces, it is completely legitimate, even desirable, to keep things fairly cool. So when you come out at work, it's reasonable to say, "I don't want to get into a huge thing about where my morality comes from and what I'd tell my grandmother on her deathbed. I really just want to be treated fairly, and in accordance with the law."

So if you've decided that coming out at work is worth the risk—or you've decided that the risks at your workplace probably aren't that great—how do you go about it?

When you come out at your job, it's an extra-good idea to think strategically about who you come out to first. That's especially true if you think your co-workers are going to have a problem with it. Specifically: Think about the people who (a) have some degree of authority, and (b) who you think will be more likely to be supportive.

Now, "authority" doesn't have to mean your boss. It might mean someone in human resources, or someone in the legal department, or just someone who lots of people like and respect. And "likely to be supportive" doesn't have to mean, "I think they're an atheist." If there's someone in authority at your workplace who has a track record of caring about fair play, or caring about the law, or even just caring about the company not getting sued and getting a ton of bad publicity—they're likely to be your ally.

So come out to them first. Give them a little time to get used to the idea. Talk with them about your plans to come out to your other co-workers. Get them on your side. And *then* start coming out to other people.

If you're just starting a new job, you might decide to hold off on coming out until people have gotten to know you. When you come out to friends and family, after all, you have that whole "these people care about me and know I'm a good person" factor in your favor. With people you're just starting to work with, you don't yet have that advantage. So you might decide to wait until you do have it. "I tend not to hide it," IasasaI says, "except when I am newly employed. At those times, I just keep quiet in general until I get to know everyone and know how open I can be. This isn't just because of religion, but because I have never been particularly comfortable around people I know poorly and when I DO get to know people, I tend not to censor what I tell them."

But you might also decide, "To heck with that." You might decide that you just want to be who you are right from your first day on the job. You might not want to search for awkward excuses to shoehorn it into the conversation later—and you might not want to make it seem like atheism is something to be secretive about. That's especially true if you're pursuing a "no big deal" method of coming out, or simply being out. Lucy Mayne, who grew up in an atheist family in Australia in an area known for being conservative by Australian standards, worked for over three years in a workplace with a number of very outspoken conservative Christians. "I went about outing myself at work," she says, "by wearing the scarlet A from the RDF [Richard Dawkins Foundation for Reason and Science] Out Campaign. I wore the pin to work every day for about a month before I had my first query about what it meant. I explained that I was an atheist, and the answer was something along the lines of 'Oh, ok'—it was no big deal. Nevertheless, my heart rate had jumped to something alarming.

"After that the queries gathered speed as people noticed that I was wearing this badge all the time. Despite the fight or flight response I had every time someone asked, I never had a bad experience. Most people didn't care. Quite a few confided to me that they were either atheists or agnostics. I got into one discussion about why I didn't believe, but it was very cordial, and didn't come up again. The most negative reaction was, 'Why do you need to tell people that,' to which I responded that I felt that there was anti-atheist prejudice in the community, and wanted to be visible as an atheist so that people didn't just deal with abstract stereotypes."

That decision is probably going to depend on your workplace. Is it more of a conservative religious hotbed where you might want to tread more carefully, or a more progressive or secular environment where your atheism probably won't be that big a deal? And, of course, it's going to depend on your personality.

Just so you know: Often, coming out atheist *isn't* that big a deal. That's true even in workplaces you'd think would be hostile. Robert B works in Maryland, in an educational supply store with Christian overtones; they carry lots of religious items, they sometimes shelve religious products with character education, and the sound system often plays Christian rock. He mostly hasn't mentioned being an atheist at work— but the conversations he's had, with both co-workers and customers, have generally gone well. He has one Catholic co-worker, he says, who "often talks about the Catholic schools she went to and her Catholic friends and family. So, religion has become, if not exactly a common topic, at least a common presence in the conversation. So, once, when she was about to explain some interesting point of Catholic ritual to me:

"Her: 'Wait, you're not Catholic, are you?'

"Me: (deliberately casual) 'No, I'm an atheist.'

"Her: (surprised blink) 'Okay.' (continues with story)"

And he's had good experiences coming out to customers as well. "Once," he says, "a customer offered me a religious tract after I'd checked her out. 'Actually, I'm an atheist,' I said. 'Oh! Well, you can just take it for interesting reading,' she answered. 'Sure,' I said, and took it. It was not interesting reading, it was pretty basic 'redemption by faith not deeds' Christian stuff—not nearly so eye-catching as Jack Chick's tracts. But aside from the unfairness of proselytizing to someone who's required by his job to be maximally polite, it went about as well as it possibly could have.

"Generally," he says, "I've had good results from treating the issue casually, as though telling people I'm an atheist was no more controversial than claiming any other religious affiliation. But then, I've been both lucky and careful about not coming out to any real fanatics."

Robert's story raises another issue. Being out or not out at work isn't just an issue in your dealings with co-workers. It can also be an issue with customers, or the general public.

Your workplace may have policies about how they want their company image to be presented by employees when they're on the job—policies that might include not bringing up controversial topics. And I don't actually think that's unreasonable. Just make sure the policy is being applied fairly—to believers as well as atheists. (That applies to relationships with co-workers as well as customers, by the way. If religious employees can wear crosses or other religious symbols, you should be able to wear atheist pins or buttons; if co-workers can post flyers about religious events they're participating in, you should be able to post flyers about your atheist events. Etc.)

Now, if policies *aren't* being applied fairly, you're going to have to decide if you want to push back. That decision will probably have to be based, not just on how bad the discrimination is and how stubborn you think your employers are likely to be, but on your own personality and situation. (Translation: Do you have the time and energy, the resources and the stomach, for a legal battle with your employer?)

But when you're making that decision, it's important to remember: Insisting on your equal rights in the workplace doesn't always have to end up in the courtroom. In fact, it usually doesn't end up there. In many cases, simply having a conversation or two with the right people—people in authority who are likely to be supportive, or people in authority who understand the law and care about not getting sued—is enough.

In fact, this is one of the best things about being an out atheist at work. It means you're free to more openly fight for rights—yours or other people's, on the job or outside of it. When Debra got a job with Hospice in Boulder, Colorado, she says, "there was some religious discussion and prayer at staff meetings—and I came out at work, because it was very uncomfortable for me to have it be part of work. (It had never been a part of staff meetings at any other place I had worked.) After that they toned it down and tried to make that part of meetings more secular or didn't have it at all."

And Amanda Knief, currently the managing director of American Atheists, tells a similar story of her first "coming out at work" experience. "I am an attorney," she says, "and I was working for the nonpartisan division of the Iowa State Legislature called the Legislative Services Agency (LSA). I drafted legislation for the state senators and representatives, the governor, and departments and agencies. About a month after I started my job, the Legislature came into session—and the first thing both the Iowa Senate and Iowa House did after gaveling in [opening the session] was pray! I was incensed. And when no one else seemed to care, I got to work looking for others who would be as upset as I was. Until this time I had not been with an atheist group or known about the atheist movement. I knew about some national organizations, but I had never been a member. That all changed.

"But first I had to tell my boss. See, to work for the LSA one has to be fairly uncontroversial. You are asked (nicely) to register as an independent to avoid the appearance of prejudice when drafting legislation for both parties. You can't belong to any group that the legislature regulates. So during my time at the LSA I gave up volunteering for Planned Parenthood and Save Darfur due to conflicts with the legislature. So if I was going to become an atheist activist, I had to tell my boss. And I did. I scheduled a meeting. I went in—and I said: 'Boss, I'm an atheist, and I want to join an atheist group.' His reaction was great. He said OK. He asked me to keep him informed of my activities and he would judge them based on how anyone in a church would be evaluated. (Employees in LSA who were in synagogues or churches, etc., had to

inform Boss about their activist and/or leadership activities as well).
Soon after, I started telling my coworkers—who were really cool about
it. Except one—who was a dick. It made for interesting conversations,
nice teasing, and better working relationships.

"This is perhaps the best decision I made," she says. "It started me
on the path of activism and my career in atheism, and it gave me the
courage to be myself with many different people: gay, straight, conservative, liberal, Jewish, Catholic, closeted atheists, and Democrats and
Republicans."

If you are pressing for your rights, and you're not getting anywhere
on your own—and you're in the United States—you can contact the
Equal Employment Opportunity Commission. States that have their
own laws about workplace discrimination also have their own state
agencies handling these kinds of complaints. Outside the United
States, you can contact the workplace discrimination agencies in your
country, or the International Labor Organization. You can also get in
touch with the Freedom From Religion Foundation, the ACLU, or
other organizations dedicated to protecting your rights as an atheist, in
the workplace and elsewhere. (See the resource guide at the end of this
book.) In fact, it's not a bad idea to contact these agencies and organizations first, before you start pushing back, to find out what exactly
your rights are. And if a couple/few conversations with your boss or
with human resources don't help, a strongly worded letter from a lawyer or government agency may do the trick.

This leads me to a difficult topic—and it's one on a lot of people's
minds when they consider coming out atheist at work. It is the case,
unfortunately, that depending on where you live and where you work,
coming out as atheist can get you fired. It can also mean getting passed
over for promotions, losing out on plum assignments, or other forms
of workplace discrimination that fall short of getting fired. And it can
create a tense or hostile atmosphere in the workplace that can make it

hard to get your job done, or for your job to even be tolerable. This doesn't always happen—but it can. William Brinkman says that at one of his jobs, "I posted a pro atheist editorial on my wall after my manager ranted against atheists. I got told that I would go to hell by one co-worker, and another tried to do a soft sell on religion. I was never on my bosses' good side after that, but, again, it was important for me to be true to myself." And Michael, who had been the valedictorian of his high school class, says, "Coming out as an atheist has caused me some problems. A good job offer was withdrawn when I told my prospective employer I was an atheist."

Yes, there are laws against religious discrimination: in the United States, anyway, and in much of the rest of the world. And these laws include discrimination against atheists. But alas—and I know this will be a dreadful surprise to many of you—not everyone obeys the law. It's shocking, but it's true. People steal from each other, beat each other up, set fire to each other's houses. Even in the workplace, not everyone obeys the law. People embezzle, violate safety standards, sexually harass employees. And in the workplace, people discriminate against each other, even when it's not legal. People in the workplace get harassed, passed over for promotion, even fired, because of their race, their gender—and their religious affiliation. Including when that religious affiliation is "none."

So if you're getting ready to come out at work, get familiar with the non-discrimination laws in your city, your state, your country. And if you do get discriminated against—document it.

In fact, it's a really good idea to document your work situation *before* you come out. If your boss has been giving you positive feedback—document it. Save your emails and your performance reviews. If your boss says nice things about you verbally, email your friends and family. "Ron just gave me a big thumbs-up on my re-organization of the warehouse! It totally made my day. Let's have a drink to celebrate!"

That way, if you mysteriously start getting hassled or demoted or fired when you come out, you'll have ammunition if you decide to fight it.

Which brings me to the next point: If you do face harassment or discrimination when you come out at work—do you want to fight it? And how? Are you willing to fight it legally? Are you willing to go through mediation or whatever internal procedures your workplace has? Are you willing to fight it in the public eye? You probably want to think about these questions ahead of time—before you come out.

If you come out as atheist and get harassed, discriminated against, or fired, you may well be able to push back against it, and win. And there are resources available for atheists who are facing bigotry in the workplace and are willing to fight it. Again: The EEOC is there for you (in the U.S.), and many states have their own agencies handling workplace discrimination complaints. The Freedom From Religion Foundation, the ACLU, and other organizations are all ready, willing, and able to support atheists in discrimination lawsuits—as well as in the all-important preliminary step of sending polite letters from lawyers, telling businesses that what they're doing is discrimination, and it's illegal, and would they kindly knock it off, please. That's a stage that almost always comes before lawsuits, and it frequently makes lawsuits unnecessary. (Again—see the resource guide at the end of this book.)

But workplace discrimination can be very hard to prove. Employers will often come up with other excuses for firing you; they'll rarely come out and say, in a documented form, "I'm firing you because you don't believe in God." There are also some workplaces that are exempt from federal discrimination laws, such as houses of worship and many faith-based organizations. And even when the case is cut and dried, not everyone has that fight in them. Lawsuits take time and energy. And a lawsuit about anti-atheist discrimination is likely to draw attention, negative as well as positive—from friends, neighbors, colleagues, the press—which takes time and energy as well. If you have kids, if you're supporting your parents, if you're sick or have disabilities, if you're putting yourself through school, if you have more than one job, the crummy reality is that you might not be able to see that fight through.

I would love to tell every atheist not to worry about coming out at work. After all, the law is on their side (in most countries, anyway). But that's not realistic. Not every instance of workplace hostility crosses the line into breaking the law. Not every case of illegal workplace discrimination is winnable in court. And not every atheist is up for a lawsuit.

So if you want to come out at work, and you think there's a real chance you'll face harassment or worse, think about whether you really have it in you to be a test case. If you don't—or for that matter, if you do—get your resume in order. Put out feelers for other jobs. Have a Plan B in place.

But it's important to remember: Most bosses aren't idiots. Okay, maybe most bosses are idiots. But people who employ other people often do know a little something about employment law. Judy Komorita, a lifelong atheist, tells the story of coming out to her boss, who is an attorney and a Christian evangelical. "The reason I told him," she says, "was because, indirectly, he asked. He enjoys talking about his faith. When I never offered my own, he began to wonder. One day, when he came in, he said 'It seems that faith doesn't play an important role in your life.' I replied 'No.' I don't remember how he phrased his next question, but he wanted to know what I was. I said 'I'm an atheist.' It didn't occur to me to lie. I'm not a good liar, and I don't like to lie. But I knew this could cause problems between us.

"I got lucky. He took it silently, and didn't lambast me. He didn't fire me. As I look back on it, I believe one of the reasons he didn't is because he is an employment law attorney, and knows quite well that any kind of retaliation against me is illegal."

In fact, depending on your workplace, being more out can actually give you more protection. If you're a very visible atheist, and you run into discrimination, your employer won't be able to claim that they didn't know about your atheism—and any unfair treatment you get is going to look highly suspicious. Mathematician, the screen name of a mathematician and physicist at a Catholic college in the Midwest, makes a point of including his involvement with Camp Quest (the summer camp for kids of non-believing families) on applications for promotion and tenure. "I specifically included the information," they say, "to preclude my removal on religious grounds, should an attempt be made. In such a case I would have the following points readily available to me.

"1. I am known publicly, through letters to the editor and newspaper articles, to be an atheist.

"2. Faculty, including religious faculty, are well aware of my position.

"3. I have been given tenure and promotion having fully disclosed my beliefs and I was chairperson of the department for several years under these conditions."

And, of course, lots of atheists have come out at work expecting a fight—and didn't get one. carolw, a former Methodist in Austin, Texas, says, "at first I was scared to come out... that was Mom's doing. She's so concerned that I'm going to post something on Facebook that's going to get me fired. I've told her probably a million times that if they fire me for being Atheist they'll have a big fat lawsuit on their hands." But her mom's fears—and hers—weren't realized. "I'm SO glad I came out! At work, my close friends know that I'm the skeptic, debunker, atheist. They tease me—'look it up on Snopes!'" She adds, "It's great to say 'I don't believe in god' or 'I'm atheist' and have whoever you're talking to say, 'me too.' One of my best girlfriends at work is atheist also, so I feel like it's me and her against the goddists. I don't feel so alone."

And schoolteacher dezn_98 has a wonderful story about coming out as atheist to his students, when they have were having a conversation during free time about a student they thought was gay. "At this point," he says, "another kid comes in and says...

"'My mom said that being gay is a sin, and that it is against the bible.'

"At this point I am like... crap... so I say...

"'Well... I don't know what to tell you. Everyone has different beliefs and to be honest I would not believe everything in the bible. I don't really believe all that stuff.'

"At that point more kids jump in and say:

"'ooooooo!!! Mr. ___ does not believe in the bible!'

"'Mr. ____ do you believe in god?'

"'No, in fact. I do not believe in god. Bunches of people have different beliefs.'

"Then all the kids get rowdy...

"'OMG Mr. ____ is an atheist!'

"'He said he does not believe in god!'

"'Mr.____ how can you not believe in jesus!'

"'Mr. ____ do you believe in an afterlife?'

"'Mr. ___ how can you be an atheist... you think we all came from nothing!'

"'Mr.____ how do you explain the big bang and evolution!'

"etc... etc... These kids were adorable with all their questions. So I said...

"'Look... just learn some science. When you get older you going to learn some more science to answer all that stuff. In the meantime... do not be homophobic, and don't be using your religion to be a bigot.'

"'What is a bigot?'

"'ahh... look... just don't be little racists... you know how I don't like that stuff. Now get outta here peoples.'

"'So I shoo them away. Then a few minutes later some student come up to me and says...

"'Mr.____ I wanna tell you something.'

"'What do you want to tell me?'

"'I don't think I believe in god either... I think I am atheist too.'

"Then I was like... awww shit!!!! I am gonna get fired now! So I say...

"'...umm... that is cool. Why don't you like... you know... keep it to yourself. I know your mother and she seems kind of religious. Keep an open mind and stuff... and you know... that is all chill with me. Keep thinking things through though.'

"Which was freaking scary. Damn kids. Anyway, I talked to some faculty members after and I asked if I did the right approach. I was afraid this was gonna come back and bite me on the bum—I would get a bunch of angry parents telling me that I was trying to make their kids atheists. Most staff said I was gonna be OK, and another said that she just does not reveal to the kids what her religious beliefs are because they are so impressionable at that age. After that we all went to a bar and got drunk. I ended up having a debate about god with another faculty member who was a christian fundamentalist. We had a good time, and we all still chill."

"After that, I just come out and say I am an atheist everywhere and I am officially 'out.'"

Given the less personally intense, "keeping things cool" approach that's considered appropriate for most workplaces, a more casual, "no big deal" approach to coming out can fit into that professionalism nicely. Brandon, who lives in Western Pennsylvania ("where there is a church on every block and no one ever talks about religion"), used the Reason Rally as an opportunity to come out as an atheist to his co-workers without any fallout. "People did not seem to care either way," he says. "When I was asked 'what did you do over the weekend?' I told them that I was in Washington DC over the weekend where I attended an atheist rally. There were no negative consequences, I did not lose my job or get any flack from my co-workers. The responses I got were mostly along the lines of 'I love DC!' or 'That sounds like it must have been fun!' They couldn't have cared less." He adds, "My casual attitude garnered casual reactions. I didn't make a big deal about it and people didn't think it was a big deal. Humor was effective in at least one situation. A co-worker was talking to me about big deals that we were both about to close. He said 'I'll be praying for you,' and I responded, 'Funny you should mention that, I'm actually going to be at an atheist rally over the weekend so I'll be... hoping really hard for you.' He laughed, I laughed, no worries."

But there may be times when getting more personal might be the right thing to do, even necessary—especially if your co-workers are getting personal with you. Judy Komorita tells this story of her Christian evangelical boss. "He did massively tick me off over his beliefs one time," she says, "late in 2009. Sometimes when something bad was going on in my life, he would ask to pray for me. I knew it was worthless, but since it seemed to make him feel better, I said sure, it being no skin off my nose. But when my mother passed away, before I left the office for four days to take care of things, he gathered me up with the bookkeeper into a prayer circle. I knew it was stupid (and wrong), and I was shaking with grief. But with his and her arms around me, he said something like 'Lord, even though Judy doesn't believe in you, I know you will take care of her and help her...' That set me off. I didn't say anything at the time. I got out of there ASAP, and stomped to my car vibrating with rage. All I could think of was 'how dare he, when he has absolutely no evidence!'

"When I got back to work the next week, the bookkeeper asked me how I was. I told her that I was still angry about what our boss had said. She must have told him, because he never offered to pray for me again.

"I don't regret that I came out to him," Judy says. "If I hadn't, I would have to (1) continue to hide, (2) put up with his incessant talk about religion and his faith and his walk with god and how this god guides him and teaches him lessons, ad nauseam, and (3) bite down on all my anger and sarcasm even more often than I do now. But I do realize I was lucky. It could have been much worse."

It's worth noting here, though, that even difficult conversations can lead to positive results. Yes, it can be frustrating to do Atheist Mythbusting 101 for the hundredth time, and if you don't feel up for it, that's entirely reasonable. But if you do feel up for it... well, that's how a lot of people are going to get educated. Remember—for you, this may be the hundredth time you've had the conversation about "How can you be moral without God?" and "Isn't it a safer bet to believe?" But for the person you're talking with, it may be their first time. And that's a huge part of how we're going to change people's minds about us—through thousands upon thousands of one-on-one conversations. Again—it's not your responsibility to do Atheism 101 education on demand for everyone you encounter, and nobody has the right to expect it of you. But if you do decide to do it, it can have very positive results.

Jeff Pedersen tells this story of coming out in the workplace in the famously conservative Orange County in California. "The one conversation I remember well from that time," he says, "was with a co-worker while I was finishing college. We both worked in the Student Union building as janitors, and he was speaking of going into politics, and wondering at his chances as we mopped floors. A study recently out about the general electability (or lack thereof) of atheists had been going through my mind, so I asked 'Well, you're not an atheist, are you?'

"'Oh, no, no,' he replied, 'I believe in God.'

"'Well, you've got that advantage then,' I told him. After a bit more talking, he asked if I had ever thought of going into politics.

"'No, I probably couldn't get elected,' I let him know.

"'Why not?'

"At this point, I remember getting that sense of anxiety and adrenaline before I answered. I'm pretty sure this had been the first time I'd ever admitted to anyone of my lack of belief, and my body was treating it as if I was going to get into a fight. 'I'm an atheist. I'm the least electable demographic,' I told him, trying to pass it off as much more casual than I felt. At this, he was a little shocked, and it led to that sort of peppering of questions that you often see on earlyish episodes of The Atheist Experience, where I had to correct various misapprehensions of what I did actually believe ('How can you not believe that there must be "something greater?,"' 'You don't think there's any intelligence outside us? Do you not think aliens could exist?' and the ever popular 'what keeps you from just going out and killing people?').

"I'm glad that I did let him know, because after that, it became a lot easier to admit to other people, and it led to interesting discussions that involved more of my co-workers as well."

"After that, it became a lot easier to admit to other people." Remember those words. It's an important point. Each time you come out as an atheist, it's practice for the next time. Several people told stories like this; they had their heart in their mouth the first time they said they were an atheist, but each time after that became easier and easier, until eventually it became second nature.

But if you don't want to have those more sensitive conversations—don't. Again: You get to draw boundaries, and in the workplace especially, it is totally reasonable to keep things from getting too personal. Judy Komorita says, again about her Christian evangelical boss: "Over the next five years or so, he did proselytize to me occasionally—in a 'loving christian' manner, trying to show me 'god's love.' A few books (one of which I read), a song or two, a couple of bible verses. It never fazed me. I don't believe in it, I don't want it, and his examples left me cold. He finally said something about 'This is not the direction you want to go in your life, is it?' I answered 'No,' (fearing to say too much; he has a bit of a temper). He then said 'Well, I won't bring it up anymore.' He never proselytized to me again."

Plus—once again, just like coming out to family or friends—coming out at work can open the door to other atheists coming out to you. Rosie, who lives in southwestern Wisconsin where almost everyone she knows has a Christian upbringing, tells this story: "I recently came out to my manager at work," she says, "because we're having a team-building day, including meditation and mindfulness facilitated by a former Buddhist priest. My manager was soliciting opinions and objections, and I said I was fine with it as long as we don't discuss religion or beliefs. Surprisingly, my boss said that he's an atheist, too. I've worked for him for eleven years, and neither of us knew that about the other, although we've discussed lots of things in social settings such as our families and parenting."

Daff, who worked at one time for a government agency, actually became a minor office hero when she came out. "An older contractor at work said, 'I can't believe people believe in the theory of evolution,'" she says, "so I explained the usage of the word 'theory' and that evolution is a scientific fact. It grew into a half-hour long debate about atheism and evolution vs. creationism and we gathered a small audience. The next day I told my supervisor, worried that I might've come on too strong with my atheism at work, and she was kicking herself that she missed the action and I got congratulated by some of the people who had been there (they were atheists too but were perfectly happy to let me have the floor to myself!). Now everyone knows about it."

And Suzanne, who worked at a university campus in Oregon, has a great story about how coming out encouraged other co-workers to come out—one of the funniest and most dramatic stories I've heard. "The clarifying incident," she says, "came while me and three co-workers were hanging out at a coffee shop after work like we often did. The conversation had turned slowly toward religion's effect on science education. I don't remember the exact words, but I remember that, though we all were in agreement on the subject, all of us were acting strangely cagey all of a sudden. There was this change in the atmosphere, like we were all holding our breath a little while trying to casually carry on this conversation. I realized later that we were all, at that moment, about to explicitly come out to each other as atheists, and we were all doing the same thing: sizing each other up. 'is it safe for them to know?' 'will this change how they see me?' 'will this affect how we work together?'

"We each starting dropping hints, 'I was raised Catholic, but...' 'I haven't been to church in years, so...'

"Finally, one of my co-workers came out and said it: 'I'm an atheist, so I really don't get it.' and I almost jumped out of my seat in excitement, 'me too!'

"Suddenly, everyone was admitting they were atheists. The mood changed, we all laughed in nervous relief, we started talking excitedly and loudly over one another. One of us said, 'wow, I've never met another atheist besides my husband, who knew we were all in the same office?'"

"Not too much changed with the group of co-workers," she adds, "except that we felt bolder and more relaxed about talking about atheistic views in the office and out of it. One religious woman in the office would get very quiet whenever we'd mention something in her earshot that was atheist-sounding, and I'd think, wow it's weird to be in a place where I'm the majority. It was liberating. A breath of fresh air. Even though I'd been lurking on atheist websites/blogs for several years and didn't feel alone, it was so much better to talk to another atheist in person."

And while coming out atheist in heavily religious workplaces can be difficult and scary, those are exactly the places where coming out atheist can be especially powerful and valuable. That's partly because it educates religious co-workers, of course. But it's also because it empowers other atheist co-workers who might be having an even harder time than you, and it makes it possible to form a bond with them. Speedwell, a corporate trainer in an oilfield engineering firm in Texas, says that "in Texas, especially in the oil industry, it is hard to be openly atheist. It is still regular and winked at for religious people to send mass e-mail with Bible verses and to talk about God and church at work. It isn't as bad in the facility I normally train at, but in other facilities, such as those in the Odessa-Midland area of West Texas, they have religious art in the reception area. I was massively uncomfortable there and my boss (a European atheist) will not send me back again.

"On my car I have a bumper sticker that reads, 'Atheism—Because Honesty Compels'… It's notable to say that no damage has happened to my car because of it. But I park near the door of the facility and people know it is my car. Six members of my ten-person work team (including the boss) are also atheists, and we found each other out in casual conversation where one person or the other would drop a telltale sign of exasperation with clergy, or laugh at the Bible-verse-spouting secretary, or let slip an anecdote about not being terribly comfortable in church. On my team it really does not matter, and should not. The religious members of my team are as respected and valuable as the atheists are.

"However," she says, "because people know me through training, and I am fairly popular with the engineers, and they are used to coming to me with software problems, many atheists, agnostics, and nonreligious people at work seem to treat me as sort of an atheist chaplain. I've had people e-mail me to vent their feelings about the latest religious mass mail. We got together informally a few years ago and registered a protest to mandatory Christmas donations to the Red Cross and Salvation Army. THEY come out to ME even when they can't do so to their family, friends, co-workers, or church. I'm not a leader by nature, but I am always happy to post a secularist joke or quip to a co-worker who is dealing with the humorless fundie elements in the industry."

You may or may not want to be "sort of an atheist chaplain" at your job. You may find it rewarding to educate your co-workers about atheism, and to start a wave of mythbusting that will ripple through their lives and into the lives of the people they know. Or you may just want to do your job already, without the stress and anxiety of being in the closet. Whatever your reasons, coming out can be totally worth it. Be careful; don't screw up your life. And then, if it won't screw up your life, come on out.

CHAPTER THIRTEEN

Strangers

In theory, total strangers should be the easiest people to come out to. They have little or no power over your life; they can't fire you, they can't kick you out of your home, they can't keep you from seeing your kids or your grandkids. The worst thing they can do is glare at you over the checkout counter, or try to convert you on the plane.

And coming out to strangers has tons of potential to change the world, and the world's views of atheists. Lots of people harbor myths and bigotry about atheists. Lots of people think they know what atheists are like because their clergyperson told them so. And lots of people think they've never met an atheist. So simply being an out atheist at the airport or the coffee counter—an atheist who seems to enjoy their life, who has morality and respect for others, who tips well and is polite to the staff and doesn't barge to the front of the line—gives a living, breathing counter-example proving that these myths are wrong. And the more of us who do this, the more powerful this becomes.

What's more: Coming out to strangers doesn't just have the power to change believers' minds about us. It can have power for other atheists. I remember a time that I was in an airport, getting coffee before my flight and chatting with the barista. He asked where I was coming from or going to (as chatty people in airports often ask)—and I hesitated. I was coming home from an atheist conference, and I was tired, and I didn't know if I felt up to having that conversation. But we'd been talking at the conference all weekend about how important coming out was, and I felt like I'd be a hypocrite if I didn't take this opportunity. So I went ahead. I said that I was coming home from an atheist conference, that I was an atheist writer and speaker and had been giving a talk.

And he got the biggest surprised smile on his face, and said, "Thank you. Thank you for doing that work." He'd never heard of me before; he didn't know anything about my work except that I wrote and spoke publicly about atheism. I'm not sure he even knew atheist conferences were a thing. But he does now. Maybe he even went to the next regional conference in his area. And if not, it still clearly made him happy to know that there were atheists in the world who were open about it, and who were writing and speaking about their atheism. It clearly made him feel safer, and less alone.

Yet many atheists still feel reticent about coming out to strangers. Some associate it with religious proselytizing, which they abhor. Others have fears about making a scene in public. And some people just aren't extroverted, and don't like talking about serious personal topics with strangers.

If any of that is true for you, I'd like to try to persuade you out of it. The first two, anyway. Simply saying that you're an atheist is not proselytizing, any more than saying anything else about how you think the world works would be proselytizing. Being an out atheist doesn't mean trying to persuade everyone you meet that God doesn't exist. It just means being honest about your own atheism. And you can get into the debates and finer points as much or as little as you want. Sure, being out to strangers can mean getting into long conversations on the plane about how atheists cope with death. (I've done that.) It can also simply mean wearing an atheist T-shirt or button in public. And that isn't proselytizing, any more than it is to wear a T-shirt with Star Wars or Obama or the Periodic Table of the Elements.

As for creating a scene: That hardly ever happens. Hardly anyone responds to a stranger telling them, "Actually, I'm an atheist," by pointing their finger and screaming, "Heretic! Apostate! Demon!" (Not unless you're in a theocracy, anyway.) Making a scene in public isn't necessarily a bad thing—that's part of the reasoning behind political demonstrations. But if you're reticent about doing it, you're not the only one. Most people are.

And this reticence works to our advantage. Even if someone doesn't like atheists, the social pressure to be civil, and the psychological barriers we have against being horrible to someone to their face, make people unlikely to pitch a fit when you tell them you're an atheist. This puts them in a position where they feel obligated to treat you with at least a base level of humanity and courtesy. And that plants the seed of the idea that atheists are human beings who deserve to be treated with courtesy. Researchers in psychology have long known that one of the best ways to get someone to think well of you isn't necessarily to do something nice for them—it's to get *them* to do something nice for *you*.[1] So putting someone in a position where they'll feel obligated to be decent to you will probably make them feel better about you—and it's likely to make them feel better about other atheists.

As for the introverts among you: I feel you. I am one of you. I'm reluctant to get into conversations with strangers about the weather, much less my atheism. What I would encourage you to do, though, is to base your level of out-ness to strangers on your general level of comfort with social engagement—and not make a special case for your atheism.

I don't have loads of stories about coming out as an atheist to strangers. When you ask atheists to tell their coming out stories, for some weird reason they usually want to talk about coming out to the people they know and care about. But the stories I do have about this are beauties.

Speedwell lives in Houston, Texas. And if there were any place where you might actually expect people to respond to someone saying, "I'm an atheist," by pointing their finger and screaming, "Heretic!," it's Texas. But that hasn't been Speedwell's experience at all. "I have to say," she says, "that other than my mother's reaction, and the reactions of her friends, I have honestly never had any angry or offended or upset response to me saying I'm an atheist. I think my appearance is disarming and my manner is friendly and matter-of-fact. Even the Mormon kids who come around on bicycles seem to think I'm a guilty pleasure; one of them said they tell each other secretly about 'the nice atheist lady.' I treat them with respect, give them cold water and cookies, and answer their questions about atheism. They have plenty of questions, after they get over my calm, smiling, 'Not interested in being religious today, honey, but I'm willing to talk about it if you want.' I think it's a relief to them to look like they're spending time 'converting' me but actually relaxing and cooling off. (Heh.) Atheist people need to be more friendly to the Mormon and JW [Jehovah's Witness] kids (and others). Many of them are freethinkers waiting to happen. We can present ourselves as caring people who don't need to lie, and a great contrast to judgmental people in their church being liars and manipulators all around them."

Another lovely story about coming out to strangers comes from Jonathan Wood, who grew up in southern Missouri as a member of a Southern Baptist church. "I was riding the streetcar home one day," he says, "and saw an elderly woman struggling down the steps with two heavy bags of groceries. I hopped off and offered to carry them for her. She accepted and we made small talk as we walked to her flat. When we got there, out of the blue, she asked me, 'Are you a Christian?' For the first time in my life, I said, 'No, I'm not. I don't believe in God.' She nodded without showing any emotion, went into her home and I never saw her again.

"As I went away, I wondered what made me say that to a stranger and I realized it was something that I'd been wanting to say for quite a while. It felt good and I walked home feeling happy."

Jim Newman, who has come out as non-religious to family, friends, and the guy at the tool rental center, points out that coming out to strangers gives you practice in coming out to the people you care about. "Use less harmful scenarios to out yourself," he advises. "Missionaries and unfamiliar proselytizers aren't going to ruin your life. I know it seems like it's giving them time but outing yourself to a JW will help you get comfortable with expressing yourself contrarily."

And Amanda Knief, currently managing director of American Atheists, has what may be my favorite "coming out to strangers" story of all time—coming out to the President of the United States. "As the government relations manager for the Secular Coalition for America," she says, "I was invited to a town hall meeting with President Barack Obama at the University of Maryland. I was seated to the left of the stage at the end of the first row of bleachers in the basketball stadium. After a sweltering morning waiting to get in, I waited another two hours for the president to speak. Then, President Obama said he would take questions—girl, boy, girl, boy. And I jumped up from my seat and put my hand straight in the air. And he picked me. And I told the President of the United States—and about 2,000 people—on live CSPAN that I was an atheist. Before I told him, he was smiling at me. After I told him, he stopped smiling. But I smiled—bigger and better. This coming out was the scariest and the best. I did it because no one else had—and I wanted to show anyone who was afraid to say they are an atheist that it can be done—to one of, if not the, most important persons in the world, a couple thousand witnesses, and on TV. I also asked the President a question about employment discrimination based on religion by faith-based organizations that receive federal funds—which he flubbed a bit. But it was saying that I was an atheist that had people friending me on Facebook, emailing me from around the world, and coming up to me at conferences and events and saying 'thank you.'

"I wouldn't change a thing!"

CHAPTER FOURTEEN

The Internet

The great thing about being an atheist on the Internet: You can say anything, to anyone.

The lousy thing about being an atheist on the Internet: You can say anything, to anyone.

The early 21st century is an amazing time to be an atheist. And that's largely, although not entirely, because of the Internet. The Internet has made it much easier for atheists to talk, rant, share ideas, commiserate, congratulate, get support, get advice, and organize. You can do any or all of this at whatever time and place is convenient for you, at four in the morning in your bathrobe if that's what works for you, with a reasonable degree of anonymity if you want that, with people from all over the world. You can take baby steps into coming out as an atheist, using handles and pseudonyms to discuss your atheism until you're ready to come out more fully. And once you're ready to come out fully, you can come out like a fireball if you want, and tell hundreds or thousands or millions of people, as proudly and fiercely as you like.

And largely because of the Internet, it is now virtually impossible to keep the existence of atheists a secret. If you're a 15-year-old in Forkville, Mississippi, and you think you don't believe in God or you just have doubts about your faith, you don't have to rely on your preacher and family and classmates, most of whom will probably tell you some truly stupid lies about atheists. You can type "people who don't believe in God" into Google, and get (as of this writing) 1,680,000 results. Some of which, granted, are religious sites telling you why religion is awesome and atheism is dumb—but many, many, *many* of which aren't. So even if you live miles away from the nearest in-person atheist community, you can, within a couple of minutes, be connected with an atheist community and an atheist movement, comprised of tens of millions of people (if not more). You can be connected with thousands of communities and organizations, and pick the ones that work best for you. And you can switch between them with the touch of a finger, if one stops working for you so well. I often wonder where the LGBT movement would be today if we'd had the Internet in the early 1970s, when that movement was just beginning to get seriously visible, vocal, and organized.

Plus, as many atheists will tell you, atheists own the Internet. (Of course, we would say that...)

But there are some downsides to coming out atheist on the Internet. People often assume that they have more privacy and anonymity on the Internet than they really do. The "coming out atheist" stories that I collected are full of people saying things like, "I didn't realize my grandmother read Facebook!" "I thought I was being sly by using a pseudonym, but my posts gave too much detailed information, and people figured out who I was!" "I meant to just write to my spouse, but I accidentally hit 'Reply All'!"

And online atheist communities can often be more... shall we say, abrasive, than in-person communities. A lot of atheists need that and want it—having a space where you don't have to be deferential to religion and can say any damn thing you want about it can be hugely liberating. But if you've just recently left religion, or if you're still in the final stages of questioning your faith, or if you simply have a lot of religious friends and family, the venom that often gets aimed at religion in online atheist spaces can be hard to take. What's more, some online atheist communities can also be... shall we say, abrasive—even with each other. A lot of atheists enjoy that; they like the rough-and-tumble, Wild West atmosphere, where they can critique other people's ideas bluntly and unapologetically, and know that their own ideas will be subjected to the same blast furnace. But if that's not how you roll, you may want to look around for online spaces that are more civil. And cyber bullying and online harassment are real, in atheism as well as elsewhere. Especially if you're a woman, and double especially if you're an openly feminist woman. (More on that in the chapters on diversity and on atheists who are already marginalized.)

But the upside, again, is that there are lots and lots and *lots* of online atheist communities. So if you're willing to do a little digging and ask around, chances are good that you'll be able to find one that feels like home for you. Probably even more than one.

So how do you go about this? How do you use the awesome power of the Internet to come out as an atheist?

So far in this chapter, I've been talking a lot about online atheist communities. But when atheists are coming out online—or are simply being out online—a lot of what they're dealing with is how to be out in non-atheist spaces. Whether it's your own Facebook page where your atheist and religious friends all hang out; whether it's other people's Facebook pages; or whether it's the online forum where you talk about knitting or socialism or Linux, you'll have to figure out how you want to talk about your atheism.

It's likely that you'll be dealing with some online spaces that aren't very atheist-friendly. OurSally grew up in England, where atheism isn't anything special. But she encountered a different attitude when she went on the Internet. "Now on the interwebs," she says, "it's entirely different. I have been thrown (quite nastily) out of a forum (a software forum!) for being atheist, so I keep to software in fora like that. (That forum is dying out because people are stopping going there. Ha!)"

Maria has had similar experiences: not being thrown out of online forums, but being targeted with anti-atheist bigotry and ignorance in them, and having to decide whether she feels like doing Atheism 101. She grew up in Sweden where she still lives, and where, she says, "you're in the majority if you don't believe in God, and there isn't really a closet to come out of." But when she started making friends and joining communities online, her atheism became more of an issue—and coming out became something she had to think about more carefully. "I had never before met a Christian who was shocked to learn I was an atheist and who peppered me with questions about it," she says. "She asked if I was really telling the truth, and how I could find any meaning in life, and how I could even find the strength to get out of the bed in the morning if I didn't believe in God, and that it was okay if I didn't believe in God, he still believed in me, and so on. I tried to answer, but I was mostly just sitting at the screen with a O__O look on my face, going 'What? Uhhh... what?? No meaning in life...?? Uh... Must be depressed because of lack of belief in a fictional character... ??? Uhh... What??' She spoke as someone whose beliefs are in the majority, and now her new Internet friend had just come out as a (gasp) atheist!"

Maria is honest about her atheism in online forums whenever it comes up. But she doesn't make a point of bringing it up herself. "I actually do often find myself hoping it won't come up," she says, "because I might really enjoy to be on that craft forum, or whatever. And even though I'm SO MUCH MORE prepared for answering questions like the ones above these days, I didn't really join those places only to get all focus shifted from beads and mixed media art techniques onto how it can be possible that I can find meaning in my life without a silly storybook character."

Here's a general guideline that lots of people have found useful: You get to curate your own online spaces.[1] You get to curate your own

Facebook page, Twitter feed, blog, etc. You get to decide how much you want to talk about atheism versus other things; if you're ranting about atheism a lot and your friends don't want to hear about it, they don't have to follow you. In your own spaces, you also get to decide what kinds of conversations you want to host and participate in; do you want vigorous but civil debate, snarky ranting, gentle respectful discussion, no contention at all? And you get to decide who you want in your space. If believers are evangelizing on your Facebook page or spewing insults about atheists—and you don't want to hear it any more—you can block them or ban them. If you do want to do Atheism 101 and patiently explain why they're mistaken, that is awesome. But it's not a moral obligation. The right of freedom of speech does not give people the right to barge into your spaces and abuse or insult you, whenever they want, for as long as they want. People have the right to speak—but they don't have the right to force you to listen.

But the flip side is that other people get to curate their online spaces, too. If people don't want to hear you talk about atheism at all in their spaces, that is totally their right.

Now, if it's a fairly public community space, such as an online forum about knitting or what have you, it's reasonable for you to ask for fairness. If it's a space where vigorous debate is encouraged, or else where standards of civility are strongly enforced; if it's a space where off-topic meanderings are a standard part of the conversation, or else where meanderings are discouraged as derailing—it's reasonable to ask that these standards be applied fairly, to atheists and believers alike. If moderators are coming down on you for criticizing religion or even just talking about atheism too much—and they're not saying those things to believers—that's worth pointing out. Ultimately, the hosts and moderators do have the right to moderate however they want—it's their space, and if they want to be arbitrary and biased, that's their right. But public online communities typically try to apply their standards equally—if they get a reputation for unfairness, they won't last very long—and if they're not living up to that when it comes to atheism, it's reasonable to call it to their attention. (Politely, and respectfully; being demanding and entitled towards moderators of online spaces is a douche move, and will get you nowhere.)

But if it's someone else's personal space, such as their Facebook page or Twitter feed or blog, they have the right to not listen to you blather about atheism, just like you have the right to not listen to them blather about religion. In their own space, they have the right to tone-troll, to shut down discussions that are making them unhappy, to ban atheists or *Star Trek* fans or people whose names begin with W. You can make your own decisions about whether their guidelines are okay with you, and whether you want to participate in their space. And of course, you can try to persuade them that their guidelines are problematic. But do it with a basic respect of their right to curate their space any damn way they please. Pulling the "You can't handle the truth!" number just makes you look like an entitled douchebag who thinks they have the right to spew anywhere they want.

There's a big advantage to coming out atheist online, one that a lot of people don't talk about—which is that when you come out in writing to lots of people at once, it can save a certain amount of time and energy. In her interview for *The Ebony Exodus Project* by Candace R. M. Gorham, Bria says, "When I decided to let everyone know that I was an atheist, I changed my religious belief on Facebook. That's how I told everyone I was an atheist, I said, 'Fuck it!'"[2] This works very well if you're using the "no big deal" method: just being out rather than making a big dramatic conversation out of it, and letting other people deal with it or freak out however they want. As Kat Car says, "'Coming out' was easy to people my own age (university students, 18-24 age band). You just change 'religious views' on Facebook, and lo and behold, your whole friend group knows."

But coming out online can also work well if you want to do it more thoughtfully. It gives you the chance to think carefully about what exactly you want to say, and how exactly you want to say it. Bob Barnes came out to all 500 people in the gated community where he lives in Sarnia, Ontario, Canada—and he did it by letter, carefully and reflectively explaining his deconversion process, explaining why it was important to him to come out, and asking other nonbelievers in the community to contact him. And when you come out online, you can even show a rough draft to people you trust, to get feedback on how it reads. That's what Rocky Stone did. "I sent an email to virtually everyone that I know," he says. "It was lengthy and quite detailed. I'd pondered the issue for months and talked with a couple of close friends (and my Christian wife) about it. My primary reason for sending it was to try to counteract the impression that all atheists are vile, immoral, devil-worshippers.

"I sent a rough draft to a half dozen or so friends and family members who already knew my beliefs and received constructive criticism from them. I made a few revisions based on those responses.

"I received email or in-person responses from about a third of the 117 people that received my 'manifesto.'... Many of my family members and acquaintances are pretty conservative and some are quite religious. I received a handful of responses that were supportive, but that also said, 'I'll pray for you.'... [But] all have been supportive and 'nice.' No one yet has damned me to hell."

Being out on the Internet—especially on social media like Facebook and Twitter, where you can identify as atheist to anyone who looks at your profile—can also head off bad conversations, as much as it can start them. When you let people know about your atheism right up front, people who don't like atheists can select themselves right out of your life before they've even met you. Alexander, a Hispanic-American ex-Catholic and a Ph.D. student in biology at the University of Ottawa, says on the Scribbles and Rants blog, "It wasn't really until I got a

Facebook account in 2005 that I was 'out' in any real sense. I did not hesitate to designate myself 'Atheist' on my profile. I wanted people to see that, and to weed themselves out if it was a problem. I wanted to stop facing the tragic, unpleasant question of whether to eventually share that fact with someone who might make a scene or stop talking to me if they knew, so I set up that mechanism of quick, passive rejection. If I could not steel my heart, I would steel my Facebook."[3]

Coming out online can also give you a place to practice. As Hemant Mehta says in *The Young Atheist's Survival Guide*, "Even if you're not ready or able to tell people close to you that you don't believe in God, find a way to come out online, even anonymously. For example, you can use a throwaway account on Reddit to explore and comment on its /r/atheism forums. By doing this, you might find that it's easier to come out later in your life without the cloak of anonymity."[4]

And, of course, coming out on the Internet can dovetail nicely with the "coming out gradually" method: dropping hints, talking about your questions and doubts, and getting people used to the idea before you say the "A" word. Hunter, who used to be an evangelical Christian, says that after he came out to his father, his sister, and his closest friend (who he later married), "Finally, there was my outing to the general public on Facebook. I started posting things here and there that would gradually introduce my Atheism. Pastafarian jokes were my favorite. The majority of my friends in the church were really cool about it. I received a couple of the standard 'I'm praying for you' replies, but even those ceased if I politely explained why I thought that was offensive. To be honest, the majority of the fights were fights that I went out and started."

So the Internet can work great for a gradual coming out. Except for the times when it really, really doesn't. The Internet also greatly increases the chances of an accidental outing. This can happen when other people forward or share or Reply All, accidentally or carelessly or in some cases even maliciously. And it can happen with your own careless clicking of Send or Post. On the Scribbles and Rants blog, Alexander says that he didn't hesitate to designate himself as "Atheist" on Facebook, and he discussed his atheist opinions and activities there at length. "But I still banked on one big, ultimately erroneous assumption," he says: "that my family would remain tech-illiterate enough to never see my Facebook page.

"My parents remain barely capable of computer use," he says. "They can use Microsoft Word for basic letter-writing tasks (though they might need someone to open it for them); they can use Gmail to send and receive messages. They were very proud of themselves when they internalized how to operate Gmail's video-call feature and could use it to keep in touch with me during my graduate work. But they spent virtually no time on Facebook, even after Mom got a profile. My siblings are, of course, avid users, but they regard my personal details as mine, and none of their business. It was an uncle who apprised my parents of the 'Atheist' designation in my profile summary, and of the torrent of anti-religious messages that circulate on my newsfeed."[5]

H. Beaton, a former Jehovah's Witness, says he has two regrets about his coming out process. One is that he wished he'd done it more suddenly when he was finally ready to do it. "My other regret," he says, "is my behavior online. In my 'shouting to the rooftops' phase I feel looking back that I was far too reckless with my personal information. I wrote about my experiences online with very specific details, thinking I was safe because I didn't name any names. I overlooked the fact that I had decided to be brave and attach my real name to some of these articles. A few JWs typing my name into Google was all it took to alert my parents (and everyone they knew) to my online activity. I wish I wouldn't have seen it as a matter of my own bravery and instead considered the consequences to my parents. If I could go back, I would have probably done a better job scrubbing the details to be more generic, and above all, not using my real name online."

And Delphinium, who lives in a very conservative suburb of Atlanta, Georgia, tells this story of coming out to a friend with a slip of the finger: "Only one of my fellow 'stay at home mom' friends knows my religious beliefs and it happened quite accidentally. One day she sent me an email asking if my husband and I would like to go see Bill Maher's movie, *Religulous*, with her and her husband. She suggested that afterwards we could grab dinner and discuss our thoughts about the movie. I forwarded the email to my husband, adding, 'I would rather cut off my arm than watch, and then discuss, this movie with her.' Only, I didn't actually forward the email to my husband. I inadvertently replied to her with those comments instead.

"Aaaahhhh! I knew I had made the mistake a microsecond after clicking 'send'! I immediately replied, again, with a full confession about my lack of religious beliefs. I explained that I didn't want to spend the evening pretending to believe, but I also didn't want her to know I was an atheist for fear of rejection of me and my kids. I told her I would have been more than happy to see every other movie in the theater other than that one. And then, I waited for the fallout."

As it happens, Delphinium's story ended very well. "It turns out," she says, "that she had suspected I was an atheist and hoped that seeing this movie would spark a discussion about it so she could ask me everything she ever wanted to know about non-believers. Throughout the years since my outing, she has asked many questions from 'What do you think happens when we die?' to 'If you don't believe that Christ is our savior, why do you celebrate Christmas?'" The two remain close friends to this day, to the point where Delphinium says, "How nice it would be if all atheists and believers could live in this sort of harmony!"

But of course, positive experiences like that aren't universal. And in general, it's much better to come out on your own, and on your own timetable, rather than being outed—either by other people, or by your own careless slip of the finger or the brain. So if you're talking about your atheism on the Internet—be careful out there, people.

A thorough discussion of cyber security and online privacy is outside the scope of this book. But I'll go over the most important rule of thumb: Assume that anything you put on the Internet will be seen by everyone. If you wouldn't want it on the front page of the *New York Times*—don't post it on Facebook or an online forum. If you're using an online handle or are otherwise keeping your real name unconnected with your atheism for the moment—be consistent about it. And if you live or work with nosy people who might snoop on your computer to see what you're up to—be extra-careful. Clear your browser history; surf in the private browsing window or "incognito" mode that some browsers have, so people snooping on the computer you're using can't see where you've been surfing. Protect yourself, until you're ready to come out to everyone, and don't have to protect yourself any more.

Of course, anyone who's spent any time on the Internet knows that one of its greatest strengths is also one of its greatest weaknesses: It loosens inhibitions. It makes people feel comfortable saying things they wouldn't say in person. And this is a big part of why so many atheists are willing to come out as atheist online—and why we're willing to question and criticize religion online. It's easier to say, "I think your religion doesn't make sense, and here's why"—or even simply, "I am an atheist"—when you don't have to see the looks of hurt or disappointment, anger or rejection, on people's faces. The fact that people feel less bound online by social convention than we do in person gives us license to tell the truth as we see it, when we would otherwise feel pressured to go along with socially acceptable lies—or stay silent in the face of them.

But this is a double-edged sword. The loosened inhibitions that the Internet gives people can also lead us to say things we really shouldn't say. And I'm not just talking here about the obvious examples of online harassment, abuse, and threats. I'm also talking simply about being more harsh, more snarky, more offensive for no good reason, than we need or want to be. And I'm talking about the tendency to focus entirely on the intellectual content of a discussion—the ideas, the evidence, the logic—while ignoring or forgetting the emotional content, and the relationship you have with this person.

Mark from Chicago says, "My method of 'coming out' as atheist was basically just posting and reposting all manner of atheist propaganda publicly on my Facebook Wall. Some of it was thought-provoking, some humorous, and some just downright crude and admittedly offensive to most believers. Most of my Facebook 'friends' had no reaction (or just ignored me) but a handful of fellow nonbelievers cheered me on. A few people (including a portion of my immediate family) reacted negatively. I'm happy to be 'out' but regret the mildly hostile manner in which I got here. For example, many of my posts and reposts simply ridiculed believers and their beliefs. I think this really turned a lot of people off... I have no way of knowing how many people have unsubscribed from my posts but I'm sure a lot did. I know two members of my immediate family did because they told me they did.

"If I had it to do over again," he says. "I would stick with thought-provoking questions and quotes, and avoid anything that could be construed as offensive or hostile. I would also try to be more cognizant of which people are interested in having that conversation and which are not. I don't think I realized how much I was turning people off to me until a couple people privately called me out on it. These days I am much more selective about what I post and repost and I use the 'lists' feature in Facebook to control which friends see which posts. I think it's unfortunate that I need to censor myself... but it's either that or damage relationships with people I care about."

This kind of regret is not uncommon. When I collected "coming out atheist" stories and asked people what, if anything, they regretted about how they came out, one of the more common themes was, "I was too harsh." And that's especially true for people who came out online. Hunter, a former evangelical Christian, says of his online experiences,

"To be honest, the majority of the fights were fights that I went out and started... Since then I've calmed down considerably. Which isn't to say I'm no longer militant. I still get enraged by stupid posts that could have been fact-checked in five seconds on Google, but I've gotten much better at managing my anger."

These regrets aren't universal, though. Many angry atheists are fine being public about their anger, and welcome the Internet as a place where they're comfortable being honest about it. Many even see the weeding-out of people who object to their anger as a feature, not a bug. Hunter again: "Being a Christian for many years meant I had collected a number of batshit insane acquaintances. People who literally believe the earth is 6,000 years old. People who literally believe their god will torture you for eternity if you vote for Obama. You name it. I had long had problems [with people] using religious claims to justify idiocy, and now I was free to voice those thoughts. I got pretty militant for the first few months. I chased away a good deal of acquaintances, and I can't say as I regret it. At least now my newsfeed isn't flooded with racist/homophobic/transphobic/etc. posters anymore."

If that's true for you—great. If it's not true for you—be careful. Remember that online conversations about sensitive topics have a tendency to go south, even if nobody involved wanted that or intended it. So if you're talking online about your atheism with people you don't want to alienate, think before you type. Wait before you hit Send. Run what you're writing by someone else, and get a tone-check on it. If you're getting upset or angry—stop. You don't necessarily have to stop the conversation entirely—although you might do that—but think carefully about how, exactly, you want to have it. And remember that there's a human being on the other end of the communication. Don't just focus on their ideas and arguments. Imagine that you're having this conversation in person. Picture their face.

For some people, though, coming out online is actually calmer and less confrontational than doing it in person. They can think more carefully about what to say and how, and they don't get impulsively sucked into emotional confrontation. Kevin Wells, an Asian American man who was living in the Washington, DC suburbs at the time, came out by changing his "religion" status on Facebook to "de facto atheism." "I made sure the change was displayed on my Facebook wall," he says. "I also know that my family lurks on Facebook, so they would see it." His parents, who are not extremely religious, have been accepting; his hard-core Christian relatives are seemingly ignoring it; and he now discusses atheism with his brother, who turned out to be a closeted atheist. "I think I did everything right," he says. "It was a non-confrontational way to inform people that are important to me of my changing world view." He wishes he could sit down with his parents and discuss their religion—but, he says, "I find it difficult to have calm discussions and to remain humble during discussions about religion with theists, and I don't want to agitate my parents."

Anna Geletka, who grew up in a moderate United Methodist community, had a similar experience. She had previously come out to her parents as a polyamorous person in an open relationship with a man and a woman. "I told them in person," she says, "which is one of the hardest things I've ever done. This probably influenced how I chose to come out as an atheist as I did not want to repeat the experience." So with her atheism, she says, "the process of my coming out has been long and slow, and I never actually sat down one-on-one with anyone and flat out told them I was an atheist." Instead, she came out gradually and slowly, starting by giving hints about questioning religion—what she calls leaving a "trail of crumbs." And she used the Internet for much of this process. She started with a blog post that was dismissive of faith; she then wrote a blog post about anti-atheist prejudice in which she identified herself as an atheist and discussed the reasons she doesn't believe in God (a post she knew her family would read); and she then came out on Facebook and changed her religion status to "atheism." Her feelings about her coming out process are mixed. "I don't know if I'd do anything differently if I had to do this again," she says. "I still feel like I have one foot in the closet sometimes... I feel like I'm being more honest, but my parents already had a pretty good idea and time to get used to it."

Finally, and very importantly: When you're coming out as an atheist online, and when you're just being an atheist online, don't forget atheist communities.

Take a look at the resource guide at the end of this book. Among all the other resources listed there, the books and organizations and whatnot, you'll see atheist forums. Facebook groups. Newsgroups. Blogs and podcasts and videoblogs, many with commenting communities. There are dozens and dozens of online atheist communities listed there. And that list isn't anywhere close to exhaustive. The chances are excellent that you'll find one that'll work for you. Maybe even more than one.

If you're holding your tongue around your relatives, you can rant on Pharyngula. If you're exploring your newfound atheism and your family is freaking out about it (or you haven't told them yet), you can get empathy and advice on Recovering From Religion. If you're interested in the intersection of atheism and other social justice issues, you can find discussions and plan actions on Atheism+. If you're an atheist who's grieving, you can get support on Grief Beyond Belief.

And very importantly, the Internet allows for anonymous organizing among people who have to protect their privacy and be extra cautious about who, if anyone, they come out to. You need to be careful with this, of course—again, it's easy to out yourself with a careless slip of the finger, and it's impossible for cyber privacy to be perfect. But within those limitations, the anonymity of the Internet lets people who need to stay closeted not only find community and human connection, but do organizing and activism to change their worlds.

There are hundreds of atheist communities on the Internet. Maybe thousands. And more are getting started all the time. By the time this book is published, there might be online forums for atheist sports fans, atheist computer programmers, atheist stamp collectors, atheist anarchist bowlers from New Jersey.

And here's what some folks in online atheist communities have to say about them.

David Viviano: "Most loved ones wanted nothing to do with me, and as a social creature, I sought out a new community. I discovered the world of Twitter and quickly met some amazing people there, which has propelled me to where I am at today and very thankful for it."

carolw: "FTB [Freethought Blogs] has been my Atheist community. I'm kind of a lurker on most of the blogs I read. I rarely comment, because usually someone has already said what I was thinking. But it feels good to have my virtual friends out here on the interwebs."

Pink Atheist in Albuquerque, on the Coming Out Godless Project website, says that when he started coming out as an atheist, "I found the Brights, and discovered a like-minded group of people with a much more positive attitude than I have ever considered for atheists."

In her interview for *The Ebony Exodus Project* by Candace R. M. Gorham, Bria says that when she came out, "I just took to the Internet to look for a community where I could be an atheist and it was OK... After I came out, I created Black Freethinkers on Facebook. And that grew to about 350-400 people, then I took it off Facebook and brought it to a main site. So we got on Tumblr because there are so many people who are like, *I'm an atheist. I'm black. Now what?*"[6]

Cris, also on the Coming Out Godless Project website, grew up in a Pentecostal "speaking in tongues" Assembly of God church. When Cris started having questions about religion, the Internet provided information and ideas that sped along their deconversion—and also provided community. "Over a period of about 2-3 months," they say, "I studied religions, philosophy, I went on Christian/atheist discussion forums and learned. My mind was like a vacuum, I could not get enough. So here it is two years later and I look back and realize that my problem with depressive episodes disappeared with religion. This is something 'God' could never fix. Apparently 'God' may have been the problem all along..."

And finally, Alexander Ryan, on the Coming Out Godless Project website: "I'm hated in my school and my family, sans my dad. I must say though, the internet is a wonderful salvation. In a place where there are no Atheists, having a place where you can go where there are countless others, and especially vocal ones, is a, pardon the pun, Godsend."

There are hundreds of atheist communities on the Internet. Maybe thousands. And they can make a huge difference in your life.

CHAPTER FIFTEEN

— ❋ —

Conservative Communities

The bad news... well, I probably don't have to tell you the bad news. You know it a lot better than I do. The bad news is that if you live in a religiously conservative part of the world, where religion dominates the social and political and economic life, coming out as an atheist can be a lot more difficult. It can have more serious practical effects on your life; it can affect whether you get hired or fired or promoted, or whether you can get elected to the school board. That's not just because of overt anti-atheist bigotry, either—although it certainly can be. In many conservative parts of the world, much of the business and political networking is done through churches or other religious institutions. If you're not taking part in those institutions, you'll be shut out of the networking. And, of course, in conservative parts of the world, much of the social life happens through religion. Even if you don't face overt hostility for your atheism—which, again, you certainly might—not participating in religion can result in de facto ostracism.

What's more, if your family and friends are part of a very conservative, very religious community, they may be pressured to proselytize to you or otherwise not accept your atheism—or, in extreme cases, to cut you off entirely. Even if they don't give in to that pressure, it may create tension between you.

Brian Nolan has always been a nonbeliever, and has recently decided that it's important to come out about it. But, he says, "it is very hard to be an Atheist in Eastern Kentucky, where I live. I have been shunned by family and friends. My step-son, a devout Catholic, no longer speaks to me. But I have to stand up for what I see as the most important issue of my life. We need more people to think about the subject critically and speak their mind... I always live by the motto: I would rather be hated for who I am, than loved for who I'm not." He goes on to say, "I have had some who have sent me private messages of support, and they told me they share my beliefs, but they are not brave enough to say so publicly."

In conservative regions, even people who are reasonably progressive or moderate on other issues will often still be resistant to atheism, or even shocked by it. Jesse Daw is a gay atheist in Fort Worth, Texas. "Coming out to coworkers can be tricky in Texas," he says. "It's usually easier to come out as gay than as a heathen. Once they know I'm gay, they already know something is wrong with me, so atheism is less of a surprise. But I never use the word 'atheist!'

"A typical conversation:

"Them: 'What church do you go to?'

"Me: 'I'm not religious.'

"T: 'But you believe in god, right?'

"M: 'No, actually I don't.'

"T: 'What do you believe then?'

"M: 'I believe that logic, rationality, and science can tell us what we need to know about the universe, without resorting to unprovable claims written by people thousands of years ago.'

"T: 'But you aren't an ATHEIST are you?'

"Where I live, it's mostly ok to be gay, to not go to church, and even to not believe in god, as long as you aren't an atheist... Once you get there, god doesn't try to save you anymore, apparently." But, he adds, "I don't generally regret being honest with family, friends, and coworkers."

And moving to a conservative religious community from a more progressive or secular one can be something of a culture shock. (To put it mildly.) Paul moved to the United States from the United Kingdom, where he grew up. "In the U.K.," he says, "it's not an issue because religion just doesn't get talked about as much and differing views are more accepted. In the U.S., religion is so embedded in the political discourse and in everyday conversation that it is hard not to face an 'outing' situation... Usually I try to avoid telling people unless asked directly. I don't lie, but I know that it makes people uncomfortable and living in the heart of the bible belt, it is usually easier to ignore opportunities to make my views known." And he points out that if he does want to be out, he has to keep coming out again and again, every time he meets new people—since the general assumption is that everyone is religious.

David Viviano has had a similar experience. He grew up non-religious, raised by non-religious parents, in a liberal area of New York, and never had any problems related to his atheism—until he moved to North Florida. "I was not informed," he says, "that North Florida is also part of the Bible Belt. Within my first week I quickly realized what would be the norm. Everyone that approached me asked me the same three questions; what's your name, your favorite college football team and what church do you go to? I remember the first time I was asked these questions, I answered them truthfully. When I got to the last question I answered with, 'Oh, I don't go to church. I don't believe in God.' I heard gasps and even heard another man begin to pray for me. I chuckled at first, but then realized they were serious. My presence alone offended them. They never spoke to me again, and that is when I realized that if I was going to keep a job I needed to go into the 'closet' with my lack of beliefs. That day I shut the door and locked it." He remained in the closet for about four years—until he met another atheist at his job.

But this story actually shows a key point about being an atheist in a conservative community: Finding other atheists may be extra important for you. Connecting with atheist communities may be extra important. And that's easier to do if you're willing to be at least a little bit out.

Which brings me to the good news. If you live in a religiously conservative part of the world, chances are excellent that you'll have a strong atheist community available to you.

When I first started traveling around the United States, giving talks to atheist conferences and local atheist groups, I was struck by what seemed to be a paradox. The groups that seemed to be strongest and most flourishing, with the numbers and resources to bring in speakers from out of town, were hardly ever in the more progressive secular cities on the coasts. They were almost always in the Midwest or the South, in cities dominated by conservative religion. There are exceptions, of course—but in general, it's a very noticeable pattern. I can't tell you how many groups I've visited whose organizers claimed that their city was "the buckle on the Bible Belt." (There seems to be quite a competition for that title!) There are definitely some great atheist communities in more progressive cities—but as a rule, the strong ones tend to be in places where religion is prominent.

This surprised me at first. Wouldn't it be easier for atheists to organize in a place like New York City or Los Angeles? But the more I thought about it, the more it made sense. There just isn't as much of a need for atheist community in New York City and Los Angeles. Life there is already pretty secular; there's plenty to do if you don't belong to a church; you don't need to be very religious or even religious at all to flourish in the social and economic and political life; and religion isn't as much in people's faces. There's more of a need for atheist community in cities like Omaha and Dallas. Being an atheist there is more stressful, more isolating. It can have more serious practical effects. So atheists are more likely to turn to each other, and to create strong organizations to help them do that.

In conservative regions, atheist communities aren't just extra strong—they can also be extra valuable. Even if you're not planning to come out, or to come out very much, they can give you help and support. And they can tell you lots more about the ins and outs of being an atheist in your particular region than anyone else. If you have a complaint about religion being pushed in your kids' public school, they can tell you who on the school board is likely to be sympathetic, and who is the hardline creationist. If you're planning a humanist wedding, they can tell you which halls you can rent that won't give you a hard time about why you're not getting married in a church. If you're looking for a job, or are thinking about changing jobs, they can tell you which workplaces are hotbeds of religious extremism, and which are more atheist-positive, or at least are indifferent about it. If you're looking for a good buffet restaurant, they can tell you the one that's owned by an atheist.

And if you do want to come out in your conservative community, or you want to be more open about your atheism than you are, having other atheists in your life can make a big difference. David Viviano again: "I remained in the 'closet' for about four years; I finally met another atheist on my job. Not only was he out but he was outspoken. Not afraid to call out the ones around us. He introduced me to The Atheist Experience, Ricky Gervais and Bill Maher. I was blown away, by not only the information but to find out I wasn't alone." The presence of an out atheist in his life—and an outspoken one at that—is what gave him the courage to finally come out himself. And when he did come out, it had that wonderful ripple effect that so often happens. He came out because another open atheist inspired him—and his coming out inspired still more atheists to do it. "Coming out was the most freeing experience I have ever been through," he says. "No longer did I have to hide who I was. After coming out that day, my dad, mom, step-mom and brother since have come out as atheists. You could say my strength gave them strength."

For any atheist, being out is more of a spectrum than an either/or thing. But for people in conservative regions, their exact place on that spectrum—the question of *how* out to be, and to whom—is likely to be both more important, and more delicate. Finding the place on the spectrum you're comfortable with—and making sure other atheists respect it—matters more when moving just a little too far out can have a strong negative impact on your life. So people who are out to their family might not come out at work, or vice versa. People who will happily do behind-the-scenes work with their local atheist community might not want to be a public face at events, or have their names on the website. Even people who are mostly out will sometimes choose to be discreet in some situations. While David Viviano is now a very outspoken atheist activist and is heavily involved in the secular community, he also says that "because of my surroundings I will not put a sticker or magnet on my car in fear of vandalism—or worse, that they would follow me to my house. Just a chance I can't take with two daughters."

And in conservative regions, even atheists who are mostly or entirely out will often be less confrontational about it. Brian Nolan again: "My advice to people who live in my area or any area as conservative as mine is, read up on the subjects thoroughly first; be educated in your beliefs. When you speak about why you feel this way, make sure you are honest, accurate and civil; it will be the most effective approach." And while David Viviano doesn't regret coming out, he does regret the very confrontational way that he did it. "I was still very young into my outspoken atheism," he says. "I was planning to 'officially come out' on Facebook on Blasphemy Day. I scoured the internet weeks before finding my favorite quotes from our most brilliant secular minds and to grab the attention of the religious; I also found some of the darkest anti-theist memes I could find. The day came and I unleashed the wrath of secular posts onto my Facebook world. Within minutes I was receiving threats, prayers and everything in between from friends and loved ones. One of my family members asked me to take the posts down because it was offending her as she scrolled through her feed. I politely told her to block me or unfriend me, but I wasn't removing my posts. It was the first time in my life I was proud to stand up for my nonbelief. After that day most unfriended me, and out of that group, I have never spoken to most of them.

"Looking back on it now," he says, "I know it wasn't the best way to come out, as I have matured into my atheism I have learned quite a bit since then. Now I will never say that I regret my decision for coming out or how I handled it, just if I were to do it now I would handle it with more professionalism."

And while I probably don't have to say this, I'll say it anyway: When you come out in a region where religion dominates the economic and political life, you probably want to be extra careful to have your practical and financial ducks in a row first.

But that being said, I'm going to finish with the refrain I keep singing throughout this book: It's often not that bad. Look at the chapters on coming out atheist to family, to friends, in the workplace, at school. A lot of these stories take place in very conservative, very religious regions. And more often than not, they turn out more or less okay. Sometimes more, sometimes less—but generally okay. So like I keep saying throughout this book: Take care of yourself, take care of your family, take care of your safety. Use your own judgment. But don't automatically assume the worst.

Judy Komorita lives in Houston, Texas, and works for an evangelical Christian boss. "Houston has a wide variety of races, faiths, and cultures in it," she says. "But I am in a very conservative, religious work community... most everyone is some type of fundy christian." For the most part, she keeps a low profile about her atheism; she describes herself as "half-hidden." Yet her experiences with coming out have mostly been fine. "Very early on," she says, "I admitted to non-belief (didn't use the word 'atheist' at that time) to another legal assistant. I'm sure she told her boss, who is an elderly and gentle man. Nothing bad came from that. One other time, a Jewish attorney (at the lunch table with a bunch of the christians) asked me why christians are so against halloween. Although I knew the answer, in an effort to duck a long, possibly painful conversation I just said 'I don't know. I'm not a Christian.' She laughed, and said 'Neither am I.' I sometimes regret not answering properly. Another time, one of the very elderly attorneys walked out of the office while I was relieving the receptionist for her lunch. He joked 'Don't let the infidels in while I'm gone.' I smiled and said 'I am one.' He stared at me for a moment, then kept going. Nothing came of that, either.

"One of the attorneys who has since retired comes to visit us sometimes. He mentioned something about religion or church one time, and I said something mildly negative. He asked 'You're not a Christian?' I said 'No, I'm an atheist.' He said 'You're brave, to come out and say that.' I think I just smiled in return."

And finally, I'll point out once again: Lots of the atheists in this book had some hard times. Some of them had some very difficult, very upsetting times. But in the hundreds of coming out atheist stories that I read for this book, literally one person said that they regretted it.

Give the people in your life some credit. Coming out as an atheist might change their minds about you for the worse—but it might also change their minds about atheists, for the better. And even if it doesn't, you'll probably feel better about yourself, and enjoy your life more.

Even in the Bible Belt.

CHAPTER SIXTEEN

— ✸ —

Progressive Communities

You'd think that coming out atheist in a big progressive city would be pretty easy.

And compared to coming out in the Bible Belt or an Islamist theocracy, you'd be right. In San Francisco or New York or Seattle, you probably won't lose your job or get your kids taken away if you tell people you're an atheist. As lifelong nonbeliever John Horstman says, "A lot of the ease I have around openly identifying as atheist is likely due to living in a large city, spending time and working at a public university, and traveling in radical leftist social circles that generally regard religion as yet another vector of authoritarian control."

But being an out atheist in a progressive stronghold has its own set of challenges. I'm definitely not saying, "Poor us, boo hoo, we are such sad atheists in the progressive strongholds." Mostly, it is easier to be an atheist in the big bad Babylonian cities. I'm saying that there are some interesting challenges to the experience, and they're worth being aware of.

Religion in progressive regions tends to be... well, progressive. It tends to be interfaith, or leaning in that direction. And progressive believers of the interfaith variety can be weirdly hostile to atheists and atheism.

The whole interfaith thing rests on a foundation of not criticizing other beliefs and affiliations. It's dependent on the idea that the variety of world religions is a rich and beautiful tapestry of faith; that all religions have at least some piece of the truth; that all religions have a partial but incomplete perception of God (like in the story of the blind men and the elephant—interfaith believers freaking love that story); that the history of religion shows an evolving understanding of God that's moving ever closer to a clearer picture of the truth of the divine.

So when atheists come along and say, "Nope, we think you're all wrong, we don't think you're perceiving anything real, we think your tapestry is a fiction, we think the truth of the divine that humanity's moving toward is the understanding that it doesn't exist"—that rubs some people the wrong way. Even if we're not saying it explicitly, the implication is inherent in coming out as atheist. Like I keep saying, there's no way to say, "Don't believe in God? You're not alone!" without implying, "Do believe in God? You're wrong!" For the Kumbaya/interfaith/rich tapestry crowd, that doesn't always go over so well.

Be aware that in progressive regions, you're also more likely to be dealing with New Age religion, almost as much as traditional religion, and maybe even more. So the anti-atheist stigma you run into is less likely to be, "You're going to burn in Hell!," and is more likely to be, "How can you let yourself be so cut off from the spiritual essence of the Universe?"

Conservative believers aren't the only ones who try to convert their atheist friends, either. Progressive believers sometimes do this as well. Liz H. figured out that she was an atheist by early high school, and talked openly about it to friends and teachers. "Some of my religious friends," she says, "(and interestingly, *the most pushy were some of my UU [Unitarian Universalist] friends*) repeatedly tried to convince me of god, or that it was worthwhile to attend their church-ish thing." [Emphasis mine.]

And it isn't just conservative religion that causes serious or even permanent rifts between family or friends. Karla grew up in the late '60s and early '70s, in the famously progressive Marin County, California, with a blend of Unitarianism and New Age religion. But as her atheism was developing, her sister was getting more deeply involved in New Age belief. Her sister's beliefs were very intense and important to her, and she interpreted any argument against them as a personal attack. But Karla's need for a rational explanation of those beliefs was just as important to her. The arguments they had about it resulted in a rift that lasts to this day. Karla's sister cut off all contact, and hasn't spoken to her in 21 years.

And speaking for myself, the worst fights I ever had with friends about my atheism were with a Wiccan, a super-progressive Christian, and a progressive interfaith gay convert to Islam. (Of course, those are the kinds of believers I know: I just don't have many fundamentalist believers in my life. Or any, really.)

Progressive religious culture, and the interfaith philosophy's supposed tolerance, can stifle coming out as atheist in other ways. On the Coming Out Godless Project website, vjack tells of getting into a Ph.D. program in psychology that emphasized multiculturalism—to the point where any expression of disagreement with religion was considered intolerant. "As you can imagine," vjack says, "this put me in an excruciatingly difficult position. It was made clear to me that successful completion of the program would depend on my ability to keep my disbelief to myself. Trust of my peers became an issue, as I learned that statements I had made outside of school got back to a professor. Clearly, this was not a safe environment to be open about atheism... On one hand, I was told that I was being evaluated on my openness, willingness to self-disclose, and exploration of how my beliefs impacted my work with others. On the other hand, I learned the hard way that questioning someone's religious beliefs equated with criticism of someone's race—it was a marker of serious intolerance. To survive this program, I would need to bury my atheism and profess respect for religious belief."

And if you're looking for community to help support you through your fights with progressive interfaith gay Muslims, be aware: Atheist communities are often not as strong in progressive regions as they are in the Bible Belt. Like I said in the chapter on conservative communities, there's just more need for atheist community in Dallas and Omaha than there is in Los Angeles or New York City. In parts of the world where nobody cares that much about your atheism, where some believers will get irritated or condescending but you probably won't get fired or lose custody of your kids, and where religion doesn't dominate the social life and isn't constantly being shoved in your face, atheists are less likely to cling to each other for support, and are more likely to just get on with their lives. The very things that make being atheist easier in progressive regions also make it harder to do community building.

For lots of atheists, this may not be an issue. They may actually see it as a feature rather than a bug. (I've heard this more than once: "What would I want with an atheist community? The good thing about atheism is that I don't have to get up on Sunday and go to meetings!") But for some atheists—if they've recently left religion, if their experience leaving religion was traumatic or isolating, if the religion they left was oppressive or abusive, if they still have deeply religious family who they feel alienated from, if religion is central to their racial or cultural identity and leaving it makes them feel uprooted, or if their atheism is just really important to them—the lack of a strong atheist community may be more of a problem.

So what do you with all this? Well, for starters: Be aware of it. Don't assume that everyone will be hunky-dory with your atheism just because you live in Babylon. It's true that it's easier to do "no big deal" coming out in progressive regions, to simply be out rather than making a production of it. And in progressive regions, you can often get away with the "Of course I'm an atheist—aren't you?" method I talked about in the "No Big Deal" chapter. But chances are good that if you do this, you'll raise some hackles. That doesn't mean you shouldn't do it, of course. Just be aware of the possible consequences.

You might look at doing community building that isn't based on replacing religious institutions. When churches don't dominate the social life like they do in conservative regions, people don't have as much need for atheist substitutes to fill that void. And when there are lots of secular options for activities, there's also more competition for people's time and commitment. So when you're doing community building, don't just think, "What do people get from religion, and how can we replace that?" Instead, think, "What do people in our region need and want?" That's what Chris Hall and David Fitzgerald and I did when we started the Godless Perverts in San Francisco, a performance series and social community based on atheist views of sexuality. We never would have come up with that if we'd been thinking, "What does religion provide for people?" (I go into this in more detail in the chapter on community building.)

In progressive regions, you may also experience atheist community in a looser, less structured way. "Atheist community" doesn't have to be an official organized group, with official atheist picnics and panel discussions. It can also be a birthday party where half your friends are atheists, and you talk about the Reason Rally and the latest controversy eating the atheosphere and the great article you read on Skepchick— and you also talk about chili recipes and socialist politics and Project Runway.

Don't forget online communities, either. We often talk about how valuable online communities are to atheists in small towns or isolated rural areas, where there isn't an in-the-flesh atheist community for a hundred miles, and the only place people have to talk about their atheism is the Internet. But online communities can also be valuable to atheists in jaded big cities, where there is an atheist community but it doesn't have a huge amount going on, and even other atheists don't care that much about atheism. And in jaded big cities, people tend to be joined at the hip to the Internet, which makes it easier to connect with other atheists in your area.

And if in-the-flesh atheist community is really important to you—get involved in it. Help make it happen. Get involved with the existing groups, and spearhead new projects for them. My experience in San Francisco is that for lots of atheists, it often doesn't occur to them to get involved with atheist communities—but if those communities do things that are fun and intriguing, they'll get on board. (I don't think it's an accident that the first ever Atheist Film Festival was started in San Francisco.) And if the existing groups are moribund and you really can't cope with them—start a new one.

But the main thing I want to say, once again, is that this usually turns out fine. And for those of us in progressive strongholds, that's doubly true.

So come on out. Look both ways before you cross the street, make sure there aren't any oncoming trucks, and come on over. And if you're ever in San Francisco, look up the Godless Perverts. We're having a blast.

CHAPTER SEVENTEEN

—— ✹ ——

The U.S. Military

Step One: Contact the Military Religious Freedom Foundation, and the Military Association of Atheists and Freethinkers.

Step Two: Follow the rest of the guidelines in this book.

I probably don't have to tell you this—but because you're in the U.S. military, you're in a weird position. On the one hand: You're an employee of the federal government, and the federal government has seriously strict standards of employment fairness. Especially when it comes to freedom of religion—including the freedom not to have one. So in theory, you have a lot of legal protection.

On the other hand: You're an employee of the U.S. Army, Navy, Marine Corps, Air Force, National Guard, or Coast Guard. So you signed away a bunch of your rights the day you signed up. A greater level of internal discipline, loyalty, and obedience is expected of you than if you were working in an office or a warehouse or a supermarket. Your commanding officers have a lot more leeway than an average boss would to enforce that discipline. You do have a lot of legal protection—but you may have to fight hard to actually benefit from it. And if you do fight that fight, you'll be doing it in a culture that really does not want people to rock the boat. (Especially in the Navy and the Coast Guard. Sorry—couldn't help myself.)

What's more: Much of U.S. military culture and many official military policies are strongly biased towards Christians—especially evangelical Christians—and against atheists. Again—go to the websites of the Military Religious Freedom Foundation,[1] a legal and media organization protecting freedom of religion and belief and church-state separation for all; and the Military Association of Atheists and Freethinkers,[2] a community organization created by foxhole atheists for foxhole atheists. You'll see story after story after story of military units saturated with right-wing Christian proselytizing. Christian service members being given preferential treatment. Christian evangelizing programs being openly sponsored by the military. Non-Christians being openly pressured to participate in these programs. Atheist service members—or even religious service members who aren't part of this evangelical Christian culture—being shunned, given onerous work details, passed over for promotion, and even threatened with violence. (And the degree to which the War on Terror is being framed as a religious war isn't helping this.)

On the Military Association of Atheists and Freethinkers website, where open nonbelievers in the U.S. military share their experiences, accounts of official prayer and proselytizing abound—prayer and proselytizing that atheists often can't opt out of.[3] On that site, Navy Petty Officer 1st Class Francy Legault (currently serving) says, "I was deployed on the USS Dwight D. Eisenhower for 8 months to the Gulf and every night over the 1MC (the announcement system) was prayer. I found it intrusive. I felt like a captured audience. Also, in boot camp, we were learning commands—right face, march, all that and one command is 'Let Us Pray' and we were told it didn't matter what we believed, when we heard that command, we HAD to bow our heads. So prayer is a command." *(Note: If people in this chapter are quoted with specific rank, position, and dates of service, their stories came from the MAAF website. Statements by military personnel are personal only and do not reflect official positions of the Department of Defense or any government agency.)*

Incidents like this are maddeningly common. Army Sergeant Kayla Williams (dates of service: 2000 – 2005) says, "While studying Arabic at the Defense Language Institute, one of our professors passed out Christian materials in class, and then called every Christian student up to hold a prayer circle immediately before our oral proficiency exams— leaving the Mormons, Hindu, and me sitting in our seats, mouths agape at how wildly inappropriate it was." Captain Neil Moody Jr. (dates of service: 1984 – present) says, "There is an interesting culture of religion in the Army, wherein the entire mission is stated in terms of service to the U.S. and god, the implication being that the two are one and the same, or at least inextricably linked. Those who do not believe are actively berated, left out of social functions, etc. Most official functions are opened and closed with prayers from Army Chaplains. If you go to the PX, the book section is full of spiritual guides (all Christian, by the way, no Muslim or other faiths represented)." Air Force Tech Sergeant Kenneth Labelle (dates of service: January 2, 2002 – present) says, "My biggest issue currently is the tendency of the military to trot out a chaplain at every major event—be it a commander's call, change of command ceremony, drill competition, etc.—and have them ask everyone to bow their heads and pray to 'the Lord,' apparently meaning Jesus. It's bad enough being an atheist and having to hear that (not that I bow my head, I usually spend the prayer looking around to see how many other non-praying people I can spot), but I can't imagine how offensive it must be to people there who may privately worship other things." And Navy Petty Officer 2nd Class Nicholas McFerran (dates of service: February 2007 – present) says, "I have had to sit through countless ceremonies where we are subjected to some religious service or prayer. I end up just staring around the room while most others bow down. And none of these ceremonies are optional."

These stories are just a drop in the bucket. On the Military Association of Atheists and Freethinkers website, there are dozens more. Army Sergeant 1st Class Chad Brack (dates of service: August

2003 – present) makes a compelling and unsettling point about this shift in military culture: "Recent overtly Christian prayers at change of command ceremonies, award ceremonies, and graduation ceremonies have caused me to step back and ask questions about how the Army can justify incorporating religious belief or tradition into its daily activities when our country is supposed to have a clear separation of church and state. Every time I'm asked to bow my head I'm reminded of the religious officers of Afghanistan who force their soldiers to partake in daily Islamic ceremony and wonder how different we really are."

Eric Paulsen has an appalling story of anti-atheist bigotry in the military—ironically, in the context of what was supposed to be training on respecting religious diversity. "I don't remember the date my grandfather died," he says, "but I was in Hospital Corpsman 'A' school in Great Lakes, Illinois at the time. A few days previous to getting the news of his death a female Chief Petty Officer had started us on, of all things, medical ethics, and in particular she was going on about respecting the religious beliefs of your patient when it came to their treatment. Good information and necessary, but things went off the rails when she decided to ask the students what their religion was. Most were Catholic, a few Baptists, miscellaneous Christian sects, and one or two Jews. When she said 'atheist' almost as an afterthought, my hand went up and after a second or two another more timid student off to my right raised his hand to half mast. I can't blame him especially considering what followed.

"I noticed a fleeting look of consternation pass over her face," he says, "but nothing followed immediately. After a few more stabs at locating a Hindu or Buddhist in our midst she came back to me and as if she were merely curious began a dialogue with me about my atheism during class in front of all of the students. I was only uncomfortable because of the venue, I really hate being the center of attention and the grilling went on for at least half an hour if not more. And she kept getting madder and madder at my replies. I was asked the typical 'so what do you think happens when you die' and I got Pascal's wager thrown at me, I was asked to explain why we were here if there was no god, and on, and on. The longer the questioning went on the more mocking her tone and the more confrontational she became—I was beginning to worry, with her being a Chief Petty Officer and me being a lowly HN [hospital corpsman], if I didn't just sign up to three months of kitchen duty or some such punishment. She had finally calmed down and resumed her lecture but was completely out of sorts, like I had just attacked her instead of the other way around. I went back to taking notes and after a 15 minute break where several of the students came up to me in the hallway with a commiserating 'What the fuck happened THERE' we were back for the last half of the class.

"About 10 minutes into the class there was a bit of commotion, someone from the front office had come in with a note and was talking to the Chief. He left and she looked at the note in her hand and then at me and I swear I could see smugness, some look of triumph that settled into her grinchy brain. Waving the slip she called my name and told me that my grandfather had died. In retrospect her flip manner was pretty cold, but knowing that he was sick with cancer and in the hospital it didn't come as a shock to me. She then said, and while this is not a direct quote it is pretty close, 'Well, since you don't believe in god I guess you won't have any need to go to his funeral, I mean you believe he is just going to rot in the ground, right?'"

As profoundly messed-up as this incident was, however, the story did end reasonably well. "I actually heard gasps from several of my classmates," he says, "so if she was trying to make ME out to be the unfeeling monster in this scenario she was really going about it the wrong way... After I got back from the funeral my classmates welcomed me back, expressed their regrets, and told me how that Chief had been removed from that class later that day and hadn't been seen since. I'm guessing that someone with a brain was trying to make this whole ugly event go away because even if the local command didn't see anything wrong in her conduct there were several people in the chain of command that might."

I should emphasize, though, that this story took place in 1988. Paulsen now says, "I think I was seeing just where the military was headed back then with all of the evangelical corruption seeping in. It wasn't terrible back in my day but I think it is entrenched now, just like in the schools, and in the courts, and in our government."

This Christian culture in the U.S. military—with its anti-atheist hostility—has practical effects as well, very often in the form of non-believers being given extra work or more onerous work, and Christians being given extra time off or other special privileges. Marine Sergeant Adam Dunigan (dates of service: April 1, 2008 – present) says, "I think the most egregious offense that religion perpetrates in the military is that it asserts itself (and is thus treated) as an integral part of military life. When I first entered basic training and we were given time off contingent on attending religious service, I was shocked." Marine Lance Corporal Steffen Camarato (dates of service: June 2006 – June 2010) says, "An Atheist in the military? Well, good job, now you get to work on Sunday because you obviously have nothing to do on Sundays right?" Army Warrant Officer Christopher Roberts (dates of service: August 2006 – present) says, "Another side note I found to be very coercive was that all Service Members who were married were allowed to visit with family members during Sunday worship services while those who weren't religious or those who weren't married were stuck on work details during that period of time." And Air Force Staff Sergeant Johnathan Napier (dates of service: September 13, 2005 – August 21, 2011) says, "I also remember going through basic training and being given the option of 'going to church' or 'cleaning.' That's not a real option. Of course everyone chooses church... Frankly, I was quite annoyed at how positively I could be viewed as a soldier, but so negatively as an Atheist."

One of the most troubling aspects of coming out atheist in the military is that if you're seeking help—medical, psychological, practical—and you tell the person you're seeking help from that you're an atheist, you may be subjected to proselytizing rather than given the assistance you need. That sometimes happens in the civilian world as well—but unlike civilians, you can't just request another doctor or therapist or what have you. Air Force Senior Airman Nathan Lewellen (dates of service: August 2008 – present) says, "I'd have to say the worst experience I've had was a time during tech school that I was being questioned about some trouble in which I had found myself. My MTL (military training leader) asked me directly, and behind closed doors, 'do you believe in god?' I just told him 'no' and he proceeded to explain to me rules of the Air Force regarding my situation with undertones of the morals reflected in those rules and where they 'came from.' I don't remember specifically as to whether or not he quoted the Bible or tried to bring up biblical stories, but this was one of the most emotionally prominent memories I have of the Air Force."

Army Specialist Dennis Bailey (dates of service: February 2008 – present) has a similar story of needing care and getting religion instead. During his last deployment, he says, "I was struggling with a lot of stress and personal issues. I let the command know that I needed some help and asked to speak to mental health. The next day the chaplain shows up at our site and proceeds to counsel me. I didn't get any help from him because I just couldn't take him seriously. I told him I was Atheist and all of his advice became about giving my problems to the lord. When he found out I was a non believer and having a rough time he saw the perfect opportunity to exploit my weakness and turn his efforts to converting me rather than helping me. I later got to see the actual combat stress [recovery specialist] and got the help I needed at the time, but the 'help' from the chaplain only succeeded in discouraging me more." And Army Sergeant KJ Kendall (dates of service: 2000 – present) tells this extremely chilling story: "In leader development training, I got severely dehydrated during land-navigation... some flunkie failed to stick an IV needle in my arm five or six times then volunteered to escort me to the hospital. During the entire 1-2 hours that he was with me, he vehemently tried to proselytize me. He had a very creepy approach... I wish I was armed with the information and resolve that I have today."

You might read this and think, "Well, forget about coming out, then. I don't want to deal with that crap—especially if I'm dealing with injury or sickness or trauma." I can definitely see how you'd feel that way. But in a sense, this is actually an argument for coming out sooner rather than later. Like I said in the chapter on coming out to family: When a crisis arises, it's better for the "I'm an atheist" conversation to already be behind you. It's better to not add the uncertainty and possible trauma of coming out to whatever other difficulty you're going through. And it's better if the people around you already know you're an atheist. Even if you have to deal with evangelical jerks, the initial shock-and-horror, "you're going to burn in Hell/don't you want to come to the loving arms of Jesus?" phase will be behind you. More importantly, you'll already have forged a bond with other nonbelievers—as well as with believers who are supportive and don't give a damn that you're an atheist.

Unfortunately, it's common for atheists in the military to have to fight even for the right to be out at all, and to have their atheism recognized. Atheists in the U.S. military have the right to have "Atheist" recorded as their official religious preference, on official records, ID tags, and military headstones. But it's common for atheists to be pressured to list "No Religious Preference" instead—or even for their preference to be ignored. Air Force Staff Sergeant Johnathan Napier again: "The most common intolerance I got was when I would order dog-tags. For religious preference I would select 'Atheist.' But the clerks would give me this dirty look and ask if I wanted 'No Preference' instead, as if it was shameful to have Atheist on dog-tags." Army Sergeant Kevin

Dare (dates of service: March 28, 2007 – present) actually had his express wishes about this ignored. "I do remember," he says, "when my recruiter asked me which religion I was and I strongly emphasized "NONE!!" and I ended up with 'no pref recorded.' At the time I didn't know any better."

This business of "not knowing any better," by the way, is one of the biggest reasons it's important to contact the Military Religious Freedom Foundation, or at least look at their website. They know in detail exactly what your rights are—and they can help you get them recognized.

It's important to point out, though, that these negative experiences aren't universal. In talking with atheists in the military, I've heard stories that have varied hugely. I've heard stories of units saturated with pro-Christian and anti-atheist bias—and I've also heard stories of atheists who were totally out to their unit, and where it was no big deal at all. And I've heard lots of stories in between. Experiences seem to vary hugely from unit to unit. Navy Petty Officer 2nd Class Bobby Daugherty (dates of service: April 2006 – April 2011) says, "I was fortunate enough to not have to endure any form of discrimination due to my lack of faith. I was afforded the opportunity while in the United States Navy to work amongst some of the finest people I have ever known. My only regret is that I am no longer with them."

Army Specialist Charles Hawes (dates of service: September 2010 – present) concurs. "I have not experienced any real discrimination from my unit," he says, "and even have a leader who for the most part shares many of my views on religion, with the only difference being he is more agnostic where I am a total atheist." Navy Petty Officer 3rd Class Marc Latou (dates of service: February 2003 – May 2006) says, "From my fellow sailors, I would say that I had no issues with discrimination or intolerance." Navy Petty Officer 2nd Class Joel Wheeler (dates of service: April 2001 – March 2007) says, "I've been lucky and only had a few run-ins with particularly religious persons, and not been discriminated against on a general basis." And Air Force Staff Sergeant

Derek Traywick (dates of service: July 2003 – present) says, "My experience with religion in the military has been nothing but positive. I've been able to have discussions about various religious ideas with many other military members. My beliefs have always been respected by the military religious community (to include chaplains). It saddens me to hear that this is not the normal way we atheists are treated."

But the pro-Christian, anti-atheist bias in the military is real. It's common. And in recent years, this evangelical Christian culture in the military is very much on the rise.

And you know how in the chapter on coming out at work, I said that even though workplace discrimination against atheists is illegal in the United States, it sometimes happens anyway? You know how I said that workplace discrimination is often hard to prove, and that if you do decide to fight back, you're likely to get a lot of flak, and things may get worse before they get better? In the military, all of that gets dialed up to eleven. The Military Religious Freedom Foundation has extensive documentation of anti-atheist and other religious discrimination in the U.S. military, and of how much work it often takes to get it handled. And when I asked Jason Torpy, president of the Military Association of Atheists and Freethinkers, to comment about atheists coming out in the military for this book, he immediately responded with a series of stories about atheists fighting for their rights: their right to have humanist alternatives to church[4]; their right to have student secular groups at military academies[5]; their right even to be identified as atheist[6] or humanist[7] on their official records, ID tags, and military headstones; their right to have humanist chaplains[8]; their right to not have their one and only one-day break from basic training be sponsored by a Baptist church, with a hellfire-and-brimstone sermon at the end of it.[9] "These all sound like 'activist' stories," he says, "but that's the point. You can either sit quietly in a corner and get bullied less or you can fight for your rights—and probably get them, but only after a fight. That's just where we are now."

So if you come out in the military, and you want to not be treated as a second-class citizen, you may have a fight ahead of you.

I know. This is a lot of really crappy news. Except it's probably not news. You probably know more about this situation than I ever will.

The good news, however, is that fighting for your rights, or even simply asserting them, often works. Army Sergeant John Gill (dates of service: April 2005 – present) says, "My first glimpse of Army belief pushing came when I was standing on a parade field as a brand new private, refusing to bow my head for the chaplain's prayer. My platoon sergeant told me afterward that even if I didn't believe in God, I should bow my head out of respect for those around me. I agreed as long he would bow his head with me and pray to some other god he didn't believe in. He wouldn't and since then I've made it a point to stand extra straight with my chin up during every prayer I'm forced to listen to. I don't face too much discrimination, possibly because I'm very outspoken and set in my beliefs."

Army Reserve Captain Neil Moody Jr. has also successfully resisted pressure to take part in military-sponsored religion. "I don't participate in unit prayer," he says. "When the benediction is given, I am upright, with head high and eyes open. This has gotten me a few comments from other soldiers who reflexively bow their heads when asked to do so. I tell them, 'I choose not to bow to anything or anyone,' which will usually end the conversation." Air Force 2nd Lieutenant Madison Scaccia (dates of service: August 2011 – present) says, "I was given the opportunity to give an invocation at an ROTC event a few years ago, and not once did I reference a god. It IS possible to remind your fellow service members to think about their deployed buddies, to keep their families in your thoughts, to remember the ones you lost without going through a deity first." And Army National Guard Sergeant Donald Ferguson (dates of service: 1998 – present) is one of many military atheists who ran into opposition over religious identification on dog tags. A former Mormon who could no longer tolerate being affiliated with the Mormon church after their involvement in passing Proposition 8, he says, "I formally requested my name be removed from the church roster. At that point I was refused new dog tags to update the religion block with 'atheist' or 'humanist' so I just had my own made online. One says 'atheist' the other says 'secularhumanist' (had to make it all one word, but it fit)."

When you come out as an atheist in the U.S. military, you don't just have lots of legal rights. You have entire organizations specifically created to help you defend those rights, and to support you while you do. Have I said, "contact the Military Religious Freedom Foundation" enough times? Well, I'll say it again. They know in detail exactly what your rights are. They know what you can do to get them recognized. And they can help you make it happen.

The Military Religious Freedom Foundation isn't an atheist-specific organization. They exist to defend religious freedom for all members of the United States Armed Forces, including nonbelievers and believers alike—and in many ways, that makes them a stronger force for atheists' rights in the military. It is an uphill battle to defend religious neutrality against the increasing right-wing evangelical Christian culture in the U.S. military. But they've had plenty of important successes: both publicizing unconstitutional promotion of religion and religiously-based harassment in the military, and putting a halt to it. They don't just engage in widely-publicized battles, either—much of their work involves individual cases,[10] many of which stay anonymous. If you're coming out as an atheist and are experiencing discrimination or abuse—or if you want to come out as an atheist and a hostile environment is making you reluctant to do so—contact them. Now.

Plus, depending on where you're stationed, you may be able to find an immediately supportive community. There are Military Atheists & Secular Humanists (M*A*S*H) groups being formed at lots of bases. As of this writing, there are M*A*S*H groups at Fort Bragg; Camp Pendleton;

Hawaii; Eglin/Hurlburt; and the North Bay area of California. If there isn't currently one at or near your base, try contacting the ones that exist elsewhere, and find out from them how to start your own.

If there is initial shock, resistance, bigotry, or hostility when you come out as atheist? Don't assume that it's going to be that way forever. Aaron Wiebusch first came out as an atheist in 2007 while still in the Marine Corps. "I was a Staff Sergeant," he says, "serving at the Mountain Warfare Training Center. The specifics are as follows: the first week of April the command Chaplain's assistant was making his way around the command post inviting Marines to attend the Easter mass later that week. When he got to me I was in my office doing paperwork and he asked if I would like to attend. Initially I had planned to simply say no thanks, but instead I said, 'no, I don't believe in any of that stuff. I'm an atheist.' You know the thing that happens in the movies when someone says something no one expects and they play the sound effect of crickets chirping? That is what the next few seconds felt like."

"The assistant's response was first to pick his jaw up off the floor, then cross his arms and look at me like I'd just sprouted antlers, before saying, 'What do you mean, you're an atheist?' I replied that, after careful consideration, I had concluded that, because there is no evidence whatsoever for the existence of a deity or deities of any sort, that none exist. 'No evidence?' he said, to which I responded; 'yes, that's correct.' He blinked several times and then said 'What about the bible?' To which I replied; 'You mean the book written over a period of about 1,200 years beginning in the mid Bronze Age by numerous authors, some of which just copied what others wrote or made stuff up in order to add credence to what previous authors wrote, and which contains stories about talking snakes and donkeys, people living for hundreds of years, a global flood that somehow left behind no evidence, a guy with super-human strength contingent upon the length of his hair, flying flaming chariots, endorsement of things like slavery, misogyny, infanticide, incest, genocide, human sacrifice, infinite punishment for finite offenses, capital punishment for trivial crimes, homophobia, not to mention unicorns, dragons, disease being caused by demonic possession, a decree that a raped woman shall marry her rapist, and people coming back from the dead? That book?' He was not pleased with my reply, and promptly left.

"The next day," he says, "I was called in to see the command Chaplain. He asked me to explain why I was an atheist. I told him that I had looked very critically at the various claims made for the existence of a god and found that each one of them contains logical fallacies of one or more types, the most common being circular reasoning or special pleading. I said that in the end any argument for the existence of a god requires that one must have faith. I said that faith, as it is defined, is the belief in something in the absence of evidence or even in the face of evidence to the contrary. Because of that, saying one must 'have faith' is no different than saying one must 'believe in whacky shit for no good reason.' Faith is nothing more than deliberate gullibility, and I refuse to live as a gullible person. At this point the Chaplain's assistant cut in by saying 'you're not respecting people's beliefs!' I said that his, and everyone's, beliefs are only ideas, and we criticize ideas all the time. We're critical of ideas about politics, economics, science, art, which car to buy or what store to shop at. Why can't we be critical of a religious idea too? And that criticizing a religion is not the same as criticizing the person who believes it. I told him that he is free to believe whatever he wants, just so long as he doesn't insist other people believe it too without evidence. After I said this he shook his head and left the room. He didn't speak to me after that."

Not the greatest welcome in the world. But eventually, Aaron says, "the rest of the command learned I was a non-believer, and most of them appeared not to care. Some did ask me a few questions, most of them dealing with just what atheism is, and overall, my time at that unit was not made difficult because I didn't believe in a god."

And very importantly—like I keep saying—when you come out as an atheist, it makes it easier for other atheists to come out, either to you privately or to everyone else publicly. And that makes things better—both for them, and for you. Lisa, who was stationed in Omaha, Nebraska, says, "I was quite closeted about atheism when on duty, although I talked about it while off-duty with a few geeky gamer types and the dude with a big ol' confrontational Richard Dawkins book on his desk... We were all Airmen who were not non-commissioned officers, so it felt very safe because there was a culture in place preventing anyone from having power over anyone else.

"Then a non-commissioned officer and outspoken atheist was transferred over to our shop," she says, "and I came out to everyone, pretty much counting on him to shield me from any bigotry, and saying so. When people asked me why I had been worried I pointed out that bigotry against atheists is a thing that happens in the military, and pointed out some examples, some of which I had read on your blog [Greta Christina's Blog]. (Thanks!) I also added that it is hard to tell how much someone cares about religion just by talking about other things, like how Catholics and Methodists have different definitions of non-believers, and different fates for them besides. Also like how few people noticed I was an atheist.

"It was all very reasonable according to the military culture. I used the chain of command to support my decision, when questioned gave answers at least as thoughtful as the questions. Nobody felt the need to escalate any conflict beyond just talking."

It can be especially helpful if officers and people in leadership positions come out as atheist. Army Master Sergeant Michael Hammond (specialty: Military Police; dates of service: August 1988 – present) says, "I've held off actively participating in MAAF because I haven't felt the need to belong to anything—just wanted to show that we exist, you know? Now, however, being 'strongly encouraged' as a leader to attend yet another prayer breakfast has pushed me past the point of tolerance." And Air Force Major Rodger Nelson (dates of service: May 1999 – November 2008, presently in the Air National Guard) says, "As an Officer, I've found it relatively easy to be a military non-theist, but I imagine it would be quite a different story for a young Enlisted member. I've decided now that I've got over 10 years under my belt I need to make myself available to other service members who may need some help with issues related to being a non-believer in today's military."

And of course, as an atheist in the military, you are in a uniquely powerful position to disprove the insulting myth that there are no atheists in foxholes. Air Force Major Rodger Nelson again: "Some of my best friends are Mormons and Southern Baptists, and while we completely disagree on theology, we still live, work, and fight right alongside each other. I personally think we atheists sometimes do ourselves a disservice by distancing ourselves too much from our religious peers—make them like you for who you are and the work you do first, then hit them with your beliefs if it happens to come up." And Army National Guard Sergeant 1st Class Casey Braden (dates of service: June 1999 – present), says, "I recently had someone learn that I was an atheist and say, 'But you are one of the nicest, happiest people I know! That doesn't make any sense!' I aim to change people's opinions about what it means to be an atheist, and to show that you don't need belief in some supernatural being to be a good person."

I know it can suck to be an out atheist in the U.S. military. I know it can be hard. If you decide not to do it, I sure won't blame you. But one of the things you can do to make it easier in the long run, and even in the medium run, is to come out anyway. It'll make it easier for yourself, and it'll make it easier for others. (Which will also make it easier for yourself.)

You may have to fight hard. You're in hostile territory, and you're likely to get a lot of flak. It's an uphill battle.

You're in the military. You should be really good at that.

CHAPTER EIGHTEEN

The Clergy

Step One: Contact The Clergy Project.
Step Two: Update your resume.
Step Three: Follow the rest of the guidelines in this book.
(Note on Step One: If you've only recently decided that you're an atheist, you may also want to contact Recovering From Religion.)

I probably don't have to tell you this—but you're in an unusual position, and an unusually difficult one. Many atheists worry about letting down their family, their spouses or partners, their friends, when they come out as an atheist. As a clergyperson, you have to worry about letting down your entire community. At the same time that you're completely re-thinking your career and your future, your livelihood and indeed your very survival, you have to worry about a whole community feeling betrayed.

There's another factor that's likely to make this harder for you. One of the main ways that religion perpetuates itself is through authority. Human beings have an innate, hard-wired tendency to trust people in authority. (Some of us less so, others more, but we all have it.) And people have a strong tendency to trust figures of religious authority. They assume that if their clergyperson—their priest, their rabbi, their pastor, their imam, their guru—is telling them things about their god or gods or the supernatural world, then they must know what they're talking about. If people are having questions or doubts about their faith, they often assume that their clergyperson has the answers—and that therefore those answers exist, and they don't have to worry about them. For many people, "understanding their religion and asking hard questions about it" is a job they're perfectly willing to outsource. (And many clergypeople are all too willing to play into this: saying things like, "have faith," "let go of doubt," "trust in the Lord," "mysterious ways," and so on, when people come to them with difficult questions about their religion.)

So when you come out as atheist, you're not just disappointing your membership in you, personally. You're making them question their own faith. You're weakening one of the main pillars that their faith is founded on. When their clergyperson takes on that outsourced job of understanding religion and asking hard questions about it—and the result of that job is, "Oh, wait a minute, none of this makes sense and there's no good reason to think any of it is true"—most people aren't going to like it.

That doesn't mean you shouldn't do it. Not in the slightest. That is a perfectly fine and reasonable thing to do, and you don't have to feel guilty about it. The truth is that there *are* no gods, that religion *doesn't* make sense, that there *isn't* a good reason to believe that any of it is true. Once you've accepted that, it's right and honest to be willing to say so. But most people aren't going to like it.

Some people may even get ugly about it. When former local Methodist pastor Teresa MacBain came out as an atheist, she was shunned by her community; she got hateful emails, voicemails, letters, and Facebook posts and messages; and the church where she had pastored for over three years changed the locks, and for two months wouldn't let her on the property to get her belongings.[1] When former Pentecostal preacher Jerry DeWitt (*Hope after Faith: An Ex-Pastor's Journey from Belief to Atheism*) came out as an atheist—or, more accurately, when he was outed by a relative who saw on Facebook that he'd been to a Richard Dawkins talk—he became a pariah in his small Louisiana town; he received a steady stream of hate mail and threats; and he was even fired from his secular job, by a boss who told him, "The Pentecostals who run the parish are not happy, and something's got to be done."[2] These stories are extreme—but alas, they're not uncommon.

Less extreme but still hostile reactions are common as well. On the Clergy Project website, Jeffrey Olsson—formerly an Anglican priest in Canada—says that when he was starting to come out as an atheist, "The next step was to tell my father, who is also a clergyman. I'll never forget his reaction as he tried repeatedly to convince me I was destined for hell. Some of my former parishioners phoned and tried to convince me I was wrong. 'You're going to hell, Jeff,' some of them said. My head pounded. No one would listen. It's as if they were immune to my reasoning. I'm not a bad person, I just don't believe anymore. I felt very alone."

So when you come out as atheist, you'll probably have more than your job on the line. More even than most other atheists, you'll likely be risking your entire community and your entire social support network. And chances are good that you'll be facing more hurt feelings—and more anger, even hatred—than most atheists do when they come out.

And especially if your deconversion is fairly recent, psychologically you may be in a somewhat fragile and shaky place—more so than many other atheists who have left religion. Clergypeople tend to take religion very seriously and experience it very deeply. Obviously. You're probably not going to go into the clergy if religion isn't important to you. So the process of questioning religion, examining it, doubting it, and eventually letting go of it, was probably extremely intense for you. More than many atheists, religion may have left a large hole in your life that you'll need to figure out how to fill, and you may be feeling very vulnerable.

"For members of the Clergy Project," acting Executive Director Catherine Dunphy told me, "coming out as an atheist can be a rather long and arduous process. Our members spend years cultivating their religious beliefs and identities; for many the transition to unbelief involves years of disentanglement from their religious tradition. Members of TCP have given much thought to the what, why and how of their beliefs, attempting to excavate their religious traditions for nuggets of truth and it is only after much discernment that they arrive, independently, at unbelief."

Plus, of course, your job *is* going to be on the line. There are very few careers where "believing in God" is a legitimate job requirement—but "clergyperson" is one of them. For most religions, anyway.

So even more than other atheists, when you come out as atheist, the chances are excellent that you're really going to be starting over from scratch. And so even more than other atheists, you'll need to plan carefully. Get your financial ducks in a row—pay off your credit card bills, and get some training in another skill, or think about which skills you already have that can transfer to the secular job market. Think carefully about who you want to tell first, and in what order. Be ready for the dam to burst; if you tell one person, be sure you're ready for them to tell everyone else. And definitely, definitely, definitely, make contact with the atheist community, and put down some roots in it.

The good news?

The atheist community *loves* ex-clergy.

The chances are excellent that if you come out as an atheist, and come into the atheist community, you will be embraced with enthusiastically open arms.

Some clergypeople are reluctant to come to the atheist community when they realize they're atheists. That's especially true if they're coming out of a more conservative religion, one with values that go against those commonly held by atheists, or one that's actively hostile to atheism. When local Methodist pastor Teresa MacBain—now former pastor Teresa MacBain—made her dramatic "I'm an atheist" announcement at the 2012 American Atheists convention, she was overwhelmed with guilt for how she had treated atheists in the past. In fact, she opened her announcement with an apology. "First of all," she said, "I want to apologize to all of you. I was one of those crazy fundamentalists, right-wingers, haters. That's the only word I can use for it. I want to say that I'm sorry to each of you for knocking on your door—you know what I'm talking about—trying to weasel my way in so I could convince you how wrong you were and how right I was. I want to apologize for verbally abusing you from the pulpit; for using the pulpit as a bully pulpit to just... hate. I can't think of a better word for it: hating. I want to apologize to you for believing that you were godless, heathen, slimy, immoral, and drunken."[3]

But in fact, most of us are going to be fine with it. More than fine. Most of us are going to be super-excited about it, and will think that you are mega-awesome. Most atheists were, at one time, religious believers—especially in parts of the world where most people are believers, and most kids are brought up to believe. Most of us get how hard it often is to let go of religion, and to come out about it. And we get how hard it is for a clergyperson, especially, to take this step—to come to the conclusion of atheism at all, much less to say so in public. For the most part, atheists have a lot of respect for people who are willing to admit that they're wrong. We are a community largely made up of people who have had to admit we were wrong. We are, for the most part, a community that values honesty, and that prioritizes truth over what we want to be true. So most of us will have great respect for your passion for the truth, your integrity in letting go of a faith that must have been enormously important to you, and your courage in coming out about it.

And, frankly? Those of us who are actively opposed to religion, and are actively engaged in persuading people out of it? We think atheist clergy and ex-clergy are the cat's pajamas. When the people whose job it is to understand religion, the people who think about religion the hardest and care about it the most, are coming to the conclusion that it's bunk—that could cause the whole house of cards to collapse. At the very least, it's going to give a hard push to some of the cards at the house's foundation. Even if you're not interested in doing that yourself, your simple existence is helping those of us who are. The very reasons that your membership is likely going to be disappointed and pissed at you are the same reasons that a whole lot of atheists are going to embrace you—you put a serious dent in religious faith, simply by your very existence.

What's more, and very importantly: You almost certainly have skills that the atheist community needs. As a clergyperson, you probably have skills in public speaking, community organizing, counseling, media production, media management, publicity, fundraising, all of the above, and more. And depending on which religious community you're coming out of, you may be able to connect with people—individuals, communities, demographics—that organized atheism has traditionally not been reaching. We need that.

We won't always be able to offer you a job. Organized atheism is growing fast, but it's still not big enough—or financially solvent enough—to offer a job to every skilled person who wants to be a professional atheist. (And you may not want to be a professional atheist, anyway.) But we will help you in any way we can. We'll give you connections. We'll share our experience and our collective wisdom. We'll help you find job training. We'll help you network. We'll give you emotional support. We'll give you... well, community. And some of you will be able to find work in organized atheism, if that's what you want.

Did I mention The Clergy Project? I did? Well, I'm going to mention it again. This is your Number One source of emotional support, practical advice and assistance, and sympathetic ears who know what you're going through. The Clergy Project is a confidential online community for current or former religious leaders—including pastors, ministers, priests, nuns, monks, rabbis, imams, and theologians—who no longer believe in God or the supernatural. After a careful screening process to protect the anonymity of all the members, you can freely discuss the challenges you'll be facing in leaving ministry and establishing a new life. People in the Clergy Project give each other emotional and psychological support—help wrestling with ethical and philosophical issues that often come with becoming atheist, ideas on coming out as atheist to family and friends, and so on. But they can also give you practical advice and support. Members of the community share ideas on finding a way out of the ministry and looking for new careers. And if you're a newcomer to atheism, they can let you know about resources you may not be aware of. They can tell you far more about coming out as a clergyperson than I possibly could.

The Clergy Project isn't going to give you a specific set of directions for coming out as an atheist, any more than I am. Maybe even more for non-believing clergy than other atheists, coming out is a very personal decision that everyone has to make for themselves. No one at the Clergy Project can tell you how to do it. But they can talk you through making your own decisions, and give you some ideas of what you might be facing, based on the benefit of their own experience. And they can give you empathy and support that's much better informed than anything anyone else could give you.

Now, if you haven't completely left your religious beliefs, if you're still in the process of questioning or doubting, the Clergy Project aren't the ones to talk to. They're not in the business of talking you out of your faith, or even helping you make the decision about whether to leave your faith. They're really just there to support clergypeople who have already made that decision.

Recovering From Religion, on the other hand...

Did I mention Recovering From Religion? I did? Well, I'm going to mention them again. If you've only recently realized that you don't believe in God, Recovering From Religion is there for you. And if you're questioning your faith, Recovering From Religion is there for you, too. They're not in the business of talking you out of your faith, either—if you're looking for people to talk you out of your religion, go to the atheist blogosphere—but if you're having doubts about your religion and aren't sure what to do with those doubts or where to go with them, they can give you support in thinking things through for yourself.

And Recovering From Religion can be tremendously valuable to atheist newbies—all atheist newbies, not just clergypeople. Some atheist communities, especially online, will assume that the people there have been atheists for a while—so they can be pretty snarky, even harsh, about belief and believers, in a way that's not always welcoming to people who have just let go of their belief, or are still in the process of questioning it. For those folks, Recovering From Religion provides support: online, with in-person groups, and soon on a 24-hour phone hotline (as of this writing, volunteers for the hotline are being trained). They're made up of recovering Baptists, Mormons, Catholics, Hindus, Jehovah's Witnesses, Muslims, Lutherans, Pentecostals, Evangelicals, and many more. Like the Clergy Project, they provide emotional support, practical assistance, and advice based on experience. And like the Clergy Project, they can tell you way more about how to handle being newly atheist than I possibly could.

If you're in the clergy, chances are that coming out is going to be extra hard for you. But you don't have to do it alone. The atheist community is dying to help.

CHAPTER NINETEEN

— ✹ —

Theocracies (Overt and De Facto)

Step One: Overthrow theocracy.

Step Two: Follow the rest of the guidelines in this book.

I don't know what to tell you. I wish I did, but I don't. If you live in a part of the world where coming out as an atheist means you could be beaten or murdered, imprisoned or executed? I don't know what to tell you. I have a few ideas, as do other people—but I don't know any atheist in the world who would blame you for keeping your atheism to yourself.

It's certainly true that pushing back against the theocracy you live in is the only way it's ever going to be defeated. But that's very easy for me to say, from the safety of my very secular San Francisco. You have to take care of yourself. I'm sure I don't have to tell you this, but there are parts of the world where simply being an atheist is a crime—and where atheists have been arrested and imprisoned for it.[1] Recently. In Egypt in 2012, Alber Saber, the atheist activist and reported administrator of the Egyptian Atheists Facebook page, was attacked by a mob, arrested, attacked in prison, convicted, and sentenced to three years in prison, for the crime of blasphemy.[2] In Indonesia in 2012, atheist Alexander Aan was attacked by a mob, arrested, convicted, and sentenced to two and a half years in prison, for criticizing Islam on Facebook and saying he was an atheist.[3] In Tunisia in 2012, atheists Jabeur Mejri and Ghazi Beji were arrested and sentenced to seven and a half years in prison for posting cartoons of Muhammad on Facebook.[4] In 2013, the governments of 31 countries were found to openly incite hatred against atheists, or to systematically fail to prosecute violent crimes against atheists. In 12 of those countries, religious authorities can put atheists to death for the crime of leaving religion.[5] Fatwas are a real thing, of course; to give just one example, atheist and feminist writer and human rights activist Taslima Nasreen has had numerous Islamist groups call for her death, and she has had a price on her head since 1993, when the Council of Soldiers of Islam in Bangladesh offered a cash award of 50,000 Taka to anyone who would kill her.[6] She has had several more fatwas issued against her since then, in both Bangladesh and India.[7] To this day, she lives in exile.

And there are parts of the world where simply being an atheist and defying religion can result in your family beating you, personally imprisoning you, or worse—as atheist activist Amina discovered, when she posted a topless photo of herself with the slogan "my body belongs to me, and is not the source of anyone's honour" and "fuck your morals," and was kidnapped by her family, denied contact with friends and supportive organizations, beaten, taken to a psychiatrist, drugged, forced to read the Koran and taken to imams, and given an invasive "virginity test."[8]

Elsewhere in this book, I've advised atheists to build a safety net before they come out, as much as they can: to find an atheist community in case they lose their religious one, and to build some savings and get their resumes in order if coming out could mean losing their job.

For you, that safety net should probably include a plan to get out of the country. Make sure your passport is in order. Make contact with people in other countries. If you possibly can, acquire job skills that you can take with you anywhere. And of course, for you, the whole "be careful who you tell, as soon as you start telling people the dam could burst, don't tell anyone you don't profoundly trust unless you're willing for everyone to know" thing is a whole lot more important. It could be a matter of life or death.

"I lived in the middle east 23 years," says Coolred38, "and came out in that country though I kept it to just a few people. Not a safe thing to do for an apostate from Islam. I had no wish to antagonize anyone when the consequences could have been dire. I had my children to think about... as well as myself. The people I came out to were from there as well (muslim/arabs mostly)... but since being back in the states I don't hesitate to tell anyone and everyone." He goes on to say, "As many will know here, muslims can be dealt with harshly for apostating from Islam and so caution is necessary; however, I have found that most arab/muslims don't care as long as you keep it to yourself. Don't broadcast the fact that you have given up Islam as it is a shame based society. You shame yourself then you shame your whole family. It can be very dangerous if the wrong person/people find out so it's best to keep your status secret or between those you trust with your life."

That being said: It is possible for you to find other atheists, and even other atheists in your area. One of the most powerful things about the Internet is that it makes it possible for people to connect, communicate, and even organize, while maintaining a fair degree of secrecy. As al-Razi from the Council of Ex-Muslims of Britain told me, "Even though atheists in theocratic societies are lonely and oppressed, the Internet offers lots of possible solace. For the first time in history atheists can connect with other atheists from around the world, and at least discuss their conscience and experience despite difficult circumstances. This is a great comfort to individuals who feel lonely. Atheist communities can do more to be receptive to this, outreach to those dissenters and sceptics in difficult circumstances. To connect online can be to hold someone's hand, and that really is important, more important than it seems."

But for atheists living in theocracies, all the advice in this book about maintaining Internet privacy is even more crucial. At the same time, all the warnings in this book about how Internet privacy is never perfect—they're even more crucial as well. (Again: A thorough exploration of the ins and outs of cyber security is outside the scope of this book. And of course, the details of maintaining cyber security change on a regular basis. Make sure you're up to speed.)

It is the case that different theocracies have different levels of severity. The legal and social penalties for atheism do vary somewhat between different theocracies. There are even somewhat different degrees of theocracy. I don't usually think of India as theocratic, for instance, and in fact its government is officially secular. But as of this writing, Indian mythbuster and paranormal investigator Sanal Edamaruku has nevertheless been in exile for a year, and he faces arrest if he returns home—because he disproved a supposedly Catholic "miracle," and has been charged with the crime of blasphemy.[9]

And even in relatively free societies, there's an unfortunate reality of de facto theocracies—insular, intensely controlling religious cultures within the larger culture. Fundamentalist polygamist Mormon cults; large, overwhelmingly Muslim neighborhoods that are essentially run by Sharia law; large, overwhelmingly Orthodox Jewish neighborhoods that enforce strict Jewish codes; Jehovah's Witnesses. Even if the countries these communities live in are more or less secular and guarantee a fair degree of religious freedom, the communities can control people's lives almost as completely as an overt, official, government-entwined theocracy.

Corey A. Henderson was raised in Ontario, Canada, in a rural congregation of Jehovah's Witnesses—a sect that preaches the complete shunning of anyone who leaves the faith, commanding its members to cut off all contact with friends, parents, brothers, sisters, and even children who no longer believe. "There are few Christian denominations more conservative, fundamentalist or evangelical than the Jehovah's

Witnesses," he says. "Witnesses consider their church a theocracy that lives in secular countries (or communist, or Islamic) only temporarily until the 'end' comes. It is difficult to convey how absolutely families and elders control members in this faith, especially in the most fervent congregations. It doesn't matter that Canada is a free and (mostly) secular country. The faith is a theocracy."

For Corey, and for many Jehovah's Witnesses, coming out atheist and leaving the church didn't just mean angering his co-workers and making his mother cry. When he came out as atheist, he says, "I lost contact with my four younger siblings, my parents, and my large extended family. Most of the friends I grew up with have never spoken to me again. It's been 20 years. I had to start my life completely over from nothing."

So if you're an atheist in a theocracy—a de facto theocracy or an overt one—it's that much more important than it is for other atheists to prepare a safe place to land, as much as you possibly can. Before Corey came out, he says, "I worked in Toronto at the time, and I had secretly rented an apartment there in the days leading up to when I left... I planned it out and did it at a time of my choosing when I had a place to live, and enough money hidden to live on for a short time." And he was careful to keep his atheism private until he was ready to come out. "I wanted to be in control of which day the news broke," he says, "so I could be sure I had a place to live."

If you're in a de facto theocracy rather than an overt legal one, you'll probably have a somewhat easier time getting out. You won't have to travel physically as far; you can get help more easily from outside communities and even law enforcement if you need it; you won't need a passport to leave. Just plan carefully. And if you can, make contact with atheist communities, online or in the flesh or both, and put down roots in them before you leave.

Now, it is the case that there are probably more people around you who are sympathetic, or even nonbelievers themselves, than you're probably aware of. Speedwell, a corporate trainer for a multinational oilfield engineering firm, has a fascinating story to tell about this. "Interestingly," she says, "I 'came out' to a local as an atheist while on a business training trip to an Islamic country, with a cultural exhibit that includes traditional crafts and artifacts, and photos of the nomadic way of life before the state was founded (hilariously, many of the people in the photos are still living). One of the employees is the grandson of a prominent imam, he told me, and while I was visiting, he gave me a personal tour of the little exhibit. He asked me if I found it difficult to be an American businesswoman in the Middle East, and I admitted casually that it was not as uncomfortable as being nonreligious in such a religious country.

"He seemed impressed," she goes on, "and said a couple times that he thought thinking people in any religion or no religion got along better than did fundamentalist believers even within the same religion, something I've always felt to be true. We had a nice talk about the role of religion in culture, and I was struck by the beauty of the traditional muezzin call to prayer that was played at the exhibit at one point while I was there. But even though he was religious (he has to be to hold a post like that) he never once made me feel harassed or looked down upon for being an atheist."

And there are communities and organizations that can help you: the Council of Ex-Muslims of Britain, Ex-Muslims of North America, Jehovah's Witness Recovery, and more. It might also be worth touching base with activists and writers who are familiar with the kind of situation you're in. Taslima Nasreen, Maryam Namazie, Wafa Sultan, Vyckie Garrison (of the No Longer Quivering site for women leaving Quiverfull societies and families), John Sargeant and Vicky Simister (ex-Jehovah's Witnesses and part of the Apostasy Project)—read their blogs, check out their websites, and contact them if they make contact information available.

That is, if you feel reasonably secure that you can surf the Internet and send email, without compromising your safety.

So yeah. You're in a bind. The things you need to do to make your life better as an atheist in a theocracy—getting information, contacting other atheists, finding sympathizers, creating community, organizing—are the very things your theocracy is going to punish you for doing. That's pretty much how theocracy works. The overt kind, and the de facto kind.

So the main thing I would say is this.

You know how throughout this book, I keep saying, "Don't tell anyone unless you're ready to tell everyone"? That has a special meaning for you. If you plan to stay in your theocratic country, or in the de facto theocratic community in your secular country, keep the number of people you tell about your atheism to a bare minimum. If you're going to come out any more than that—if you're going to do online organizing with other atheists in your area, or even just start coming out to more people—have an exit strategy ready.

I'm not going to tell you not to organize. Organizing is how you're going to make things better. But unless you're willing to be a test case or a martyr, remember that for you, "being ready to tell everyone" means being ready to leave.

CHAPTER TWENTY

— ✦ —

Students: College, High School, and Earlier

Step One: Contact the Secular Student Alliance, CFI On Campus, and/or the national atheist student organization in your country (if there is one).

Step Two: Read *The Young Atheist's Survival Guide: Helping Secular Students Thrive*, by Hemant Mehta.

Step Three: Follow the rest of the guidelines in this book.

If you're an atheist student who's coming out or who wants to come out, you have an enormous set of advantages that other atheists don't. (At least, if you're an atheist student in a part of the world that isn't a crushing theocracy. If you are, see the chapter on theocracies.) Your peers are far more likely to be atheist-positive than any other demographic. Heck—your peers are far more likely to be atheists than any other demographic. (According to a 2013 Harris poll, 36% of Americans under age 35 don't believe in God[1]—a number that's going up rapidly,[2] and a trend that seems to be true around the world.[3]) If you're in the United States and you go to a public, government-run school—whether that's college, high school, grade school, whatever—you have a fair amount of legal protection and legal rights. (You do still have rights if you go to a private or religious school, by the way—you just don't have as many.) And you have a couple of seriously awesome organizations behind you, whose specific job it is to give you support and help you organize a supportive community with other atheist students.

You also have one big disadvantage that other atheists don't. If you're dependent on your parents (which many students are, although not all of them), then you're... well, dependent on your parents. So if your parents have a hard time with your atheism, it can have a profound and direct impact on your everyday life, in a way that isn't true for adults who have left the nest. If you're a high school student, or a college student living at home, your parents can make your life difficult in a wide assortment of ways: from berating and guilt-tripping you about your atheism, to dragging you to religious services and events (or trying to, anyway), to severely limiting your freedom. In some extreme cases, parents have even been known to cut off their atheist children entirely. That's rare, but it does happen.

And while you have lots of legal protection and legal rights, getting those rights enforced can be a hassle at best and a battle at worst.

Let's get to the good news first. And there is a lot of good news.

The main piece of good news is the same one I keep repeating throughout this book: For most people in your situation, coming out atheist turns out fine. It's true that if you're dependent on your parents, and they're seriously religious—or if you go to a school where the students and/or administration are seriously religious—coming out atheist can feel daunting. And you should listen to that: I don't want you ruining your life because Aunt Greta, Knower of All Things, said it would all come out in the wash. Listen to your instincts—and if those instincts are telling you to hold off until you graduate, do that.

But in writing this book, and in reading the coming out stories I collected for it, I was astonished at just how many atheists came out at a young age. Way more people than I'd expected came out in college, in high school, in junior high, in middle school, even in grade school. I think the youngest age someone reported coming out was six. And very few of these people said, "I came out, and my worst fears were realized." "I came out, and my fellow students started bullying and harassing me." "I came out, and my teachers or professors started picking on me." "I came out, and my school administration fought me tooth and nail on every piece of illegal promotion of religion I asked them to remove." "I came out, and my parents disowned me and threw me out of the house." That happens. I won't deny for a second that it happens. But it's not what usually happens.

It's not always sunshine and cupcakes. There can be fights, tension, alienation, guilt-tripping, pressure, and other unpleasant results. But the outcome is rarely horribly dire. And both the dire and the less-dire-but-still-no-fun stuff usually gets better with time.

Another piece of good news: You are part of the most secular generation in history. There are almost certainly lots of other atheist students at your school, even if you don't know it yet. You know how I keep telling people throughout this book that if they come out as atheists, there's a good chance that other atheists will start coming out of the woodwork? If you're a student, multiply that chance by at least two or three. (About 5[4]–15%[5] of Americans don't believe in God, depending on which poll you look at. For Americans under 35, that number jumps to 36%.[6]) And even your fellow students who aren't atheists are more likely to be familiar and comfortable with atheism than older folks. If for no other reason, they're more likely to live large parts of their lives on the Internet—and atheism is all over the Internet.

Yet another piece of good news: If you're in the United States, you have the Secular Student Alliance on your side. As of this writing, there are Secular Student Alliance affiliates at 376 schools—331 at colleges or universities, and 45 at high schools. And if you don't already have a Secular Student Alliance group at your school, it's really not that hard to start one. The SSA has tons of information, materials, resources (including financial resources), and advice: on how to start a group, maintain it, grow it, and keep it going after you've graduated.

And if you're pretty much anywhere in the world, you have CFI On Campus (the student branch of the Center for Inquiry) on your side. As of this writing, they have affiliates at 324 colleges and universities—including in Nigeria, South Africa, Brazil, Kenya, Nepal, Ghana, the United Kingdom, and Australia, as well as Canada and the United States, with 60 groups outside the United States—and they can also give you information and resources to help you with your group. (Lots of student groups belong to both organizations, by the way—that's a really good idea, it hooks you up with even more resources.) If you're in Australia, there's the Freethought University Alliance; if you're in the United Kingdom, there's the National Federation of Atheist, Humanist and Secularist Student Societies. There are almost certainly other countries with national organizations of atheist students that I don't know about. So if you do come out, and other atheists at your school start coming out too, you can probably organize. And "organize" can mean anything from just hanging out, to setting up fun social activities, to doing service projects and charitable work, to doing atheist visibility and activism, to organizing and hosting conferences (free student-run atheist conferences are popping up all over), to fighting your school administration if they're being jerks about promoting religion and discriminating against atheists.

Still another piece of good news: You have the larger atheist movement on your side. People in the atheist movement are thrilled at how powerful the student movement is, and at how fast it's growing. And most of us are dying to help. Many atheist conferences have inexpensive student rates for attendance. Many atheist organizations have inexpensive student rates for membership. Local non-student atheist groups are often eager to support student groups, and to partner with them on projects and events—partnerships that can benefit both sides. And at your school itself—depending on the school, of course—there may be atheist teachers or professors or other adults who'd be delighted to lend a hand to the student atheists on their campus.

In *The Young Atheist's Survival Guide*, Hemant Mehta—high school teacher, atheist blogger/activist/speaker, and former board member of the Secular Student Alliance—talks about how high school atheists have a much less difficult time now than they did in the past, even less than ten years ago. Comparing the 2004 story of Nicole Smalkowski with the 2011 story of Jessica Ahlquist—both of whom fought discrimination and bigotry from their school administrations—he says, "Both young women stood up for their atheism and dealt with social ostracism and threats as a result. But only one had a positive outcome. Why was that?... I would argue that there's one reason that towers above the rest: The difference was *almost entirely due* to the rise of a support system for young atheists that has only recently blossomed. Jessica Ahlquist is only one of the many beneficiaries of a revolution in the way Secular Americans support young atheists in this country—and that revolution wasn't quite ready to help Nicole Smalkowski in 2004."[7]

And one more piece of good news: Even if you are in a genuinely difficult place? Pretty much by their very nature, the difficulties you're in are temporary. You won't always be in school. You won't always be dependent on your parents. I know, I know; young people freaking hate it when older people tell them, "This is just a phase, you'll get over it." That's not my point at all; if you're having a hard time because of your atheism, I don't mean to minimize that even for a second. I get that it sucks, and it's not okay, and you have all my empathy. I'm not saying, "Yeah, yeah, this isn't going to last, quit making such a big deal about it." I'm saying, "Hang in there."

Let's talk about parents first. I've already said a lot about coming out to family. Look that chapter over again; a lot of the stories there are from atheists coming out to their families while they were in college, high school, or even younger, and a lot of the ideas there will probably be relevant to you. But there are a few more specific points that I want to make.

If you're under age, living in your parents' home, being financially supported by them, or are otherwise dependent on them, you may find yourself in a situation where they can essentially force you to keep enacting the rituals of their religion: praying at the dinner table, observing religious laws and customs, attending religious services, etc. (This can be an issue for lots of younger atheists, whether you're in school or not.) Even if they can't force you, they can lay on some serious pressure. Many of the biggest fights young atheists have with their parents revolve around going to church, temple, mosque, etc. (It's an interesting phenomenon, actually—when people openly state that they would rather have you lie and pretend to believe than be honest, it shows how essential social consent is to keeping religion propped up.) Lexie, an Australian university student who grew up in a religious community, tells of the enormous fight she had with her mother over whether she would go to church. "I did go to church that next morning," she says, "albeit yelling, screaming and basically being dragged out of the door (picture a teenager and mother behaving basically like a young mum and tantruming toddler)."

Lauren, who grew up in a predominantly German Lutheran area of upstate New York and came out to her Lutheran family and church at age 12, had a similar experience (minus the screaming tantrum). "I had become an atheist two years earlier," she says, "after failing to reconcile the old testament with the idea of an omni-everything god. At that time, I asked my mother to be excused from Sunday School because 'I didn't like it,' and was naturally refused. Even at that tender age I knew a shitstorm would follow any departure from orthodoxy, so I was too chicken to declare my atheism then. However, once I faced the prospect of having to declare a lie in front of the whole congregation, I couldn't stand the hypocrisy of my silence any more.

"First I told my mom (a believer but not much of a church goer) that I didn't want to be confirmed or go to Sunday School because I didn't believe in god. She was really pissed, and I basically got the 'my roof, my rules' routine. I think that my defiance plus dumping one more headache into her already busy schedule was what she reacted to—my immortal soul did not seem to be on her agenda. It was more 'shut up and go because I said so,' and not 'you're going straight to hell.'

"Next I told Pastor Luther Knauff after confirmation class that I didn't want to be confirmed because I didn't believe in god.

"Pastor: 'Everyone has doubts sometimes.'

"Me: 'I don't have doubts, I'm positive.'

"Pastor: 'Pray for faith.'

"Me: 'I can't get up there and say stuff I don't believe.'

"Pastor: 'Please stop disrupting class with your questions. This is a special time in everyone's life—don't ruin it.'

"The upshot was that mom forced me and Pastor Knauff acquiesced, so I had to go through with the confirmation ceremony. I did remain silent through the responses. This was quite a traumatic experience because two people who were supposed to be my moral guides knowingly tried to make me profess a lie, and I felt like the world's biggest hypocrite and coward for even appearing in the ritual."

Lauren adds, though, that "other than that, being an out atheist has proven fairly easy. Turns out there were a lot of other closeted atheists in the family."

Even if your parents don't try to force you into attending religious services, some atheists will voluntarily choose to do it—or give in to pressure to do it—in order to keep family peace. You have to decide for yourself whether you'd be okay with that, and whether you'd be okay with the consequences if you don't, and which will suck for you less. You'll have to make that decision based, among other things, on your own priorities and values—and on how severe the consequences of defiance are. Will your parents actually disown you if you don't go to church? Or will they just guilt-trip you to death?

If you decide to stand firm and not attend, it may be useful to frame it as an honesty issue. That won't always work; as Lauren discovered, and as I talked about in the chapter on family, some families see religion less as a serious spiritual devotion and more as a family ritual or duty, and they'll often want you to keep showing up for it even when you no longer believe. But if your family takes religion more seriously than that, it may help to make it clear that you take it seriously as well—too seriously to fake a faith you don't have. In either case, as I talked about in the family chapter, it may help to suggest other family togetherness activities: to give both yourself and your family a sense of continuity and connection, and to reassure all of you that your atheism doesn't mean you're disappearing.

And if you decide to go ahead and attend services, you may find it useful to see yourself as an "undercover anthropologist" or "undercover psychologist." That's the advice given by Richard Wade, a retired Marriage and Family Therapist living in California, who writes the "Ask Richard" advice column for the Friendly Atheist blog. Attending religious services when you don't believe is a very different experience from attending when you do. You can come at it from an outsider's perspective; it can give you insight into the phenomenon of religion, help you understand the motivations driving it, even sharpen your arguments against it. It's been demonstrated that atheists, on average, are better informed about religion than believers—in fact, we're better informed about specific religions than those religions' adherents.[8] That's very powerful; it arms us against the accusation that we're rejecting religion out of ignorance, and it makes us better debaters if we choose to debate. As Hemant Mehta told me, "If you have to go to church, it's helpful to use that time to 1) fact-check the pastor, 2) see if you can figure out what methods the pastor is using (rhetorically, psychologically) to win over the crowd, and 3) figure out the toughest questions to ask the pastor afterwards. Pretend it's a game—or training grounds for becoming a future activist!"

Deciding what order to tell people in, by the way, may be very helpful for you. Lots of atheist students have found it useful to tell their siblings and get their support before they tell their parents, and many have made careful decisions about whether to tell Mom or Dad first, depending on how they think they'll handle it. Just be prepared for the secret to get out. Siblings might let it slip, and if they're religious, they might even tell on purpose, out of concern for your non-existent immortal soul. And it's not reasonable to expect your parents to keep secrets from each other for very long.

Student atheists also have to wrestle with the question of whether to get into arguments about religion with their parents. That's true for most atheists; the question of debating religion with the people in our lives is a common one, and a big one. But the issues can get dialed up to eleven if you're financially dependent on the people you're arguing with, or if you're living under the same roof.

I go into this in a lot more detail in the chapter on family, as well as in the chapter on arguing about religion. With students, though, I think there's an additional dynamic. Your atheism, and your arguments for atheism, may be dismissed as just part of your youth: as teenage rebellion against authority, or as snot-nosed know-it-all-ism. It may take some time for your parents to take your atheism seriously, and accept that it isn't just a fad or a phase. That's pretty unfair—if for no other reason, it's common for people of all ages to change their religious affiliations and ideas, and in fact these often evolve throughout people's lives—but people may lay it on you anyway.

I'm not sure what to tell you about how to handle that. On the one hand, making your case for atheism, and explaining your reasons for rejecting religion, can make it clear that you've thought about the question sincerely, and aren't taking it lightly. On the other hand, like I said in the chapter on family, it can be tricky to draw the line between "explaining why you're an atheist" and "explaining why religion is bunk." And you may have decided that you don't want to argue with your parents about why religion is bunk. All I can say is that if you've decided to avoid debates about religion, but you do want to explain why you're an atheist so they understand that you're not just a snotty teenager trying to be outrageous—keep a very careful eye on the line between the two. Especially if you're living under the same roof, and can't really get away from each other, and arguments are going to create ongoing tension. (Also, like I keep saying, acceptance of your atheism may take time. So give it time.)

There are different issues here, by the way, for college students than for high school students or younger. For college students—especially if you're living away from home—your parents may already be feeling sadness and loss over you growing up and leaving. Your atheism may feel like part of that loss, or like salt in the wound. That's true to some extent for high school and younger students as well—but for you, the issues may have to do more with your parents' transition from seeing you as a child for whom they're responsible, to seeing you as an independent adult who's making their own decisions. In many religions, bringing up children in the faith is one of the most important duties of a parent. Your parents may have a hard time letting go of that role, and accepting that you're now enough of a free agent to decide about religion for yourself.

If your parents' issues seem more about learning to respect your autonomy: Show them in other ways that you're responsible, and that when you think for yourself and make your own decisions, you generally show good judgment. If their issues seem more empty-nesty: Work to reassure them that you aren't disappearing from their lives.

Finally—what if you think your parents are likely to seriously flip out? What if you think they really might cut off your tuition, severely limit your freedom for as long as you live with them, stop talking to you, kick you out of the house? What if they belong to a culty sect like

Jehovah's Witnesses, where cutting off apostates is actually required by the religion?

I hate to encourage you to be paranoid. But if you think your parents are likely to give you a genuinely horrible time about your atheism, to the point where they might actually cut you off or otherwise screw up your life, then don't tell anyone unless you're prepared to tell everyone. That includes siblings, friends, teachers and school administrators. And for the love of Loki, if you're looking up stuff about atheism on the Internet, clear your browser history. (The same is true, by the way, if you're thinking of coming out at your school, and you think bullying is a likely thing.) When Damon Fowler asked his high school administration, confidentially, to not have a school-sponsored prayer at his public high school graduation, the news of his atheism mysteriously got leaked—resulting in him being bullied by teachers as well as fellow students, and resulting in his parents kicking him out of his home and dumping his belongings on the lawn.[9] That is nineteen kinds of messed-up, and he didn't deserve that for a second. He deserved to have his school administration respect his privacy when he confided in them. He also deserved to have his school administration not violate the Constitution and force religion on him. He didn't get any of that. So be careful out there.

Now, in general, for a lot of atheists (including atheist students), telling some people and not others, being out in some circles and private in others, is a totally workable strategy. That's especially true if you don't live at home any more, and the circles of your life are unlikely to overlap. Lots of atheist students are completely out to other students, even becoming leaders in their atheist student groups, and never breathe a word to their parents—and that works out fine for them. I'm just saying: Dams do burst. Friends break trust; parents snoop. If the worst that's going to happen when word gets out is a big tearful scene and months of phone calls begging you to come back to Jesus and not break your mother's heart, that risk might be worth it. But if word getting out is going to seriously ruin your life—don't tell anyone unless you're prepared to tell everyone. Be careful, until you're on your own, and don't have to be so careful anymore.

So speaking of peers—let's talk about peers.

For college students coming out as atheist, peers are often not that much of an issue. After all, one of the best things about college is that you get to start over with an entirely new peer group, and make a whole new set of friends with values and interests and outlooks that your newly adult selves all share. And again—in case I haven't said this enough—unless you're going to a heavily religious college, chances are excellent that a third of your peers and potential friends are atheists or some other sort of nonbeliever. (And even if you are going to a heavily religious college, more of your fellow students are atheists than you might think.)

Joshua Brose had been an intensely devout Christian, deeply involved in youth ministry and planning to stay in the ministry. "At Campus Atheists Skeptics and Humanists (A.k.a. CASH)," he says on the Coming Out Godless Project website, "I thrived. First—they answered all my questions until I was satisfied with the answers. Second—they gave me a place where I could meet more people like me. Third—they knew how to party. I began to see what a life free from religion was like. A life without Christianity was still full, happy, and virtuous—but it wasn't only good, it was better. Atheism doesn't really seem to offer anything—the word itself is only concerned with something that doesn't exist. However, I soon discovered that Atheism does actually have something to offer. It offers freedom from religious guilt. An Atheist doesn't have to worry about God knowing their every thought. An Atheist doesn't have to consult the bible to make sure they are following arbitrary sexual norms. An Atheist doesn't have to take things on authority—instead they can freely use evidence to discover the truth about our universe."

Lots of college and university students have similar stories about their atheist groups. David A. Bishop, president of the Secular Student Alliance at Florida Tech (Florida Institute of Technology), says, "This group has helped so many people, myself included, find a group of people where they feel comfortable talking about our non-theistic view points." Carol, of the Society of Freethinkers at University of California Merced, says of her group, "This is a wonderful opportunity for students trying to make a difference in their worlds." Stephanie Parker, president of the New Mexico State Secular Student Alliance at New Mexico State University, says, "Our campus has, if I recall, over 30 religious groups and as of now only two secular groups. I wasn't sure what to expect from it but so far after our rocky start, we are on a roll."[10]

And Flora, who realized she was an atheist when she was 24 and was about to start graduate school, says that her on-campus community didn't just make her life better—they specifically helped her come out. "There was a campus atheist group that I joined," she says, "and one of the topics that we often discussed was whether or not we had told people that we were atheists. Being involved in the group and participating in functions made it pretty easy for me to come out to strangers and acquaintances."

I think this may be one of the reasons the student atheist movement is as powerful, as vibrant, and as fast-growing as it is. At least in the United States, college students are among the few demographics who can come out as atheist with a fair degree of confidence that they'll get plenty of social support. In addition, most colleges and universities have some sort of diversity policy—so openly atheist students and student groups typically have a fair degree of official protection, and even official support. (If you have an atheist student group, chances are good that you'll be able to get funding for it from your school.)

It's not that atheism is never an issue at college. Religious life can be a big deal on campuses, especially in more conservative regions, and religion can be totally in your face. But finding atheist and atheist-friendly peers at college should be as easy as falling off a log. See if there's a Secular Student Alliance or a CFI On Campus group at your school. If there's not, see what you need to do to start one. Or just wear an atheist T-shirt. Your peers should start coming out of the woodwork.

The exception, of course, is religious schools, or schools in heavily religious countries. (For the latter, see the chapter on theocracies.) Even there, chances are good that many of your fellow students are atheists—but if coming out means risking expulsion, being outed to parents, or worse, it'll be a lot harder to find them. It isn't impossible, though. The online world makes it possible to privately connect with other atheists, and organize groups with them. Just be careful. (See the chapter on the Internet for more on cyber privacy.)

If you're really finding the situation at your school intolerable, you might look into transferring—or even just getting the hell out, if your safety or mental health or basic well-being is being endangered by where you are. Safron, who was raised Mormon by very religious parents (including a father who she describes as a fanatic), attended the intensely Mormon Brigham Young University for two years. "I was manipulated by my dad," she says, "and too young or naive to realize I had other options." Eventually she transferred to another school, "one where no one assumed I was Mormon and most people just didn't talk about religion. If it ever came up, I told people I was not religious and did not volunteer my Mormon past. It was very liberating for me to not have to confront religion and religious culture every day." And if you don't want to transfer or can't, remember: School is not forever. Hang in there.

Even if you're attending a religious school, you may still be able to join an atheist group. As Hemant Mehta pointed out to me, "Even religious schools (certainly many religious colleges) now have atheist groups, even if they're underground, as is the case at Brigham Young University. A lot of religious colleges that are Religious In Name Only (RINO?) like DePaul and Loyola in Chicago—Catholic-affiliated, but not *really*—have LGBT and atheist groups that get the same rights as other groups. So there's hope!"

High school is somewhat different. Compared to college or university students, high school students don't have as much independence, or as many rights. High school culture also has more emphasis on conformity, whereas college culture is usually more supportive and rewarding of individuality. Bullying is more common in high schools (although it does happen in college as well). And while you commonly have at least some choice about where you go to college, most high school students are pretty much stuck where they are. (Ditto all of that for junior high, middle school, and grade school.)

Marnie came out in middle school when she started refusing to say the Pledge of Allegiance. "Sometimes classmates would press me," she says, "and I'd explain that I don't believe in god and I don't believe in blindly repeating a promise of loyalty. I was sometimes called a communist and/or satanist, which both seemed like odd insults but I was a painfully unpopular individual already and standing my ground neither lost me nor gained me any friends so I don't recall being particularly bothered either way, which made the taunting pretty short lived. In other words, I gave a lot more f**ks about what I believed than I did in what others thought of me, which made the process largely painless." And Will tells a story of coming out at age nine in Terre Haute, Indiana. "One of these other kids brought the 'G' word up," he says. "I remember chuckling and saying 'Why do you believe that? There is no such thing as God.' They reflexively recoiled and looked at me like I was carrying the Bubonic plague. They even seemed to withdraw from me physically and decided to not play in the same general area with me… At that point I began to realize that this was a taboo position that I was unknowingly staking out."

Finding other atheist students, of course, can be hugely helpful. High school culture may make that more difficult than it is for college students, but lots of high school students are doing it—both informally and in organized groups. As of this writing, the Secular Student Alliance has 45 high school affiliates, and that number just keeps going up. These can make a big difference in your experience as a high school atheist. William Epperson, president of the Socrates Society of Hudson at Hudson High School, said to the Secular Student Alliance about his secular group, "It's made our school a little more reasonable and more of a safe zone for skepticism and rationality." And just so you know: If you attend a public school in the United States, and your school allows other extra-curricular student groups, they are legally required to allow atheist groups as well. (Talk to the SSA to learn more about your right to organize.)

Hemant Mehta agrees. In *The Young Atheist's Survival Guide*, he says, "Having these groups for atheists can be the difference between being accepted and feeling isolated, between having a safe venue to discuss your religious doubts and having to keep them suppressed. In schools where being an atheist automatically puts you at a disadvantage, it is vital to have a community of like-minded students who can prove the stigmas wrong and educate the student body on why atheists, too, can be good, kind, moral people."[11]

And if a secular group at your school isn't an option, you still may be able to find support networks. As middle-school counselor and Grief Beyond Belief founder Rebecca Hensler told me, "If there is no club or student organization devoted to secularism at the student's school and they aren't up for starting one, they may still find a safe refuge in a Gay Straight Alliance, Diversity Club or Ally Club. It isn't a guarantee that kids and educators who are LGBTQ or support LGBTQ students will also support atheist students, but the odds are better than in the general population, particularly in conservative regions of the U.S."

Depending on your personality—and on your school culture—a "Why should I care what you think of me?" attitude can be a powerful shield against hostility. Ostracizing atheists is unacceptable and messed-up—but it has less power if you make it clear that you don't want their society in the first place. Liz H. came out as both bisexual and atheist in her suburban Massachusetts high school. "[I] had made it clear," she says, "that I had no interest in the popularity contests you get in high school. I hung out with the people I found interesting, and the 'popular' crowd apparently actually feared me once they figured out they didn't have any power over me. Shouting gay slurs at me was ineffective when my response is 'and?'; telling me I was going to hell got old when I laughed them off with 'I think you missed the part where I don't believe in your fiery doom' (fiery doom said with spooky fingers and a dramatic eye-pop). Mostly it amounted to this: I had been hated in middle school for no discernible reason beyond being new and intelligent. When I changed schools in high school, I came in with the attitude that what mattered was that I was myself, and people who didn't like it could go fuck themselves. So the atheist thing was just one small piece of me."

But some students will flourish better if they treat their peers as... well, as their peers. They do well with a more affable, good-natured approach, extending respect and expecting it in return, and not treating religious disagreements as any different from any other standard school squabbles. Jont Musiteur, who came out at a Catholic boarding school, says, "It began in earnest as telling other students in confidence. I didn't think it would be that big of a thing. Others around me had come out. Responses were varied, but nothing spectacular. Some were good with it, some joined in a debate, sometimes it turned into trading insults the way internet debates go (You're stupid! vs. You're evil!). It also led to some really interesting philosophical discussions... One or two of the other students thought I was trying to be special or controversial. Well, people do at that age, and maybe there was an element of that in my coming out if I'm honest. I had no seriously bad direct reactions from it on telling people, but word got around—well, I wasn't making a secret out of it." He adds, "Most people I came out to directly were fine with it. I got called 'atheist' (as an 'insult'), 'heathen' and similar, but not in actual animosity as far as I could make out."

And conversations about religion, even arguments and debates, don't have to be hostile; they can be friendly and even productive. James was raised attending a variety of churches and Sunday schools; he tried at first to believe, but was identifying as an atheist as early as third grade. When he came out in high school in 1986, he says, "I was sitting with my friends at high school before classes. We had formed our own clique. It was a 50/50 mix of boys and girls, juniors and seniors. Our group consisted of one female Pakistani, one female Indian (India), two/three female Caucasians, four male Caucasians, one male Indian (India). The conversations ranged anywhere and everywhere, seeking opinions, validation or just discussing world events. On this particular day, the topic of religion came up; those around the table matter-of-factly volunteered their religion background, ranging from Hindu, Islamic, Presbyterian, Methodist, Episcopalian, Catholic to finally me, an atheist. This is when the table went into a stunned silence of sorts followed by a rapid fire Q&A of the soulless one. The concept of atheism was totally alien and here was a prime specimen in front of them, hiding in plain sight."

But, he goes on to say, "None of the questions were antagonistic although deeply probing, looking for a hint of agnostic or doubt. We were all pretty tight as friends, been to each other's houses, met everyone's family, did social events outside of school, so they already knew my character. Now, there were some moments of discomfort while this was all digested and some of them had to reconfigure their viewpoints of me. This did not last long as I did not change any of my mannerisms or challenge their faiths nor proselytize my own worldview. I went on being me. It lasted about a week, with the occasional clarification question but it settled down to being just another adjective when thinking of me."

Now, he, says, "after 25 years, having reconnected through various social media, we are still friends. I am glad I was surrounded by my friends who Q&A my views as it helped solidify my position without being adversarial."

Bullying of atheist students can and does happen, though—both verbal and physical. If you've been following news stories about high school atheists—such as Jessica Ahlquist or Damon Fowler—then you'll be depressingly unsurprised by stories of bullying, threats of violence and rape and even death, teachers joining in with public humiliation, and administrations being unresponsive or even complicit.

Now, it is the case that these very public news stories haven't just been about atheist students coming out of the closet, or even coming out of the closet and organizing groups. The horror stories have mostly been about atheist students pushing back against some school policy or tradition, and drawing public attention to it: Jessica Ahlquist fighting to get a prayer banner taken down from her public high school auditorium,[12] Damon Fowler fighting to stop a school prayer at his public high school graduation.[13] Which, of course, they absolutely had every right to do, without being bullied or threatened. It's also worth remembering that these news stories have been... well, the stories that made the news. Speaking from years of experience as a writer and reporter, I can tell you that "Atheist Student Comes Out, Gets Death Threats" makes a great headline. "Atheist Student Comes Out, Gets Glared At"—not so much. "Atheist Student Comes Out, Gets Pretty Much Accepted"— even less. These horror stories are important, they're worth reporting, but that doesn't make them universal.

But anti-atheist bullying isn't just limited to high school activists demanding their constitutional rights and getting in the news. Kate Restivo, a lifelong atheist with non-believing parents, came out in seventh grade, in a conversation about different religions during art class. Her school was multi-cultural, with many denominations of Christian, Muslim, Hindu, Buddhist, and more, and while some students' reactions to her atheism were more guarded than they were to other religions, with some people seeming offended, she didn't think much of it. "The people who reacted negatively were acquaintances more than friends," she says, "and everything seemed fine after class.

"The next day after school, I was waiting for my Mom to pick me up, and another student approached me, yelling. It's worth noting that he was a pretty big male, and I was a tiny, scrawny girl who was still four years away from puberty. I recognized him, but he wasn't in my class so I didn't know who he was. He started pushing me around until I fell to the ground, and then stood over me, swearing loudly, yelling some stuff about Jesus and Christianity. He left to meet his friends, and I tearfully continued waiting for my ride. The next day, the same guy pushed me down again until another student came over and dragged him away—that was the last time. I wasn't hurt at all, but I was seriously shaken. What I gathered from his yelling was that word got around about that discussion from art class, and he was personally offended by something I had said about Christianity. I scoured my brain, trying to think if I had said anything offensive about religion, but my friends assured me that I hadn't—I was just expressing my beliefs, as everyone else did. I think there was some broken-telephone gossip and it culminated in someone who professed to love Jesus deciding that I needed to have that knowledge beaten into me."

Unsurprisingly, the experience made her more cautious about coming out to her fellow students. "Needless to say," she says, "I didn't discuss my beliefs as openly after that, outside of my immediate group of friends... Throughout the rest of middle school and high school, I never actively hid my atheism, but I never offered it."

A complete exploration of school bullying, and what both adults and students can do to prevent it, and how people can respond when it happens, is beyond the scope of this book. Some organizations that are working on this issue include Public Justice, the Bullying Prevention Center, the International Bullying Prevention Association,

Bullying UK, Schools Anti Bullying Web Gateway, Bully Police, and Stopbullying.gov. They can give you much more detailed and informed advice than I can. The main thing I want to say, about anti-atheist bullying specifically, is this:

More and more schools are aware of bullying, and are responding to it. And if you're being bullied at your school because of your atheism, you have every right to have it taken every bit as seriously as any other form of bullying. But anti-atheist bullying may not be on your school's radar.

So get it on their radar. Get your school informed. And get some help doing it. Contact the Secular Student Alliance. CFI On Campus. The Freedom From Religion Foundation. The anti-bullying organizations listed above. When your school gets deluged with letters from lawyers saying, "Yes, you damn well have to take anti-atheist bullying just as seriously as any other type, you'd better deal with this pronto," you'll have a lot more power than if you try to deal with it alone.

Which brings me to the last section of this chapter: dealing with teachers, counselors, principals, school administrations, school boards, and other authority figures at schools.

Like parents and peers, school authorities vary wildly: from awesome human beings who love their work and want the absolute best for their students, to total raging jerkwads or apathetic automatons, and everything in between. They're probably not as emotionally important to you as your parents or your peers (although some students do have close relationships with some teachers or counselors). But they can definitely have an effect on your life as an atheist.

The reality is that some school authorities will be supportive of atheist students, and some will be openly hostile, and a lot will be in between. And I can't help you predict which you'll get. But here are a few things to keep in mind. School administrators often are more concerned about keeping peace and order than they are about fairness.

What's more, even if they are sympathetic, as teachers or counselors may well be, they may not want to battle their bosses or colleagues over the rights of their atheist students. And of course, they may have their own religious prejudices affecting how they treat you. Jont Musiteur had mostly good experiences with fellow students when he came out atheist at his Catholic boarding school. But when he told his religious education teacher, he says, "he reacted with 'You'll live a life of sorrow and perdition.' I still don't know how to place that answer, whether it was a snap off-the-cuff retort, attempted banter that was unintentionally heavy-handed (he was known for that) or a serious threat." And when his school administration found out, he says, "I had to fight for everything—absolutely no privileges (even privileges just for being a senior student). I don't know whether that was only due to coming out as an atheist, or just generally being an outcast, and how much one was due to the other, it was all a blended smoosh. Anyway I was one too many, a nuisance, and they let me know it."

And in *The Young Atheist's Survival Guide*, Hemant Mehta tells the story of high school atheist Micah White, who was told that his atheist group couldn't announce their meetings over the public address system or put up signs to advertise. When Micah objected, his vice-principal Bill Chittle told him, "Stop worrying so much about the law and worry about what Grand Blanc High School allows." ("Months later," Mehta says, "the principal admitted that American law did, in fact, apply to the Michigan school."[14])

This isn't always how administrators respond, though. In *The Young Atheist's Survival Guide*, Mehta also tells of one of his blog readers, Andrew, who spoke to an assistant principal about a substitute teacher who had been preaching the gospel in his public high school band class. "I gave her a quick rundown of the situation," Andrew says. "Her eyes widened when she heard that he was preaching and she said, 'That's not right. I'll take care of this,' and marched out of the office and down to the band room. I went to school in a small town in Indiana where religion is generally considered as American as baseball and apple pie, but the assistant principal knew what the law was and reacted as soon as I let her know what was going on with a minimum [amount] of fuss."[15]

One specific bit of practical advice about school authorities: Don't ambush them. If you go to a school where religion is a big part of the culture (a religious school or otherwise), and you think your fellow students are likely to give you a hard time about your atheism, talk with your school counselor first. If you're planning to form an atheist student group, talk with your school administration ahead of time. (Andy Cheadle-Ford, High School Specialist at the Secular Student Alliance, told me about an atheist group being denied the right to form—because they hung flyers and organized a meeting before they were allowed to.) If you have an issue with your school illegally promoting religion, talk with administrators privately before you alert the media. And as Mehta says in *The Young Atheist's Survival Guide*, "Many students get to know their teachers and counselors well over the course of their high school careers—but they don't make an effort to get to know their administrators. That outreach, from both sides, could do wonders."[16]

School authorities can seem like they wield a ridiculous amount of arbitrary control over your life. And there's truth to that. But it's also the case that, in the United States and in much of the rest of the world, there are clear, firm rules about how students are supposed to be treated. Religious and other private schools have more leeway than government/public schools, but they have rules and laws they're supposed to follow, too. If you're having serious problems as an out atheist in school—not just bullying, but public school teachers using class time to proselytize, or religious students being given preferential treatment, or outside religious programs being brought in under the guise of education, or the administration blocking you from organizing an atheist group—you have recourse.

You may or may not want a fight. You get to decide that. If you don't have a fight in you, if you decide to just hang in there until you're done, that is totally reasonable, and totally your right. You know your personality, and your situation, better than I do. But if you are facing actions by your school that violate your rights, and you do decide to push back, you have help. Contact the Secular Student Alliance. CFI On Campus. The Freedom From Religion Foundation. The ACLU. As Mehta says in *The Young Atheist's Survival Guide*, "When students are aware that groups like the Secular Student Alliance and the Freedom From Religion Foundation specialize in dealing with these issues... the controversies usually come to an abrupt end. All it takes is an email informing the national atheist groups what's happening in your school and their staffs will handle it from there."[17] And if you want publicity for your case, it should be no problem to find atheist bloggers and other writers who'll help shine a spotlight on what you're dealing with.

You have help. Pretty much the entire atheist movement has your back. As Secular Student Alliance Director of Campus Organizing Lyz Liddell says: Students are the future of this movement—but students are also the present of this movement. We're dying to see what you're going to do with it.

CHAPTER TWENTY-ONE

Parents

Step One: Read *Parenting Beyond Belief: On Raising Ethical, Caring Kids Without Religion* (Dale McGowan, editor), and *Raising Freethinkers: A Practical Guide for Parenting Beyond Belief* (Dale McGowan, Molleen Matsumura, Amanda Metskas and Jan Devor).
Step Two: Find a secular parenting support group in your area—or start one.
Step Three: Look up Camp Quest.
Step Four: Follow the rest of the guidelines in this book.

If you're a parent, it may be tempting to stay in the closet to try to protect your children. Especially if you live in a part of the world that's dominated by religion, and where atheists face bigotry or even open hostility. If you're a parent, of course you'd want to protect your kids from that.

But if you're a parent, you probably also want to give your children a role model of pride, confidence, ethics, and honesty. You might also want to participate in atheist communities and bring your kids up in them—which will be much harder to do if you're in the closet. You'll almost certainly want to get support from atheist parenting groups if you possibly can—which, again, is harder to do if you're in the closet. And I'm guessing you don't want to teach your kids that atheism is something to be ashamed of. Your kids may grow up to be atheists themselves; chances are good that they will. If they do, you want them to feel comfortable, natural, and proud about their atheism. And you don't want them to feel like they're alone. Coming out atheist may feel like you're exposing them to ugliness—but you're actually strengthening them against it.

In *Raising Freethinkers*, Dale McGowan has this to say:

"Q: **Why is it so important for nonreligious parents to "come out"? Won't my child benefit from a lower profile?**

"A: One of our main goals as parents should be the creation of a saner world for our kids. One of the best ways nonreligious parents can do this is by working toward a world in which religious disbelief is no big deal. That's the goal, of course—not to dominate the culture, not to wipe religion off the map, but to simply make religious disbelief no big deal.

"We can learn a great deal from the progressive movements that have preceded us. Racism becomes difficult to support once you know and love someone of a different race. Homophobia falls apart when you learn that your neighbor or your child is gay. The same is true for religious disbelief. Religious people are currently surrounded by closeted nonbelievers. This makes it possible for them to retain a caricature of the nonreligious as someone 'out there,' far away, wild-eyed and repugnant, alien and threatening. When instead they learn that sweet, normal cousin Susan doesn't believe in God, a powerful shift must take place to accommodate the new information.

"Many nonreligious people think the shift will downgrade them in the eyes of the other person. After talking to literally hundreds of nonbelievers about their 'coming out' experiences, I am happy to report that it generally works in reverse: instead of downgrading the friend or relative, most religious people will upgrade, however slightly, their overall opinion of the nonreligious. Their caricature becomes less supportable when a face both known and loved is placed on it.

"If every nonreligious person were to reveal her beliefs to those around her, gently and with a smile, the predominant cultural attitude toward religious disbelief would be profoundly altered overnight. Fear and mistrust would not change to instant approval by any means, but the simplistically-drawn image of the nonreligious would necessarily become more complex, more nuanced, more accurate. It almost always goes better than you think it will."[1]

For some atheist parents, being a parent is actually a big part of what drives them to be more out. Naomi, whose family are conservative Southern Baptists, says, "I could have gone my whole life riding that ambiguous fence, but I am a mother. I had to eventually take a stand with my identity... I also want my daughter and son to have confidence and a strong identity within our larger religious family, as freethinkers."

Some parents are reluctant to come out to their families—to their own parents and siblings and cousins and so on—for fear that it will poison their families' relationship with their children. But it can actually work the other way. Not being clear about your atheism can make it harder to enforce boundaries about what behavior you will and won't tolerate towards your children. Denise grew up Christian, and lives in a place that she calls "entrenched deeply in religious culture." But despite that, she says, "Over time, I've become much more confident about who I am and how I identify." And she says that her experience with how her mother dealt with her kids was the object lesson she needed about why coming out confidently was so important. "With my mother," she says, "she has been adamant that I'm 'not REALLY' an atheist—that I'm more like the prodigal child, that if she just prays long and hard enough, I'll return to the fold. If it were just ME that she pressed on, I would just ignore her. However, her push continues with my two older children (and I have no doubt that she will start with the youngest when he gets older). She has no sense of boundaries, regarding them. She faults me for not teaching them about heaven and hell."

Of course, you know your circumstances better than I do. You know better than I do whether your open atheism will expose your kids to real hatred, harassment, bullying, or ostracism—or whether the response will probably be more moderate. And you have to do your own cost/benefit analysis about that. Omaar Khayaam is an ex-Muslim living in Bradford—a city in northern England with a large Muslim minority. "What makes it a little bit more tricky for someone from my ethnic background," he says, "is that religion is tied up with culture and is part of your identity. Although I don't live in a theocracy, I might as well! I think things would have been different if I was single. I could very easily pack my bags and move. But my wife and kids' reputation is more important to me than my open atheism. I guess the option to move out of the city is open to me. But I'll cross that bridge once my kids are adults."

That can be a hard decision. And if the religious environment you're in is truly horrible, it's not unreasonable to stay more in the closet. But I'll say the same thing I've been saying again and again in this book: Most of the time, this turns out okay. Re-read the chapters on coming out atheist to family, to friends, at work. It usually turns out fine. "Fine" can vary from "sucked a lot but got better eventually," to "somewhat difficult but not as bad as I thought," to "really not that big a deal," to, "eighty zillion atheists I never knew about suddenly came out, too." But horribly dire outcomes are fairly rare. They happen, and I won't dismiss that. But they're not what usually happens.

And you do have resources available. Atheist parenting groups are popping up all over. Lots of atheist communities that don't specifically have parenting groups are still very family-friendly, and many of their events are welcoming to families with kids. There's also Camp Quest, the summer camp for children of secular families—so even if you live in a place where there aren't a lot of resources for atheists with children, for one week a year your kids can be surrounded and supported by people who accept and celebrate atheism. (Camp Quest is mostly based in the United States, but as of this writing they have two overseas part-ners—one in Switzerland, and one in the United Kingdom.) There's a useful website and online forum, Atheist Parents at atheistparents.org, that can point you to resources and give you support. There's a great parenting blog on the Skepchicks network, Grounded Parents, loaded with information, ideas, perspectives, empathy, and humor. And defi-nitely check out the excellent books *Parenting Beyond Belief* and *Raising Freethinkers*. They have given enormous help to thousands of parents before you. If you're an atheist parent who's coming out of the closet, the best thing you can do is to find these resources, and take advantage of as many as you can.

All of this is assuming that you and your spouse or partner are both atheists (or in the case of poly relationships, that you're all atheists)—or that if you're not, you're okay with your religious differences. But if you have a contentious relationship with your partner or spouse—or your ex-partner or ex-spouse—there unfortunately is a real possibility that they might use your atheism as a weapon in battles over your kids. There have even been cases where judges have explicitly cited one par-ent's atheism as reason to deny them custody.[2] And we have no way of knowing how many other judges have let this color their decisions, without saying so in the open. Timid Atheist has privately told a few friends and family members about her atheism. But, she says, "I am not out publicly due to my fear of my ex using it against me for custody... Once my daughter is 18 and a legal adult, I'll add my real name to this online tag and continue onward. Until then, I simply don't trust her father to not use this against me in some way."

Denise echoes this as well. The first person she came out to was her ex-husband. "At the time," she says, "the ex acted as though he didn't really care one way or the other, since he was not actively religious—I would (even still) classify him as more agnostic than anything. However, he came from a semi-religious upbringing, and I should have antici-pated a few things that happened down the road... The ex attempted to use my status as an atheist against me in court, in an attempt to obtain custody of our children. He lost—but it had nothing to do with religion or lack thereof."

We don't really know how often this happens. It doesn't seem to be the norm, but it probably happens more than we hear about. And again, we have no way of knowing how often atheism and religion affect custody decisions without it ever being stated openly. If you think this is a real possibility—if you think your ex-spouse or ex-partner is likely to pull this on you, and you live in a part of the world where judges arc likely to be biased against atheists—it may be wise to wait to come out until custody is settled.

Of course, if you're an atheist with kids, you don't just have to decide about coming out to your neighbors and family and workplace and community. You have to decide about coming out—or being out—to your kids. And you have to decide how to talk with your kids about religion: about beliefs that other people have, and about their own beliefs or lack thereof.

LD from Queensland, Australia says, "Even though my girls' father is a non-believer, and I, not wanting to be a hypocrite, had quit participating in Catholicism after the oldest of our three had made her First Communion, I was still nervous about actually sharing my thoughts with them. I broached it casually one afternoon, saying as I flipped through a Watchtower, that I was sorry, after a year studying the bible intensely with our dear Jehovah Witness friend (while simultaneously reading Dawkins, Hitchens, and The Counter-Creationism Handbook), it just made more sense that there was not One True Religion, more likely they were all false and I supposed I must be an atheist though they were free to believe or not believe whatever they wanted. The oldest (16) and the youngest (8) said they thought the same way as I did but they didn't want to hurt our friend's feelings. My 13 year old replied, 'Jeez, it took you guys long enough! I always just believed in science.' We kept our non-belief quiet so as not to offend, but still participated in friendly debates." She goes on to say, "We have extended family members, fundamentalist Christians (some who attended Liberty U [the evangelical Christian university founded by Jerry Falwell]), and several times the kids have entered into conversations where I have had to kick them under the table or drag my finger slowly across my neck. The extended family is aware of my atheism and liberal social leanings via my Facebook posts. We have a silent truce."

One of the biggest questions facing atheist parents is how to talk with their children about religion: not just their own lack of religious beliefs, but the topic of religion in general. Do they try to teach their kids to be atheists? Let them make up their own minds? Support them in making up their own minds, but teach them about critical thinking and skepticism, and talk about their own reasons for rejecting religion? Do they talk about mainstream religions differently from other unfounded myths, or do they treat them all pretty much the same? Lots of atheists want to let their kids decide about religion for themselves, and that's understandable, especially if they had religion foisted on them in their own childhood. That's what my own parents did. And I understand why. But I do think they made a mistake; they never really talked with me and my brother about why they were nonbelievers, or about the thought processes that led them to reject religion. We hardly discussed religion at all. So when I went to college and got exposed to New Age spirituality, I wasn't armed against it. I picked up a whole passel of unsubstantiated beliefs: in Tarot cards, astrology, reincarnation, lots of stupid woo crap. It took years to shed those beliefs, and shedding them was somewhat traumatic. I think it's great that our parents wanted to let us make up our own minds—but I wish they'd given us better tools for doing so. That's a tricky balance, though, and you'll have to find your own place on that spectrum where you're comfortable.

As your children get older, you'll have to accept that they may make different decisions about being out than you do. (Assuming they're atheists themselves, of course.) If you've decided to be discreet with your parents, they may decide to be open. If you've decided to be out but not to argue about religion, they may decide to be more confrontational. At some point, you'll have to decide when your parental rights and responsibilities to make decisions for the whole family stop, and when your children's rights to make their own decisions start. You might want to stay fairly private with your neighbors about your atheism—but your kids may chafe at this if they feel like it's dishonest. You might want your relationship with your parents to be fairly conflict-free about religion—but your kids have their own relationship with their grandparents, and at some point they get to base that on their own values, not on yours. As your kids get older, your conversations about this will have to change from "parental decider" to "people on more equal footing, negotiating each other's rights to autonomy and privacy."

In addition, if you don't want to be out about your atheism to the general public, you'll have to decide about asking your kids to keep the secret. Some parents are fine telling their kids (when they're old enough to understand, of course) that there are some things they don't discuss outside the family. (Parents and kids have been having these conversations for decades about things other than atheism, of course. Smoking marijuana is the classic example, and when my own father was organizing a union at his workplace, I had to keep it a secret until the union was successful.) If you tell your kids about your atheism and ask them to keep it secret, that can strengthen the bond between you—but it also puts a burden of secrecy on them that may be too much.

On the other hand, if you don't tell your kids about your atheism, they won't have to worry about keeping a big secret that might hurt the family if it gets out. But they may pick up on the fact that you're keeping something important from them, which can put a strain between you. Secrecy with your kids will also make it harder to talk with them clearly about religion—talks that would help them better understand religion, and help them make up their own minds about it. Of course, being out in general makes that decision unnecessary. But if that's really not best for you, you'll have to decide whether you're going to ask your kids to keep your atheism a secret, or just keep it secret from them.

That can be a tough decision. When you're making it, though, there's something important to remember: Your kids may be having doubts and questions about religion themselves. They may already be nonbelievers. And if they are, they may be having their own feelings of isolation, stigma, social pressure to participate in religion, and all the rest of it. If you're open with them about your atheism, it'll make things easier for them.

Helena, who grew up in an upper middle class family in a fairly wealthy community in Minneapolis/St. Paul, said that she'd felt pressured to be confirmed into her Lutheran church, even though she knew she was an atheist and had tried to make that as clear as she could. Afterwards, she says, at an Easter service, "my mom signed us in on the church members card at the end of the pew—me and her, not my younger brother (not confirmed) or my dad. That last was a surprise.

"'Dad's not a member,' my mom said when I asked.

"'Wait, really?' I said. 'I didn't know that.'

"'You didn't?' Dad said.

"'If I'd known that, I wouldn't have gotten confirmed,' I said. 'I'm obviously an atheist.'"

After this, she says, "I immediately felt closer to my dad (we were already really close, but this was another level); we talked about our lack of religious beliefs and our moral philosophies constantly."

Sevtap tells a similar story, but about rather more extreme circumstances—growing up in a non-believing family in the heavily Muslim-dominated country of Turkey. On the Coming Out Godless Project website, she says this: "My family are 'followers of Ali' [the cousin and son-in-law of Islamic prophet Muhammad], but my parents soon became atheists so I grew up with atheist parents. Even my relatives which are still 'followers of Ali' say they don't take it too seriously, I believe it's much easier for them with that label in Turkey compared to being an atheist over here. Two years ago, I was at a relative's funeral where nobody said they thought that he is in heaven or he is watching us or any of those things. My father told me that none of our relatives would say such outrageous stuff without being ashamed of so much stupidity."

And Lauren tells of how, at age 12, she confronted her pastor about her atheism and her unwillingness to be confirmed and publicly lie about believing in God. After her pastor and her mom forced her to go through with the confirmation, she says, "I discovered later in life that my dad was a closet atheist who was under a gag order from mom not to infect her kids with that claptrap. Turns out he was proud as a peacock of his little logician for figuring things out by herself and having the courage of her convictions. Gee, thanks—I could have used a little backup at the time, even if it was just, 'let's go along to get along for now.'"

For kids who are nonbelievers, having parents they know are atheists is one of the most powerful forms of support they can have. And if you can do it, being parents who are out and proud atheists is one of the best ways you can help them be out and proud themselves.

And if you do think being out is the right decision, but you're having a hard time getting up the nerve to do it, remember this: This stuff is getting better. Most of the world is getting more atheist-friendly, and indeed more atheistic, every year. The world your children are growing up into will be a much better place for atheists than the world you and I grew up in. And being as out as you possibly can be, being as out as it's safe to be, is going to help make that world even better—for your kids, and for everyone.

CHAPTER TWENTY-TWO

— ✹ —

*The Already Marginalized: People of Color, Women,
LGBT People, and Others*

Step One: Find atheist writers, bloggers, videobloggers, podcasters, organizers, speakers, teachers, etc. who are also part of your marginalized group—and follow their work, and get ideas and inspiration from them.
Step Two: Find atheist communities and organizations—in person or online—specifically of, by, and for your marginalized group. (If there aren't any, and if you have time and energy and are okay with that degree of visibility, consider starting one. For more thoughts on that, see the chapter on building community.)
Step Three: Follow the rest of the guidelines in this book.

I probably don't need to tell you this. You probably already know this. But I'm going to say it anyway: If, in addition to being an atheist, you're part of another marginalized group—a group that's pushed to the edges of society, seen as second-class or "other," treated with bigotry or discrimination or disempowerment—coming out as an atheist can be an extra challenge.

That's partly just because of the math. Two or more marginalizations are harder to deal with than one, and if you're already ground down or frustrated or have reached the end of your rope dealing with racism or classism or sexism or whatever, you might not want to pile one more stigma onto the one (or ones) you already have.

Then add to that all the entertaining things that happen when these marginalizations intersect. If you're looking at the complications of being a black atheist... think about being a black gay atheist. A black lesbian atheist. A black lesbian blue-collar atheist. Multiple marginalizations don't just add onto each other; they interact and intertwine and bump up against each other in all kinds of interesting ways. And atheism specifically—and the specific set of stigmas connected with it —can have special implications and resonances with different marginalized cultures. (A thorough exploration of intersectionality is outside the scope of this book; Google the term if you want to read more about it.) What's more, organized atheism isn't always super-excellent at being welcoming to people from marginalized groups, or at dealing with our own -isms. It's all a rich tapestry...

There are lots of different ways to be marginalized, of course. They all intersect with atheism and religion in different ways. And unfortunately, there's no way for me to discuss every marginalized group here. I could write an entire book about how atheism intersects with marginalization, and how atheism is different for different demographics. Entire books have been written on just a single one of these intersections, such as the experiences of African Americans with atheism and religion. (See the Books list in this book's resource guide.) And much as I might like to, I really can't shoehorn an entire other book into this one. I might write that book someday. For now, for this chapter, I'm just going to touch on three fairly broad categories of marginalization —people of color, women, and LGBT people—and talk about what coming out as atheist might be like for these folks, with some strategies and options for doing it. And I'm going to touch on the role that the greater atheist community plays in all of this.

LGBT People

Let's start with LGBT folks.

You might think that coming out as atheist for LGBT people wouldn't be that bad. After all, the atheist community is generally pretty progressive, especially on sexual orientation stuff. And to a great extent, you'd be right. Atheists generally are a lot more gay-positive then the world at large, and many atheist organizations and thought-leaders have taken up gay civil rights issues very much as their own—especially when religion is a major source of the oppression. (To clarify, the atheist community is often a lot more LGB-friendly than it is T-friendly —a lot more supportive of lesbians and gays and bisexuals than of trans people—a point I'll get into more in a bit.)

But even when the atheist community embraces us, there's often a flip side going on. And that's that LGBT people can often be very religious. It's rare for that religion to be conservative or dogmatic, of course—it's generally more progressive, fluid, and/or interfaithy, and obviously it's almost always LGBT-positive. But it's still there.

That may seem weird, given how homophobic so much religion is. But actually, I think that's a big part of the reason behind it. Many LGBT people feel very damaged by religion—by homophobic religious teachings they were hammered with as children, or by homophobic religion in society generally, or both. So for many LGBT people, it can be very healing to be part of a gay-friendly religion, and to believe in a god who unconditionally loves and celebrates their sexuality and gender identity. If you've been brought up believing that God hates fags, it can be comforting to hear a religion tell you that God loves fags—more comforting in some ways than accepting that God doesn't hate fags, because God doesn't exist.

And the organized LGBT movement often emphasizes this religiosity—particularly in recent years—as part of a larger strategy to present LGBT people as "just like everyone else." That's especially true in the United States. Many LGBT organizations have had a deliberate strategy to gain acceptance by presenting us as mainstream, ordinary people next door, with kids and dogs and lawns and mortgages and so on... and since in the United States, being religious is seen as part of being mainstream, trotting out clean-cut All-American gay people means showing that we go to church. Or synagogue. Or some sort of religious thing. One of the ways that anti-gay forces have marginalized us has been to slur us as atheists who are destroying religious values—and all too many LGBT organizations and leaders have been willing to counter this by throwing their atheists under the bus.

So for many LGBT atheists, coming out as atheist means going against the grain of our LGBT community and movement, and even feeling isolated or ostracized by them. In LGBT spaces and events, I've been exhorted to pray. I've been told about "our Creator." I've seen comments in LGBT blogs listing bigoted anti-atheist canards that could have come from the religious right. I've heard inaccurate statistics bandied about regarding how many nonbelievers there are—statistics that diminish our numbers and strength. I've heard the inaccurate and insulting canard about "fundamentalist" atheists, and when I've pointed out how inaccurate and insulting this is, had the language firmly defended. I've seen atheism get sorted into two distinct categories: the reasonable ones who want to work with religious groups, and the unreasonable ones who think religion is a delusion. (As if you couldn't think religion is mistaken and still want to work with religious groups.) I've seen atheism get sorted into two distinct categories: the good "live and let live" ones who don't criticize religion, and the bad ones, the intolerant "fundamentalist" ones who think they're right and say so. (And depressingly, I've heard these artificial divisions trotted out by LGBT people who know, and deride, the history of these same divisions when it comes to our own movement.) I've heard LGBT leaders say how important it is to reach out to people of different religious faiths, with no mention at all of reaching out to people with no faith. Not even in lip service.

This stuff isn't usually as intense as the identification African American communities typically have with religion, or the cultural disconnection many black atheists experience. But it's there. And since many LGBT people identified as queer and connected with the queer community before we identified as nonbelievers, being dissed by that community when we come out as atheist can leave us feeling hurt, betrayed, and uprooted from the place we saw as our home.

I don't have a great answer for how to deal with this. But if the LGBT people or communities or movements in your life start pulling this crap on you, it's worth pointing out to them just how crappy it is. LGBT folks often take pride in how we've created alternative families for people who are alienated from their original ones; we know how painful it can be to get shut out from the place you call home, and we're sensitive—even touchy—about our created family embracing all LGBT people with open arms.

So if you gently inform them—let's not call it guilt-tripping, that's such an ugly word—that pushing religiosity so hard is leaving their atheist brothers and sisters out in the cold, it's going to sting. And it should sting. Of all the lousy experiences I've had being an atheist in the LGBT community, the most unsettling have been the times that LGBT people have come to me, privately, to tell me about their atheism, because they didn't feel comfortable saying it in the open. If you're an LGBT atheist, you may have experienced this, too. And LGBT people know—or they should know—that this means something is wrong. They know what it's like to be the out LGBT person who others come out to in private. And they know full well that this is a sign of a serious problem. They know something's going on in that group that's making LGBT people talk to each other in whispers, and think twice about coming out.

So when they find out that this is happening for atheists in the LGBT community, it's going to sting. It's going to make them feel ashamed of themselves. Or it should.

Work that.

For some LGBT people—especially those who come out of homophobic religions—their atheism isn't a separate issue from their sexual or gender identity. They're often very much tied together. This doesn't mean that we became atheists so we could reject religious rules about sexuality, or anything like that. Being queer doesn't turn you atheist, and being atheist certainly doesn't turn you queer. But the two identities are often closely connected. Bigoted religious views on sexuality and gender are often what start LGBT people questioning religion. Accepting atheism often makes LGBT people feel liberated about their sexuality and/or gender identity. And bigoted religious views on sexuality and gender are often a big part of what drives LGBT people to become atheist activists.

Midori, a queer-identified trans atheist and college student, says, "I find it interesting that I can't really talk about my experiences coming out as an atheist without talking at least a little about my experiences coming out as queer, or vice-versa. These experiences are very closely related and intertwined for me, if for no other reason than that they happened during roughly the same time frame. However, my atheism is not at all related to my queerness, except insofar as being an atheist made it easier to explore my gender and sexuality. When I was religious, I assumed I was straight, because that was the 'right' way to be, and, had I known what it meant, I would have assumed I was cisgender for the same reason. I'm really glad I became an atheist before I figured out that I'm queer, because I got to skip the whole religious guilt step. It does, however, rather complicate considerations of if/when I want to come out to my very religious parents. I would rather not come out to them as an atheist at all... but I highly doubt I could come out as queer without god coming into the conversation, and I'm not willing to lie if I'm directly asked about my attitude towards god and religion."

This connection is often made by our families and communities as well. When you come out as both LGBT and an atheist, to people who aren't wild about either, all the assorted issues—parents feeling like failures, families and communities feeling like you're abandoning them, etc.—can get multiplied. And sometimes, the people we come out to will lump our atheism and our sexuality or gender identity into one giant bundle of apostasy. Marina Stolting, who grew up in Canada with a Roman Catholic family on her mother's side and a Pentecostal one on her father's, tells the story of coming out as a lesbian to her mother (who then outed her to everyone else). "The first question on everyone's mind," she says, "was 'what about God?' Nobody asked 'how do you know you're gay' or 'have you tried getting a boyfriend?' It was painfully obvious to all that I was as queer as they come. They wanted to know how I reconciled my faith with my girlfriend. 'What *about* God?' I asked back, emphasis on the word 'about.' That's when they knew." And her relationship with her father ended then as well—again, with her lesbianism and her atheism being irrevocably tied together. "It was a surprisingly short conversation," she says. "What do you say to your obviously gay daughter who knows more about your own religion than you do?

"You stay the hell away. You stay away because she might influence the children you have left. You stay away because you don't want the church to know that she left and is successful; that she isn't pregnant and still paying most of her salary to some slumlord like every other girl her age in that church. You stay away because you can't build an argument on implications.

"You stay away because she might convince you that you're wrong. And you've already lived most of your one and only life."

Midori had a similar experience with coming out as both atheist and trans. For most of his friends and fellow students, it's not much of an issue; his college is relatively diverse, and people of different religious affiliations—including "none"—get along with little or no contention. But when he came out as trans to a Christian roommate, her rejection of his trans identity was very much tied in with her religion—and showed little respect for his atheism. "Although it was clear that she was trying to be supportive and accepting," he says, "it was also clear that this conflicts with her religious beliefs and that, even though she respects me enough to try to use my preferred name and pronouns, she still thinks of me as female.

"She left me a card right before she went home for the summer that basically said 'I totally support whatever you decide to do, but I'm going to quote bible verses at you and tell you that I think you are a wonderful person "just the way you are" (read: female) and I pray you will come to accept yourself "as you are."' This was painful to read. I don't think she meant to be offensive, but intent is NOT magic. I wish she would have said these things to my face or at least given me a chance to respond. I really wish she would not apply her religion-based morality to me or quote bible verses like they're evidence when she knows I am an atheist."

But while atheism and LGBT-ness are closely intertwined for many people, the two experiences are obviously not the same. And for many gays and lesbians, coming out atheist is harder than coming out gay, and people typically are more accepting of the latter than the former. This isn't surprising; gays and lesbians have been a visible, vocal, mobilized movement for many decades now, and we've had many decades to change people's attitudes about us. (That's somewhat less true for trans people—the world isn't nearly as accepting yet of trans people as it is of gays and lesbians.) Atheists haven't been super-visible and super-activist for nearly as long, so when it comes to creating social acceptance, we're a few decades behind.

Jesse Daw, a gay man whose father is the minister in a conservative Church of Christ congregation, says it was easier to tell his parents he was gay than to tell them he was an atheist. Not easy, but easier. And that was true even with a very spiritual mother and a father who's the minister in a conservative Church of Christ congregation. "I came out as gay to my parents when I was 21," he says. "While 'accepting' would be too strong a word to describe their response, they are fairly tolerant... Coming out as a nonbeliever was a slower process, and harder on them." And the same is true in his workplace. "Coming out to coworkers can be tricky in Texas," he says. "It's usually easier to come out as gay than as a heathen."

But he finds that he can use the double-threat to his advantage. "Humorously referring to myself as a gay godless heathen," he says, "seems to help defuse the occasional bit of tensions."

Ryan had a similar experience when he chose to come out as atheist and gay in the same conversation. "I was 18," he says, "almost 19, living at my parents' house. They were beginning to be annoyed by my complete lack of ambition, and getting ready to kick me out of the house. One evening at dinner, I brought up college, and mentioned a few I would apply to. They nodded approval and continued eating.

"'Oh, and also,' I said, 'I'm gay.'

"'Really?' said Mom, sounding more surprised than hurt and more surprised than I expected. We had a long conversation about that, just discussing how I came to realize it and so forth.

"Then Dad, the most religious of us, asked if I had any conflicts about this with church. 'Oh yeah, that's another thing. I'm an atheist, too, so that won't be a problem.'

"Later that night, Mom would tell me that Dad was more shocked and hurt by the atheist thing than the gay thing. Oh well, he got over it."

Now, when it comes to coming out, LGBT atheists do have an advantage. We've usually done one round of coming out already, about our sexual or gender identity, and we can learn from those experiences and get confidence from them. But it can be a mistake to assume that coming out atheist and coming out LGBT will be exactly the same. Mark from Chicago says, "It's been interesting going through the 'coming out' process all over again, this time as an atheist. When I started coming out as gay I was terrified, and I spent about five years coming out to myself before spending another five years coming out to others. And pretty much everyone ended up being totally fine with it and I couldn't help wondering what I'd been so afraid of. Coming out as an atheist was very different: there wasn't really any fear and I did it in a relatively short period of time—but my friends and family were far less enthusiastic and supportive this time around."

And there's an important difference between coming out atheist and coming out gay—a difference that can make coming out atheist harder. When you come out as gay, you're not telling straight people they're wrong to be straight. But as I've said elsewhere in this book, there is no way to say, "I don't believe in God," without implying, "If you do believe in God, you're wrong." No matter how nicely we say it, that's still what we're saying. So relations between atheists and believers may always be a bit strained, with some topics that are always a bit touchy—in a way that isn't necessarily true for gays and lesbians.

Again, I don't have a magic button to make that tension go away. I'll just say what I've been repeating throughout this book. Stay calm and empathetic, without being apologetic. Reassure them that your disagreement about this one issue doesn't mean that you don't love or respect them. Have patience, but draw clear boundaries over unacceptable behavior. Make your own decisions about how much patience you're willing to have, and who you're willing to have it with. Give the people who care about you some credit. Find communities of like-minded people, who can give you support if the going gets rough. It's okay to hold off on coming out until it's relatively safe. And when you are ready to come out, remember how much power it has to change your life, to change the lives of the people around you, and to change the world.

And stay fabulous.

It's different from coming out as LGBT. But it's not all that different. If you've already come out as gay or lesbian or bisexual or trans, you have a pretty good handle on this.

Women

Now, let's talk about the women.

There's a lot of pressure on women to be religious. There's a lot of pressure on everyone to be religious, of course... but that pressure is different for women, and in many ways it's stronger. In most of the world, the job of raising children and teaching them values is primarily seen as women's work. And that includes the job of teaching children to be religious. Women are expected to believe, to show up at religious services, to participate in religious communities, to do a lot of the organizing and scut work and day-to-day business of making religious communities happen—because they're expected to pass all this on to their kids. This gender expectation doesn't just affect mothers, either; it splashes over onto women who, for whatever reason, don't have children.

What's more, in much of the world, the job of preserving morality—and again, of passing that morality on to children—is seen as women's work. Women often get seen as the guardians of virtue, especially the gatekeepers of sexual virtue, while men get seen as beasts who would run wild if women didn't keep them in line. And in cultures that equate morality with religion—which is to say, most cultures right now —this adds to the idea that being religious is women's work. (And yes, I know that many of these same religions also teach that women are the font of all sin; that we're morally weak, inherently corrupt harlots, tempting men away from the path of righteousness with our seductive ways, and bringing sin and disobedience into the world by listening to a talking snake and eating a magic apple. Hey, I didn't say these religions were consistent. If you're looking for someone to reconcile the internal inconsistencies in religion, don't ask an atheist.)

And in sexist societies—which is to say, pretty much all societies—where women are cut out of the power structure and have little or no access to political or economic power, or where the access we do have is a heavily guarded obstacle course loaded with landmines, organized religion is often one of the few arenas where women can have some authority and power and respect. Women are rarely the ultimate leaders of traditional organized religion, but they do a huge amount of running things on the ground day-to-day, and they get a lot of respect and admiration for it. So being religious isn't just pressured onto women —it can actually be very appealing.

A lot of people have commented on the relatively low proportion of female atheists. Pretty consistently, polls show that among atheists and the non-religious in the United States, women make up about 40%[1] (although globally, the numbers for men and women are almost the same, with women actually having a slight edge[2]). This seems somewhat surprising at first, given how grotesquely sexist, oppressive, even brutally misogynistic religion so often is. But when you look at the pressure on women to be religious, or at least to participate in religious structures even if we're not feeling it—and when you look at how attractive organized religion can be for women, even when it teaches that we're weak, sinful, second-class harlots—it begins to make a lot more sense.

Ironically, though, all these pressures on women to stay in religion also provide excellent motivations for us to leave. That whole thing about being treated by our religions as tempting, wicked seducers who are nevertheless responsible for maintaining the morality and faith of our family—and how either way, we're the ones who get blamed for other people's screw-ups—that hasn't escaped us. A lot of us, anyway. It's a game we can't win, and a bunch of us are quitting.

But these expectations can make it uniquely difficult for women atheists to come out. For many women, coming out as atheist doesn't just mean upsetting people's view of us as good Christians or Jews or Muslims or whatever. It means upsetting their view of us as women. If we're married, it upsets their view of us as wives; if we're mothers, it upsets their view of us as mothers. In a lot of cases, it even means challenging people's fundamental ideas about womanhood and motherhood and marriage. (And frankly, when women become atheists, our own ideas about these things often change as well.) Some people aren't going to like that. To put it mildly.

And if the job of passing religion to future generations is resting in your hands, and you drop that ball, that's likely going to cause some hard feelings as well. Like I said in the chapter on coming out to family: Even if your family doesn't take the religious part of religion very seriously, they may still see it as an important part of family tradition. Now, if that tradition is so important to them, it's not very fair of them to make preserving it your responsibility. But even though it's unfair, they may see things that way anyway—and they may be upset when you break that chain. And of course, if they do take the religious part seriously, they're probably going to be angry with you for endangering not only your own immortal soul, but your children's, and their children's, and all the generations to follow.

That may not just be a problem for your family, either. When you come out as an atheist, other religious people in your community may feel like one of their pillars is crumbling. Other parents in your community may fear that your little heathens are going to corrupt their little angels. And they won't be wrong. One of their pillars *is* crumbling. One of their pillars has crumbled. And even if you and your kids never say a single bad word about religion to anyone... well, like I say in the chapter on visibility, and the chapter on how coming out atheist creates other atheists, and the chapter on how coming out atheist has a snowball effect, the mere presence of open atheists is often a big part of what persuades religious believers out of religion.

If that's your situation, there are a couple of ways to handle it. You can go with the reassuring, "I'm still the same person I always was" route. Remind them of other values and interests you all still have in common; reinforce traditions that aren't religious. Or you can go with the more confrontational, "Yes, things are changing, they bloody well should change, your expectations of me were totally unfair and unreasonable, your expectations of all women are totally unfair and unreasonable" route.

You can go in different directions with different people, at different times, over different issues, and in different combinations. You can cheerfully hang the Christmas ornaments that were handed down to you from your grandmother and your mother—but be damned if you're going to make your daughter go to confirmation. You can keep wearing the headscarf because that's what all the women in your Muslim family do—but have long conversations with your siblings and cousins about why Islam is bullshit and God doesn't exist. You can keep taking your kids to synagogue—but also take them to churches and mosques and covens and Buddhist temples and humanist meetings, to expose them to lots of different religious views, and let them put the pieces together themselves. Or you can tell your family that you don't believe anymore, and if they still believe then taking the kids to synagogue is their job—but when they get back from synagogue, teach them how to make potato pancakes, and show them the menorah your great-grandmother brought with her when she fled from Germany.

And, of course, you can remind everyone that passing along traditions, and teaching and enforcing ethical values, is everyone's job. Tradition and morality are human traits, and treating them as women's work insults and dehumanizes men, even as it oppresses women. It's bad for everyone. And when we come out as atheists, and push back against the arbitrary gender roles that are demanded or reinforced by religion, it makes everyone's life better.

Race and Ethnicity

And finally, let's get into race and ethnicity.

This is a topic that many people avoid. White people especially. There's a common misconception that simply talking about race is the same as being racist—and there's a common fear of saying the wrong thing and stepping on landmines. (And of course, white people are the ones who have the luxury of ignoring race, or pretending to ignore it.)

But this is a hugely important topic for atheists and atheism. For anyone, really. I'd be doing our community a disservice if I didn't get into it. Obviously, writing about racial and ethnic marginalization puts me in a somewhat strange position: I'm white, and I haven't lived through these experiences myself. So I'm basing this section on numerous conversations (online and in the flesh) with atheists of color, and on lots of their writings that I've read on the subject. And I've made a point of getting feedback on early drafts of this book, from people with more experience in the areas I'm talking about—including with this chapter. If I'm getting some stuff wrong here, please accept my apologies.

For many families, of all races and ethnicities, religion is a central part of the family identity, and the two can be deeply interwoven. And this can be even stronger in African American families, Hispanic families, families of Middle Eastern or Southeast Asian descent, and other families of people of color, as well as immigrant families or families with other marginalized identities. For folks in these families, coming out atheist can seem like a betrayal—not just of their god, not even just of them personally, but of the entire family, and the family history and identity.

Liam, a mixed-race atheist raised as a socialist-left Catholic in Britain, talks about the reasons he thinks his father was so upset over his atheism. "There are issues of family identity," he says. "My father stressed... how I completely lacked loyalty to my ancestors. I am mixed race—although people so often identify me as black that sometimes I even self-identify that way. I am a second generation immigrant: the vast majority of my family is Irish, but my father's father was Ghanaian. To the best of my knowledge, on both the Ghanaian and Irish sides of my family there are not now, nor have there ever been, other atheists. I suspect atheism is seen as yet another example of English decadence, of the sort which we as immigrants are to define ourselves against. Indeed, my dad often says things to the effect that 'The bloody English don't believe in anything,' certainly intending the widespread atheism of English culture to be implicated in this, and derides the Church of England for being closet atheists. That I came out as an atheist involved betraying this aspect of my heritage, and rendering myself no better than the colonialists."

And for many cultures, religion is an important part, not only of the family identity, but of the cultural and racial identity as well. Many African American atheists talk about how tightly woven religion is with African American culture, and they say that coming out atheist can get them treated as race traitors. In *Moral Combat: Black Atheists, Gender Politics, and the Values Wars*, Sikivu Hutchinson says, "In the moral universe of mainstream African American communities, essentialism dictates that those who violate the tacit contract of religious observance are somehow 'less' than African American."[3] Ditto with many Hispanic people. Alexander, who figured out that there was no God as "a precocious fourth-grader" and came out to his Catholic family almost immediately, was met with hostility and confusion—and quickly went back into the closet. "True to form," he says on the Scribbles and Rants blog, "my parents dropped the matter as long as I went through the motions and didn't bring it up myself. Religion was a cultural necessity more than anything else, part of how they tried to keep us Hispanic in the face of Anglo-American hegemony."

It's also true that cultural norms, not just about being atheist but about discussing religion at all, can be different in different cultures. And that can also make coming out as an atheist tricky. An atheist originally from New Zealand, MMC is "now in South Korea, meeting people from all around the world—Christian, Muslim, Buddhist, Hindu and plenty of non-religious people too. Both in Korean society and in the international communities of Korea, religion is seen as a very, very personal matter—as it should be. I'm rarely asked about religion, if I am then I give a brief answer and keep off the topic. If somebody were to try to proselytize to me then I'd give them a piece of my mind, but it doesn't happen."

But it's important to remember that coming out atheist isn't always a problem. As dezn_98 says, "I have no white friends, so everyone I came out to was either black or brown." He then goes on to say, "I did not encounter any serious trouble while coming out, so these stories are almost all positive... No one, except one, really cared that I was an atheist."

Plus, you know how I keep saying that coming out atheist makes it easier for other atheists in your life to come out? How you won't have any idea how many atheists you already know until you come out to them? How realizing that you're both atheists is a huge relief for both you and them—and can strengthen a bond between you? That's extra true in communities where coming out is extra hard. dezn_98 feared that his family would have a negative reaction to his atheism; he finally got tired of not being able to talk about it, and called his cousin on a whim. "The convo went like this," he says:

"'Yo, I got to get this sht off my chest. You ready? I got to tell you somethin real serial.'

"'What's up?'

"'I think, that I do not believe in god no more'

"After a brief silence...... 'mmm... OK, neither do I. so what?'

"WTF? Really son? How come you neva told me?'

"'Sht never came up. I did not think it mattered.'

"'Well, it does fcking matter asshole. I have been keeping this clogged up for months and now I find out you one too? You little sht... you should of told me!'

"'Aight, so now what? Is that all you had to tell me?'

"'I mean, yeah that was all. Hold up hold up... when did you stop believing?'

"'Man, I stopped a long time ago. Religion is just fcking stupid.'

"'Does _____ know (my other cousin who I am tight with), and does your mom know?'

"'_____ is a fcking atheist too!'

"'WHAT? Word... y'all are asses... keepin this sht from me. What about your mom?'

"(bursts out laughing) 'Hell no my mom don't know! She would kill me! Your mom know?'

"'FCK NO! I can't tell her. I might tell her later tho... to be real. We see how dat would go...'

"That was how my first coming out went.

"From there," he continues, "we just started to explore the issue of religion together, and I made my cousin into an even stronger atheist than before. Before he simply did not believe because he thought it was silly, I am an academic and he is not. So over time as I read philosophy, and I discussed various issues with him, I noticed he became a stronger advocate for atheism himself. Instead of not caring [enough] about the issue to even mention it, he started coming up to me sharing stories about how he is frustrated with religious thinking as well. I sort of influenced him into becoming a skeptic. He used to believe in ghosts but not god, and as we explored the rationale to stop believing in gods, he stopped believing in ghosts too. My 'coming out' actually influenced him, someone who was already an atheist, to be more outspoken and more rational about his atheism while making him drop other super-natural beliefs."

That's a really important point as well. Coming out as atheist doesn't just encourage other atheists in your life to come out. It can encourage them to be stronger and more visible advocates for atheism. And having other atheists to talk with can sharpen everyone's thinking about atheism and religion—which will make conversations with believers in your lives go better.

You may also find that the people you come out to about your atheism are entirely unsurprised by it. Here's dezn_98 again, on coming out atheist to his sister:

"'Yo, I want to tell you something.'

"'What is it?'

"'I am an atheist.'

"'mmm... Yeah, I kind of knew that already.'

"'Wait... what? Fck you talkin about? How you know?'

"'Meh, it was kind of obvious. I mean, you do not believe in ghosts, or luck, or astrology... I mean, you don't believe in anything. I kind of just figured you did not believe in god too.'"

And you know how I keep saying that coming out atheist doesn't just get existing atheists to come out to you—it can help believers re-think their beliefs and become atheists themselves? Here's dezn_98 once again, on what happened after he came out to his sister: "After that conversation, my sister started to come to me over time and ask questions about her religious beliefs. In that, she used me to explore what she believed herself, because apparently, she never thought about it. I was the only one who ever had thought about it, and she just sort of started to think about it, instead of going with the flow, with me. As we explored the issues together, she started to see more of my side of things and became less and less religious. As she did, I pretty much just validated her lack of belief, and eventually she turned atheist as well. So now me and my sister are atheists. She was a fuzzy agnostic/liberal believer who never explored Christianity and instead believed simply because it was tradition. Upon realizing that yes, there is an actual option to just not believe, she sort of just ran towards that option, with my support."

But dezn_98 acknowledges that things were easier for him than for others. He lives in New York, which is very progressive, and "everyone I knew, except one, was a liberal christian who probably believed you can get into heaven merely for being nice (you do not have to believe in the jebus)."

He points out that "Churches have traditionally been the staging point for many POC [people of color] communities when they want to speak out. As a result of this embedded history, churches in POC communities usually offer lots of social services related to helping brothas and sistas out. It is no small thing to distance yourself from the very foundations that frequently give you a hand on social justice issues. As a result, in POC communities, it is very hard to be an atheist because you are giving up a lot of social support that was previously your primary support mechanism when facing oppression.

"The other point," he says, "is that because churches are so ingrained within POC cultures, many POC's can not imagine life without them. They relate their strengths to their belief in god, their belief that strong faith can give them strength to [prevail] over the unfair bigoted ways this society works. So when you challenge that belief, you may be shaking the very foundation that they believe is their greatest strength. Considering that they are not taught about other ways to cope, and the fact that closing the door on the church means closing avenues to get social justice.... this is not a fcking game. This kind of stuff hurts, and it runs deep."

Jamila Bey, an African American atheist speaker, journalist, and activist, gave a talk at an American Atheists convention where she described the African American community as "low-hanging fruit, surrounded by thorns." She pointed out that African American men are already staying away from church in droves; they may describe themselves as religious, but they're not putting their butts in the pews. She pointed out that it isn't news to African American women just how sexist their churches are; they're well aware that while women may be running church business day-to-day, it's still overwhelmingly men who are the leaders, who get the attention and the glory and get to be the deciders. She pointed out that the traditional homophobia of most African American churches is unsettling to many folks in the community, who have been re-thinking their views on gay people and becoming more accepting of them. She pointed out that African Americans are very familiar indeed with the role religion has played in slavery and the history of racist oppression. And she says that all these people are ripe for picking by atheism—if it weren't for the thorns of the intense cultural identification of so many African Americans with their religion, and the fact that so much community building and political organizing and just day-to-day practical support is done through the churches.[4]

Like I keep saying to everyone throughout this book: You need to make your own decisions about this. You get to make your own decisions. You get to decide for yourself whether the need to not upset or alienate the family and community you rely on, and the desire to not weaken or stress the ties that bind you together, are more important than the need for you to be honest about your atheism and your feelings about religion—and the value that coming out will have, for you and other atheists in your community, in helping you find and support each other.

If you do decide to come out—to some folks in your community, or to everyone—I strongly encourage you to make contact with atheist communities and organizations that are specifically of, by, and for people in your culture. (Many are listed in the resource guide at the end of this book.) They can help you a lot more than I can. They can give you some of the social and practical support you may have been getting from religion. They can give you better-informed and more nuanced advice on coming out to believers in your life, and maintaining relationships with them. They can help you feel less uprooted from your culture, less disconnected from it. They can help remind you that you are not bloody well a race traitor just because you don't believe in God. And in any conversations you have with believers in your life about why your atheism doesn't bloody well make you a race traitor, the people in these communities can be Exhibit A.

In her interview for *The Ebony Exodus Project: Why Some Black Women Are Walking Out on Religion—and Others Should Too* by Candace R. M. Gorham, Heather says that when she started coming out as an atheist, "the first people I looked to were the atheist groups. I typed it in and they were predominately white. I felt like I couldn't really get with their issues or whatever they had going on. But then I typed in 'black atheists' and some shit came up! And I was like, 'Oh, shit!' There was the Black Atheist Alliance and that's when I started seeing more black folks. Facebook has really been my saving grace, as far as the whole atheist movement."[5] And in her *Ebony Exodus Project* interview, Ivori says that when she started researching atheism, "I was very delighted to find that there were people like myself on Facebook. I was like, 'A Black person! Yes!'"[6]

Which brings me to my next point: When you're talking about your atheism with believers in your family or community, it may help to point out that the connection between their religion and the culture you share isn't as all-encompassing as they might think. Point out the long history of African American atheism, freethought, and resistance to religion, and the many prominent historical figures in that history, from A. Philip Randolph to Zora Neale Hurston.[7] Point out that the Hispanic community's identification with the Catholic Church is weakening; Hispanic people are leaving Catholicism at an unprecedented rate, either joining Protestant churches or leaving religion altogether.[8] (Getting this kind of info is where organizations and websites dedicated to atheists in your demographic can be seriously helpful.) You might also insert whatever rant you may have about religion's role in racist oppression: the role it played in slavery and Jim Crow; the role it's played in undermining public education; psychics and other religious frauds preying on Hispanic neighborhoods; filthy rich megachurch pastors preying on impoverished blighted communities. Remember: low-hanging fruit.

And you can point to polls showing that the numbers of atheists in your community aren't actually all that low. In the United States anyway, the proportions of disbelief for people of color are pretty much the same as for white people; they're a little lower, but not that much.[9] It's true that among African Americans, the proportion of people—especially women—who identify as strongly religious are higher than average. But those numbers are mostly being sucked from the "meh" category, the "religious but don't care that much about it" crowd—not the "non-religious" crowd.[10] African Americans and Hispanic Americans disbelieve in God at about the same rate as white Americans.[11] And Asian Americans are actually more likely to be non-religious than white people. A *lot* more.[12]

So point out that religion isn't as dominant in your culture as they think. It's just that the atheists are closeted. And ask if that's what they want. Ask if they want the atheists in your community to feel isolated, to be afraid to speak their minds and tell the truth for fear of being shunned.

And remember this: The same strong family and cultural ties that may make your atheism hard for your family and friends to handle? There's a good chance that these same ties will get them to accept you in the long run. They don't want you out of their life, out of the family and community and culture, any more than you want to be out of it.

In her interview for *The Ebony Exodus Project* by Candace R. M. Gorham, Janet says, "When I told my grandmother that I didn't believe, she said she loved me no matter what."[13] And in her own *Ebony Exodus Project* interview, Raina says that while family acceptance took time, her nonbelief isn't an issue now—and it's even resulted in some surprising family apostasy. "When I told my mother I was agnostic," she says, "she said the same thing I did to her when I was trying to get her to go to church: 'I don't want you to go to hell.' And she cried. It was really sad and I felt bad that I was doing it, but, I couldn't help it. But my mom is cool with it now." She adds that, "My father's side, they don't really care. They're all like, 'Okay, you're still a good person. You're not out there killing people. You're in school getting an education. Good for you.'" Her discussions with her aunt got her aunt rethinking religion; when Raina explained why she didn't believe, her aunt said, "'You know, I never thought about that before, I have to think about that for a while before I come back to you.'" And she adds that "my grandmother, the one who took me to church at 7:30 sunrise services for three hours and Bible study, she's agnostic now."[14]

These happy endings aren't universal, of course. *The Ebony Exodus Project* has plenty of stories of black atheists having problems with their families when they came out, or even being cut off by them entirely. But while the happy endings aren't universal, they're not uncommon, either. You know your family better than I do, and you need to make your own risk/benefit analysis—but when you do, don't automatically assume that coming out atheist is going to ruin things with the people in your life forever. Give the people who care about you some credit.

And when you do all of this, no matter how you choose to do it, you can always get support from the atheist community.

Yeah. About that...

Isms in Atheism

I wish I could tell every atheist of color, without any reservations, to connect with the atheist community. I wish I could say that to every atheist from every marginalized community and identity. I wish I could tell every atheist who's a woman, an immigrant, African American,

Hispanic, of Asian or Pacific Islander descent, transgender, disabled, blue-collar or working-class, that the atheist community will welcome them with open arms and a completely understanding heart. I wish I could tell them that they were never going to deal with racist remarks, or people giving them crap for pointing out racist remarks. I wish I could tell them that they were never going to deal with online sexual harassment and in-person sexual harassment, or with people flipping their wigs when they try to do basic anti-harassment prevention and education.

I also wish I had a pony who flew to the candy factory every day to bring me chocolate truffles.

One of my saddest experiences as an atheist speaker was when I gave a talk to a group of high school atheists—most of whom were Hispanic or African American or mixed race or otherwise not white, and many of whom were young women—and during the Q&A, they asked me what the heck was up with all the controversies in atheism over gender and race. I so wanted to tell them that it wasn't a problem and things would be totally fine for them—and I couldn't. The reality, unfortunately, is that the atheist community and movement are not free of racism, sexism and misogyny, classism, transphobia, and other forms of bigotry and marginalization, whether conscious or unconscious. Even homophobia and biphobia rear their heads at times (although that's less common).

I'm not saying that atheists and organized atheism are worse with this stuff than society at large. In some cases, I think we might be somewhat worse: I think that for women, we suck somewhat worse than average, along with the tech, gaming, sci-fi, comics, and other communities that have traditionally been male-dominated and have recently had an influx of women that they're flipping out about. In some cases, I think we're better: I think we're definitely more welcoming to gays and lesbians and bisexuals than the world at large (although we still often suck when it comes to trans issues). But for the most part, atheists and atheist communities are reflective of... well, of people, and of the societies these people come from. It's disappointing that we're not better than that, just like it's often disappointing when a marginalized group doesn't get it about how they might be marginalizing others. But alas, it's not really surprising.

Atheists can also have an unfortunate tendency to think that because we're right about atheism, we're right about everything. We have a tendency to think that because we figured out the right answer to one very large, very important question, therefore we're smarter than anyone else—and that if someone tells us we're being thick-headed, we can safely ignore them. We often tend to think that because we're familiar with logical fallacies and cognitive biases, therefore we're somehow miraculously free of them. And while most atheists are fairly progressive on most social justice issues, too many of us tend to think that this makes us entirely free from bias. We tend to think that because we're gay- and lesbian- and bi-positive, therefore we must be trans-positive as well; that because we have one black person and two women speaking at our conference, therefore we're being inclusive; that because we aren't overtly and consciously bigoted and we have more or less the right opinions about the broad social issues of the day, therefore our work here is done, and we can relax and pat ourselves on the back. So when atheists say or do something racist or sexist or classist or transphobic or ableist or whatever, and get called on it, the squawk of defensive, righteous outrage can be deafening.

And this can make it harder for atheists from other stigmatized demographics to come out. Kelly, who grew up in a devoutly evangelical Protestant family, talks of her difficulty getting support from the atheist community. "I would have loved some resources and support from atheists when trying to figure out how to come out to my parents," she says. "While I do read many atheist blogs (and have since before coming out), I would not say I am connected to the online atheist community—mostly because I am a little scared of online comment boards.

I've seen a lot of nasty comments, particularly geared towards women, so I tend to just read and personally reflect."

Kate says something very similar. She had an intense religious upbringing, with a father who was (and is) a vicar in a hardcore evangelical/fundamentalist wing of the Church of England. At the time she came out, she says, "I was connected with an online atheism forum, which I stayed part of for many years. Nowadays I have drifted away from online atheism because a) I don't need it any more, and b) the hostility to feminism and social justice gets me down."

And dezn_98 says, "Look—atheists do get discriminated against. We all know this and have all felt it. However, if you think that being labeled as an atheist is anywhere near the level of oppression other minorities like gays, women, people of color, and trans people feel, you are a giant fcing idiot... I will make that clear. While yes, atheists do get discriminated against, it is nowhere near the sheer amount of volume other minorities face. So do not try to say things like, 'I know how it feels to be black because of my atheism, blah blah.' FCK YOU RACIST FOOL. So there, that is the starting point."

If you need more confirmation of this, if you need to see any more stories about the kind of crap marginalized people often deal with in the atheist community, take a look at Chapter 30: Diversity, or, Making Communities Welcoming to People Who Aren't Just Like Us.

So yeah. All that sucks. I've been saying for a while now that it sucks. A lot of us have been saying for a while now that it sucks. I'm not going to say anything different here.

What I will say—because I'm a relentlessly optimistic Pollyanna cheerleader—is that things are getting better. In just the last few years, at atheist events and on speaker rosters and in blogging networks and at local groups and more, the representation of women, of African Americans, of Hispanic people, of young people, of people who have left religions other than Christianity, has been going up and up and up. Many atheist communities are eager to encourage diversity, and to welcome different faces. (Sometimes a little too eager; the tendency for atheist groups to glom onto the one black person who shows up has been reported by many.) Many atheist communities are taking specific, positive action to make this diversity thing happen, instead of sitting back and hoping that it does. And I am seeing way, *way* more atheists speak up about social justice stuff than I ever have in the years I've been with this movement. White folks are speaking about racism; cisgender folks are speaking about transphobia; middle-class folks are speaking about classism; men are speaking about sexism and misogyny. Etc.

If you're an atheist who comes from another marginalized community or identity or group or thing, there are almost certainly organizations and communities dedicated to other atheists like you, created by and for and about other atheists like you. There are lots of them listed in the resource guide; there are probably more that I'm not aware of or didn't find out about before I finished this book. I passionately encourage you to check them out, whether you decide to come out of the closet or not. But there are also organizations and communities—and a whole lot of individual atheists—dedicated, not specifically to atheists like you, but to making organized atheism as a whole more welcoming to a wider variety of atheists. Including atheists like you. And it's making a difference. It's getting better.

I won't blame you if you decide to take a pass. I won't blame you if you decide that it's not your job to do Social Justice 101 in the atheist community. I won't blame you if you decide that the community you go to for emotional support and practical support and continuity and connection can't be a place where you're constantly having to get people up to speed on basic issues of respect and humanity. I won't blame you if you decide that it's more important to you to build community with people who share your racial or ethnic or gender or sexual identity than it is to build community with people who share your opinion about whether God exists.

But if you do decide that organized atheism is worth a shot—there are a whole lot of us who have your back.

And even if you don't? You can still come out as an atheist if you want to. And you can still get lots of different kinds of support for that. I just wish we could give you the full-fledged support of the entire community that you deserve.

CHAPTER TWENTY-THREE

— ✺ —

Arguing About Religion

When you come out as an atheist to religious believers—should you get into arguments about religion?

This is a question that's come up again and again in this book: in the chapters on coming out to family, to friends, to classmates, and more. When atheists come out about our atheism, one of the most common responses is for people to try to talk us out of it. And when we come out, many of us burst right out of the gate by railing against religion and spreading the good news that there is no God.

Is this a good idea? When you come out as an atheist, should you let yourself get drawn into arguments about whether God exists—or even start them yourself?

I'm going to go out on a limb here. I'm going to make what may be a controversial statement.

The question of whether to get into arguments about religion? It's not a question of "whether." It's a question of "how much."

I've said this several times throughout this book, but it's crucial to this chapter, so I'll say it again: There is literally no way to say, "I don't believe in God," without implying, "If you do believe in God, you're mistaken." No matter how nicely you say it, no matter how many pretty pictures of blue skies and clouds you put behind the words, that's still what you're saying. Belief or disbelief in God isn't a subjective opinion, like what kind of music you like or whether cauliflower is awesome, where you can disagree with someone and both be right. There either is a god, or there isn't. Asserting that one position is true means asserting that the other is false.

So there is literally no way to say, "I am an atheist," without starting an argument. The mere act of saying, "I don't believe in God," *is* starting an argument. (Unless, of course, the person you're talking with says, "I don't, either!")

So when you're deciding whether to get into arguments about whether God exists, it may be helpful to bear that in mind. You're not deciding "whether." You're deciding "How much?" "What kind?" "With whom?" "In what tone?" "For how long?" "Where do I draw the line?" And you're probably thinking about your priorities with different people, and in different situations. Is it more important to make your case and try to win the argument, or to preserve the relationship? How do you preserve the relationship, while still feeling like you're being honest and authentic and true to yourself?

That's what this chapter is about. It is not—repeat, NOT—about how to win arguments about religion with believers. It's more about the emotional side of debating religion. It's intended to give you an idea of some of the personal issues that often arise when atheists and believers debate. It's intended to show you some of the landmines you might step on, so you can avoid them—or so you can step on them deliberately and thoughtfully, rather than by accident. It's intended to help you recognize people's boundaries about religious disagreements—and to help you draw your own.

Before I talk about how to proceed with arguments about religion, I want to take a moment to defend doing it at all. Many atheists are strongly resistant to the idea of talking believers out of belief; they think it's too much like religious evangelizing, which they see as intolerant or obnoxious or other bad things. And many atheists are convinced that it never works. They say that religious beliefs are too irrational; they're held for emotional reasons, not intellectual ones, so there's no point making rational arguments against them. Or else they say that religious beliefs are too entrenched; people hold on to them too deeply, and they'll never be persuaded out of them.

To the idea that debating religion equals evangelizing equals badness, I want to say this: Religion is an idea about how the world works. (As is atheism.) So why shouldn't we treat it like any other idea: ideas about science, medicine, philosophy, politics? Why shouldn't we question it, debate it, point out when it doesn't fit the evidence or doesn't make sense? Why, alone among all other ideas that humanity has come up with, should religion be treated with kid gloves? If we think it's a mistaken idea, why shouldn't we try to talk people out of it?

The problem with believers evangelizing isn't that they think they're right and are trying to change minds. The problem is how they go about it. They base their persuasion on fear: the normal fear of death, and the trumped-up fear of Hell and eternal torture. They base it on a false hope for immortality they have no good reason to think is true. They base it on falsehoods: denial of reality, denial of the idea that reality even matters, gross inaccuracies about history and science, even out-and-out lies. They base it on lousy evidence and worse logic; on emotional manipulation, extreme social pressure, appeals to authority; on the manipulation of every cognitive bias in the book. They base it on the suppression of other ideas. They knock on people's doors at eight o'clock on Saturday morning. (And, of course, the conclusion they're trying to persuade people into is wrong.)

The problem with believers evangelizing isn't that they think they're right and are trying to change minds. That's the only decent and honorable thing about it. And I see no reason that atheists shouldn't change some minds ourselves. (As long as we're honest, and aren't manipulative or coercive, and don't knock on people's doors at eight in the morning.)

As for the idea that debating religion never works?

Bollocks.

Go to any atheist gathering with a decent number of people. And ask for a show of hands, or just start asking around. Ask how many former believers were persuaded out of religion—at least in part, not necessarily entirely, but in part—because of arguments against religion that they heard, read, saw on YouTube, listened to in a podcast, got into with their friends or family, whatever. Ask how many of them had their deconversion process started, or moved forward, or had the final nail in the coffin driven in, by somebody's argument for why religion is mistaken and atheism is correct.

I can pretty much guarantee you that the number will be large. I've asked this question at oodles of talks I've given, and I've never gotten a response that wasn't significant. It's usually at least half the crowd. Often more.

It is true that arguments against religion rarely work right away. A single argument is rarely, by itself, going to convince someone that their religion is mistaken. It takes time; it's usually an ongoing progression, involving lots of different thought processes. But it can work. It has worked, plenty of times. It is a huge part of why the number of atheists in the world is going up at such a dramatic rate.

If you don't want to get into these debates (beyond the point of simply asserting your atheism, that is), that's totally your business. I don't think arguing people out of religion is a moral obligation or anything. I just want you to make that decision based on an accurate understanding of the ethics behind it—and its potential to work.

Okay. Moving on. Now that you've been persuaded that debating religion is morally acceptable and potentially effective—how do you make your decisions about it?

There are lots of reasons for atheists to argue with believers about religion, or to simply explain our reasons for our atheism. Some people do it, obviously, to persuade believers that God doesn't exist. Others do it to give believers a better understanding of what exactly we think and why—and to get a better understanding of what the believers in our lives think and why. Still others do it simply to show that we take the question seriously: that we haven't become atheists on a whim, out of rebellion, or so we can reject our religion's rules. And still others do it to sharpen our own understanding of our atheism. In the same way that some believers will think, "I'm not afraid of debate, I don't want a weak faith that won't permit questioning, I want my faith to be tested," some atheists debate with believers to make sure we've really thought our atheism through, and that we've considered all the best arguments against it.

If you're going to argue about religion, it's a really good idea to clarify what you want to get out of it. That'll help you decide how to proceed. And it'll help you decide how, and when, to knock it off.

If you argue about religion with believers, there are likely going to be times when they get upset. Especially if you're even somewhat successful, and you get them doubting their faith or considering difficult questions about it. Many people have never seriously questioned their religious beliefs or even thought about them very carefully. And letting go of them can be scary. It can be emotionally scary—you have to think about life, death, meaning, your place in the universe, in radically different ways. And as we've been discussing in much of the rest of this book, it can be scary in more practical ways; it can mean alienating your family and friends, risking your job, maybe risking your safety.

So when you're debating with believers, remember that they're not just calmly considering the intellectual value of your case. In the back of their minds—maybe in the front of their minds—they might be wondering, "What if they're right? What in my life would have to change? What would I tell my mom? Where would I be without my church? What would my life mean, anyway? How will I deal with death? Oh, crap—if they're right, then my dad is really dead, and I'm never going to see him again!"

Don't be surprised if they get upset.

That's not necessarily a reason to avoid the debates. Even though the process of questioning religion can be upsetting, most atheists are glad that they did it. And again, merely saying "I am an atheist" is in some sense the start of a debate, and there may be no way to avoid the upsetting ideas it can raise. But you might want to cut the argument short if they—or you, for that matter—are starting to get really distressed. If the conversation is important, you can always come back to it later. Part of being patient and being the bigger person is recognizing when conversations are going south, and accepting that you may get into some frustrating encounters where you don't get closure in one conversation.

And you may hit some serious brick walls. You may hit denial of evidence, of logic, of reality, of the very idea that evidence and logic and reality matter. You may hit thought processes as convoluted as the earbud wires in your gym bag; circular reasoning that runs in tiny little loops no bigger than a donut. You may hit infinitely moving goalposts. You may hit refusals to listen at all. You may hit emotional ugliness: personal insults, anti-atheist bigotry and slurs, threats from people who have power over you (like parents), recriminations for raising the question at all. So with some people, you may decide to drop it. At least for the time being; maybe indefinitely or permanently.

Now, I'm most emphatically *not* saying, as some atheists argue, that some people need religion, and it's bad to talk them out of it. That is a load of dingo's kidneys. Among other things, it's totally patronizing to believers; it treats them like they're weak, like their delicate sensibilities can't cope with the full weight of reality. "You can't handle the truth!" To hell with that. You're presumably arguing with grownups, and they can decide what they can and can't handle.

I'm saying, as a purely practical consideration, that some people are not going to change their minds. Not in the course of one argument, anyway. Some people, when they get backed into a rhetorical corner, are going to cover their eyes and stick their fingers in their ears. Or else they'll pull out the sharp teeth and claws. They may be able to handle the truth—but right now, they're not going to. As a purely practical consideration, it's worth recognizing when you've reached that point. If you care about the person and the relationship, that's probably a good time to drop it.

It's also worth considering whether this is the best time for a debate. For myself, I have a policy that I don't debate believers if they're in a crisis and are using religion to help get through it. I don't debate believers who are in acute grief, for instance, or are using religion to help recover from alcoholism or other drug abuse. I don't agree at all that some people need religion permanently—but I think it may be true temporarily. If someone in crisis presses me for my opinion, I'll give it—but I won't pursue an argument very far, and I'm not going to bring it up. (Anyway, my friends already know my opinions.)

Of course, it's also worth considering how important this relationship is to you, and what you're willing to do to preserve it. Some people, with some relationships, may think, "This relationship is too valuable to sacrifice over a fight about God. Let's drop it." Other people, with other relationships, may think, "This relationship is too valuable to keep my mouth shut over something this important." And, of course, not all relationships matter the same. You may go further in a potentially destructive argument if it's with an old school chum from years ago—and dial back if it's with your mother.

Which brings me to an important point. When you argue about religion with the people you're close to and see every day—your friends, your family, your partner or spouse, even your co-workers or fellow students—it's not like arguing with strangers on the Internet.

When you argue with strangers or loose acquaintances on the Internet, you're probably going to focus mainly on... well, on the arguments. The logic (or lack thereof); the evidence (or lack thereof). You're more likely to be blunt; if their arguments are convoluted or ridiculous or based on lousy evidence, you're more likely to say so. If they get offended at the very fact of your criticism, you're more likely to use that as a chance to skewer religious privilege. If they fall back on emotional arguments, you're more likely to use that to show that their actual arguments don't hold water. When they back themselves into a corner, you're more likely to go in for the intellectual kill. (I am, anyway!)

But when you argue about religion with people you're close to, chances are you'll want to dial back a bit. You'll probably want to pay attention, not just to your rhetorical successes and failures, but to the emotional dynamics between you. If the person you're arguing with is getting emotional, that might be your signal, not that you should go in for the kill, but that you should step back or change the subject.

At the same time, though, there are directions you can go in with people you're close to that you probably won't go in with strangers. If your in-laws are dragging out the old "How can you be moral without God?" chestnut, it is totally appropriate for you to respond with, "That is really hurtful. You've known me for four years, and by now you should know that I am a good person. Even if you don't understand *how* I can be a good person, can you at least accept that I am one? Can you please stop treating me as less than fully human just because I don't share your religion?" You probably won't say that in an online debate with JesusIsLord278.

And there's another difference between debating religion with people you're close to, and debating with strangers on the Web. With people you're close to, you might seriously consider whether you want to argue online at all: on Facebook, in email, in online forums, or anywhere on the Internet.

As I said in the chapter on the Internet—as thousands of people have said before me—when we communicate online, it's easy to stay abstract, and forget that we're having a human interaction with an actual human being. This does have a strange and valuable power; the Internet frees people to say things we're afraid to say in person, including saying, "I'm an atheist" in the first place. But with people we care about, it can be very risky. It's easy to focus on the ideas and forget about the person; to focus on winning or losing the argument rather than keeping or losing the relationship. For myself, after several bad experiences with serious disputes in email or Facebook, I pretty much never do this with people in my personal life, unless there's no choice. You might not go that far—but it's worth thinking about. And think about how you'll feel if the argument gets ugly or painful, and one of you pulls the plug partway through. Will you be okay with that? If not—think twice about starting the argument in the first place.

And with people you're close to, you'll have to decide how to handle it when they make truly terrible arguments for religion. None of the arguments are great, obviously—if there were great arguments for religion, we wouldn't be atheists—but some are worse than others. Some have a vague rooting in the idea that evidence and reason matter; others are just flatly stupid, brain-torturing, ridiculous, or all three. (Exhibit A: Pascal's Wager. Shoot me now.)

Sally M, who's been an atheist since she was a child, tells this story of a coming out that turned straight into an argument about religion, a coming out that was an argument about religion from its very inception. "My parents assumed it was a phase," she says, "when I made them aware. We were in the car one day and I said, 'Wow, we could have just crashed into that pole and died horribly, that would have been absolutely awful, and (my sister) wasn't even wearing her seatbelt, her body would have killed you for sure!' (I was in a mood, and I was a teenager...)

"My mother was horrified and responded, 'What would you do if that really happened?'

"I said, 'Well, I'd be dead, so I guess I wouldn't notice?'

"And she said, 'I mean when you get to heaven!'

"I was kind of taken aback at this point because she sounded pretty serious, and said, 'I'd be dead and there is no heaven, it's fine. What are you talking about?'

"'The Bible! God!'

"'Um. Mom, those are just stories. They're not *real*.'

"She got all hushed and stared at me. 'How do you know? What if it is and you just said that and God HEARD YOU??'"

I know. Pascal's Wager. Shoot me now.

You have to decide how to respond to that. And you may respond differently with people you care about than you do with strangers on the Internet. With strangers on the Internet, there is considerable power in pointing out how ridiculous their arguments are. If it doesn't persuade the person you're debating, it may make someone else who's watching sit up and take notice. But with people you care about, you need to be cautious. No matter how careful you are about saying "That is a ridiculous idea," instead of "You are a ridiculous person," they may not get it. They may feel personally attacked. If you don't want that, you'll need to be careful about how you word your responses to their laughably bad arguments.

And very importantly: You don't have to show up to every fight you're invited to. You get to decide who you're willing to argue with, and when. You get to decide if you think it'll be productive, if you think the people you're talking with will be open-minded, if you're in the mood. And if things start to go south, you can opt out any time you want.

Naomi, who was raised in a politically conservative Southern Baptist home, came out to her family in a four-page email explaining her deconversion, making it clear that she had read Biblical history, and showing that she had real convictions based on deep study. But when her father said he wanted to spend an evening discussing it with her, she declined. "I am very non-confrontational by nature," she says, "and even a benign debate leaves me flustered and shaken. I wasn't about to go head to head with my loved ones for many reasons, but basically because I thought it would be damaging to our relationship and pointless." What's more, she adds, she didn't think the conversation would be a sincere debate. "I knew that I would be in for a full on theological assault," she says. "My dad does not 'discuss' these matters. I already saw what my sister went through when she came out as 'catholic'—she offered to be open for discussion about the changes in her beliefs and was subjected to hour long lectures about how she had gone off the rails... I knew agreeing to disagree while gaining mutual understanding was not the objective."

And Naomi knew that her own atheism was not going to change. She knew she had considered the question carefully and at length, and she knew her father was not going to say anything she hadn't already thought out. "I did not want to open that door," she says, "to even feign the possibility that I could be convinced to go back to faith. I don't see how that would be possible—the clarity you have when you close the door forever on 'faith' is astounding."

Of course, the flip side of that is also true. If you get into arguments with believers, they get the same "opt out" option you do. Remember that. If they back out of an argument or change the subject, don't pull the "You can't handle the truth!" number on them. Respect them for recognizing their emotional state—and respect their right to draw their own boundaries.

And if you argue about religion, there is one very important possibility you need to be prepared for—the possibility that you'll win. Debates about religion do sometimes persuade people out of it. This almost never happens in a single conversation, so don't expect it to. But if you ask former believers what changed their mind about religion, a whole lot of them will say, "Conversations with atheist friends." (Or family members, or colleagues, or strangers on the Internet.) So if you're debating someone you know about religion, and a month or a year later they come to you and say, "You're right, there is no God— now what do I do?," be prepared to give them support if they need it. Be prepared to point them to atheist philosophies of life and death and the universe and whatnot. And be prepared to point them to some resources. (There's an atheist resource guide at the end of this book; it's not an all-inclusive listing of every atheist resource on the planet, but it should help get people started.)

Finally, it's important to remember that arguments between athe-ists and believers don't always go south. And I'm not just talking about times when the arguments are successful, and we persuade them out of their religion. Atheists and believers can debate, and both keep their views on religion—and stay close for years. Hunter was at one time an actively evangelical Christian, knocking on people's doors to win souls. By the time he came out as an atheist to his incredibly devoted Christian father, he says, "he had suspected for some time that I was no longer a Christian.

"On his deck one night, he said, 'but you still believe in the spiri-tual realm, right?' I said that I didn't and that certainly seemed to freak him out. I remember going off on a monologue at that point. I tried to explain that, for all the good things in life to be true, it didn't especially matter if God was real or not. Even if he wasn't real, everything that people felt on Sunday morning was real. The fact that it probably came from their own minds, and not from any external source, didn't make it any less powerful. My father was actually pretty receptive to the idea. 'Huh,' he said. And he was silent for a while. He's still a Christian, and we still debate the merits of religion from time to time, but things are very much as they were before. I would say we still have a very good relationship."

Hemant Mehta agrees. In *The Young Atheist's Survival Guide*, he says, "I can say from experience that some of my closest friendships in high school and college formed with religious people because we both enjoyed debating the topic. We could talk about faith and challenge each other, never with malice."[1]

And in fact, a willingness to argue about religion can increase people's respect for you, and strengthen the bonds between you. Sally M again: "The results of my being open about my atheism were negligible, except that a couple of my religious friends would take me with them to their church to argue with their pastor when they felt he was getting arrogant. I was the go-to atheist, the one people came to when they were freaking out about a crisis of faith or when they just wanted a logical answer to a question. I think it actually made some of my friends trust my opinion more, because they knew I'd give them the objective viewpoint on their problems, and not try to preach at them about the morality of the situation, like some of their other friends."

So remember that. Debating religion with believers doesn't have to be a death sentence to the relationship. Just keep an eye on the ball. Remember what you want to get out of the argument. Remember what you want to get out of the relationship. And keep an eye on whether the argument is taking you away from where you want to go—or is actually bringing you closer.

CHAPTER TWENTY-FOUR

— ❋ —

My Own Coming Out Story

It wouldn't be much of a "coming out atheist" book if I didn't tell my own coming out story. I'll warn you now, it's not hugely dramatic or exciting. But people do seem to want to hear it. It's something atheists bond over; get three open atheists in a room together, and sooner or later, we'll be telling each other our coming out stories. I've heard more than I can possibly recall. I've been asked to tell mine more times than I can remember. And it wouldn't be right to ask other people to bare their deepest feelings and tell their intensely personal stories of trauma and triumph with family and friends—and not tell my own.

I'm lucky. My family are almost all nonbelievers. Both of my parents were agnostics, and in fact my father stopped calling himself agnostic and started calling himself atheist long before I did. My brother is an atheist. To the best of my knowledge, all of my aunts and uncles and cousins are atheists or some sort of nonbelievers. My grandparents were religious, but not very, and anyway all of them were gone by the time I came out. (I doubt it would have been much of an issue with them anyway—again, all their kids were nonbelievers, so I don't think their grandchildren's atheism would have come as a great shock.)

So coming out atheist to my family was a non-issue. In fact, the opposite was true; when I was in college and decided to major in religion, they were worried that I'd found Jesus. I had to reassure them that no, this was an entirely academic study of religion, and Jesus remained well and truly lost.

I did, as it happened, pick up some religious beliefs in college—not of the Jesus variety, but of the New Age variety. It was a fairly typical "college student on too many drugs" mishmash of Tarot, reincarnation, astrology, occultism, synchronicity, friendly trickster spirits who planted joints in our apartment, the idea that subatomic particles must be conscious and have free will since their behavior isn't predictable... you know the drill. And I did have to go through a process of letting go of those beliefs. This was a gradual process of moving from some fairly specific junk ideas (like the invisible spirit of the Tarot moving the cards as they were shuffled—no, really), towards a vague, generalized belief in some sort of immaterial spirit that animated all living things and survived in some form after death. It was a gradual process that ended very abruptly indeed, when I had minor surgery, went under general anesthesia—and completely abandoned any shred of an idea I might have had about having a consciousness separate from my brain. This was a somewhat traumatic experience, especially since it involved letting go of any notions I was still clinging to about an afterlife. So since this is me, and I'm a writer, I wrote about it. My first piece of explicitly non-believing writing, "Comforting Thoughts About Death That Have Nothing To Do With God," was published in *Skeptical Inquirer*, Vol. 29 #2 (March/April 2005).

Again—this is me. Writer since 1989. Blogger since 2005. Known largely for (a) writing about very personal things, and (b) writing about things other people don't want to write about, because they're too controversial or too stigmatized. (Among other things, I was a sex writer for decades before I became an atheist writer.) So as my nonbelief developed, writing about it was an obvious, natural thing to do. This meant that my continued process of coming out as a nonbeliever—identifying as an agnostic, as a skeptic, and then finally (after reading *The God Delusion*) as an atheist—all happened largely in public, on my blog and elsewhere on the Internet. My continued process of becoming an increasingly ardent atheist, and becoming increasingly involved with atheist communities and the organized atheist movement, also happened largely on the Internet.

And my process of getting into confrontations with friends—and in a few cases losing those friends—happened largely on the Internet.

I don't want to get into too much detail about the lost friendships. Those are other people's stories as well as mine, and while I'm generally comfortable airing my own dirty laundry, I'm a bit hesitant to air other people's. The bottom line: Some believers from the very progressive San Francisco Bay Area, people very much into the ecumenical/interfaith/"it's all a rich tapestry of faith"/tolerance-and-acceptance version of religion, were initially quite supportive of my atheism, and even of my atheist writing. But once my atheism became more outspoken—once I moved into questioning and criticizing religion, pointing out its flaws and implausibilities, and trying to persuade people out of it—these people's tolerance got stretched to the limit. I'd thought I could disagree with friends about religion, the same way we might disagree about politics or science or any other idea, and still remain friends. And with some people, that's been true. But for a few people, people for whom religion was very important, my outspoken anti-theism was a dealbreaker. I suppose I can't blame them (except to the degree that I blame anyone for holding religious beliefs at all, since I think they're indefensible). If I had an idea about the world that was central to my approach to life and even to my identity, and a friend of mine was dedicating their life's work to demolishing it, I'd have a hard time, too.

None of the friends I lost were intensely close. But a couple of them were people I'd spent a lot of time with, and were part of groups and communities I felt an important connection with. These were people I respected and cared about, friendships I didn't want to lose. It was sad, and it still makes me sad.

But it's also the case that coming out as an atheist, and being so public about my atheism, helped other friendships grow stronger. With many friends who already accepted the non-existence of any gods, or who became atheist at about the same time I did, our atheism became a bond between us. And my public atheism drew me into other friendships, new friendships, friendships with people I'd never even have met if it weren't for the atheist movement. One of the things I love most about being in organized atheism is how much it's widened my circle of friends: I'm now friends with people from a much wider range of ages, backgrounds, races, occupations, economic classes, geographical regions, than I ever have at any point in my life. That's kind of awesome. What's more, some friends and family members who already identified as atheist became more open about it, in part, because of me. Still others have let go of their religious or spiritual beliefs, in part, because of me. And that feels pretty darned cool.

And when it came to coming out at work, I got lucky there as well. When I first came out as an atheist, I worked at a hippie/punk rock/anarchist/freakazoid book publisher and distributor, and a good half (at least) of my co-workers were atheists, who thought my atheist writing was awesome. If there were believers there, it mostly didn't come up. I did have one difficult conversation with one co-worker who wanted to convince me that audio recordings of dead souls were real; we had one somewhat intense argument about it, and afterwards we just avoided the subject. And I did have a weird situation where another co-worker started commenting on my blog—and turned into one of my most irritating, nasty, persistent religious trolls, someone I actually wound up banning. (The first commenter I ever banned, actually.) That was awkward as hell; when we had to work on projects together, we pretty much had to pretend that our contentious online relationship didn't exist.

But overall, my atheism was totally fine at work, and even positive and supportive. I was never in any fear of being fired, or passed over for promotion, or anything remotely like that. It actually strengthened bonds between me and many of my co-workers—bonds that are still there, even after I left that job. I feel very grateful for that.

If I had it to do over again, would I do anything differently? I'd probably be more cautious about getting into arguments about religion with friends. I *am* now more cautious about getting into arguments about religion with friends. I'm more likely to keep my religious debates out of my personal life, and to limit them to my public writings. And when I do argue with friends about religion, I back off and change the subject a lot sooner than I used to. (I'm also less inclined to debate religion with friends in email, on Facebook, on my blog, or anywhere online, since I know how quickly online arguments can go south, and how ugly that Southland can be.)

But even if I'd done all that, I'm not sure things would have turned out much differently. Even if I hadn't engaged with these particular people about their religion in any way, I was still being very public, not only about my atheism, but about my active and vehement opposition to religion. It was all over my blog and my email blasts and my Facebook feed. It was pretty much impossible to ignore. It still is. And for at least one person, the fact that I made arguments against religion at all—not only with him, but in public spaces, and with anyone ever—was unacceptable. In his eyes, the very act of treating religion as just another conclusion about the world was not simply disrespectful, but intolerant, hateful, even fascistic. (His words. He even compared me to Joseph Stalin and Glenn Beck.) Even if I had always diplomatically backed out of debates with him personally, he was never going to be okay with my atheist blogging and reporting and Facebooking.

I know I keep saying this, but it keeps being relevant, so I'll say it again: I'm not sure there's any way to come out as an atheist without upsetting somebody. There is literally no way to say, "I'm an atheist," without at least implying, "If you believe in God, you're wrong." So I don't think there was any way to do the work I care about, the work that's become so important to me, without alienating at least someone.

But am I happy that I came out as an atheist? Do I think it was the right decision? Absolutely. No question. I am not a person to whom secrecy comes naturally. I can do it: I've kept secrets in my life, and will continue to keep more. But it's not comfortable for me. I would much rather just say what's on my mind. I have made a career out of saying what's on my mind. And I am, without a doubt, much happier being open about my atheism than I ever could have been being secret about it.

PART THREE: HELPING EACH OTHER COME OUT

— ✹ —

So far, I've mostly been talking about how we can come out in our own lives, and what we can do to make that process easier on ourselves and the people we're coming out to. But there's something else, something huge, that we can do to make coming out atheist easier:

We can change the world.

We can make the world one in which it's easier to come out—not just for ourselves, but for all atheists.

I know. You're rolling your eyes and thinking, "Sure. Easy, shmeezy. We'll get that done in an afternoon. And when we're done with that, we'll have dinner, and then we'll fix poverty and global climate change."

But there are, in fact, lots of things we can do that make it easier for other atheists to come out: practical, down-to-earth things, with concrete effects. They're not going to rid the world of anti-atheist bigotry overnight—but they can make a real difference, and sometimes faster than we might think.

In fact, in just the last few years, we've already made it easier to be an atheist. In 1999, polls showed that only 49% of Americans would vote for an atheist for President. In 2012, that number had jumped to 54%.[1] That's still pretty pathetic; we're still at the bottom of the list, below every other marginalized group in the poll.[2] But it's an increase of

5% in just thirteen years. In thirteen years, we got to the point where a majority of Americans consider us trustworthy enough to be President. That's not trivial. That's pretty freaking dramatic.

And coming out has a snowball effect. When we come out as atheist, other people will feel safer coming out. Then they'll make the next wave of people feel safer. And so on, and so on, and so on. The more of us who come out, the easier it is on all of us.

So what can we do to help each other come out? What can we do as individuals to support our atheist friends or family members who want to come out? What can we do as a community to make atheism a safer place to come out into? What can we do as a movement to change the non-atheist world and make it a better place for atheists?

Let's talk about that.

CHAPTER TWENTY-FIVE

Visibility and Role Models, or, Step One:
Come Out Your Own Damn Self

Do you want to help other atheists come out? The Number One most powerful thing you can do is to come out yourself.

This theme comes up again and again in this book: Having open atheists in our lives makes it easier for us to come out. When we see that other atheists exist, it makes us feel less alone, and lets us know that we'll have support if we have a hard time. When we see that other atheists not only exist, but are happy and good, with joy and meaning in their lives, it helps us get over whatever messed-up myths we might have learned about atheism. And when we see that other atheists not only exist, and are not only happy and good, but are open about it—and when we see that it hasn't messed up their lives, that in fact their lives are generally better now that they're out—it gives us courage to come out ourselves.

briansawilddowner grew up near Houston, Texas. "Hardly the most friendly part of the country for non-believers," he says. When he told his mother that he was an atheist, she started telling her siblings and parents about it—with surprising results. "For quite a few of them," he says, "their response was 'so are we.' Everyone had just been too afraid to talk about it, so it was something no one really knew about each other. My grandmother even talked to me and told me that she'd been having a lot of doubts about it as well!"

Being an out atheist doesn't just help other atheists to come out. It helps other atheists to be *more* out. Again: Being an out atheist isn't an either/or thing. It's a spectrum. And if we're more open and visible to more people, other atheists will often move closer to the "out" end of the spectrum themselves. dezn_98 says that after he came out to his close friends and family, he decided he didn't need to come out to anyone else. "What changed my mind," he says, "was that my cousin, the first one I told, started telling me how he is just plain out. He had no qualms about telling people he did not believe. I asked him how it went and he said for the most part people did not care... He actually empowered me to be more or less nonchalant about my atheism, [and to be] just full blown out there with no inhibitions of calling myself an atheist."

Coming out doesn't just help other atheists come out. It helps other atheists simply *be* out. It helps create a culture where being an open atheist isn't a big deal, and coming out doesn't have to be a big dramatic event. naathcousins, who was raised Catholic, says, "I've never really 'come out' as atheist as such (as in, a dramatic 'hey everybody, I'm an atheist' moment) so no-one has individually 'helped me come out.' But the fact that many of my friends are openly atheist, and none of the others are the sort of people who try to convert one to their faith; that's the thing that has made me never need a 'coming out' moment with my friends."

Being an out atheist can also help other atheists understand their own atheist identity more clearly—and that can help them publicly claim it. antialiasis never really believed in God, but they convinced themselves that they did, and later identified as agnostic. "I started calling myself an atheist," they say, "when a person I respected explained that what I was describing as 'agnostic leaning towards atheist' was exactly the same thing she meant when she called herself an atheist... For me, the instrumental factors in that realization were 1) people I already liked and respected who were openly atheists, and 2) being educated about what atheism actually is."

And, of course, coming out as an atheist can change believers' minds about atheists, and make them less likely to believe ridiculous and damaging stereotypes about us. And that makes it easier for *all* of us to come out. Kevin Wells is a mixed-race Asian American man with both Bible-thumping Christians and closeted atheists in his family. "Now that I'm out as an atheist," he says, "I feel like I want to set a good example as a friendly atheist. I'm extremely happy I came out, and I have had at least a couple of theists tell me that they enjoy reading my comments relating to theism/atheism that I post on Facebook, and that I'm the only atheist they know. I want to squash the negative generalizations that many people place upon atheists."

Some atheists are reluctant to come out and be visible because they feel like they aren't good enough to be role models. We sometimes think that we have to be a credit to our atheism (horrible phrase): that if we show our flaws, or reveal that atheism and being an out atheist can sometimes be hard, we're letting down the side. But being role models doesn't mean presenting ourselves as completely happy atheists with perfect lives. Revealing our struggles and our vulnerability can actually be encouraging to others. It makes being an out atheist seem more accessible, like something anyone can do.

And being a visible role model for atheism doesn't have to mean being confrontational or in-your-face. If that's your style, that's fine. If that's not your style—that's also fine. steffp, who grew up in a Catholic family in a very Catholic-dominated village in Germany, talks about what happened when he was age ten. "We moved in with mom's brother," he says, "who was a closeted gay and the first atheist I ever met. Strange records and books on his bookshelves. Classical and Jazz music, poetry, art picture books, a complete history of fine arts and philosophy. He held papers and magazines that we had never heard of, and political convictions (timid labor party) that were totally different. And he did not attend church on Sundays. He did not mention his atheism at all, but he would patiently explain the difficult words in his history of philosophy, and did not object when we kids sneaked into his room and marveled at his van Gogh and impressionism picture books. He taught us mental discipline, and Kantian audacity of inquiry. This was, I think in retrospect, the foundation of atheism for all of us."

If you have internalized atheophobia or residual guilt about your atheism, coming out—and the encouragement it gives others to come out—may cause some initial qualms. Eric Paulsen came out at age ten, largely because he found Sunday school "a depressing waste of time," and "going to church had begun to give me nightmares, terrible dreams of desolation and torture; even the dreams of heaven were of a sterile unemotional place where you were forced to sing the praises of a god I had grown increasingly doubtful of." His parents were much more accepting than he'd expected, and after a serious conversation they let him quit Sunday school. After that, he says, "the only result of my coming out that worried me was that shortly after I stopped going to church my brother also fought to stay home and I was always a little worried that he only did it because of me. See, back then I was more of a weak agnostic and was afraid that if I was wrong I could be condemning him to an eternity in hell next to me and I felt guilty for that. I don't feel that way anymore, of course, I have gone from weak agnostic to strong atheist, but I still wonder if he would have come to the conclusion that he too was an unbeliever if I hadn't first."

And if your own experiences of accepting atheism or coming out about it were troubling or traumatic, you might feel some guilt about encouraging others to do it—even if that encouragement simply takes the form of coming out yourself. Evelyn grew up in the relatively non-religious United Kingdom, in a family that wasn't particularly religious.

But despite that, she says, "After deciding I didn't believe in God there was still a period where I was not comfortable describing myself as an atheist. It had been painful acknowledging that I didn't believe and I was uncomfortable causing similar pain to others."

That's up to you to decide, obviously. But it's worth thinking about whether, even with any troubling experiences you may have had accepting atheism or coming out about it, you still regret it. If you don't regret it—don't assume that other people will. After all, most atheists don't. Think of it this way: Having surgery is traumatic, but you'd still encourage your friend to get it if you thought they'd be healthier and happier afterwards.

And if you're having these qualms about coming out, it's worth thinking about whether atheism, or even outright opposition to religion, is important enough to you to overcome your qualms. Evelyn again: "A conversation with a hardline Muslim changed my view. The guy said that he thought that Salman Rushdie deserved to be executed if he went to a Muslim country. Later in the conversation he admitted after some evasion that he had no problem with the death penalty for adultery. When I disagreed he said, 'It's divine law, you can't question it.' I realised that the only reasonable answer to that was, 'No it's not and yes you can,' although I did not have the courage to say so at the time.'

"My husband, colleagues and atheist friends all gave me confidence to describe myself openly as an atheist," she adds. "However, I still credit the Muslim guy with making me realise it was necessary." Evelyn is now not only more open about her atheism—she's also gotten involved in secular activism.

And finally: When we come out as atheists, it doesn't just encourage other atheists to come out. It encourages other atheists to speak out against anti-atheist bigotry—and to take action against it. Here's Miriam's story, one of my favorite stories in this book. It's a story about coming out as an atheist under trying circumstances, while being put on the spot, and in the face of an authority figure—and in the process, giving courage to other atheists to come out, inspiring them to question institutionalized religion and to demand their rights as atheists, informing people about secular support systems, and initiating policy change into the bargain. She pretty much hit a grand slam with this one.

"I recently started an intensive outpatient treatment program for chemical dependency," she says. "We meet three days a week—there's two group therapy sessions and a 'skills' session, which has had themes like assertiveness, anger management, or depression. I had a hard time finding a program that wasn't explicitly religious... as an atheist, being told that I need to surrender to my 'higher power' clearly isn't going to be helpful to me at all! After a fair bit of searching, I was able to find a clinic-based program that promised an individualized treatment program, so I hoped that it would not get too much into the 12-step woo. I was very open about being atheist through the intake and when meeting with the therapists, but it hadn't come up in any of the group sessions.

"The most recent skills session was—you guessed it—spirituality, and was led by an Episcopalian minister who's also in recovery. (The regular counselor told me about the topic beforehand, apologized to me, and gave me a list of non-12-step meetings and programs.) I wasn't excited about it but I did my best to go in with an open mind. I figured that while the topic might not be applicable or helpful to me, maybe it'd be helpful for others in the group. So even if I didn't get anything out of it personally, I wasn't going to be argumentative or disruptive. I planned on taking the same attitude I do towards the Serenity Prayer that closes each meeting—I don't participate, but I'm not disrespectful. I just stay quiet and let everyone else do their thing.

"The session started with the minister introducing herself and sharing a bit about her view of addiction. She framed this with what seemed to me to be a false dichotomy: on one hand, there's the material world: always struggling and striving for more and more, competitive, self-centered, and materialistic. On the other hand, you have spirituality: community, love, altruism, and being part of something bigger than yourself. She said that she sees addiction as both a physical and a spiritual disease, and if you only address the physical/material dimension while neglecting the spiritual, you're going to be left with a pretty miserable life. She then asked us to introduce ourselves and say a bit about what had brought us there. As I was sitting to her right, she turned to me and asked me to go next. So I did.

"After stating my name and what had brought me to the group, I said, 'And just so you know, I'm an atheist. I don't believe in a soul; I don't believe in any supernatural beings or higher powers; I don't believe in mind-body duality or anything like that at all.' I also told her that I was frankly put off and offended by the idea that my atheism condemns me to a life of misery. She quickly backtracked that no no, that wasn't what she meant at all! On to the next person now please!

"As she attempted to lead us through a discussion of spirituality, I saw several other people in the group pushing back—some gently, some not so gently. One person challenged her statement that AA/NA and other 12-step programs are open to everyone regardless of beliefs, saying 'There's a lot of god in that book. They may call it a higher power, but really they're talking about god.' Another person wondered out loud whether it was okay for courts to order people to go to AA meetings (it's not!).

"At the end of the night as we were getting ready to go, one person approached me and asked me about non-12 step meetings that he might be able to attend. Another said that he'd noticed I don't say the Serenity Prayer (and he's stopped saying it since then, too). During the next session, our regular counselor asked which of us was made uncomfortable by the references to spirituality, and almost every. single. person. raised their hand. It led to a really good discussion about why the traditional 12-step programs have such an emphasis on spirituality, and how we can find the same resources and community support outside of a religious framework.

"At the beginning of that night, I hadn't planned on coming out to my group as an atheist, but I'm really glad that I did. My hope is that those of us in the atheist community who are struggling with addictions can support each other and help each other find secular, evidence-based treatment, so that we aren't forced to grit our teeth and put up with the 12-step woo that so many believe is the only way to treat addiction."

There is nothing I could possibly add to that. She said it perfectly.

Coming out helps other atheists come out. And that makes things better for all of us. For them, for you—for everyone. That's not going to be our only motivation, or even our primary one. But if that matters to you, if it gives you encouragement and inspiration—remember Miriam's story. And remember every other story in this book.

CHAPTER TWENTY-SIX

Support or Pressure? How to Tell the Difference

For as long as I've been involved in the atheist movement, I've been hearing the cries, "Come out, come out, wherever you are!" Lots of people who care about atheism—organization leaders, thought leaders, local community leaders, just folks in the community—are exhorting one another to come out about our atheism. We're saying that it's a powerful way to improve our own lives and the lives of people around us. And we're saying that it's the most powerful political action we can take.

I'm one of those people. I'm totally on board. That's the whole reason I'm writing this book. Yes, we should support each other in coming out. We should encourage each other to come out. We should even work to create a culture where coming out as atheist is seen, by both atheists and believers, as natural and normal; a rite of passage; a question not of "if" but of "when." The LGBT community has done this very successfully—and I think it's a great idea for atheists to do it, too.

At the same time, I've also been saying throughout this book that we should understand our differences—which includes understanding that some atheists are going to have an easier time coming out than others. Some atheists are in situations that make coming out more difficult—in some cases, even more dangerous. We should have sympathy,

336 • COMING OUT ATHEIST

and accept that other people have to come out on their own timetable. We shouldn't pressure them to come out before they're ready. We
shouldn't pressure them to come out to a greater degree than they're
ready to. We should be careful about their privacy if they're preserving
it. And we should definitely not out them.

So how do we reconcile these goals? How do we support and encourage people to be out—without guilt-tripping them if they're not?

I don't have a magic formula about how to draw that line. It's a line
I've been trying to draw throughout the writing of this book, and I'm
still not sure that I got it right. (I'm assuming that readers of this book
have already decided that they want to come out, so I've been leaning
in the direction of encouragement and cheerleading—which I hope
you haven't experienced as peer pressure.)

I don't have a formula for drawing the line between encouragement
and pressure. But I have a few ideas about how to keep an eye on it.

One way to manage that line is to have empathy. If you're exhorting
other atheists to come out, think about how you'd feel if you weren't
out, and you were hearing this message. If you heard, "You owe it to
other atheists to come out"—would you hear that as encouragement,
or pressure? Would it be more encouraging to hear, "Coming out helps
other atheists—do it if you can"? What about, "Other atheists made
it easier for us—let's try to pass that along"? What kind of language
makes you feel defensive, and what do you hear as supportive? What
language makes you think, "Yeah, this is hard, but others have done it,
and others have my back"? Think about that—and craft your language
accordingly.

Related to this: Listen carefully to *why* the people you're talking
with are having a hard time coming out. Different people face different
obstacles. Sometimes, coming out is hard for personal reasons; some
people are more independent, more comfortable on the fringes of society, while others are more socially-oriented and care more about what
people think of them. Sometimes it's for pragmatic reasons; it can be

harder to come out if people are financially dependent on their parents, if they live someplace where religion is ingrained in the social structure, if they don't have a financial safety net and losing their job could mean ruin. Sometimes it's for larger social and cultural reasons; it can be harder to come out for people who are already part of a marginalized group—if they're gay, a person of color, an immigrant—and they don't want to alienate the supportive culture they rely on, or don't want another stigma piled onto the ones they already have. Sometimes it's hard because community matters a lot to some people, and the place they live doesn't have a strong atheist community to come out into.

So pay attention to what obstacles they're facing—and tailor your encouragement accordingly. If their concerns are more about ostracism or social isolation, let them know about atheist communities. (And help build them! For ideas on that, see the chapter on building community.) If their concerns are more pragmatic, hook them up with job training, job counseling, networking in whatever atheist community you're part of. If their issues are more about their cultural identity, let them know about atheist communities specifically by and for whatever groups they're part of. If they're in need of community, let them know about atheist communities, and help build them. I said that already, didn't I? Well, there's a reason for that. For many people, their anxieties about coming out—even the pragmatic concerns—are about isolation. One of the strongest encouragements you can give is reassurance that they won't be alone—and assistance in making that true.

I also think that when we're encouraging people to come out, it's often helpful to acknowledge how hard it can be. That might seem totally backwards; wouldn't saying "Yeah, coming out can really suck" be discouraging? Wouldn't it put a damper on people who'd otherwise be excited about it? But I don't think that's true. I think if we act like perky cheerleaders and exhort people to come out without acknowledging its difficulties, people will think we're out of touch with their reality, and will dismiss what we're saying. If, on the other hand, we recognize how rough it can be—if we say things like, "Yeah, I know it can be hard, I'm happier now that I'm more out, but it was rough there for a while," or even, "Yeah, I know it can be hard, I had a relatively easy time of it, but I know I was lucky and that isn't true for everyone"—then our message seems more realistic, and the goal seems more attainable. So I think it's helpful to word our "come out, come out!" exhortations in a way that's both encouraging and sympathetic. We can say things like, "Come out if you can." "Come out if it's safe." "Take a step outside your comfort zone."

Related to that: Understanding that coming out is a continuum, and a process, can help us encourage it in a way that's compassionate. Instead of simply saying, "Come out!" as if that were an either/or thing, we can say things like, "Come out as much as you can." "Take a step towards coming out." "Come out to one person you've never come out to."

And finally: This business of being encouraging without guilt tripping, and keeping an eye on the difference? It doesn't just apply to one-on-one conversations with the people in our lives. It applies to writers, bloggers, videobloggers, podcasters, etc., who are crafting a "Come out! Come out!" message for a wider audience. And it applies to groups and organizations creating visibility and coming out programs. If we're encouraging atheists to come out, let's make sure that what we're saying doesn't make people feel like they're being dragged out through the closet door. Instead, let's make them feel like they're being invited into a better place.

CHAPTER TWENTY-SEVEN

Don't Out People

Don't out people.

Don't, don't, don't.

You may have strong opinions about whether people should come out as atheists. You may have personal opinions about whether individuals you know would be happier if they came out. You may have political opinions about whether atheists in general should be more open about their atheism.

But you have no idea about the reality of other people's lives. You don't know if they're in a nasty custody battle with a highly religious partner. You don't know if their boss is a flaming fundamentalist bigot. You don't know if their parents would cut off their tuition if they discover they're an atheist. You don't know if they've decided to keep their mouth shut around their sick grandmother. The decision to come out can be a tricky cost/benefit analysis—and you don't get to make that analysis for other people.

Even if someone is planning to come out, they may have their own plan for doing it, their own timetable. One of the recurring themes of this book is picking a good time and place. And you don't know what a good time and place is for other people. You don't know if they'd planned to do it over a holiday visit, so they'd have plenty of time to process it; whether they'd planned to wait until some big project was done, so it wouldn't compound the stress they were already under. Again—not your cost/benefit analysis to make.

And even if this moment would be a perfectly good time and place for them to come out, even if they were ten seconds away from doing it themselves, being outed is a very different experience from coming out. It can make people feel ambushed; it can leave them emotionally and psychologically unprepared. It makes their coming out a reaction, not an action: something that was done to them, not something they did on their own. It takes away the ownership of the coming out experience. It can feel like a violation.

Most atheists do report that they're happier after coming out, and that coming out was a good decision. Even if it has some bad outcomes, such as alienating family members, they overwhelmingly say it was the right decision. But very few atheists who were outed involuntarily say they're happy about it. Most of them are happy about the basic fact that they're now out—but they wish they'd been able to do it themselves. They tend to think it would have gone over better with their family or friends, or that it would have been less stressful on themselves. Or both.

Don't out people. It sucks. johnkarpf was brought up in an evangelical fundamentalist Christian family where religion dominated life, but started having doubts at age 16. "I confessed my feelings to my brother who was 13 at the time," he says, "sort of stream of consciousness, I was just trying to work it out aloud, and although I told him in confidence, he immediately ran into the living room and said to my mother; 'John doesn't believe in God.' I was momentarily breathless. I don't know what I expected. My brother outed me and I was NOT ready for it. I wasn't even sure what I was thinking." The result was that his father laid down a harsh and rigid set of restrictions and punishments; he threw out all of John's science fiction books, made him attend church but wouldn't let him sit with the family, forced him to quit his job to spend all his spare time reading the Bible, made him surrender his driver's license, refused to let him talk on the phone (so he wouldn't tell any other family members), and refused to let him spend any time alone. This went on for two months, at which point his parents returned his driver's license to him—and kicked him out of the house. "He talked," John says, "in an unfamiliar measured tone that sounded rehearsed: 'Your mother and I have decided that having you here is much too dangerous for your brothers and sister and too much of a burden on our family. We as parents are responsible for the souls of our whole family.'" John and his family were estranged for years; he eventually forgave them so they could see their grandchildren, but they didn't apologize for kicking him out until they were in their seventies.

Even if the consequences aren't that dire, being outed still sucks. "Coming out to my grandmother was by far the worst," says Kat Car. "I was outed against my will. I never intended to tell her. She is an active church member; not a fire and brimstone guilt type, but very firm in her views. She is also one of the people I love most in the world, and I had recently lost my grandfather. I had no intention of ever telling her I thought he was just gone, that the world we can see is all we have.

"I was at university, and she and my dad had come to take me and my boyfriend out to dinner. My boyfriend made a silly joke about my atheism, as he often does. My dad had known for years, and was if anything slightly bored by it, but my nan turned to me and said 'Oh, you're being an atheist now are you?' like I'd decided to be a Goth, or a footballer. Another silly phase I would grow out of.

"I laughed, slightly hysterically, and said yes, but I wasn't about to begin worshipping Satan or eating babies. She nodded, disappointed. I was caught out in a situation I had already decided never to deal with... I suggest you brief the people that [you] know if you don't intend to come out to certain people. Let them know you're not going to tell person x, and why."

Don't out people on purpose—and don't do it by accident. Be careful with other people's privacy. Check with them before you forward their email about the atheist meetup, or tag the photo of them at the atheist conference, or mention the atheist group they're organizing when you're visiting their family.

If someone is a very public atheist, you're probably safe. It's probably safe to mention that Richard Dawkins is an atheist. Or the president of the American Humanist Association. Or me. You hereby have my permission to tell anyone you want that I'm an atheist.

But if we're not talking about very public professional atheists, you don't always know. Some people have "atheism" all over their Facebook page—but they still haven't told their grandparents, and they know their grandparents don't read Facebook. I've met presidents of atheist student groups who weren't out to their parents. Heck, I've met directors of national atheist organizations who weren't out to their parents.

The only people I would consider it legitimate to out are public figures who are secretly atheist but are publicly opposing atheist rights or separation of church and state. (I have the same policy about closeted gay politicians who are opposing gay rights.) Even then, it's morally dicey—and it's strategically problematic. Is a self-serving, morally bankrupt political hack getting dragged out of the closet kicking and screaming really the image of atheism we want to present to the world?

So don't out people. Don't do it intentionally. Don't do it accidentally. Just don't.

CHAPTER TWENTY-EIGHT

— ✺ —

Understanding Our Differences

This is a very short chapter, and it consists of pretty much one piece of advice:

Go back and re-read the first part of the book.

All of it. The whole thing. Even the chapters that don't apply to you. If you're not a student, read the chapter on coming out in school. If you're not in the military, read the chapter on coming out in the military. If you're not a marginalized minority, read the chapter on coming out for marginalized minorities.

Coming out is different for everyone. There are different challenges faced by people coming out in different circumstances. If we want to support other atheists in coming out, we need to understand these differences, and have empathy about them.

If we're creating an atheist community, or we're trying to make an existing community grow and flourish, we need to know what different atheists' needs are. We can't assume that what works for us is going to work for everyone. We may like listening to talks and lectures—but other people may need more socializing and emotional support. We may enjoy hanging out in bars—but other people may need activities that are more kid-friendly, or that just don't involve alcohol. We may want a meeting space with ample parking—but other people may need meeting spaces near public transportation.

Omaar Khayaam's community members are mostly Muslims; he comes from a Muslim family, and the city in England where he lives has a large Pakistani Muslim minority. It took him "over twenty years of struggling to believe in God and in the religion of family (Islam)" before he finally accepted and embraced his atheism. He now says that being out would be easier for him if more people in the atheist community had a better understanding of the Muslim world—and the ex-Muslim world. "What would be useful," he says, "is a greater understanding of the dynamics of being an ex-muslim and ways to help those from this community. I do sometimes get the impression that atheists and freethinkers who are not from the ex-muslim community have a naive understanding of the ex-muslim situation."

If we're going to make atheism a safer place to land for a larger number of people, we need to make our communities more welcoming to people who aren't like us. And we can start by learning what other atheists' experiences are. So go back and re-read the first part of the book—including any chapters you skipped. (It's a good idea anyway, just for your own sake. The categories in this book aren't that clear-cut, and lots of ideas from one chapter apply to others.)

But don't stop there. Read blogs and books, watch videos and listen to podcasts, attend workshops and go to talks, from atheists who aren't like you. Even better—get into conversations with atheists who aren't like you. (I get into this more in Chapter 30: Diversity, or, Making Communities Welcoming to People Who Aren't Just Like Us.)

And speaking of building an atheist community...

CHAPTER TWENTY-NINE

— ✳ —

Building Community

Creating, supporting, and participating in atheist communities is absolutely one of the most important things we can do to help other atheists come out.

The reasons people stay in religion often don't have that much to do with actual religious beliefs. When believers are polled on why they belong to the religion they belong to—not the broad categories like Christian or Muslim, those are mostly influenced by what they were brought up with as children, but why they picked their particular house of worship—they typically say things like, "The people were friendly." "My family and friends go there." "They take good care of my kids." "The rabbi is an inspiring speaker." "The pastor gave us good advice on our marriage problems." "I like the music." People pick their religion partly because of spiritual growth and religious doctrines, but it also has a lot to do with the community that religion provides: emotional support, practical support, and companionship.[1]

And the social isolation that often happens when people leave religion can be intense. H. Beaton, who was raised as a Jehovah's Witness, makes this point all too well. "If a Jehovah's Witness ceases to follow the religion's rules," he says, "and are not deemed to be adequately 'repentant' by the local church elders, they are excommunicated. Except in a few specific situations, no Jehovah's Witness is allowed to say so much as 'hi' to them anymore. That is what I grew up with. Anyone in my life, no matter how important they were to me, could be taken from me in an instant. One day, I could be hanging out with my best friend, the next day I might never be allowed to speak with him again, or else I myself would face excommunication. More than anything, more than Armageddon itself, I feared disfellowshipping.

"Long story short," he says, "I overcame that fear and decided to leave my religion, but I insisted on doing it 'right.' Since Jehovah's Witnesses don't condone friendships outside their organization, I had no social structure outside the religion. I recognized the need to build up a replacement for it first. I was already talking to other ex-JWs on the internet, but I had nothing 'offline' as it were. I had no idea even how to make friends on my own. All my friendships previous to that were meeting someone at the Kingdom Hall (what JWs call Church), with our guaranteed mutual religious beliefs as a convenient ice breaker. Without that, I had no social 'tools.'"

Jehovah's Witnesses are an extreme case, of course. But some form of exclusion or rejection is common when people leave religion. Even if it doesn't rise to the level of outright shunning, many atheists find that when they come out, connections with religious friends or family become strained, or they simply don't feel welcomed. And even if everyone is trying their best to be nice and keep things together, atheists ourselves may just not feel like part of things anymore.

Many atheists come out without being part of any atheist community. Some connect with atheist communities after they come out; some don't. But the atheists who were part of a community before they came out generally say that it helped them, and they're glad they did it that way. When Chris H. came out, his uncle reacted badly, initially responding by saying, "so you think life has no purpose?," and continuing to email him about what a shame it was that he saw no value in life. "Fortunately," he says, "I was somewhat involved in atheist communities online when I came out, and had a large circle of friends who were at least not religious by the time my uncle flipped out on me... They both helped me sort through the issue to some degree."

For Kenneth Smith, connecting with an atheist community was actually part of what helped him accept his atheism. On the Coming Out Godless Project website, he says that while personal examination of his faith led him to reject the Christian mythology, "I didn't immediately realize I was an atheist until about ten years later when I became affiliated with a freethinker group in southwest Missouri. Through open discussions and exposure to leaders in the godless society, it was like a beacon of light had been turned on within my brain."

And many atheists who didn't connect with an atheist community until they came out now wish they'd done it earlier. Coolred38, who was brought up as Muslim in the Middle East, says, "When I came out I was not connected with any atheist community as such. I didn't know any personally but read their thoughts online etc... Now I'm quite involved and it was amazing to learn that I was not alone anymore."

Atheist communities can also create atheist visibility—and we already know how visibility helps us. When briansawilddowner moved to Denton, Texas, he immediately searched for non-religious groups, and found two—both of which he ended up becoming the head of. "I remember someone attending one of the student group meetings," he says, "and saying that they never really thought about it until they saw our group on campus and thought 'oh, I guess I am an atheist.' I know a few other people who started identifying as atheist while I knew them. That never came from me arguing with them or showing them why their reasons for believing were bad, it just came from me being honest about who I was and being visible."

So we need to create communities—in the flesh as well as online—that provide what religions provide: guidance and counseling, safety nets, day care, places for rituals and rites of passage, activities for families, avenues for charitable and social justice work, events that are inspiring and fun, ongoing companionship, continuity. We need to create communities that just give people basic human contact if their religion cuts them off. If we're asking atheists to consider coming out, we need to give them a safe place to land.

A lot of people are already doing this—and that's awesome. I think it's a huge part of why atheism has been growing so fast and doing so well. There is now, as of this writing, an atheist group in just about every major city in the United States, and lots of smaller cities and towns as well. That wasn't true even a few years ago when I was first starting in organized atheism. We have come amazingly far in just a few years. Let's keep it up. Let's do it better. And let's do it more.

Not everyone is a joiner, of course. If community isn't that important to you, that's fine. If community is important to you, but you don't need it in the form of structured groups, that's also fine. And if you like structured groups, but don't feel a need for them to be atheist-specific—again, that's totally fine. "Atheist community" can mean an official, organized, identifiable atheist community, either in person or online. But it can also simply mean having friends and family who are atheists—people you can talk with about atheism, or even people you don't have to keep it secret from. If you go to the weekly gathering of the West Virginia Atheist Anarchist Bowling League, that's atheist community. But if you just throw a birthday party and half the people who come are atheists, that's atheist community, too.

So even if you're not into the meetups and picnics and panel discussions of your local atheist group, you can still be part of this community-building thing. John Horstman, a lifelong nonbeliever in Milwaukee, Wisconsin, says, "I only discovered FtB [Freethought Blogs] a year or so ago, and it is my sole specifically-atheist 'community,' so I have both been not connected to and connected to an atheist community. That said, many of my friendships through my life have been with other atheists, so I've always had an informal community of atheist friends. This has doubtless contributed to coming out being a non-issue for me—I have no fear of being 'outed' and rejected by family and friends." And Alan, who became an atheist at age 17, says that at the time he came out, "I was not connected to an explicitly atheist community, but I was at a math/science/engineering school, and atheism was very common and perhaps the majority there. It was a non-issue, which helped me feel much more comfortable with it than I had felt in high school (where atheism was rare)."

Even having one or two atheist friends can make a difference. Kevin Wells, who came out by changing his religion on Facebook to "de facto atheist," says, "When I came out, I was not connected with an atheist community at all, but I have a very close friend in real life who is an atheist. As a person I love and respect, after I learned of his lack of belief, I felt more comfortable accepting my own deconversion."

And online communities do count. They don't offer all the same benefits of in-the-flesh communities, of course (and vice versa—in-the-flesh communities don't give you everything that online ones do). But people get a huge amount from online atheist communities: emotional support, practical advice, role models, encouragement during hard times, people to bounce ideas off of, the benefit of other people's experience, entertainment and laughs, a place to commiserate, a sense that they're not alone.

CD from TX, a former passionate Christian and worship leader, lives "smack in the middle of the Bible Belt. Four of the 25 biggest churches in the country are within an hour's drive of my house. About ten more are close enough for a weekend road trip. As an atheist I'm a member of a small minority." He says that "the online atheist community has been incredibly helpful to me. There are several blogs and forums I could point to, including this one [Greta Christina's Blog], that have opened my eyes and made me think. I don't always agree with what's being said, but unlike in church, I can disagree out loud and that's an accepted position (provided I have logic and evidence to back my position). So far I'm still trying to work up the courage to find an in-person group to meet with—there are several nearby but for some reason that seems like a final step that's too big to take at this point."

When H. Beaton was questioning and eventually leaving the Jehovah's Witnesses, he says that, "throughout this entire ordeal, I got a lot of great advice and support from the ex-Jehovah's Witness community online. So many people leave that religion while still buying into their beliefs, and what they believe about outsiders is not pretty. Not being involved with 'Jehovah's Earthly Organization' means that you are a loathsome, immoral creature who has no hope for the future; someone caught up in a world of sex, drugs, and materialism. So many former Jehovah's Witnesses get into terrible things simply out of a belief that it is what they're 'supposed' to be doing. Everything they learned about the outside world came from an Organization dedicated to keeping them sequestered from it. Talking to other former Witnesses online helped me to realize that things didn't have to be that way. I wasn't 'supposed' to be doing anything. I was responsible for my own life and my own happiness. Above all, I learned that I could live a happy and productive life outside the Watchtower Organization."

And Debra, who figured out that she was an atheist as a teenager in Anaconda, Montana, says, "There were no atheist groups that I knew of when I came out. I felt very alone as an atheist until I discovered groups online."

I can't possibly tell you everything there is to know about building atheist communities in one chapter of one book. I can't even tell you most of what there is to know, or even a significant fraction. And that's outside the scope of this book, anyway. Fortunately, there are organizations that are dedicated to doing exactly that. The Secular Student Alliance, the Center For Inquiry, the American Humanist Association, the British Humanist Association, Atheist Alliance International, all sponsor and support local communities, and they can give you excellent materials on how to start them, build them, and keep them going. They can't tell you everything you need to know, but they can give you a good start. (And there are almost certainly lots of organizations doing this work that I don't know about.)

That said, I'd like to make a few specific points about community building.

I've been doing a lot of traveling around the United States and Canada, giving talks to atheist groups and getting a sense of what those groups are like. And it seems that the strongest groups are often the ones with the widest range of activities. If your group only does socializing, or you only have speakers, or you only do visibility and activism, you're only going to attract a small portion of the atheists who might be out there looking for a group to join. Of course you have to balance "having a variety of activities" with "overextending and spreading yourself too thin"; you can't be all things to all people. It's fine to expand gradually, especially when you're just starting out. But if you diversify your activities as much as you can, your group will become a safe place to land for more people.

I've also noticed that the strongest groups are often the ones where local and student groups are working together. The student atheist movement is huge, it's growing rapidly, it's active and well-organized and highly motivated. They're doing a ton of atheist visibility and on-the-ground community building—and they're doing it for a demographic that's very receptive to our message. As Secular Student Alliance Director of Campus Organizing Lyz Liddell says, students are the future of this movement—but they are also the present of this movement. The skyrocketing rate of religious nonbelief is overwhelmingly driven by young people.[2] People over 25 are leaving religion in dribs and drabs; young people are leaving it in droves. And the student movement is there to catch them. In fact, they're almost certainly a big part of why young people are leaving religion in the first place.

But there's this problem—which is that a lot of students don't stick with the atheist movement after they graduate. The ones who do stick around are often already in the habit of working with their local group. And the local groups with a more diverse age range tend to be ones that work with students.

So build bridges between the two. You don't have to do everything together, or even most things. But you can promote and publicize each other's events, even co-organize a few events. Student groups can give local groups energy, new ideas, warm bodies for projects. Local groups can give student groups continuity, mentoring, money. (Student groups usually operate on shoestring budgets, and a donation that seems small to non-students can make a real difference.) If you want some more specific ideas on how to build these bridges, talk with the Secular Student Alliance.

When you're building community, it's important to strike a balance between making the community familiar and stable for long-term members, while still being welcoming to new ones. Speedwell, a 45-year-old woman in Houston, Texas, says, "I don't belong to an atheist community in Houston now. It seems difficult to join a group, for me. I tried a couple times, but everyone had pre-existing relationships and dynamics, and they tended to be either much younger or significantly older than me, and I didn't feel that I could fit in."

This can be a difficult balance to strike—but keep an eye on it. Do you find that lots of newcomers check out your group, but that hardly any stick around? Or do you have lots of turnover in your group, with very few people lasting more than a year or two? Keep an eye on that balance. Newcomers and long-timers are all important for the health of a community, and you really do need both. It's a good idea to have some regular activities that stay more or less the same for years, while also trying new activities fairly frequently. Make sure newcomers get a good welcome; say hi and chat with them, without glomming onto them. And if they come back a few times, make sure they feel not only welcome, but valuable. Encourage them to participate in projects, or to spearhead their own.

On a closely related note: It is *hugely* important to make your community welcoming to a wide variety of people—including people who don't look just like the people who are already in it. If your group is mostly white, middle-class, college-educated, middle-aged or older, and male, there are a whole bunch of atheists in your neck of the woods who you're not reaching. That is an enormous missed opportunity.

It's fine—more than fine, in fact—to have a community that's dedicated to a particular demographic, like an atheist student group or a group for African American atheists. But within that demographic, diversity is still important. Do you have a wide range of races in your student group, or a wide range of ages in your African American group? The whole next chapter is about diversity, though, and it goes into this topic in a lot more detail, so I'll just mention it here and move on.

And one of the hardest things about building atheist communities—in person and online—can be balancing the needs of people who are viscerally angry at religion and want a community where they can safely express that, with the needs of people who are more recent deconverts from religion, or who have religious friends and family, and who don't want to sit around and gripe about how awful religion is. When Kelly decided to come out to her conservative evangelical Protestant family, she had difficulty figuring out the best way to do it. "I have attended a few atheist gatherings," she says, "but I found them uncomfortable and not particularly enjoyable. My largest problem was the amount of time the people in these particular groups spent simply mocking the religious. While I value thoughtful criticism and love a fiery debate, this just seemed mean—particularly to someone who was once religious and still has many devoutly religious friends."

Speedwell echoes this sentiment. "I have a what-not-to-do story," she says. "One time, long before I was consciously questioning my faith, when I was in my early 30s, I went into an atheist chat room. I had been an admirer of Ayn Rand since I was a teenager, and the chat was an Objectivist room. I had the idea of trying to answer some questions I had about how Christianity was regarded in Objectivism and whether some synthesis could or could not possibly be achieved. I had an open mind and really wanted to know, and if the chat had treated me kindly and told me where my reasoning was wrong, I think I would have understood. But I didn't last ten minutes in the chat before my innocent question, 'What do you think of people who honestly believe they have faith' was judged not-so-innocent and I was banned. I was upset and thought 'atheists are assholes' for a few years after that."

At the same time, though, plenty of atheists find both great comfort and great freedom in having a place where they can say any damn thing about religion that they want. Many atheists feel very damaged by religion, and when they finally leave it, they have a huge amount of rage and pain they need to talk about. Other atheists feel like they've been silenced about religion by the social conventions that protect it from criticism, and when they finally get into an atheist community, they feel like they can finally let their hair down. For many atheists, the freedom to rag on religion is one of the main things they want from an atheist community. Demanding that all atheist communities be gentle and respectful is going to leave a lot of atheists out in the cold. At the same time, though, so will demanding that all atheists be fine with the "We Hate Religion" venom bath.

I'm not sure how to resolve this conundrum. My best suggestion might be to try to serve both these needs—separately. If you're an in-the-flesh community, it might be worth having dedicated events or sub-groups or caucuses; have a "Sunshine and Rainbows" night once a month, and a "Let's List All the Reasons Religion Sucks" gathering on another night. If you're an online community, your best bet might be to direct people to another community that might be better suited for them, rather than blasting them for not adhering to your standards. Both of these needs are valid—the need for a gentle space to explore your doubts or your loss of faith, and the need for a free space to express your true thoughts and feelings about religion—but it's hard to make them mesh and overlap. Recognizing that these really are different needs might be the best way to serve them.

Finally: When we're looking at how to build community, we tend to ask, "What does religion provide that we're not providing?" I think that's an excellent and worthwhile question. But I'd like to see us reframe it. Instead of asking, "What does religion provide?," maybe we should be asking ourselves, "What do people need?"

I'd like to reframe it this way for a couple of reasons. For one thing, I don't want to give religion any credit that it doesn't deserve. I don't think religion actually provides all that much that people can't get in other ways. In fact, I would argue that there's exactly one thing, and only one thing, that religion uniquely provides: a belief in the supernatural. Religion gives people a belief in a supernatural creator or creators, a supernatural caretaker or caretakers, and/or a supernatural afterlife. Period. Everything else that religion happens to provide—social support, rites of passage, a sense of tradition, a sense of purpose and meaning, safety nets, networking, companionship and continuity, etc.—none of that is particular to religion. All of it can be gotten elsewhere.

And we need to remember that the social support provided by religion can actually be very toxic. The "support" can be toxic in and of itself: when it promotes hatred and ignorance and intolerance, or makes outrageous demands as the cost of belonging. And when you no longer accept the beliefs that the bonding is based on, the "support" can become intolerable. H. Beaton says that when he was first beginning to consider himself an atheist, "I went to a bonfire with my brother and people I knew from my old congregation. By then I had been reading a lot, but having friends and a social life was something I felt I couldn't lose at that point. At one point I convinced myself that

I would stay in the religion just for the social aspects, and not concern myself with whether or not my beliefs were true. I saw the beliefs as a 'price of admission.'"

But once he finally let go of his religious beliefs, he says, "not even the social interaction was enough. In fact, I began to crave it less and less. It eventually got to the point where I couldn't stand to be in their company. Another bonfire is where I realized it. I realized that 99% of their conversation was negative. They'd make snide remarks about gay people, snide remarks about evolution, and constant reiteration of how things are so bad and that can only mean the end of the world is 'so close.' I only liked that social circle because I made those same comments. What I craved was not the social interaction with those particular people, but the feeling of camaraderie that came with being part of an elite group with special knowledge the rest of the world is too stupid, ignorant, and blinded by the Devil to understand. Not sharing those beliefs made that feeling impossible."

And in *Moral Combat: Black Atheists, Gender Politics, and the Values Wars*, Sikivu Hutchinson says something similar about how religious "support" in the black communities can often be toxic and harmful. "Because religiosity is evidence of 'authentic' blackness," she says, "it is difficult for black non-theists to publicly criticize the Black Church's special trifecta of religious dogma, greed, and hubris."[3]

Now, I do think it's interesting to ask why so many human needs have traditionally been met by religion. Is it a historical accident? Is it because religion has been so relentlessly dominating? Is there something about belief in the supernatural that makes it easier for people to organize around? But when we look at more secular societies and the ways that they're flourishing, it becomes clear that, whatever the reasons are that these needs have been met by religion, they certainly don't have to be.[4] And when we ask ourselves, "What does religion provide?," I think we're buying into the idea that religion does something special.

But mostly, I'd like to reframe this question because I think it'll help us be better organizers. I think it'll help us be more nimble, and more flexible. What people need varies tremendously: depending on their region, their culture, their subculture, their upbringing, their economic status, just on the individual person. And what people need from atheist communities varies tremendously, depending on all these things—and depending on how dominant a force religion is in their area, and what religions are or aren't currently doing for them.

In San Francisco where I live, there's lots of stuff available for people who aren't religious. There's tons of secular social events, political organizing, charitable work, activities and entertainment, which have nothing to do with religion. So if people aren't religious here, they don't have to turn to an atheist community for all that. And they won't be treated as pariahs. There's sometimes conflict between atheists and believers, but coming out as an atheist here isn't a social death knell.

But in the Bible Belt, that's a lot less true. In the Bible Belt, a huge amount of social support, charity work, family activities, etc. are done through the churches. You can't turn around without someone asking, "What church do you go to?" Religion there is a hugely dominating force in people's everyday lives. And coming out as an atheist really can mean becoming a pariah: losing jobs, homes, custody of kids, the love and support of family and friends.

So atheists in San Francisco, on the whole, need something very different from their godless communities than atheists in the Bible Belt.

These questions were very much on our minds when we started organizing the Godless Perverts Story Hour. I was talking with atheist writer and organizer David Fitzgerald about atheist community in San Francisco, and how we could bring more people into the mix. We were thinking out loud, "What will get San Franciscans to come to an event? What do San Franciscans like?" And the answer popped into both of our heads at once: "San Franciscans like sex." (Obviously people outside San Francisco like sex, too; but in San Francisco, people are generally more willing to be public about it.) So we thought: What if we organized an event where atheist writers do readings about our godless views of sex? We touched base with Chris Hall, who'd already launched the Godless Perverts thing with a well-attended and well-received panel discussion—and the three of us put together the Godless Perverts Story Hour, an evening of depictions, explorations, and celebrations of godless sexualities, along with critical, mocking, and blasphemous views of sex and religion. And it brought in a nearly sold-out crowd. We've turned it into a regular event, and we've expanded it into a social community, with meetups and parties.

Now, if we'd been thinking, "What does religion provide?," we never would have come up with this. We would have come up with picnics, coming-of-age ceremonies, something like that. There are lots of things that religion traditionally provides, but "explicit sexual entertainment" is not generally among them. But because we were thinking, "What do people need and want?"—and because we were specifically thinking, "What do people in the San Francisco Bay Area need and want?"—we could think outside the box, and come up with an idea that Bay Area atheists responded to.

What people need from an atheist community in San Francisco is different from what they'll need in Tulsa. It'll be different in Austin and Manhattan, Minneapolis and Dallas, Montreal and Tokyo, Saskatoon and Seattle and Sydney and South Africa. If we keep asking ourselves, "What does religion provide?," we'll focus too much on what religion already provides, and overlook creative ideas that religion is missing out on. If instead we ask ourselves, "What do people need?," we'll be better able to, well, meet people's needs—the ones religion is currently filling, and the ones it doesn't have a clue about. And we won't be giving religion credit that it hasn't earned.

CHAPTER THIRTY

— ✹ —

*Diversity, or, Making Communities Welcoming to People
Who Aren't Just Like Us*

So I've talked about helping other atheists to come out. I've talked about how being out ourselves makes it easier for other atheists to come out. I've talked about how to support other atheists in coming out, without pressuring or guilt-tripping them. I've talked about understanding the differences between atheists, so we can give them better support in coming out. I've talked about building communities that atheists can come out into.

We now come to an important question—a question that is unfortunately very sensitive, and often very explosive:

Which atheists?

Are we interested in broadening our horizons? Are we interested in expanding the atheist community and movement beyond the kinds of people who are typically involved in it? Are we interested in making the atheist community and movement more welcoming to more people— and to a wider variety of people—than are already participating in it?

I do a lot of writing about feminism, racism, and other social justice issues, within organized atheism as well as outside of it. I'm not alone in this; a lot of atheist writers, videobloggers, podcasters, etc. are doing this. And we get a lot of resistance from other atheists. Some of that resistance is not worth addressing; it comes in the form of ad hominem insults, flat-out falsehoods, racist/sexist/classist/other slurs, ongoing harassment, even threats of violence or rape or death. But some of it comes from people who are probably well-meaning, and who simply don't understand why the social justice crowd keeps hammering on about this stuff. They see how explosive these issues are, how divisive. And they want atheists to all get along. They want us to focus on the ninety-five percent we agree on, instead of on the five percent that we don't. They want us to just focus on the atheist stuff—church-state separation, atheist visibility, anti-atheist bigotry and discrimination, etc. They see the social justice stuff as mission drift.

I have a certain amount to say about this. But the Number One thing I want to say, the one thing I want you to remember from this chapter if you don't remember anything else, is this:

Social justice *is* atheist stuff.

Sexism, racism, classism, ageism, transphobia, disability issues, and more—this *is* atheist stuff.

It's atheist stuff because there are female atheists. African American atheists. Hispanic atheists. Trans atheists. Working class and blue collar atheists. Young atheists, old atheists, disabled atheists, atheists with mental illness. Atheists of Asian descent, Middle Eastern descent, Native American descent. Making the atheist community and movement welcoming to all these people, and more—that is not mission drift. That is one of our core missions.

And this is why the social justice crowd keeps hammering on about it. When the atheist community and movement fails to be welcoming to a large and diverse population of atheists—we have failed at our mission.

When women show up at our meetups and never come back because creepy guys were invasively creeping at them—we have failed at our mission.

When African American people show up at our conferences and don't come back because almost all the speakers were white—we have failed at our mission.

When Hispanic people come to our meetups and don't come back because they got asked, "Are you in this country legally?"—we have failed at our mission.

When people of Asian descent come to our meetups and don't come back because they got told, "You speak the language so well!"—we have failed at our mission.

When people without a college education come to our meetups or online forums and don't come back because they heard patronizing talk about how college-educated people are more likely to be atheists and this means atheism is smarter and better—we have failed at our mission.

When young people get invited to give input to local groups and don't come back because every idea they offered got shot down by old-timers who don't want to change anything—we have failed at our mission.

When trans people come to our meetups or online forums and don't come back because they got asked invasive questions about the state of their genitals—we have failed at our mission.

When the very idea of having sexual harassment policies at atheist conferences turns into a firestorm of bitter controversy that eats the Internet for months, and when women outside organized atheism hear about this and say, "Screw that, I'm an atheist but I sure as hell don't want to be part of that movement"—we have failed at our mission.

When poor and working-class people don't show up for our meetups or conferences because they're too expensive or aren't near public transportation—we have failed at our mission.

When parents don't show up at our meetups or conferences because we don't provide child care and they can't afford a babysitter—we have failed at our mission.

When people with disabilities don't come to our meetups or conferences because they're not accessible—we have failed at our mission.

When deaf and hard-of-hearing people don't come to our meetups or conferences because we don't have sign language interpreters—we have failed at our mission.

When people with mental illness come to our meetups or conferences and don't come back because speakers or members were using the words "crazy," "cuckoo," or "insane" in mocking and derogatory ways—we have failed at our mission.

When African American people talk to organizers of overwhelmingly white groups about possible racism and get told, "We don't exclude anybody," as if "not physically barring the door to black people" was all anyone needed to do to make their group inclusive (as opposed to the absolute bare minimum)—we have failed at our mission.

When women come to online forums and don't come back because they were called bitches and whores and cunts, and the people who complained were told to lighten up and grow a thicker skin—we have failed at our mission.

When marginalized people of all varieties don't participate in our meetings, conferences, blogs, videos, podcasts, forums, chat rooms, and more, because they were all about issues that primarily concern white, middle-class, middle-aged, college-educated, cisgender men—we have failed at our mission. When marginalized people of all varieties point out this omission and ask us to pay more attention to atheist-related issues that are more relevant to them, and get told that organized atheism can't do this because it would be "mission drift"—we have failed at our mission.

And when marginalized people of all varieties point out any or all of this, and get gaslighted or dismissed or told to stop talking about it—we have failed at our mission. When marginalized people point out ways they felt excluded by our meetings and conferences and blogs and videos and chat rooms and so on—and get told, "No, you didn't," or,

"You're being divisive," or, "You're blowing things out of proportion," or, "We didn't mean to exclude you, therefore you didn't feel excluded, therefore you should stop asking us to change"—we have failed at our mission. When people's right to be treated with dignity and humanity gets called the "five percent we disagree on," and people get asked to shut up about it so we can work on issues that really matter—we have failed at our mission.

All of this, by the way, is stuff that actually happens. I'm not making up any of it. I have heard of, or have personally seen or experienced, every one of these incidents in organized atheism. In some cases, I've seen them again and again and again and again and again.

There are a zillion ways that we show unintentional bias towards marginalized people. There is more than ample research pointing to this conclusion; do a Google search on the terms "microaggressions"[1] and "unconscious bias"[2] if you want to see it. That doesn't make us bad people; it means we've unconsciously picked up the biases of our culture, and that's entirely understandable. It would be surprising if it weren't true.

But it does mean that we have to accept this reality, and take responsibility for it, and work to be better. And it means that, since we have a zillion forms of unconscious bias, we have to make a conscious effort to overcome them. There's no other way it's going to happen. There's no other way for organized atheism to become genuinely inclusive, genuinely diverse, genuinely representative of all atheists as opposed to a very small sliver of us.

So let's talk a little about how to do that.

First, let's talk about some of the ways that this bad stuff happens. Let's talk about some specific ways that imbalances of race, gender, class, and more can perpetuate themselves, even if there's zero conscious intent to discriminate. (I'm mostly going to focus on race and gender here, by the way—a thorough exploration of biases in organized atheism is outside the scope of this book, it would take an entire book to really get into it. I do realize that not all -isms and marginalized groups are the same, and I apologize for not being able to expand this further. But these ideas do have a lot of general application.)

1: Unconscious bias. Even with the best of conscious intentions, people tend to be more comfortable, and more trusting, with people who are more like them. This has been well and thoroughly documented.[3] It's one of the most important reasons for affirmative action; people in charge of hiring tend to gravitate towards people who are more like them. So if the people doing the hiring are white men, they're more likely to hire white men... and as the people they hire rise to positions of power, they in turn will be more likely to hire white men... and so on, and so on. If there's no conscious attempt to seek out qualified women, people of color, etc., the process will perpetuate itself indefinitely.

This isn't just true in hiring. It's true in any community or movement. If a movement starts out being mostly made up of white men, and there's no conscious attempt to seek out women and people of color, it'll have a strong tendency to stay mostly white and male.

What's more, people can have racist or sexist attitudes without being aware of them. You don't need to be in the KKK or Operation Rescue to say and think stupid things about race or gender. (As someone who's said and thought plenty of stupid things—believe me, I speak from experience.) A lot of racism and sexism isn't grossly overt; it's subtle, it's woven so deeply into our culture that we often don't see it until it's called to our attention.[4] It might not occur to some white people that saying, "You speak the language so well! What country are you from?" to an Asian American is racist; it might not occur to some men that bombarding a woman they've never met with repeated compliments on her appearance is sexist. But you can bet that the people on the receiving end of this stuff are aware of it—and it can put them off from participating in a community they might otherwise be drawn to.

2: Focus. People have a natural tendency to focus on the issues that concern them most directly. And if a movement—however unintentionally—is being dominated by white men, it'll tend to focus on issues that primarily concern white men, at the expense of issues that are more important to women or people of color.

As just one example, I'll cite our failure to offer the kinds of support that make religion so central in many communities of color. It's true that we've been doing a much better job creating atheist communities in recent years, in the flesh as well as online. But these communities often don't provide the kinds of practical support routinely offered by black and Hispanic churches: job counseling, food banks, day care, and so on. What's more, when we routinely shoot down areas of social change activism because they aren't what we've traditionally worked on, we fail to offer one of the biggest things many marginalized people get from religion—a platform they can use to fight back.

Here's what dezn_98 has to say about this. "It is just a brute matter of fact that the churches in POC [people of color] communities are strongly connected to social justice issues. While yes, churches can be the ones that cause discriminatory views to other people, they also work really hard to promote a lot of social justice within that group. Churches have traditionally been the staging point for many POC communities when they want to speak out. As a result of this embedded history, churches in POC communities usually offer lots of social services related to helping brothas and sistas out. It is no small thing to distance yourself from the very foundations that frequently give you a hand on social justice issues. As a result, in POC communities, it is very hard to be an atheist because you are giving up a lot of social support that was previously your primary support mechanism when facing oppression. Know that before you enter minority spaces begging them to come out—you are asking them to risk a lot."

So when we ignore issues that are important to women or people of color, these folks are less likely to get involved in the atheist movement. And when they aren't involved, it's that much easier for the movement to ignore issues these folks care about. It's a nasty self-fulfilling prophecy. Which leads me to:

3: Self-fulfilling prophecies. For the sake of argument, let's pretend that #1 and #2 aren't happening at all, that there are no racist or sexist attitudes in the atheist movement—not even subtle or unconscious ones. Let's pretend that the atheist movement is largely and most visibly white and male because of pure, random luck.

Even if that were so? The movement's tendency to be mostly white and male would still perpetuate itself.

Remember what we talked about before. People are more comfortable with other people who are like them. And that's true for women and people of color, too. If a movement has mostly white men in it, and its most visible representatives are mostly white men, women and people of color aren't as likely to join up. They—we—are more likely to feel like fish out of water. We're less likely to see the movement as being about us.

What's more, if a movement is mostly white and male, a lot of women and people of color are going to assume that #1 and #2 are probably happening. I know that I'm less comfortable going to an event that's mostly male—since the chances of having women's issues ignored, or having my femaleness be inappropriately sexualized, are a lot greater. Women and people of color are often cautious about joining a community that's mostly white and male. We're going to wonder why that is.

So even if the atheist movement's homogeneity had happened purely by accident, it would still tend towards a self-perpetuating cycle. And these cycles aren't going to be broken by everyone just saying, "Okay, we promise to not be racist and sexist." They can only be broken by recognizing exactly how we *are* racist and sexist. They can only be broken by seeing that there's a problem—and taking action on it.

Plus, of course, all this is assuming that there's no overt racism or sexism in the atheist movement. And that, sadly, isn't the case. Anyone who's seen the hateful, misogynist harassment and threats that routinely get aimed at feminist women in the online atheist community will be all too aware of this.

I'm just scratching the surface here. A thorough exploration of bias and privilege is beyond the scope of this book. But here's the good news:

A lot of this is fixable.

Or at least, it's addressable.

And it's much, much easier to address in the earlier stages of a movement than it is down the line, after patterns have been established, and vicious circles have started running their course, and bad feelings have had time to fester.

So how do we fix it?

Let's start with the self-fulfilling prophecy bit. There are specific, practical steps we can take to derail these cycles, or at least to mitigate them. And self-perpetuating cycles can be used for good as well as evil.

For starters: Atheist organizations can work to reach out to women and people of color, and to get the women and people of color they have now into positions of greater prominence. Atheist leaders can work to address specific concerns of women and people of color in the community. Atheist conference organizers, and local or student groups bringing in speakers, can invite more women and people of color to speak. Atheist speakers' bureaus can recruit women and people of color. Atheist writers can do more to cite the ideas and accomplishments of female atheists and atheists of color, both from history and the current movement. Atheists can speak out when we see racism and sexism in our movement. Etc.

And as these efforts take hold and the movement becomes more inclusive, more women and people of color will feel comfortable joining.

Inclusivity can also be a self-perpetuating cycle.

There's an all-too-common idea that this sort of affirmative action—going out of our way to welcome, recruit, and promote women and people of color—is itself racist or sexist, and that we should blind ourselves to race and gender (or pretend to be blind to them). There's even a notion that affirmative action will somehow "lower the bar" and bring in less-talented people, and that we should recruit speakers and leaders and organizers based purely on merit, with no concern for race or gender. But the exact opposite is true. Unconscious biases are real; it's a delusion to think we're making decisions based purely on merit. If we don't want our unconscious biases running the show, we have to make a conscious effort to counter them. And working to stretch our sights outside the usual suspects doesn't lower the bar or dilute the talent pool. It expands it. It brings in talented people we would have overlooked.[5]

Some organizations/bloggers/writers/etc. are doing this. And it's paying off: I'm already seeing more diversity at atheist groups and events than I did even four years ago. Let's keep doing it—and let's do it more.

The "unconscious bias" thing isn't hopeless, either. It can also be addressed by taking positive steps to be more inclusive. One of the great things about having a more diverse community is that your unconscious biases get called into question: partly just by seeing counterexamples on a regular basis, and partly because there'll be more people around to call you on your crap. (And these people will feel safer in calling you on your crap, since they'll feel like they have backup.) And again, this can turn into a self-fulfilling prophecy for good instead of evil. When a more diverse membership makes a community more conscious of its biases, and inspires it to work harder to overcome them, then the community becomes even more welcoming to more different kinds of people.

And ditto with focus. Getting more women and people of color in our movement—especially in leadership—will get these groups' specific concerns heard and addressed a whole lot more. And as these concerns are heard and addressed, our community will become more inviting to a more diverse population. The power of the self-perpetuating cycle, again, can be a force for good.

There are some specific, pragmatic things we can do about all this. An important one, and one that's hard for a lot of people, is this: When someone brings up the subject of racism or sexism—listen. Pay attention. Don't just get defensive and reflexively reject the idea out of hand. We don't always have to agree with the criticism—I sometimes see accusations of sexism that I think are bull—but we should think about it, and listen to what people are saying, before we decide if their criticism has merit. As writerJames so eloquently put it in his Cubik's Rube blog, "Don't let your first response to a potentially legitimate complaint—made in as calm and reasoned and generous a manner as you could ask for, lodged by a demographic that consists of half the population of the planet and who have a history of being beaten down by the other half—be to tell them to shut up because they're wrong to feel the way they do. That should not be where you instinctively, immediately go to when someone's not happy with the way things are."[6]

Closely related to that: Don't assume that the problem is out of our hands, and that nothing we do will ever make a difference. Pessimism is an excuse to avoid responsibility. When we say things like, "The problem isn't with the atheist movement—women or people of color have special reasons for not coming out as atheists"? When we say things like, "The problem is how deeply intertwined African American culture is with religion," or, "The problem is that perpetuating religion has traditionally been a female role"? It's basically saying, "White male atheists are the real atheists. The reasons white men have a hard time coming out as atheists—those are the default reasons, the ones we should be addressing. Women and people of color are special, atypical. This should be a One Size Fits All movement—and that size should be the size it already is, a size that comfortably fits white men."

It's entirely possible—probable, even—that the nature of gender and race in our culture makes it harder for women or people of color to come out as atheists. But that's not a reason to give up. That's a reason to say, "What can we do about this?" That's a reason to say, "These folks are nonbelievers. They're part of our community—or they should be. What can we do to make being an out atheist easier for them?"

Here's another specific, practical thing we can do to help. I mentioned earlier that conference organizers, and local or student groups bringing in speakers, can invite more women and people of color to speak. As diversity strategies go, this one is easy and cheap; it gets a wider variety of ideas into our conversation; and it makes our public face more welcoming.

But I want to add something to this suggestion. If you're inviting women or people of color to speak? Don't just get us to speak about gender or race. It's fine to do that part of the time—it's important that these questions get talked about. But if the only thing we're ever seen talking about is gender or race, that marks us as Other. It implies that the only interesting thing about us is our race or gender. And it implies that the real atheists, the ones who understand atheism and get to talk about it, are white men.

We can also encourage the women and people of color who are already in our movement to step into leadership. A few years ago, I heard a presentation by She Should Run, an organization that works to get women to run for political office—and they pointed to research showing that women are far more likely to run for office if someone simply asks them to do it.[7] Women and people of color are not socialized to think of ourselves as leaders—but when someone suggests that we do it, we're a lot more likely to see it as an option. So that one act—simply saying, "You'd be great on the steering committee!" "We could use someone like you on the Board of Directors!" "The president of the group is stepping down, you'd be great at it, you should run!"—this, by itself, can go a long way towards making an organization more diverse. In fact, one of my favorite diversity stories comes from Amanda Knief, managing director at American Atheists, who took this step with dramatic results. The 2013 American Atheists convention in Austin, Texas was one of the most racially diverse atheist conferences I've been to, and along with many other forms of diversity, there were way more African American groups tabling than I'd seen at any atheist event. When someone asked Knief why she thought that was, her answer was simple: "We asked them."

This brings me to one of the best things we can do to make organized atheism more diverse—and that's to do coalition work with other social change movements. There's an important tip about this, though. When you make contact with other groups, don't frame it as "doing outreach." Do it as equals. If you're running an atheist group, don't contact the women's group or the African American group and invite them to come to your meetings. Go to *their* meetings (if it's appropriate). Ask if they'd like to co-organize a joint event. Tell them you're thinking of inviting a speaker to talk about the history of freethought in the African American community, or the role religion has played in holding back reproductive rights, and ask if they'd like to sponsor it with you. Better yet—ask if they have any speakers or events that are in your wheelhouse and that could use co-sponsorship. Ask if they're planning a service project that could use some extra hands. Don't make it about your group trying to boost your numbers and increase your diversity. Make it about their group, and the areas where you already overlap.

We can also make sure that our groups and events are accessible. Women and people of color tend, unfortunately, not to have as much money as white men. If we make our events affordable or provide scholarships, if we make sure they're near public transportation, if we provide child care, that makes them a lot more inclusive.

Here's another nuts-and-bolts strategy for inclusivity. If your organization or event has T-shirts? Print them in women's styles. I know this seems like a minor issue—and it is—but small things like this add up. The attitude that this should be a One Size Fits All movement, and that it should be a size that fits men? Not having women's T-shirts sends that message in a very literal way. Having women's T-shirts, on the other hand, clearly says, "We understand that atheist women exist, and we see them as part of our community."

Small things like this can make a big difference. It's part of your organization's public face. So make sure that this face isn't overwhelmingly white and male. Make sure that the faces on your flyers, your billboard campaign, the front page of your website, aren't overwhelmingly white and male. That's not enough by itself—but it's not trivial.

And one last strategy bit before I wind up and move on: Those of us who are already on board with this stuff? We need to keep talking about it. Making this case within the atheist movement is like the atheist movement making our case outside it—it's like water on rock. The ideas take time to penetrate.

And it's especially important for men to talk about gender, and for white people to talk about race. I know that's hard. Believe me, I know. It can feel like you're walking in a minefield; it can feel like you're going to put your foot in your mouth every ten seconds. It's uncomfortable for me, too. We have to do it anyway.

We have to do it because it works. And here's an example of how this has worked really well. When my wife Ingrid and I started hanging out in the atheist blogosphere, one of the first things we noticed was that, on the rare occasions when someone in a comment thread said something bigoted about gay people, straight people were immediately all over them. In droves. We—Ingrid and I and other gays and lesbians—didn't always have to be the ones speaking out about homophobia. We usually didn't have to be the ones speaking out. We could just sit back and watch the straight people deliver the smackdowns. That, just by itself, made us feel incredibly welcomed into the atheist community. What's more, we saw atheist writers and bloggers—straight ones—taking on LGBT issues such as same-sex marriage with great passion, very much as their own. That made us feel like the atheist movement was our movement—and it got us excited about getting involved.

But why should we care? Why should it matter so much that the atheist movement is largely white and male, with so many white men in leadership? Don't we have other things to worry about?

I'm going to answer as I so often do: with my unique blend of pie-eyed idealism and hard-nosed, Machiavellian practicality.

The idealistic reason? Because it's the right thing to do. Because women atheists, and atheists of color, matter just as much as white male atheists. Because religion hurts women and people of color just as much as it hurts white men—more so, in many ways. Because when women and people of color leave religion, they need a safe place to land, just as much as white men do. Because fighting racism and sexism makes us better people, and makes the world a better place. Because this conversation shouldn't be about Us and Them; it should be about Us. We are all Us, all part of this movement, and we should all be treated as if we matter.

The pragmatic reason?

It will make our movement stronger.

Numbers make us stronger—and making the movement more inclusive brings in more numbers. Thinking through our ideas makes us stronger—and making the movement more inclusive challenges us to think more clearly. And diversity itself makes us stronger. It brings new ideas to the table. It multiplies our ability to make alliances with other movements. It brings a wider range of views to the public debate. It makes us not look like elitist jackasses in the public eye.

In fact, I'm going to get a little harsh here for a moment. This is not rocket science. This is Political Organizing 101. The self-perpetuating reality of racism and sexism, and the necessity of taking action to counteract it? Every serious social change movement on the block knows about this, and is at least making a gesture towards working on it.

And there's a reason for that. Look at the history of other social change movements: the labor movement, the peace movement, the environmental movement, the civil rights movement, the women's movement, the LGBT movement that we so often model ourselves on. Every single one has been bitten on the ass by this issue. Every one now wishes they'd taken action on it in the early days, before bad habits and self-fulfilling prophecies got set in a deep groove that's really hard to break out of.

Atheists have a chance to not do that.

We're not going to single-handedly fix racism and sexism overnight. Even I'm not enough of a pie-eyed optimist to think that. But we have a chance to learn from the mistakes of every social change movement before ours. Our movement—at least, the current incarnation of our movement, the visible and vocal and activist incarnation—is still relatively new. We have a unique opportunity to handle this problem early: before these self-perpetuating cycles become deeply entrenched, and decades of ugly history poison the well.

Let's take that opportunity.

Let's take action on this now.

CHAPTER THIRTY-ONE

The Snowball Effect

I want to bring things back now to one of the best things about coming out atheist, and one of the most important ways that simply coming out ourselves can help other atheists:

Coming out creates a snowball effect.

The more atheists there are who are out, the larger and more powerful our community becomes. And the larger and more powerful our community becomes, the more atheists there will be who'll be willing to come out. And the more atheists there are who are out...

There are lots of ways this snowball effect works. Some of it is simply that seeing other out atheists makes people feel safer coming out themselves... and then they make the next wave feel safer... and so on, and so on. (A phenomenon we've been talking about a lot in this book.) Some of it is that coming out changes believers' attitudes about atheists and makes society less hostile to us... and *that* makes more atheists feel safer coming out... and then that changes even more believers' attitudes about us... and so on, and so on. All of this is something we can learn from the history of the LGBT movement. When more people came out as gay, being gay seemed more ordinary and acceptable... which meant there was less stigma and hostility against gays... which meant more gays felt comfortable coming out.

And some of this snowball happens, frankly, because coming out atheist is part of what makes more people become atheists. In fact, for this very reason, I would argue that the snowball effect is even more powerful for atheists than it is for LGBT people. After all, coming out gay isn't going to turn anyone else gay. It's just going to make people who are already gay feel more comfortable saying so. But coming out atheist does make other people atheist. Or rather, it's often part of the process. Religion isn't a sexual orientation we're largely born with. It's an idea, a conclusion about how the world works. And like I said in the chapter on cultivating other atheists, it's a hypothesis that relies on social consent to perpetuate itself.

So coming out does more than just make people who are already atheists feel comfortable coming out. It also makes people who aren't already atheists feel uncomfortable about religion. It makes people re-think religion. And the more out atheists there are, the harder it is for people to ignore the holes in religion. Coming out inspires more people to abandon religion... and they'll inspire even more people to abandon religion... and so on, and so on.

Coming out atheist is like the story of the Emperor's new clothes. It's very hard to be the first person to say out loud that the Emperor is naked. If everyone around you is saying that the Emperor is wearing beautiful clothes—and they're saying that not seeing his clothes makes you wicked and sinful and cut off from the true meaning of life—you're probably going to keep your mouth shut. You might even convince yourself that you see the clothes. But when a few people are willing to say it, then a few more people will say it, and a few more—until everyone who sees that the Emperor is naked is willing to say so, and the people who thought he had clothes on start realizing that he's naked.

And there's one more way that coming out atheist adds to the snowball: The more out atheists there are, the more powerful organized atheism becomes. The more out atheists there are, the more people there'll be to sign petitions, write to their representatives, show up at rallies, organize atheist film festivals, do child care at atheist events, lobby their elected officials, create local atheist communities, show up at local atheist communities, start atheist soup kitchens, donate books to atheist groups with libraries, donate money to atheist organizations who are supporting atheist students or fighting for atheists' legal rights or making atheism more visible.

Coming out atheist is like the story of the Emperor's new clothes—if there were a small but rapidly-growing organized movement dedicated to making the Emperor's nakedness visible.

Coming out has a snowball effect.

So let's keep the snowball rolling.

CHAPTER THIRTY-TWO

— ✸ —

Coming Out Is Fun

And finally, I think there's one more thing atheists can do to help each other come out:

We can remind each other that coming out is fun.

A little while ago, I was hanging out with some folks from the Minnesota Atheists after a talk I gave. We were chatting, as atheists often do, about coming out as atheists—how important it is, how central it is to the success of the movement, the various obstacles in its way.

And one of the women at the table, Robin Raianiemi, said something that struck me. She was talking about an assortment of closets she'd come out of in her life. And she pointed something out that I think we sometimes forget:

Coming out is fun.

Coming out is exciting. Coming out is an adventure. Coming out is a rush. Telling someone something true about yourself, something they don't know, something you don't know how they're going to respond to—it's exhilarating.

And living an out life is fun. Being out makes you feel liberated. It makes you comfortable in your own skin. It makes it easier to find other people who share your values and experiences, people you connect and resonate with. An honest life, a life where you're not constantly keeping track of who knows which secrets about you and how they might hurt you if they tell—it feels good. It's easier to relax, and to be yourself, and to have fun.

Coming out is fun—and being out is fun.

Yes, coming out can be hard. It can be scary, painful, even dangerous. You might upset people; you might have difficult conversations. You might even lose people you care about. In extreme situations, you might lose your job, your home, custody of your kids. Coming out can be hard, and if you're in a situation where it might seriously injure you, you should think carefully about whether to do it and how. I'm not going to pretend that any of that isn't true. It is.

But I think atheists tend to emphasize the difficult part more than the joyful part. We tend to talk about coming out as a noble duty, a rite of passage, a painful but necessary step to a better life for ourselves and the world. And there's some truth to that. But there's also truth to this:

Coming out can be fun.

I've made this point a number of times throughout this book, but I'm going to make it one more time. In the hundreds of coming-out stories I read for this book, there's a very consistent pattern that shows up—and it's a pattern that's backed up by research.[1] When you look at atheists who've come out of the closet, you see that, on the whole, they're happier. Even if they alienate friends and family, even if they lose job opportunities, even if they get treated as amoral villains or pathetic losers—they're still happier

They're happier because a life with more integrity is happier. They're happier because a life with less fear is happier. They're happier because the people who love them really love them, and not some other person who's walking around with their face and their name. Even if their worst fears are realized, and they do lose people they love—they're still happier.

Coming out can be hard. It can be scary, it can be upsetting, it can be dangerous, it can be really annoying, it can take time and work. But it can also be awesome. It can be the door to a better life.

And if we want to support each other in coming out, one of the best things we can do is to tell those stories, and get that message out.

So here are a few.

H. Beaton, a former Jehovah's Witness: "My life today is orders of magnitude better than it was when I was a Jehovah's Witness. Not having to imprison my mind is such a fantastic thing. I was a mental and emotional wreck. I very much wanted an intimate relationship with a woman and all I had managed to attain in my years of trying was a very destructive on-again, off-again... prompted more by her family and friends than the two of us. I had no idea how to talk to women or even how to date them because all of the regular kinds of dating are discouraged by the religion. It drove me into a depression deep enough to require medication.

"I have not needed a single pill since leaving the Jehovah's Witnesses. I haven't had a single suicidal thought, nor have I had the inclination to harm myself. My life, as I said, is orders of magnitude better. I'm married and own a home. I'm living the life I want to lead. I'm free."

Flora, whose family are intensely conservative Christians in Texas: "I'm extremely happy that I did come out to my family. I feel much more honest and open because of it; like our relationships are built on mutual love and trust instead of on fear or lies."

Tori, a teenager from a very Catholic Puerto Rican family, whose mother was disappointed when she came out, whose sister told her she wasn't really an atheist and that she was doing it to rebel, whose father told her she couldn't possibly know what she believed because of her age, whose aunt freaked out and called her ungrateful, and whose deeply religious grandmother ("abuela") yelled at her mother about how she should have taken her to church more and how she needed morality, says this: "Am I happy I've done this? Absolutely. I know from my experience with my abuela that keeping secrets sucks. I am able to be more honest during intellectual conversations and real life. When my family mentions something religious, I don't have to hide. I only wish I was more forthright about it."

Patrick Walsh, who had been "really into Christianity" but left his religion and began calling himself an atheist in college: "Since I've come out, my life has 100% changed for the better! I love being able to openly discuss my Atheism with my friends without having to worry about them knowing. It's also been great, because I feel I have definitely affected other people's lives and beliefs by getting them to actually think about what they believe."

David A. Musick: "I have no regrets with being honest with others about my loss of faith. There were no negative consequences to me for being honest about my atheism then, and there have not been since, as I have continued to be honest about it."

Denise: "I'm *completely* happy. Yes, there have been a few difficulties, but that is true with life in general. I don't *advertise* that I'm an atheist, but I likewise don't bother hiding it. I've found that being true to who I am is profoundly more satisfying than hiding behind the doubts and lies."

Eric M. of Louisville, Kentucky: "I'm quite happy that I came out and it was unquestionably the right decision for me. Life hasn't changed too much beyond being a bit less willing to put up with religious nonsense in inappropriate venues."

Eric Paulsen came out at age ten, when he asked his parents to stop sending him to church since he found the experience depressing and nightmarish. When they agreed to his request, he says, "I can't tell you how much better I felt once I knew I was no longer going to be forced to participate in this weekly farce. It was truly as if I had been washed clean."

Markus Ismael, who grew up in Indonesia in a strict Protestant family, came out to his mother over the phone, when he told her he had proposed to his girlfriend and she asked whether she shared their faith. "Did I regret coming out when and how I did?" he says. "No. My mom asked me a question, and I answered truthfully. That's what matters to me; the truth, and my integrity. All the positive qualities I was raised with by my parents, and imbued in basic training by the USAF [United States Air Force] I retained as an atheist. If time were rewound back to 1998, and I find myself facing the same question from my mom, I would not change a thing. Coming out to my mom became a defining moment in my life."

Jason Sciple, who lives in Kingwood, Texas in the Bible Belt, says in David G. McAfee's book *Mom, Dad, I'm an Atheist*: "I now proudly accept my atheism and am passionate about speaking up for secularism, free thought, reason, science, and logic. I've developed a passion for helping believers and non-believers alike to value secularism and equality. Every relationship is different, but with most relationships it is just becoming old news... I'm finding that as I get more comfortable with myself, others start to accept this as part of who I am."[2]

In her interview for *The Ebony Exodus Project* by Candace R. M. Gorham, Bria tells of coming out to the woman who had originally led her to religion. "She said to me, 'You are still my daughter. I love you.'" She adds: "My BFF, I told her I was an atheist, and she's gangster like me and she just said, 'So! So what? You still my sister?'"[3]

In her *Ebony Exodus Project* interview, Mandisa says, "I've had some of my high school peers actually thank me for saying the things that I do say because they've felt the same way. Even if some of them still subscribe to a god concept, they have definitely broken away from organized religion and are becoming very skeptical. It's been really great and it helps me, too, to know that there are people like me."[4]

Jessica Wood, on the Coming Out Godless Project website: "This is the happiest I've been in my life."

Midori: "Over the past few months, I've come out to my brother and his wife as queer, trans, and atheist. It seems like I am always coming out as something. Their reaction is usually something along the lines of 'We love you and support you no matter what, and if you need anything, just let us know.' They're awesome like that."

WilloNyx: "I am not lying when I say I have come out hundreds of times. I rarely come out in groups of more than two and everyone I am even kind of close to knows. I have never been openly rejected. Some friends distance themselves but none of them have said 'back devil, back.' Often when I come out I am met with [the] 'I thought I was the only one in this town' theme. Actually there are probably about 30 atheists I have personally met here. We are not alone but being out is the only way to know that."

Sam: "I am proud that I am atheist. I feel I dodged a bullet when I realize how much of my life was not wasted with religion. I've not once regretted expressing my atheism and have been pleasantly surprised by the agreement I've received, even quietly."

Liam, who comes from a mixed-race Catholic family in England, and whose father at first responded to his atheism by saying that his heart was broken: "Nowadays there is absolutely no tension between me and my father on this issue, we cheerfully discuss matters—including, even, religious matters—and debate disagreements as we always have. The only thing that has changed is I no longer go to Church for the sake of maintaining appearances, and I value the additional free time on Sunday."

Helena, who spent her formative years attending a Lutheran church in Minneapolis/St. Paul: "Things are much better now. When I went to college I became a feminist, and then I came out [as gay], so the conversation moved way beyond the religion question. Every revelation in my life/identity seems to take my mom about two years to conceptualize and move past, but I'm okay with that. I've never gotten any pushback from my friends about any of these things, mostly because they're all agnostic or atheists and feminists, too. My brother is the best person alive; even as an 18-year-old college freshman he was an outspoken and unapologetic feminist and atheist. I am so proud of him. My dad is amazingly open-minded and accepting. Even my grandparents know I'm an atheist, and it all seems to be fine."

When Lay came out to their brother in Jerusalem, where they both live, "He didn't question whether or not I was really an atheist or try to convince me of anything. He just took the knowledge in stride and has since been really accepting in the past few months since I told him. It's allowed us to be a lot more honest with each other about everything. It's been so refreshing to have someone who knows about this part of me. It's allowed us to be more respectful and honest with each other. I'm so glad I told him."

Blaine says of coming out to his parents: "They were both more than accepting and didn't seem to care one bit."

rodriguez says of coming out to their mother: "I'm generally happier now in my relationship to her... I can't imagine how trying it would be to disguise my true beliefs, to my mother, every day, in my own home."

Jeff Pedersen, who grew up very religious in rural Central California: "In actually telling people I am an atheist now... the two responses I receive are either casual acceptance, or (more rarely) a bit of surprise followed by casual acceptance. I have never been sorry that I have been open about being an atheist, and on the whole, I feel happier."

Rocky Stone: "Yes, I'm happy I did it. Perhaps it made a small difference to a few people."

Hunter: "Overall, coming out was a really painless, and sometimes very joyful experience for me. That others have suffered so much for coming out makes me recognize and appreciate the goodness of my close friends and family all the more."

Josiah Allen: "My life is great, and obviously it's nice not to have to lie every time I go home."

Terri Garrett: "I'm absolutely happy I came out. It's also helped my children to live authentic, unashamed lives."

Daniel Schealler: "The anonymous atheism ship has sailed for me, and I'm happier for it."

Coming out is fun.

Let's remind each other of that. And let's tell the world.

AFTERWORD

— ✹ —

I know that this book isn't complete. I know, with virtually no doubt, that within minutes of the final draft going to press, I'll be thinking, "D'oh! I can't believe I forgot to mention [X]!" I'm sure I'll be thinking of ideas I should have included, demographics I should have given special attention to, people or books I should have cited, cautions and encouragements I should have given. And I'm sure I'll be noticing typos that I didn't catch.

If you're reading this book, and you're having that same response— please let me know. I hope this book is successful enough to warrant a second edition, and possibly even more. If there's anything missing that you think should be in here, or anything you think I've gotten wrong, please email me at gretachristina@gmail.com. If I write a second edition, and if I agree with you, I'll include your suggestions. Thanks!

ACKNOWLEDGMENTS

— ✦ —

First, last, and always: Ingrid.

I wrote this book with a whole lot of help. That's been true for every book I've written or edited—but it's even more true with this one. This book feels very much like a collaboration, even a community effort. I can't possibly thank everyone who helped by name. But I'm going to give it a shot.

Thanks to absolutely everyone who answered my call for coming out stories: whether by posting comments on my blog, or by sending me email. This is, to a great extent, your book: I read all of your stories, and every one of them shaped my ideas. Whether I quoted you or not, your story made it into this book. So enormous thanks to: Aaron Wiebusch, akitamix, Alan, Alexander, Alexandria Farris, Alice, Amanda Knief, Amy, Andrew, Anna Geletka, antialiasis, Beth Presswood, Beyond_Dimensions, Blaine, Bob Barnes, Brandon, Brennan, Brian Nolan, briansawilddowner, bubba707, carolw, CD from TX, Chad, Chris H., Chris Hallquist, Christopher Stephens, Clarissa, Coolred38, Corey A. Henderson, Daff, Daniel Schealler, David A Musick, David Viviano, Debra, Delphinium, Denise, dezn_98, doublereed, Elena, Enkidum, Erasmus, Eric M., Eric Paulsen, Evelyn, Flora, frog, gb-james, Gilbert, grumpyoldfart, H. Beaton, Helena, Hunter, IasasaI,

Icaarus, Jafafa Hots, James, Jason, Jeff Pedersen, Jesse Daw, Jessica, Jim Newman, John Horstman, johnkarpf, Jon, Jonah, Jonathan Wood, Jont Musiteur, Josh, Joshua Brose, Josiah Allen, Judy Komorita, Karla, Kat Car, Kate, Kate Restivo, Keith Hughes, Kelly, Kevin Wells, Kim, Kimberly, Kimberly, Kristin, Lauren, Lay, LD, Lexie, Liam, Lisa, Liz H., Lucy Mayne, ludicrous, malani, Maria, Marina Stolting, Mark, Markus Ismael, Marnie, Mathematician, Matthew Prorok, Michael, Midori, Miguel, Miriam., MMC, mnb0, naath, Naomi, Omaar Khayaam, otrame, OurSally, Pat, Patrick Walsh, Paul, Phil, Ralph Serrano, Robert, Robert B., Rocky Stone, rodriguez, Rosie, rwahrens, Ryan, Safron, Sally M, Sam, sambarge, Sara, Sarah, Sebastian, Seh, Skylar Norman, Snowball, Speedwell, steffp, Stephanie, Suzanne, Taniat, Taran Meyer, Terri Garrett, Thais Camargo, Timid Atheist, tomforsyth, Tori, Tyrant of Skepsis, UDS, Wayne Schroeder, Will, William, William Brinkman, WilloNyx, zero6ix, and 1000 Needles.

Thanks also to everyone who publicized my call for coming out stories: to all the bloggers who posted about it on their blogs, to everyone who posted about it on Internet forums, to everyone who retweeted it on Twitter or shared it on Facebook or forwarded it to their friends and family. I didn't just want this book to be "how people who read Greta Christina's Blog came out as atheist, and what you can learn from them." When I was collecting these stories, it was important to cast as wide a net as I could. Getting the word spread made a huge difference.

I didn't just rely on my own solicitation for stories. I also read "coming out atheist" stories on numerous websites. So many thanks go out to the Coming Out Project, the Military Association of Atheists & Freethinkers, the Clergy Project, Reddit—and to everyone on these websites who told their stories and made them public. Thanks also to the authors of books that I pulled coming out stories from: Candace R. M. Gorham, author of *The Ebony Exodus Project*; David G. McAfee, author of *Mom, Dad, I'm an Atheist*; and Hemant Mehta, author of *The Young Atheist's Survival Guide*.

And I also have to thank anyone and everyone who ever told me your "coming out atheist" story in person. If we met at a conference, at a talk, in a pub after a conference or a talk, at a party, in a heart-to-heart, on Facebook, or anywhere else, your story shaped my ideas and my outlook. And your story inspired me to write this book in the first place. So thanks.

Ingrid had to read more drafts of this book than anyone other than me and my publisher. She has an excellent eye for grammatical errors and awkward turns of phrase—a skill that I take shameless advantage of. She has apparently infinite patience with interminably long, over-thinking debates about how to fix grammatical errors and awkward turns of phrase. She also had to put up with me while I was deeply embedded in "finishing the book" mode—which, in case you've never lived with a writer, is seriously No Fun. Writers finishing a book tend to be distracted, irritable, self-absorbed, sleep-deprived, and on an emotional rollercoaster of their own making. Ingrid has more patience with all of this than I deserve. And she only ever said, "Honey, come to bed, you've done all you could" ironically. I owe her more than I can possibly say.

And I owe an enormous debt of gratitude to the friends and colleagues who gave me extensive help with this book. Coming out is really different for different atheists, and it was hugely important to get detailed feedback on the book, so my personal perspective wasn't completely skewing my depiction of other people's experiences. This was especially true with the chapters on parents, students, clergy, people in the U.S. military, people in theocracies, and other atheists with very different experiences from mine. So I suckered a bunch of people into reading early drafts: either of the entire book, or of specific chapters on topics they had expertise on. Big thanks go out to al-Razi, Jamila Bey, Susie Bright, Andy Cheadle-Ford, Ian Cromwell, Heina

Dadabhoy, Catherine Dunphy, Dana Hunter, Ben Gamble, Debbie Goddard, Chris Hall, Rebecca Hensler, Amanda Knief, Lyz Liddell, Dale McGowan, Hemant Mehta, Ashley F. Miller, Miri Mogilevsky, Rick Muelder, Maryam Namazie, Taslima Nasreen, Jen Peeples, Chris Rodda, Alan Sokal, Jason Torpy, Richard Wade, and Stephanie Zvan. I would also like to give special shout-outs to Alex Gabriel, who did two full rounds of intensive copy editing, and to Lee Hays Romano, who thoroughly proofread the whole darned thing. You all put a whole lot of time and work and thought into a project that wasn't yours, because you thought it would benefit the community. I hugely appreciate it. Any remaining errors are entirely my responsibility and none of yours.

Many thanks to my cover designer, Casimir Fornalski. Cover art matters a lot more than many people realize, and Casimir's art is that rare combination of punchy and inviting: demanding attention in an entirely friendly way, conveying the book's essence at a glance while at the same time provoking curiosity about it. I feel more lucky to have met him than I can say.

Thanks to Amy and Rob Siders at 52 Novels for their excellent work on formatting the ebook. You made ebook publishing easy, even for non-techies like me.

I am enormously grateful to my blog readers: for supporting me when I needed it, for critiquing me when I needed it, and for giving a damn about my work. In particular, the resource guide was largely crowdsourced. Thanks to everyone who helped with that.

Thanks to my editors at *AlterNet*, *Free Inquiry*, *The Humanist*, and *Salon*, for getting my work into the public eye, and for your patience in dealing with my absences and mood swings when I was in book-completion hell.

And last, first, and always: Ingrid.

RESOURCE GUIDE

———— ✸ ————

This is by no means an exhaustive list. It's just meant to get you started. Most of these organizations are atheist or otherwise godless; the ones that aren't have missions that dovetail with the values commonly seen in the atheist community.

ORGANIZATIONS/ COMMUNITIES/ SUPPORT GROUPS

African Americans for Humanism

Supports skeptics, doubters, humanists, and atheists in the African American community, provides forums for communication and education, and facilitates coordinated action to achieve shared objectives. *aahumanism.net*

American Atheists

The premier organization laboring for the civil liberties of atheists and the total, absolute separation of government and religion. *atheists.org*

American Civil Liberties Union

The guardian of liberty in the United States. The ACLU works in the courts, legislatures and communities to defend and preserve the

individual rights and liberties guaranteed to all people in the United States by the Constitution and laws of the country.
aclu.org

American Humanist Association

Advocating progressive values and equality for humanists, atheists, and freethinkers.
americanhumanist.org

Americans United for Separation of Church and State

A nonpartisan organization dedicated to preserving church-state separation to ensure religious freedom for all Americans.
au.org

Atheist Alliance International

A global federation of atheist and freethought groups and individuals, committed to educating its members and the public about atheism, secularism and related issues.
atheistalliance.org

Atheist Alliance of America

The umbrella organization of atheist groups and individuals around the world committed to promoting and defending reason and the atheist worldview.
atheistallianceamerica.org

Atheist Foundation of Australia

The Foundation supports the rights of atheists and seeks to keep religion out of politics; includes articles, quotes and news from an atheist perspective.
atheistfoundation.org.au

Atheist Ireland

Building a rational, ethical and secular society free from superstition and supernaturalism.
atheist.ie

Australian Skeptics

Investigating pseudo-science and the paranormal from a responsible scientific viewpoint.

skeptics.com.au

Black Atheists of America

Dedicated to bridging the gap between atheism and the black community.

blackatheistsofamerica.org

The Brights' Net

A bright's worldview is free of supernatural and mystical elements. The ethics and actions of a bright are based on a naturalistic worldview.

the-brights.net

British Humanist Association

BHA works on behalf of non-religious people who seek to live ethical lives on the basis of reason and humanity. They promote Humanism, a secular state, and equal treatment of everyone regardless of religion or belief.

humanism.org.uk

Camp Quest

Residential summer camps for the children of atheists, freethinkers, secular humanists, and humanists.

campquest.org

Center for Inquiry

Their mission is to foster a secular society based on science, reason, freedom of inquiry, and humanist values. They have many local branches with regular meetings.

centerforinquiry.net

CFI On Campus

Organizing atheist, freethinking, skeptical, and secular humanist students

and faculty worldwide. A project of the Center for Inquiry.
centerforinquiry.net/oncampus

Church of the Flying Spaghetti Monster

A satirical church created to make fun of religion and point out the absurdity of teaching creationism in public schools. They hold that an invisible and undetectable Flying Spaghetti Monster created the universe after drinking heavily. Praise his Noodly Appendage!
venganza.org

The Clergy Project

A confidential online community for active and former clergy who do not hold supernatural beliefs.
clergyproject.org

Committee for Skeptical Inquiry

Their mission is to promote scientific inquiry, critical investigation, and the use of reason in examining controversial and extraordinary claims.
csicop.org

Council for Secular Humanism

Their mission is to advocate and defend a nonreligious lifestance rooted in science, naturalistic philosophy, and humanist ethics and to serve and support adherents of that lifestance.
secularhumanism.org

Council of Australian Humanist Societies

Umbrella organization for humanist societies around Australia.
humanist.org.au

Council of Ex-Muslims of Britain

Nonbelievers, atheists, and ex-Muslims are establishing or joining the Council of Ex-Muslims of Britain to insist that no one be pigeonholed as Muslims with culturally relative rights nor deemed to be represented

by regressive Islamic organisations and "Muslim community leaders."
ex-muslim.org.uk

Equal Rights Now—Organisation Against Women's Discrimination in Iran

Established to promote women's freedom, emancipation and equality between women and men in the social, economic and political arenas as well as to strive for an end to sexual discrimination.
equalrightsnow-iran.com

Ex-Muslims of North America

A community of Ex-Muslims (murtids) of various ethnic origins and nationalities that are currently residing in North America.
exmna.org

Filipino Freethinkers

An organization of atheists and freethinkers in the Philippines working for a secular Filipino society by promoting reason and science.
filipinofreethinkers.org

Foundation Beyond Belief

A charitable foundation created to focus, encourage and demonstrate humanist generosity and compassion.
foundationbeyondbelief.org

Freedom From Religion Foundation

Works to educate the public on matters relating to nontheism, and to promote the constitutional principle of separation between church and state. The Foundation is the nation's largest association of freethinkers (atheists, agnostics and skeptics) with over 17,000 members.
ffrf.org

The Freethought Society

Committed to education, investigation, and understanding.
ftsociety.org

Freethought University Alliance/ Freethought Student Alliance

A coalition of Australian atheist, humanist, skeptic and secular campus groups.

freethoughtalliance.org.au

Godless Perverts

Presents and promotes a positive view of sexuality without religion, by and for sex-positive atheists, agnostics, humanists, and other nonbelievers, through performance events, panel discussions, social gatherings, media productions, and other appropriate outlets.

godlessperverts.com/

Grief Beyond Belief

Faith-free support for non-religious people grieving the death of a loved one.

facebook.com/faithfreegriefsupport

Hispanic American Freethinkers

A non-profit national educational organization 501(c)(3) which serves as resource and support to all Hispanic freethinkers in promoting the search for truth through science, rational thought, skepticism, secular humanism, logic, scientific criticism of all un-natural (i.e. supernatural, paranormal) claims and dogmas, rational evaluation of faith-based myths, the Constitutional principle of church/state separation, secular values, and promotion of critical thinking in general, as well as absolute freedom of conscience.

hafree.org

Humanist Association of Ireland

Promote the ideals and values of Humanism: an ethical philosophy of life, based on a concern for humanity in general, and for human individuals in particular.

humanism.ie

Humanist Celebrants at the Humanist Society

Humanist celebrants conduct Humanist, secular, nonreligious, non-theistic and interreligious weddings, memorials, baby naming, and other life-cycle ceremonies.

humanist-society.org/celebrants/

Humanist Community at Harvard

Dedicated to building, educating, and nurturing a diverse community of Humanists, atheists, agnostics, and the nonreligious at Harvard and beyond.

harvardhumanist.org

Institute for Humanist Studies

A humanist think tank committed to information and practices meant to address the socio-political, economic and cultural challenges facing communities within the United States and within a global context.

humaniststudies.org

International Committee Against Stoning

Preventing the implementation of stoning sentences; fighting to abolish stoning.

stopstonningnow.com

Jehovah's Witness Recovery

An online environment that promotes positive healing and recovery from the Watchtower Society of Jehovah's Witnesses.

jehovahswitnessrecovery.com

Kasese United Humanist Association

Promoting humanism and free thought in communities around the country, with special reference to the Western Uganda region.

kaseseunitedhumanistassociation.blogspot.com

Military Association of Atheists and Freethinkers

Their mission is to provide a supportive community for nontheistic

service members, to educate military leaders about nontheism, and to resolve insensitive practices that illegally promote religion or unethically discriminate against nontheism.
militaryatheists.org

Military Religious Freedom Foundation
Dedicated to ensuring that all members of the United States Armed Forces fully receive the Constitutional guarantees of religious freedom to which they and all Americans are entitled by virtue of the Establishment Clause of the First Amendment.
militaryreligiousfreedom.org

National Federation of Atheist, Humanist and Secularist Student Societies
An association of atheist, humanist and secular student societies facilitated and supported by the British Humanist Association.
ahsstudents.org.uk

National Secular Society
Britain's only organisation working exclusively towards a secular society. Founded in 1866, they campaign from a non-religious perspective for the separation of religion and state and promote secularism as the best means to create a society in which people of all religions or none can live together fairly and cohesively.
secularism.org.uk

No Longer Quivering
Information regarding the deceptions and dangers of the Quiverfull philosophy and lifestyle.
nolongerquivering.com

Pakistani Atheists and Agnostics
PAA is about rational thought, compassion, science, freedom, and education. They provide a forum for freethinkers in Pakistan to get

together, share ideas and strive for common ambitions.
facebook.com/Pakistani.Atheists

Rationalist International
An India-based worldwide association which reports on campaigns it conducts against magic and mystification and on news of importance to rationalists.
rationalistinternational.net

Recovering From Religion
If you are one of the many people who have determined that religion no longer has a place in their life, but are still dealing with the after-effects in some way or another, Recovering From Religion may be the right spot for you.
recoveringfromreligion.org

Richard Dawkins Foundation for Reason and Science
Their mission is to support scientific education, critical thinking and evidence-based understanding of the natural world in the quest to overcome religious fundamentalism, superstition, intolerance and human suffering.
richarddawkins.net

Secular Coalition for America
The national lobby representing the interests of atheists, humanists, agnostics, freethinkers and other nontheistic Americans.
secular.org

Secular Homeschool Support
Information, resources, and a place to share and connect with secular homeschoolers across the world.
secularhomeschool.com

Secular Organizations for Sobriety
An alternative recovery method for those alcoholics or drug addicts

who are uncomfortable with the spiritual content of widely available 12-Step programs. SOS takes a reasonable, secular approach to recovery and maintains that sobriety is a separate issue from religion or spirituality.

cfiwest.org/sos

Secular Student Alliance

Their mission is to organize, unite, educate, and serve students and student communities that promote the ideals of scientific and critical inquiry, democracy, secularism, and human-based ethics.

secularstudents.org

Secular Therapist Project

A confidential service matching nonbelievers looking for therapy with secular therapists: therapists who are nonbelievers or are committed to providing secular, evidence-based therapy that does not involve supernatural or religious elements. The service is confidential for both patients and therapists.

seculartherapy.org

Skepticon

The largest free skeptical conference in the United States. They support, promote, and develop freethought, skeptic, and scientific communities through inclusive educational programming… which is really a fancy way of saying people all get together to share ideas, knowledge, and high fives.

skepticon.org

The Skeptic's Society

Their mission is to investigate and provide a sound scientific viewpoint on claims of the paranormal, pseudoscience, fringe groups, cults and claims between: science, pseudoscience, junk science, voodoo science, pathological science, bad science, non science and plain old nonsense. Publishes *Skeptic* Magazine.

skeptic.com

Society for Humanistic Judaism

Mobilizes people to celebrate Jewish identity and culture consistent with a humanistic philosophy of life.

shj.org

Stiefel Freethought Foundation

Provides financial support and volunteer strategy consulting to the Freethought Movement.

stiefelfreethoughtfoundation.org

The Sunday Assembly

A godless congregation that celebrates life. Their vision: a godless congregation in every town, city and village that wants one.

sundayassembly.com

Uganda Humanist Association

Promotes Humanism in the form of a skeptical, rational, scientific, philosophical and liberal human rights culture in Uganda.

uganda.humanists.net

United Coalition of Reason

A nonprofit national organization that helps local nontheistic groups work together to achieve higher visibility, gain more members, and have a greater impact in their local areas.

unitedcor.org

Women Against Fundamentalism

Challenges the rise of fundamentalism in all religions. Members include women from many backgrounds and from across the world.

womenagainstfundamentalism.org.uk

ONLINE FORUMS/ RESOURCES/ SUPPORT NETWORKS

Atheism+

A safe space for people to discuss how religion affects everyone and to apply skepticism and critical thinking to everything, including social issues like sexism, racism, GLBT issues, politics, poverty, and crime. *atheismplus.com*

Atheism Resource

Provides information about atheism from a historical, cultural, political, psychological, sociological, and scientific perspective. *atheismresource.com*

Atheist Nexus

The world's largest coalition of nontheists and nontheist communities. *atheistnexus.org*

Atheists of Color: A List

A list of prominent atheists of color, organizations of atheists of color, and atheist organizations predominantly focused on and/or participated in by people of color. *freethoughtblogs.com/greta/2011/03/21/atheists-of-color*

Atheist Parents

Dedicated to helping parents worldwide to raise well-educated, thoughtful, ethical, socially responsible, environmentally aware, and most importantly, godless children. *atheistparents.org*

Black Atheist Alliance

A Facebook forum where black atheists, agnostics, the nonreligious, and open minded believers can get together to express their views. All are welcome, regardless of your race or religious views. *facebook.com/groups/blackatheistalliance*

Celebrity Atheist List

An offbeat collection of notable individuals who have been public about their lack of belief in deities.

celebatheists.com

The Coming Out Godless Project

Share your godless story with the community.

comingoutgodless.com

Coping With Illness & Disability, Without Faith

A Facebook page for people who have chronic illnesses and disabilities and have learned that we don't need faith to get through it, because we know that the strength that gets us through comes from us. If you're tired of being told "It's God's plan!" then this page is for you!

facebook.com/CopingWithIllnessDisabilityWithoutFaith

ExChristian.net

Encouraging de-converting and former Christians.

exchristian.net

Free Inquiry

The magazine of the Council for Secular Humanism. Their mission is to promote and nurture the good life—life guided by reason and science, freed from the dogmas of god and state, inspired by compassion for fellow humans, and driven by the ideals of human freedom, happiness, and understanding.

secularhumanism.org/fi

The Freethinker

The voice of atheism since 1881.

freethinker.co.uk

Friendly Atheist Forums

Online discussion forum for readers of the Friendly Atheist blog.

forum.friendlyatheist.com

God Is Imaginary—50 Simple Proofs

It is easy to prove to yourself that God is imaginary. The evidence is all around you. Here are 50 simple proofs.
godisimaginary.com

Grief Beyond Belief

Faith-free support for non-religious people grieving the death of a loved one.
facebook.com/faithfreegriefsupport

Grounded Parents

Skeptical parenting blog by a team of parents from a variety of backgrounds, some less traditional than others, some extraordinarily traditional.
groundedparents.com

Hispanic Atheists Society of America

Focuses on the specific needs of Hispanic Americans breaking away and recovering from religion.
facebook.com/HispanicAtheistsSocietyofAmerica

The Humanist

A magazine of critical inquiry and social concern. Published by the American Humanist Association.
thehumanist.org

Internet Infidels/The Secular Web

A nonprofit educational organization dedicated to defending and promoting a naturalistic worldview on the Internet.
infidels.org

Iron Chariots

The counter-apologetics wiki. Collects common arguments and provides responses, information and resources to help counter the glut of misinformation and poor arguments which masquerade as evidence for religious claims.
ironchariots.org

A Large List of Awesome Female Atheists

A list of some great female atheists who you should check out if you haven't already done so.

freethoughtblogs.com/blaghag/2010/01/a-large-list-of-awesome-female-atheists

Latino/a Atheists

A space where Latino/a atheists, agnostics, humanists and free thinkers can express their doubts and encourage critical thought on religious views.

latinoatheists.com

Lawyers' Secular Society

Provides advice and assistance to individuals affected by laws which give special advantages to those who assert religious beliefs. Based in Britain.

lawyerssecularsociety.org

Outer Blogness

A former/secular Mormon blogging community. Sponsored by Main Street Plaza.

outerblogness.org

Present Moment Mindfulness

Mindfulness practice and science from a secular perspective. Podcasts, articles, meditation instructions and support, discussion forum, online practice circle, and more.

presentmomentmindfulness.com

RationalWiki

Refutation and analysis of anti-science and crank ideas; essays on right wing authoritarianism and religious fundamentalism.

rationalwiki.org

Reddit Atheism

A community in favor of scientific understanding, equality for everyone,

and positive secularism. They also oppose religious over-reaching and influence on others.
reddit.com/r/atheism

Secular Cafe
A place for mostly *secular* people to socialize, support, and discuss religion, science, politics, etc.
secularcafe.org

Skeptical Inquirer
The official journal of the Committee for Skeptical Inquiry. Publishes critical scientific evaluations of all manner of controversial and extraordinary claims, including but not limited to paranormal and fringe-science matters, and informed discussion of all relevant issues.
csicop.org/si

The Skeptics Annotated Bible/ Koran/ Book of Mormon
Passages of the Bible, Koran, and Book of Mormon are highlighted with a focus on their scientific inaccuracy, historical inaccuracy, contradictions, failed prophecies, absurdity, injustice, cruelty and violence, sexism, homophobia, and intolerance.
skepticsannotatedbible.com

The Skeptic's Dictionary
Definitions, arguments, and essays on topics ranging from acupuncture to zombies, and a lively, commonsense trove of detailed information on things supernatural, paranormal, and pseudoscientific.
skepdic.com

South African Skeptics
An online skeptic community for and by South Africans.
skeptic.za.org

Spiritual Abuse Survivor Blogs Network
Supporting and promoting spiritual abuse survivors through individual blogging efforts.

patheos.com/blogs/nolongerquivering/spiritual-abuse-survivor-blogs-network

Think Humanism

An independent humanist forum for people interested in humanism, secularism and freethought. Their aim is to offer a stimulating and supportive online environment to individuals who choose to live without religion and who wish to explore and develop humanist ideas on the web. *thinkhumanism.com*

The Thinking Atheist

Assume nothing. Question everything. And start thinking. Podcast, videos, blog, online forum, and more.
thethinkingatheist.com

Truth Saves

It's time we all become more honest and knowledgeable about Christianity and its claims.
truth-saves.com

Talk Origins

A Usenet newsgroup devoted to the discussion and debate of biological and physical origins. Also provides articles and essays with mainstream scientific responses to those advocating intelligent design or other creationist pseudosciences.
talkorigins.org

Why Won't God Heal Amputees?

If you are an intelligent human being, and if you want to understand the true nature of God, you owe it to yourself to ask, "Why won't God heal amputees?" Start your exploration here.
whywontgodhealamputees.com

BLOGS/ VIDEOBLOGS/ PODCASTS

Greta Christina's Blog
Atheism, sex, politics, dreams, and whatever. Thinking out loud since 2005. Yes, I'm putting myself first, out of alphabetical order. It's my book. Suck it up.
freethoughtblogs.com/greta

Freethought Blogs
The largest and most widely-read network of atheist, secular, freethought, and other godless bloggers.
And yes, I'm listing Freethought Blogs second, also out of alphabetical order, since they're the network I blog with.
freethoughtblogs.com

A Million Gods
An atheist medical student stuck in a land of a million gods. The blog of Avicenna.
freethoughtblogs.com/amilliongods

The Ace of Clades
Science doesn't know everything. Religion doesn't know anything. The blog of videoblogger Aron Ra.
freethoughtblogs.com/aronra

Alethian Worldview
If it isn't reality, it isn't the truth. The blog of Deacon Duncan.
freethoughtblogs.com/alethianworldview

Almost Diamonds
Stephanie Zvan has been called a science blogger and a sex blogger, but if it means she has to choose just one thing to be or blog about, she's decided she's never going to grow up.
freethoughtblogs.com/almostdiamonds

AronRa

Video blogger. "I'm just doin' my part to raise awareness of science and the growing socio-political opposition to it."
youtube.com/user/aronra

Ask an Atheist

A call-in radio show featuring atheists from the Tacoma/Seattle Area.
askanatheist.tv

Atheism: Proving The Negative

Analyses of God beliefs, atheism, religion, faith, miracles, evidence for religious claims, evil and God, arguments for and against God, atheism, agnosticism, the role of religion in society, and related issues.
atheismblog.blogspot.com

The Atheist Experience

A weekly live call-in television show sponsored by the Atheist Community of Austin, geared at a non-atheist audience.
TV show/podcast: *atheist-experience.com*
Blog: *freethoughtblogs.com/axp*

Atheist Media Blog

Your daily source of news & videos on science & religion.
atheistmedia.com

Biodork

Thoughts from Brianne Bilyeu, a Minneapolis-based nerdy, liberal, humanist progressive, on topics such as science, skepticism, religion, atheism, critical thought, politics, and local and global humanitarian and equality efforts.
freethoughtblogs.com/biodork

Black Skeptics

Spotlights the work of black skeptics, freethinkers, atheists, agnostics,

humanists and other heretics who would dare to buck the orthodoxies of blind faith.
freethoughtblogs.com/blackskeptics

BlagHag

Profound thoughts from Jen McCreight, a liberal, geeky, nerdy, scientific, perverted feminist atheist.
freethoughtblogs.com/blaghag

Brute Reason

With great snark must also come great responsibility. Ruining your fun since 2009. The blog of Miri.
freethoughtblogs.com/brutereason

Butterflies and Wheels

Fighting fashionable nonsense. The blog of Ophelia Benson, columnist for *Free Inquiry* and the co-author of *The Dictionary of Fashionable Nonsense*, *Why Truth Matters*, and *Does God Hate Women?*
freethoughtblogs.com/butterfliesandwheels

Camels With Hammers

Daniel Fincke aims to discuss atheism, ethics, religion, Nietzsche, secularism, and general issues in philosophy in ways that are both accessible to non-philosophers and yet stimulating to professional philosophers.
patheos.com/blogs/camelswithhammers/

Canadian Atheist

A group blog of atheists from across Canada.
canadianatheist.com

Richard Carrier Blogs

Blog of the renowned author of *Sense and Goodness without God* and *Not the Impossible Faith*. He specializes in the modern philosophy of naturalism, the origins of Christianity, and the intellectual history of

Greece and Rome, with particular expertise in ancient philosophy, science and technology.

freethoughtblogs.com/carrier

A Citizen of Earth

The blog formerly known as Blue Collar Atheist

patheos.com/blogs/acitizenofearth

Comrade PhysioProffe

See for yourself.

freethoughtblogs.com/physioprof

Choice In Dying

Arguing for the right to die and against the religious obstruction of that right.

choiceindying.com

Cubik's Rube

Regular blogging on atheism, skepticism, genderism, journalism, anarchism, politics, and other stuff that infuriates or inspires.

cubiksrube.wordpress.com

DarkMatter2525

YouTube channel. Humorous animations depicting the insanity of religion. Occasionally, they make a serious video.

DarkMatter2525

Daylight Atheism

Advocates secular humanism as a positive, uplifting and joyous worldview that deserves a larger following and wider recognition in the marketplace of ideas. The blog of Adam Lee.

patheos.com/blogs/daylightatheism/

The Digital Cuttlefish

The poet laureate of the atheist blogosphere.

freethoughtblogs.com/cuttlefish

Dispatches from the Culture Wars
Thoughts from Ed Brayton on the interface of science, religion, law, and politics.
freethoughtblogs.com/dispatches

Dogma Debate
A fast-paced liberal radio show and podcast designed to discuss and debate topics on politics, civil rights, science, religion, and equality.
dogmadebate.com

En Tequila Es Verdad
Blog of Dana Hunter, a science blogger, SF writer, compleat geology addict, and Gnu Atheist.
freethoughtblogs.com/entequilaesverdad

EvolutionBlog
Commentary on the endless dispute between evolution and creation.
scienceblogs.com/evolutionblog

Friendly Atheist
I think of this as the Atheist Times. If you want to stay informed about current atheist news, this is the place to go.
patheos.com/blogs/friendlyatheist

Geeks Without God
No mystical energy field controls my destiny. Podcast.
geekswithoutgod.com

Godless Bitches
This podcast was created to focus on feminist issues from a secular perspective and to help increase the presence of women's voices in the secular community.
godlessbitches.podbean.com

Godlessness in Theory
Queer left politics, pop culture and skepticism. The blog of Alex Gabriel.
freethoughtblogs.com/godlessness

Happiness Through Humanism
Short posts about the Humanist philosophy designed to encourage people to live ethical lives of personal fulfillment that aspire to the greater good of humanity.
humanisthappiness.blogspot.com

Heteronormative Patriarchy for Men
Splashes of mud from the trenches of the online gender wars. The blog of Ally Fogg.
freethoughtblogs.com/hetpat

The Indelible Stamp
Ethics, outrage, and evidence. The blog of Tauriq Moosa.
freethoughtblogs.com/indelible

Jesus and Mo
Religious satire from holy roomies Jesus & Mohammed in a twice weekly comic strip.
jesusandmo.net

Zinnia Jones
Secular trans feminist.
freethoughtblogs.com/zinniajones

Less Wrong
A community blog devoted to refining the art of human rationality.
lesswrong.com

Living After Faith
A podcast which addresses the process of coming out of religion, and how to live again after leaving the life of faith.
livingafterfaith.blogspot.com

Lousy Canuck
"Because I don't watch enough hockey, drink enough beer, or eat enough bacon." Blog of Jason Thibeault, an IT guy, skeptic, feminist, gamer and atheist.
freethoughtblogs.com/lousycanuck

Love, Joy, Feminism
Poking holes in piety, purity, and patriarchy. Blog of Libby Anne, an atheist, feminist, and progressive who grew up in a large evangelical homeschool family highly involved in the religious right.
patheos.com/blogs/lovejoyfeminism

Ashley Miller
Polemicist, activist, nerd.
freethoughtblogs.com/ashleymiller

Mr. Deity
A webshow/ podcast which looks at the everyday life of the creator and everything he must endure as he attempts to manage his creation.
mrdeity.com

Maryam Namazie
Nothing is sacred. Namazie is Spokesperson of the One Law for All Campaign against Sharia Law in Britain, the Council of Ex-Muslims of Britain, and Equal Rights Now - Organisation Against Women's Discrimination in Iran.
freethoughtblogs.com/maryamnamazie

Nirmukta on FTB
The blog of Nirmukta, an organisation which promotes science, freethought and secular humanism in India.
freethoughtblogs.com/nirmukta

No Country For Women
Humanism secularism, feminism. The blog of physician, writer,

feminist, human rights activist and secular humanist Taslima Nasreen.
freethoughtblogs.com/taslima

No Longer Quivering
Information regarding the deceptions and dangers of the Quiverfull
philosophy and lifestyle.
nolongerquivering.com

No Religion Know Reason
Caribatheist's blog. Random reflections on atheism and faith from a
born and bred West Indian.
caribatheist.blogspot.com

The Non-Prophets
An Austin-based live weekly Internet radio show.
nonprophetsradio.com

Non Stamp Collector
YouTube video channel. If atheism is a "religion"... then Not Collecting
Stamps is a "hobby."
youtube.com/user/NonStampCollector

Pandaemonium
Blog of Kenan Malik, a writer, lecturer, broadcaster, author of *From
Fatwa to Jihad: The Rushdie Affair and Its Aftermath*, a presenter of
Analysis, on BBC Radio 4, and a panelist on The Moral Maze, also on
Radio 4.
kenanmalik.wordpress.com

Pandagon
Progressive politics, feminism, atheism, other good stuff.
rawstory.com/rs/category/pandagon

Pharyngula
Blog of PZ Myers. Evolution, development, and random biological
ejaculations from a godless liberal.
freethoughtblogs.com/pharyngula

Point of Inquiry

The Center for Inquiry's flagship podcast, where the brightest minds of our time sound off on all the things you're not supposed to talk about at the dinner table: science, religion, and politics.

pointofinquiry.org

Qualia Soup

YouTube video channel. UK artist and secular humanist discussing critical thinking, science, philosophy & the natural world.

youtube.com/user/QualiaSoup

Cristina Rad

"I have many talents. Most of them fictional. Like God." The blog of videoblogger Cristina Rad, a.k.a. ZOMGitsCriss.

freethoughtblogs.com/cristinarad

Rationally Speaking

The official podcast of New York City Skeptics. Join hosts Massimo Pigliucci and Julia Galef as they explore the borderlands between reason and nonsense, likely and unlikely, science and pseudoscience.

rationallyspeakingpodcast.org

Reasonable Doubts

Your skeptical guide to religion. An award winning radio show and podcast for people who won't "just take things on faith." Its mission is to investigate the claims of religion from a fair-minded yet critical perspective. Blog and podcast.

freethoughtblogs.com/reasonabledoubts

Religion Dispatches

A daily online magazine that publishes a mix of expert opinion, in-depth reporting, and provocative updates from the intersection of religion, politics and culture.

religiondispatches.org

Scribbles And Rants

A blog about atheism, social justice, history, science, sex, sex ed, psychology, feminism, racism, bigotry, ableism, disability.
aniasworkinprogress.blogspot.com

Mano Singham

Thoughts on atheism, religion, science, politics, books, and other fun stuff, from a theoretical physicist and author of *God vs. Darwin: The War Between Evolution and Creationism in the Classroom*, *The Achievement Gap in US Education: Canaries in the Mine*, and *Quest for Truth: Scientific Progress and Religious Beliefs*.
freethoughtblogs.com/singham

Skepchick

A group of women (and one deserving guy) who write about science, skepticism, feminism, atheism, secularism, and pseudoscience. With intelligence, curiosity, and occasional snark, the group tackles diverse topics from astronomy to astrology, psychics to psychology.
skepchick.org

Skeptics Guide to the Universe

Your escape to reality. Weekly science podcast produced by the New England Skeptical Society. Also provides blogs, forums, videos and resources.
theskepticsguide.org

Spanish Inquisitor

Nobody expects the Spanish Inquisition!
spaninquis.wordpress.com

Susie Bright's Journal

Sex and politics. Stopped believing in "God" around 1968—a very big year for that sort of thing. "Could not be accused of shutting up."
—*Rolling Stone*.
susiebright.blogs.com

Temple of the Future
The blog of James Croft, committed Humanist and Humanist Celebrant.
patheos.com/blogs/templeofthefuture

This Week in Christian Nationalism
Blog of Chris Rodda, author of *Liars For Jesus: The Religious Right's Alternate Version of American History*; contributor to Talk2Action. org, Huffington Post; and Senior Research Director for the Military Religious Freedom Foundation.
freethoughtblogs.com/rodda

Token Skeptic
Bending misconceptions with her mind. Blog of Kylie Sturgess, host of the Token Skeptic podcast.
patheos.com/blogs/tokenskeptic

Uncredible Hallq
Philosophy, atheism, killer robots.
patheos.com/blogs/hallq

Why Evolution Is True
Blog of Jerry A. Coyne, Professor in the Department of Ecology and Evolution at the University of Chicago, and author of *Why Evolution Is True*.
whyevolutionistrue.wordpress.com

YEMMYnisting
Proudly feminist, proudly bisexual, proudly atheist. The blog of Yemisi Ilesanmi.
freethoughtblogs.com/yemmynisting

The Zingularity
Blog of Steven Andrew, a struggling free lance writer and regular contributor to the popular progressive website Daily Kos.
freethoughtblogs.com/zingularity

ZOMGitsCriss, a.k.a. Cristina Rad
Video blogger. "I'm a shooting star leaping through the skies , I am a satellite, I'm out of control."
youtube.com/user/zomgitscriss

BOOKS

50 Great Myths About Atheism, by Russell Blackford and Udo Schuklenk

50 Popular Beliefs That People Think Are True, by Guy P. Harrison

50 Reasons People Give for Believing in a God, by Guy P. Harrison

50 Simple Questions for Every Christian, by Guy P. Harrison

African American Humanism: An Anthology, Norm R. Allen, editor

African American Humanist Principles: Living and Thinking Like the Children of Nimrod, by Anthony B. Pinn

Amazing Conversions: Why Some Turn to Faith & Others Abandon Religion, by Bob Altemeyer and Bruce Hunsberger

Atheism: A Reader, by S.T. Joshi

Atheism: A Very Short Introduction, by Julian Baggini

Atheism: The Case Against God, by George H. Smith

Atheism For Dummies, by Dale McGowan

Atheist Voices of Minnesota: An Anthology of Personal Stories, Bill Lehto, editor

The Atheist's Guide to Christmas, Robin Harvie and Stephanie Myers, editors

Attack of the Theocrats! How the Religious Right Harms Us All—and What We Can Do About It, by Sean Faircloth

Black and Not Baptist: Nonbelief and Freethought in the Black Community, by Donald Barbera

The Black Humanist Experience: An Alternative to Religion, by Norm R. Allen

Breaking the Spell: Religion as a Natural Phenomenon, by Daniel C. Dennett

Breaking Their Will: Shedding Light on Religious Child Maltreatment, by Janet Heimlich

By These Hands: A Documentary History of African American Humanism, by Anthony B. Pinn

The Caged Virgin: An Emancipation Proclamation for Women and Islam, by Ayaan Hirsi Ali

Caught in The Pulpit: Leaving Belief Behind, by Daniel C. Dennett

The Complete Heretic's Guide to Western Religion Book One: The Mormons, by David Fitzgerald

Confession of a Buddhist Atheist, by Stephen Batchelor

Consciousness Explained, by Daniel C. Dennett

Darwin's Dangerous Idea: Evolution and the Meanings of Life, by Daniel C. Dennett

Daylight Atheism, by Adam Lee

Deconverted: A Journey from Religion to Reason, by Seth Andrews

The Demon Haunted World: Science as a Candle in the Dark, by Carl Sagan

The Devil in Dover: An Insider's Story of Dogma v. Darwin in Small-town America, by Lauri Lebo

The Digital Cuttlefish: Omnibus, by Digital Cuttlefish

Does God Hate Women? by Ophelia Benson and Jeremy Stangroom

Doubt: A History: The Great Doubters and Their Legacy of Innovation from Socrates and Jesus to Thomas Jefferson and Emily Dickinson, by Jennifer Michael Hecht

Drunk with Blood: God's Killings in the Bible, by Steve Wells

The Ebony Exodus Project: Why Some Black Women Are Walking Out on Religion—And Others Should Too, by Candace R. M. Gorham, LPC

The End of Biblical Studies, by Hector Avalos

The End of Faith: Religion, Terror, and the Future of Reason, by Sam Harris

The End of God-Talk: An African American Humanist Theology, by Anthony B. Pinn

The End of the Soul: Scientific Modernity, Atheism, and Anthropology in France, by Jennifer Michael Hecht

Faith No More: Why People Reject Religion, by Phil Zuckerman

The Fallacy of Fine-Tuning: Why the Universe Is Not Designed for Us, by Victor J. Stenger

Freethinkers: A History of American Secularism, by Susan Jacoby

From Fatwa to Jihad: The Rushdie Affair and Its Aftermath, by Kenan Malik

The Friendly Atheist: Thoughts on the Role of Religion in Politics and Media, by Hemant Mehta

God: The Failed Hypothesis: How Science Shows That God Does Not Exist, by Victor J. Stenger

God and the Folly of Faith: The Incompatibility of Science and Religion, by Victor J. Stenger

The God Argument: The Case Against Religion and for Humanism, by A.C. Grayling

The God Debates: A 21st Century Guide for Atheists and Believers (and Everyone in Between), by John Shook

The God Delusion, by Richard Dawkins

God Hates You, Hate Him Back: Making Sense of The Bible, by CJ Werleman

God Is Not Great: How Religion Poisons Everything, by Christopher Hitchens

The God Virus: How Religion Infects Our Lives and Culture, by Darrel W. Ray

God vs. Darwin: The War between Evolution and Creationism in the Classroom, by Mano Singham

Godless: How an Evangelical Preacher Became One of America's Leading Atheists, by Dan Barker

Godless Americana: Race & Religious Rebels, by Sikivu Hutchinson

God's Defenders: What They Believe and Why They Are Wrong, by S.T. Joshi

The Good Atheist: Living a Purpose-Filled Life Without God, by Dan Barker

The Good Book: A Humanist Bible, by A.C. Grayling

The Good News Club: The Christian Right's Stealth Assault on America's Children, by Katherine Stewart

Good Without God: What a Billion Nonreligious People Do Believe, by Greg Epstein

The Gospel of the Flying Spaghetti Monster, by Bobby Henderson

The Great Agnostic: Robert Ingersoll and American Freethought, by Susan Jacoby

The Happy Atheist, by PZ Myers

The Heathen's Guide to World Religions: A Secular History of the One True Faiths, by William Hopper

Hope after Faith: An Ex-Pastor's Journey from Belief to Atheism, by Jerry DeWitt

I Sold My Soul on eBay: Viewing Faith through an Atheist's Eyes, by Hemant Mehta

Icons of Unbelief: Atheists, Agnostics, and Secularists, S.T. Joshi, editor

In Defense of Atheism: The Case Against Christianity, Judaism and Islam, by Michel Onfray

In Faith and In Doubt: How Religious Believers and Nonbelievers Can Create Strong Marriages and Loving Families, by Dale McGowan

Infidel, by Ayaan Hirsi Ali

Irreligion: A Mathematician Explains Why the Arguments for God Just Don't Add Up, by John Allen Paulos

Judaism for Everyone ... Without Dogma, by Bernardo Sorj

Leaving the Fold: A Guide for Former Fundamentalists and Others Leaving Religion, by Marlene Winell

Letter to a Christian Nation, by Sam Harris

Liars For Jesus: The Religious Right's Alternate Version of American History, by Chris Rodda

Life, Sex and Ideas: The Good Life without God, by A.C. Grayling

The Little Book of Atheist Spirituality, by André Comte-Sponville

A Manual for Creating Atheists, by Peter Boghossian

Meditations for the Humanist: Ethics for a Secular Age, by A. C. Grayling

Misquoting Jesus: The Story Behind Who Changed the Bible and Why, by Bart D. Ehrman

Mistakes Were Made (But Not by Me): Why We Justify Foolish Beliefs, Bad Decisions, and Hurtful Acts, by Carol Tavris and Elliot Aronson

Mom, Dad, I'm an Atheist: The Guide to Coming Out as a Non-Believer, by David G. McAfee

Moral Combat: Black Atheists, Gender Politics, and the Values Wars, by Sikivu Hutchinson

Mortality, by Christopher Hitchens

Nailed: Ten Christian Myths That Show Jesus Never Existed at All, by David Fitzgerald

The New Atheism: Taking a Stand for Science and Reason, by Victor J. Stenger

Nomad: From Islam to America: A Personal Journey Through the Clash of Civilizations, by Ayaan Hirsi Ali

Nonbeliever Nation: The Rise of Secular Americans, by David Niose

Not the Impossible Faith: Why Christianity Didn't Need a Miracle to Succeed, by Richard Carrier

Nothing: Something to Believe in, by Nica Lalli

The Only Prayer I'll Ever Pray: Let My People Go, by Donald R. Wright

Parenting Beyond Belief: On Raising Caring, Ethical Kids Without Religion, by Dale McGowan

The Portable Atheist: Essential Readings for the Nonbeliever, by Christopher Hitchens, editor

Proving History: Bayes's Theorem and the Quest for the Historical Jesus, by Richard Carrier

Quest for Truth: Scientific Progress and Religious Beliefs, by Mano Singham

The Quotable Atheist: Ammunition for Non-Believers, Political Junkies, Gadflies, and Those Generally Hell-Bound, by Jack Huberman

Raising Freethinkers: A Practical Guide for Parenting Beyond Belief, by Dale McGowan

Red Neck, Blue Collar, Atheist: Simple Thoughts About Reason, Gods and Faith, by Hank Fox

The Scope of Skepticism: Interviews, Essays and Observations From the Token Skeptic Podcast, by Kylie Sturgess

Sense and Goodness Without God: A Defense of Metaphysical Naturalism, by Richard Carrier

Sex & God: How Religion Distorts Sexuality, by Darrel W. Ray

The Skeptic's Annotated Bible, by Steve Wells

The Skeptic's Dictionary: A Collection of Strange Beliefs, Amusing Deceptions, and Dangerous Delusions, by Robert Todd Carroll

The Skeptic's Guide to the Paranormal, by Lynne Kelly

Society without God: What the Least Religious Nations Can Tell Us About Contentment, by Phil Zuckerman

Think: Why You Should Question Everything, by Guy P. Harrison

UFOs, Ghosts, and a Rising God: Debunking the Resurrection of Jesus, by Chris Hallquist

The Unbelievers: The Evolution of Modern Atheism, by S.T. Joshi

Voices of Unbelief: Documents from Atheists and Agnostics, Dale McGowan, editor

The Ways of an Atheist, by Bernard Katz

What Do You Do With a Chocolate Jesus?: An Irreverent History of Christianity, by Thomas Quinn

What is Humanism, and Why Does it Matter? (Studies in Humanist Thought and Praxis), by Anthony B. Pinn

Why Are You Atheists So Angry? 99 Things That Piss off the Godless, by Greta Christina

Why Evolution Is True, by Jerry A. Coyne

Why I Am Not a Christian, by Bertrand Russell

Why I Am Not a Christian: Four Conclusive Reasons to Reject the Faith, by Richard Carrier

Why I am Not a Hindu, by Ramendra Nath

Why I Am Not a Muslim, by Ibn Warraq

Writing God's Obituary: How a Good Methodist Became a Better Atheist, by Anthony B. Pinn

The Young Atheist's Survival Guide: Helping Secular Students Thrive, by Hemant Mehta

ENDNOTES

Part One: Introduction

1. Greta Christina, "Coming Out Atheist — I Need Your Stories and Advice," Greta Christina's Blog, May 30, 2012. http://freethought-blogs.com/greta/2012/05/30/coming-out-atheist-stories-and-advice/; Greta Christina, "Coming Out Atheist — I Need Your Stories and Advice," Greta Christina's Blog, Greta Christina's Blog, September 13, 2013. http://freethoughtblogs.com/greta/2013/09/13/coming-out-atheist-i-need-your-stories-and-advice/; Greta Christina, "How Did People Help You Come Out Atheist — And How Did You Help Others?," Greta Christina's Blog, September 25, 2013. http://freethoughtblogs.com/greta/2013/09/25/how-did-people-help-you-come-out-atheist/

2. "Coming Out Godless Project." http://comingoutgodless.com/

3. "Clergy Project." http://clergyproject.org/

4. "Military Association of Atheists & Freethinkers." http://militaryatheists.org/

5. "Reddit Atheism." http://www.reddit.com/r/atheism/

Chapter 1: Making Your Own Life Better

1. Christopher R. H. Garneau, "Perceived Stigma and Stigma Management of Midwest Seculars," Sociology Theses, Dissertations, & Student Research. Paper 22, University of Nebraska-Lincoln, 2012. digitalcommons.unl.edu/sociologydiss/22/

Chapter 2: Helping Other Atheists

1. Candace R. M. Gorham, *The Ebony Exodus Project: Why Some Black Women Are Walking Out on Religion—and Others Should Too* (Durham, NC: Pitchstone Publishing, 2009), Kindle edition, Chapter 14.
2. Hemant Mehta, T*he Young Atheist's Survival Guide: Helping Secular Students Thrive* (Denver, CO: Patheos Press, 2012), Kindle edition, Chapter 8.
3. T. DeAngelis, "All You Need Is Contact," American Psychological Association, Vol 32, No. 10 (November 2001). http://www.apa.org/monitor/nov01/contact.aspx
4. Jeffrey M. Jones, "Atheists, Muslims See Most Bias as Presidential Candidates," Gallup (June 21, 2012). http://www.gallup.com/poll/155285/Atheists-Muslims-Bias-Presidential-Candidates.aspx
5. Mehta, *Young Atheist's Survival Guide*, Chapter 4.
6. Will M. Gervais, "Finding the Faithless: Perceived Atheist Prevalence Reduces Anti-Atheist Prejudice," *Personality and Social Psychology Bulletin*, University of British Columbia, 37: 543-556 (April 2011). http://www.patheos.com/blogs/friendlyatheist/2011/03/26/study-shows-anti-atheist-prejudice-goes-down-when-our-numbers-go-up/
7. Mehta, *Young Atheist's Survival Guide*, Chapter 6.

Chapter 3: Cultivating Other Atheists

1. David G. McAfee, *Mom, Dad, I'm an Atheist: The Guide to Coming Out as a Non-believer* (Great Yarmouth, UK: Dangerous Little Books, 2012.), Chapter 9 (Testimonials).

Chapter 5: Should You Even Come Out at All?

1. Garneau, "Perceived Stigma and Stigma Management of Midwest Seculars."
2. Carol Tavris and Elliot Aronson, *Mistakes Were Made (But Not by Me): Why We Justify Foolish Beliefs, Bad Decisions, and Hurtful Acts* (Boston: Houghton Mifflin Harcourt, 2007).
3. Garneau, "Perceived Stigma and Stigma Management of Midwest Seculars."

Chapter 6: The Basics

1. 1 Chris Hallquist, "Coming Out as an Atheist Eagle Scout," The Uncredible Hallq, May 30, 2012. http://www.patheos.com/blogs/hallq/2012/05/coming-out-as-an-atheist-eagle-scout/
2. Tracy Clark-Flory, "Dan Savage Is Coming for Your Kids," *Salon*, March 17, 2011. http://www.salon.com/2011/03/17/savage_16/
3. Dan Savage, *The Commitment: Love, Sex, Marriage, and My Family* (New York: Dutton, 2005).
4. Amanda Marcotte, "10 Myths Many Religious People Hold About Atheists, Debunked," *AlterNet*, September 13, 2011. http://www.alternet.org/story/152395/10_myths_many_religious_people_hold_about_atheists,_debunked
5. Sam Harris, "10 Myths—and 10 Truths—about Atheism," *Los Angeles Times*, December 24, 2006. http://www.latimes.com/news/la-op-harris24dec24,0,6461407.story#ixzz2nyb28VGg

6. Austin Cline, "Atheism Myths & Misconceptions: How Theists Misrepresent Atheism," About Agnosticism/Atheism, accessed December 20, 2013. http://atheism.about.com/od/atheismmyths/

7. Greta Christina, "Eleven Myths and Truths About Atheists," Greta Christina's Blog, March 31, 2009.

8. Garneau, "Perceived Stigma and Stigma Management of Midwest Seculars."

9. WIN-Gallup International, "Global Index of Religiosity and Atheism 2012," August 6, 2012. http://www.wingia.com/web/files/news/14/file/14.pdf (PDF)

10. Harris Polls, "Americans' Belief in God, Miracles and Heaven Declines," December 16, 2013. http://www.harrisinteractive.com/NewsRoom/HarrisPolls/tabid/447/ctl/ReadCustom%20Default/mid/1508/ArticleId/1353/Default.aspx

11. Phil Zuckerman, "Atheism: Contemporary Rates and Patterns," in *The Cambridge Companion to Atheism*, ed. Michael Martin (Cambridge, UK: Cambridge University Press, 2005). http://www.thechapmans.nl/news/Atheist.pdf (PDF)

12. WIN-Gallup, "Global Index."

13. Hallquist, "Coming Out as an Atheist Eagle Scout."

Chapter 7: The "No Big Deal" Method

1. CNN, "This Oklahoma Atheist Isn't Thanking the Lord," The Situation Room/ Oklahoma Tornadoes, Wolf Blitzer interviewing Rebecca Vitsmun, May 21, 2013, 06:20 PM ET. http://www.cnn.com/video/data/2.0/video/weather/2013/05/21/tsr-okla-tornado-bts-blitzer-rebecca-vitsmun.cnn.html

Chapter 8: A Few Words About Language

1. *Letting Go of God*, DVD, written and directed by Julia Sweeney (Five Sisters Productions, 2008).

Chapter 9: Family

1. *Letting Go of God.*
2. Ibid.
3. Daniel C. Dennett, *Breaking the Spell: Religion as a Natural Phenomenon* (New York: Viking, 2006), chapter 8.5.
4. Gorham, *The Ebony Exodus Project*, Chapter 9.
5. Mehta, *The Young Atheist's Survival Guide*, Chapter 4.
6. Greta Christina. "High School Student Stands Up Against Prayer at Public School and Is Ostracized, Demeaned and Threatened," *AlterNet*, May 25, 2011. http://www.alternet.org/story/151086/high_school_student_stands_up_against_prayer_at_public_school_and_is_ostracized%2C_demeaned_and_threatened
7. Seth Andrews, "Nothing More to Talk About," TheThinkingAtheist channel, YouTube. http://www.youtube.com/watch?v=_J4ZuHEYXkk
8. Gorham, *The Ebony Exodus Project*, Chapter 3.

Chapter 10: Spouses and Partners

1. McAfee, *Mom, Dad, I'm an Atheist*, Chapter 9 (Testimonials).

Chapter 11: Friends

1. Mehta, *The Young Atheist's Survival Guide*, Chapter 4.
2. Dennett, *Breaking the Spell*, Chapter 8.5.
3. Gorham, *The Ebony Exodus Project*, Chapter 11.
4. McAfee, *Mom, Dad, I'm an Atheist*, Chapter 9 (Testimonials).

Chapter 13: Strangers

1. Tavris and Aronson, *Mistakes Were Made (But Not by Me)*, 28.

Chapter 14: The Internet

1. Jason Thibeault, "You Are Free to Choose How to Use the Internet," Lousy Canuck, September 22, 2013. http://freethoughtblogs.com/lousycanuck/2013/09/22/you-are-free-to-choose-how-to-use-the-internet/
2. Gorham, *The Ebony Exodus Project*, Chapter 2.
3. Alexander, "Out into the Light," Scribbles and Rants, September 17, 2013. http://aniasworkinprogress.blogspot.com/2013/09/out-into-light.html
4. Mehta, *The Young Atheist's Survival Guide*, Chapter 6.
5. Alexander, "Out into the Light."
6. Gorham, *The Ebony Exodus Project*, Chapter 2.

Chapter 17: The U.S. Military

1. "Military Religious Freedom Foundation." http://mrff.org/
2. "Military Association of Atheists and Freethinkers." http://militaryatheists.org/
3. "Atheists in Foxholes, in Cockpits, and on Ships," Military Association of Atheists and Freethinkers, accessed December 20, 2013. http://militaryatheists.org/atheists-in-foxholes
4. Jason Torpy, "Humanist Alternatives to Church at Air Force Basic Training," Military Association of Atheists and Freethinkers, August 4, 2013. http://militaryatheists.org/news/2013/08/humanist-alternatives-to-church-at-air-force-basic-training/
5. Kate Donovan, "Secular Students of the Military: West Point," Friendly Atheist, May 25, 2012. http://www.patheos.com/blogs/friendlyatheist/2012/05/25/secular-students-of-the-military-west-point/
6. "Can I Have Atheist on My Official Records, ID Tags, and Military Headstone?," Military Association of Atheists and Freethinkers, accessed December 20, 2013. http://militaryatheists.org/about/faqs/

can-i-have-atheist-on-my-official-records-id-tags-and-military-headstone/

7. Hemant Mehta, "U.S. Army Major Wants Dog Tag to Say 'Humanist'; Military Says No," Friendly Atheist, February 9, 2012. http://www.patheos.com/blogs/friendlyatheist/2012/02/09/u-s-army-major-wants-dog-tag-to-say-humanist-military-says-no/

8. Hemant Mehta, "House Votes Down Amendment Allowing Non-religious Military Chaplains, but 150 Democrats Voted for It," Friendly Atheist, June 14, 2013. http://www.patheos.com/blogs/friendlyatheist/2013/06/14/house-votes-down-amendment-allow-ing-non-religious-military-chaplains-but-150-democrats-voted-for-it/

9. Hemant Mehta, "The 'Free Day Away' Program," Friendly Atheist, January 21, 2008. http://www.patheos.com/blogs/friendlyatheist/2008/01/21/the-free-day-away-program/

10. "A Selection of Mail Received by the Military Religious Freedom Foundation: Accolades, Acclaim, and Recognition Mail," Military Religious Freedom Foundation, accessed December 20, 2013. http://www.militaryreligiousfreedom.org/mrff_mail_reports/aar_report.pdf (PDF)

Chapter 18: The Clergy

1. Greta Christina, "Major Threat to Religion? Clergy People Coming Out as Atheists," *AlterNet*, June 10, 2012. http://www.alternet.org/story/155798/major_threat_to_religion_clergy_people_coming_out_as_atheists

2. Robert F. Worth, "From Bible-Belt Pastor to Atheist Leader," *New York Times*, August 22, 2012. http://www.nytimes.com/2012/08/26/magazine/from-bible-belt-pastor-to-atheist-leader.html

3. Teresa MacBain, "Teresa MacBain - Coming Out - American Atheists Conf. March 26, 2012," Richard Dawkins Foundation for

Reason and Science channel, YouTube. http://www.youtube.com/watch?v=Qh_eaZn_s9U&

Chapter 19: Theocracies (Overt and De Facto)

1. Council of Ex-Muslims of Britain, "Political and Legal Status of Apostates in Islam," December 2013. http://ex-muslim.org.uk/wp-content/uploads/2013/11/Apostasy_Report_Web1.pdf (PDF)
2. International Humanist and Ethical Union, "Freedom of Thought 2012: A Global Report on Discrimination Against Humanists, Atheists and the Non-religious," December 10, 2012. http://iheu.org/files/IHEU%20Freedom%20of%20Thought%202012.pdf (PDF)
3. Ibid.
4. Ibid.
5. International Humanist and Ethical Union; Matt Cherry, lead author, "Freedom of Thought 2013: A Global Report on the Rights, Legal Status, and Discrimination Against Humanists, Atheists, and the Non-religious," December 10, 2013. http://iheu.org/story/you-can-be-put-death-atheism-13-countries-around-world
6. Amnesty International, "Bangladesh: Fundamental Rights of Women Violated with Virtual Impunity," October 1994. http://www.amnesty.org/es/library/asset/ASA13/009/1994/es/2ec0258d-ac9d-4cd3-a9c8-438e717b0a32/asa130091994en.pdf.%20Page%2013%20%20-%2016 (PDF)
7. Taslima Nasreen, "Fatwabaaz and Politicians," No Country for Women, November 11, 2013. http://freethoughtblogs.com/taslima/2013/11/11/fatwabaaz-and-politicians/
8. Maryam Namazie, "Amina: 'I Will Continue the Struggle in Tunisia,'" Maryam Namazie, April 16, 2013. http://freethoughtblogs.com/maryamnamazie/2013/04/16/amina-i-will-continue-the-struggle-in-tunisia/

9. Lhendup G. Bhutia, "An Atheist in Exile," OPEN Magazine, July 6, 2013. http://www.openthemagazine.com/article/nation/an-atheist-in-exile

Chapter 20: Students: College, High School, and Earlier

1. Harris Polls, "Americans' Belief in God."
2. Barry A. Kosmin and Ariela Keysar with Ryan Cragun and Juhem Navarro-Rivera, "American Nones: The Profile of the No Religion Population," Institute for the Study of Secularism in Society and Culture, February 09, 2010. http://commons.trincoll.edu/aris/files/2011/08/NONES_08.pdf (PDF)
3. WIN-Gallup, "Global Index."
4. Ibid.
5. Harris Polls, "Americans' Belief in God."
6. Ibid.
7. Mehta, *Young Atheist's Survival Guide*, Chapter 2.
8. Pew Research Center's Forum on Religion & Public Life, "U.S. Religious Knowledge Survey: Executive Summary," September 28, 2010. http://www.pewforum.org/2010/09/28/u-s-religious-knowledge-survey/
9. Christina, "High School Student Stands Up Against Prayer."
10. All quotes in this paragraph were comments made by students to the Secular Student Alliance.
11. Mehta, *Young Atheist's Survival Guide*, Chapter 2.
12. Greta Christina, "Why Is an Atheist High School Student Getting Vicious Death Threats?," *AlterNet*, January 18, 2012. http://www.alternet.org/story/153803/why_is_an_atheist_high_school_student_getting_vicious_death_threats
13. Christina, "High School Student Stands Up Against Prayer."
14. Mehta, *Young Atheist's Survival Guide*, Chapter 3.
15. Ibid., Chapter 6.
16. Ibid., Chapter 6.

17. Ibid., Chapter 3.

Chapter 21: Parents

1. Dale McGowan, Molleen Matsumura, Amanda Metskas and Jan Devor, *Raising Freethinkers: A Practical Guide for Parenting Beyond Belief* (New York: AMACOM, 2009), 250-251.
2. Eugene Volokh, "Discrimination Against Atheists," The Volokh Conspiracy, August 29, 2005. http://www.volokh.com/posts/1125342962.shtml

Chapter 22: The Already Marginalized: People of Color, Women, LGBT People, and Others

1. Harris Polls, "Americans' Belief in God," and Kosmin and Keysar, "ARIS 2008."
2. WIN-Gallup, "Global Index."
3. Sikivu Hutchinson, *Moral Combat: Black Atheists, Gender Politics, and the Values Wars* (Los Angeles: Infidel, 2011), 40.
4. Jamila Bey (speech at American Atheists Convention, Des Moines, Iowa, 2011; summary of talk confirmed with speaker by author).
5. Gorham, *The Ebony Exodus Project*, Chapter 11.
6. Gorham, *The Ebony Exodus Project*, Chapter 8.
7. "Historic Black Humanists," African Americans for Humanism, accessed December 20, 2013. http://www.aahumanism.net/history
8. Kosmin and Keysar, "ARIS 2008."
9. Ibid.
10. Pew Research Religion & Public Life Project, "A Religious Portrait of African-Americans," January 30, 2009. http://www.pewforum.org/2009/01/30/a-religious-portrait-of-african-americans/
11. Kosmin and Keysar, "ARIS 2008.
12. Ibid.
13. Gorham, *The Ebony Exodus Project*, Chapter 5

14. Ibid., Chapter 9.

Chapter 23: Arguing About Religion

1. Mehta, *Young Atheist's Survival Guide*, Chapter 8.

Part Three: Helping Each Other Come Out: Introduction

1. Jones, "Atheists, Muslims See Most Bias."
2. Ibid.

Chapter 29: Building Community

1. Kent Shaffer and Craig Van Korlaar, "Q+A: Top Reasons for Church Attendance," Church Relevance, accessed December 20, 2013. http:// churchrelevance.com/qa-top-reasons-for-church-attendance/
2. Harris Polls, "Americans' Belief in God"; Kosmin and Keysar, "ARIS 2008"; and WIN-Gallup, "Global Index."
3. Hutchinson, Moral Combat, 74.
4. Phil Zuckerman, *Society without God: What the Least Religious Nations Can Tell Us About Contentment* (New York: NYU Press, 2008).

Chapter 30: Diversity, or, Making Communities Welcoming to People Who Aren't Just Like Us

1. "Microaggressions," Let Me Google That For You. http://lmgtfy. com/?q=microaggressions
2. "Unconscious Bias," Let Me Google That For You. http://lmgtfy. com/?q=unconscious+bias
3. Understanding Prejudice, "The Psychology of Prejudice: An Overview," article adapted from Plous, S. (2003), "The Psychology of Prejudice, Stereotyping, and Discrimination: An Overview," in S. Plous ed., Understanding Prejudice and Discrimination (New

York: McGraw-Hill, 2002), 3–48. http://www.understandingprej-udice.org/apa/english/

4. Ibid.

5. Understanding Prejudice, "Ten Myths About Affirmative Action," updated version of essay first published in *Journal of Social Issues* (volume 52, pages 25-31) later revised in S. Plous ed., *Understanding Prejudice and Discrimination* (New York: McGraw-Hill, 2002), 206-212. http://www.understandingprejudice.org/readroom/articles/affirm.htm

6. writerJames, "Isms, in My Opinion, Are Not Good," Cubik's Rube, August 11, 2009. http://cubiksrube.wordpress.com/2009/08/11/isms-in-my-opinion-are-not-good/

7. Jennifer L. Lawless and Richard L. Fox, " Girls Just Wanna Not Run: The Gender Gap in Young Americans' Political Ambition," School of Public Affairs, American University, March 2013. http://www.american.edu/spa/wpi/upload/Girls-Just-Wanna-Not-Run_Policy-Report.pdf (PDF)

Chapter 32: Coming Out Is Fun

1. Garneau, "Perceived Stigma and Stigma Management of Midwest Seculars."

2. McAfee, *Mom, Dad, I'm an Atheist*, Chapter 9 (Testimonials).

3. Gorham, *The Ebony Exodus Project*, Chapter 2.

4. Gorham, *The Ebony Exodus Project*, Chapter 14.